MW01108044

# The Rainbow of Experiences, Critical Trust, and God

# The Rainbow of Experiences, Critical Trust, and God

*A Defense of Holistic Empiricism*

Kai-man Kwan

continuum

Continuum International Publishing Group Inc
80 Maiden Lane, New York, NY 10038
The Tower Building, 11 York Road, London SE1 7NX

www.continuumbooks.com

© 2011 Kai-man Kwan

All rights reserved. No part of this book may be reproduced, stored in
a retrieval system, or transmitted, in any form or by any means, electronic,
mechanical, photocopying, recording, or otherwise, without the permission
of the publishers.

Library of Congress Cataloging-in-Publication Data

ISBN-13: 9781441174017 (hardback)

Library of Congress Cataloging-in-Publication Data
Kwan, Kai-man.
The rainbow of experiences, critical trust, and God : a defense of
holistic empiricism / Kai-man Kwan.
p. cm.
Includes bibliographical references (p. ) and indexes.
ISBN-13: 978-1-4411-7401-7 (hardcover : alk. paper)
ISBN-10: 1-4411-7401-X (hardcover : alk. paper) 1. God—Proof,
Empirical. 2. Swinburne, Richard. 3. Trust. I. Title.
BL473.K93 2011
212′.13—dc23
                                                          2011019701


Typeset by Newgen Imaging Systems Pvt. Ltd., Chennai, India
Printed in the United States of America

# CONTENTS

# FOREWORD

*Richard Swinburne*

"All knowledge comes from experience." We come to know what is happening around us by what we hear, see, and touch, and this experience of the world is mediated by visual, auditory, and tactual sensations. But merely coming to know that I have had certain sensations—for example, the sensation of a blue shape passing across my visual field—will not provide me with very much useful information about the world. I need to know for certain what constituted the shape. I trust my senses when it seems to me that what I am observing, via the shape in my visual field, is a blue car passing the window. We trust our senses and our memories about what we did and heard yesterday; and we trust other people when they tell us what they have seen and heard. All our knowledge of history and geography comes from what others have told us or written what they have seen or heard. Scientists acquire their knowledge about how the world works by making observations, especially from the results of experiments, and find the best theory to explain them. But each individual scientist relies largely for his data on what others report from their observations. Moreover, scientists trust their intuitions that the theory which satisfies their normal criteria for being the best theory will yield true predictions. As nonscientists we are entirely dependent on what they tell us. So even for information about very ordinary physical events, we have to place a lot of trust in others. Furthermore, since we think that most of our beliefs about ordinary physical events are correct, we must think that we are in general right to trust our senses, our memories, and what scientists and others tell us. Yet we also think that our sources of information are not perfectly reliable; we check them against each other. What one person tells us that they saw at a certain place and time may be contradicted by what other people tell us that they saw at that place and time; and then we justifiably doubt what the first person told us. And so generally our trust in our sources is and ought to be critical trust.

Kai-Man Kwan argues that we have no good reason for confining this principle of "critical trust" to our sources of information about ordinary physical events. We seem to be aware of ourselves as making free choices of deep significance, of other people as beings who are more than their bodies, of the compelling nature of morality, of the beauty of nature and works of art, and of the timeless truths of logic and mathematics. We should, he argues, trust our intuitions also in these respects—in the absence of counterevidence. It is to be expected, Kai-Man Kwan argues, that the world should contain the realities which I have just set out, and that we should be aware of them—if there is a God, but not otherwise. Finally many of us have at particular moments or for long periods an explicitly religious experience, which often comes as an awareness of God. To this awareness also we should give critical trust. Kai-Man Kwan argues that all the major types of human experience fit together in providing us with a reasonable prima facie case for the existence of God.

The argument relating to God "from religious experience" is often presented as an argument from a very peculiar type of experience which religious people have, quite unlike our other experiences. This book is unique in describing so comprehensively, and within one volume the data, the many different kinds of related human experience, data often hard to describe and so easy to neglect. It thus locates the "argument from religious experience" within a rich and deep background, which brings it to life and makes it much more plausible. I am very happy to commend this wide-ranging book, to what I hope will be a wide-ranging public.

## Acknowledgments

This book project began with my PhD research in Oxford under the supervision of Richard Swinburne over 20 years ago. His excellent scholarship has always been my model, and his patient supervision and enlightening criticisms have laid down the foundation of my work in analytic philosophy. The debt I owe him should be obvious in this book. I am also grateful to Charles Taliaferro, who was one of the first readers of my PhD dissertation. His constant encouragement has been a great help to me. Last, but not least, I have to thank my lovely wife, Wendy. Especially during the few months I concentrated on the writing of this book, her unfailing support and loving patience were just remarkable. I dedicate this book to her. Of course, it goes without saying that all the faults are mine.

# ABBREVIATIONS

| | |
|---|---|
| ARE | Argument from Religious Experience |
| AT | Addition Theory |
| BSJ | Basic Source of Justification |
| CE | Classical Empiricism |
| CSH | Computer Skeptical Hypothesis |
| CTA | Critical Trust Approach |
| DDP | Doxastic Decision Procedure |
| EME | Extrovertive Mystical Experience |
| ES | Epistemic Seeming |
| FT | Fusion Theory |
| FPP | First-Person Perspective |
| $H_n$ | Naturalistic Hypothesis |
| $H_t$ | Theistic Hypothesis |
| IBE | Inference to the Best Explanation |
| iff | If and only if |
| IIT | Impure Informational Theory |
| IPE | Interpersonal experience |
| ISH | Isomorphic Skeptical Hypothesis |
| ME | Monistic Experience |
| MP | Mystical Practice |
| NC | Necessary Condition |
| NDE | Near Death Experience |
| PC | Principle of Credulity |
| PCE | Pure Consciousness Event |
| PCT | Principle of Critical Trust |
| PFEF | Prima Facie Evidential Force |
| PFJ | Prima Facie Justification |
| PIT | Pure Informational Theory |
| PT | Principle of Testimony |
| RE | Religious Experience |
| RMO | Realism about Material Objects |
| RWH | Real World Hypothesis |
| SC | Sufficient Condition |
| ScE | Scientistic Empiricism |
| SDT | Sense Data Theory |
| SE | Sense Experience |
| SP | Sensory Practice |
| SSH | Superior Skeptical Hypothesis |
| STA | Selective Trust Approach |
| TE | Theistic Experience |
| TOM | Theory of Mind |

# INTRODUCTION

The question of whether religious experience (and experience of God) can be trusted has been hotly debated in the field of philosophy of religion in recent years. I survey this contemporary philosophical debate here, provide in-depth analysis of the crucial issues, and argue for an affirmative answer to the above question. First, I argue against traditional empiricism (or narrow empiricism), and defend Richard Swinburne's Principle of Credulity, which says that we should trust our experiences unless there are special considerations to the contrary. The Principle of Credulity is renamed the Principle of Critical Trust in this book to highlight the need for balance between trust and criticism. This principle is the foundation of a new approach to epistemology, the Critical Trust Approach (CTA), which admits that our epistemic base is fallible, but advocates an attitude of prima facie trust to replace Cartesian doubt. It maintains the emphasis on experience, but tries to break loose of the straightjacket of narrow empiricism by broadening the evidential base of experience. However, only those experiences that can withstand criticisms can, *in the end*, be fully trusted.

Second, I argue that the application of CTA to religious experience is legitimate. In particular, theistic experience is a well-established type of experience that is internally coherent and much more widespread than the critics suggest. Throughout this book, I will reply to various criticisms of religious and theistic experience. Moreover, I propose to replace narrow empiricism with holistic empiricism, which takes seriously our human experiences, such as interpersonal, moral, and aesthetic experience. I suggest that this whole spectrum of experiences is coherent and beautiful, and I call them the rainbow of experiences. Especially when we look at the depth dimension of this rainbow and consider it as a whole, it provides pointers to both a transcendent realm and a personal God.

There have been quite a few books on the argument from religious experience (ARE) already. My arguments are built on these previous efforts, but I also intend to further advance the ARE. Basically, I follow the lead of Swinburne's approach, but I elaborate and refine it at the same time. In particular, I propose that the distinction between Token PCT and Type PCT is important in order to defend his approach from objections. Alston has, by far, made the most sophisticated discussions about the epistemology of religious experience. His idea of doxastic practice, in fact, resembles my idea of a well-established type of experience. The strongest criticism of his approach is the alleged inability to deal with conflicting mystical practices. I agree that this is the weakest point of his system. However, I suggest that holistic empiricism, which takes into consideration various types of human experience in light of coherence and worldview considerations, can provide a fruitful and rational way to resolve the conflicts. In Part B, I gradually build up this case and conclude that theistic experience probably will not be defeated by conflicting religious experiences.

This book is the result of an encounter between a Chinese mind and the analytic philosophy of religion, taking place over several decades. From the beginning, I felt some ambivalence about analytic philosophy. On the one hand, I appreciate its rigor and clarity, and the various insights made possible by making fine distinctions. On the other hand, I am sometimes bewildered by the over-technical discussions and hair-splitting distinctions. I am also frustrated by the divorce of philosophical discussions from existential concerns, even in the area of religious experience. I am not entirely happy with the idea that religious experiences are isolated, episodic events, modeled on the perception of a table or chair. In early days, I was attracted to the approaches of Paul Clifford, Boyce Gibson, and George Thompson, among others, who advocated a broader empiricism. I am also fascinated by books like Paul Schilling's *God Incognito* or Aidan Nichols's *A Grammar of Consent*. But, as a rule, they are ignored by analytic philosophers.

In this book I try to combine the analytical ARE with existential concerns and weave them together in a cumulative *argument* from human experiences. I do believe this is a promising line of argument, but perhaps I am also influenced by my Chinese background. Cosmologically speaking, the Chinese have aspired toward the union of Heaven, earth, and human being. Epistemically speaking, the Chinese instinct is not toward analysis, but the union of knowing, feeling, and doing—a kind of holism. Although the task of integration is difficult, I do believe that the significance of religious experiences can only be fully appreciated when evaluated holistically, in the context of the whole person of the experient, the entire rainbow of experiences, and, in the end, a coherent worldview. Perhaps I have been too ambitious here, but I hope my attempt to integrate religious experience with interpersonal experience, existential experience, moral experience, and so on will be found to be enlightening by some readers.

# GOD, CRITICAL TRUST, AND HOLISTIC EMPIRICISM

# CHAPTER 1

# CONTEMPORARY RESURGENCE OF THE ARGUMENT FROM RELIGIOUS EXPERIENCE

God is not just a hypothesis for the religiously devoted. He is a Living Reality who permeates all their lives. Religious experiences sometimes convey such a heightened sense of reality that the conviction they instill transforms the lives of the experients. Furthermore, religious experiences are often world transforming as well—just contemplate the immense impact of people like Moses, St. Paul, Augustine, Wilberforce, and so forth on Western civilization. Are religious experiences trustworthy?

One of the main concerns of natural theology is whether there are rational arguments for the existence of God. The argument from religious experience (hereafter ARE) contends that, given the appropriate premises, we can derive from the religious experiences (abbreviated as REs) of humankind a significant degree of epistemic justification for the existence of God. In this book, I will defend the ARE, but I have no intention of arguing here that only a particular theistic tradition (such as Christianity) is correct. My strategy will consist of two stages. First, I offer a general defense of RE as a pointer to the supernatural realm. Then I focus on a subclass of RE, the experiences of God, or theistic experience (TE), and argue that theistic experiences provide significant justification for the belief in God. I do not claim that it is a conclusive argument, but I think it is a reasonable argument, which can contribute to the cumulative case for the existence of God.

Some clarification of terms is needed. By a *religious experience* I mean an experience that the subject takes to be an experience of God, or some supernatural being or state of affairs. (By "God" I roughly mean the supremely perfect being who is all-powerful, all-loving, and a personal ground of being.) Such an experience is *veridical* if what the subject took to be the object of his experience actually existed, was present, and caused him to have that experience in an appropriate way.[1] The claim that "S has an experience of God" does not entail "God exists." So the fact that religious experiences have happened does not prejudice the issue of the existence of God.

## 1.1 The Argument from Religious Experience in the Twentieth Century

Earlier defenders of religious experience included both theologians and philosophers, for example, Farmer, Frank, Waterhouse, Knudson. Some of them claimed that religious experiences provided immediate knowledge of

God that was *self-authenticating*. However, philosophers tended to be critical of such claims (Flew 1966, chapter 6). Keith Yandell (1993, chapter 8), himself a defender of religious experience, was highly critical of this notion. These criticisms were influential, and accounted for the rise of a form of the ARE that did not rely on claims to self-authentication. Typically, contemporary defenders only claim that religious experiences are prima facie evidence for the relevant religious beliefs, that is, they only have *prima facie evidential force* (hereafter PFEF), which can be defeated. Alternatively, we can say that religious experiences have *prima facie justification* (hereafter PFJ). They can be called *presumptive* data, too.

Albert Knudson anticipated the contemporary ARE: "The assurance that the apparent immediacy of the religious object carries with it has the right to be treated in the same way as the corresponding assurance in sense experience. It is to be accepted as valid in default of positive disproof. This...is the method actually followed by the human mind in all fields of human inquiry" (Knudson 1937, p. 100).

From the 1950s to the 1970s, able defenders of religious experience included A. C. Ewing (1973), John Hick (1967), H. D. Lewis (1959), Elton Trueblood (1957), John Baillie (1962), Rem Edwards (1972) and H. P. Owen (1969). However, at that time verificationism, roughly the doctrine that only in-principle verifiable sentences were cognitively meaningful, was still influential, and hence even the meaningfulness of religious language was in doubt. By now verificationism is effectively dead. Starting at the end of 1970s, a number of analytic philosophers had produced increasingly sophisticated defenses of religious experience. Richard Swinburne (1979, chapter 13) defended religious experience via his Principle of Credulity (hereafter PC), which said that it was rational to treat our experiences as innocent until proven guilty. In other words, religious experiences were treated as prima facie evidence for the existence of God until there were reasons for doubting them. This attracted a lot of attention in the field of philosophy of religion. There were, of course, many critics, for example, William Rowe and Michael Martin, but Swinburne also inspired the support of quite a few professional philosophers, such as Gary Gutting.

Many books on religious experience were written that basically followed Swinburne's line of reasoning, such as those by Davis (1989), Wall (1995), and Gellman (1997). Other philosophers also worked independently toward a similar conclusion, for example, Wainwright (1981) and Yandell (1993). One landmark of this debate is William Alston's *Perceiving God* (1991), which skillfully defended a doxastic practice approach to epistemology. This approach said that it was practically rational to trust our socially established doxastic practices, including the Christian Mystical Practice. His arguments were widely discussed and taken seriously.

Defenders of the ARE have made considerable progress in the twentieth century. When Swinburne first propounded his ARE via his Principle of Credulity in the late 1970s, he was greeted with incredulity (see Hesse 1981, p. 288). Nowadays, even critics among professional philosophers of religion treat the ARE with some respect. It is now regularly discussed in texts on philosophy of religion, and I think it is going to become one of the classical arguments for God. The old defenders continue to update their case (Gellman 2001; Hick 2006; Yandell 1999), and the ARE has also drawn new supporters. Of course, the ARE also has able detractors (Richard Gale, Matthew Bagger, Nicholas Everitt, James Harris), but I think they will acknowledge that their opponents are their epistemic peers. After all, Alston and Swinburne can't be dismissed as amateur philosophers. No consensus exists yet, but the ARE seems to be alive and well.

Besides the analytic defense of ARE, there is an alternative strategy of defending RE by putting it in the context of uniquely human experiences and then arguing that RE is the consummation of human transcendence. This line of argument has been developed by Paul Schilling (1974), John Macquarrie (1982), and Aidan Nichols (1991). They contend that RE is, in fact, continuous with many intimations of transcendence immanent in our ordinary experiences. Unfortunately, this line of argument has been neglected by analytic philosophers. Despite the lack of rigor in argumentation, this argument is strong in its breadth and phenomenology of human experience. The analytic ARE and the existential ARE can, in fact, complement one another, the former providing a solid groundwork of epistemological and argumentative structure, and the latter providing a broader experiential base and an existential connection to human life. This book is my attempt to integrate these two strategies.

The ARE is also exciting and fascinating because it helps us rethink deep issues in epistemology. I think contemporary defenders of ARE are exploring a new paradigm. There are also independent and consonant developments in the field of epistemology in recent decades. When Swinburne first boldly proposed his PC, it was quite novel and radical. True, it was similar to Chisholm's critical common-sensism, but few would imagine applying it directly to RE. At that time the deficiencies of traditional foundationalism were already apparent to many epistemologists, but perhaps they were still hoping for a quick fix. Now they are more open to radically different epistemological frameworks. Epistemic principles like Swinburne's PC have been accepted by diverse philosophers like Gary Gutting, William Lycan, Robert Audi, and Michael Huemer. Things like presumptive data and defeasible reasoning are now the stock-in-trade of contemporary epistemologists. Moreover, some are exploring theories that more or less resemble Alston's Doxastic Practice Approach, for example, Catherine Elgin's (very) weak foundationalism, Susan Haack's foundherentism, Nicholas Rescher's methodological pragmatism, or James Freeman's commonsense foundationalism. This kind of epistemological development certainly enhances the initial plausibility of the ARE.

## 1.2 Positions and Strategies Concerning Arguments from Religious Experience

To clarify the complicated debates surrounding RE, let us first spell out the major positions and strategies we can adopt.

### 1.2.1 Different Positions on Religious Experience

Not all philosophers believe that we can come to an objective conclusion about the epistemic status of religious experience. So we can distinguish between two major kinds of position: objectivism versus non-objectivism: *objectivism is the position that it is rationally possible to arrive at an objective conclusion about the epistemic status of religious experience.* Most analytic philosophers presuppose objectivism when they argue for the reliability of REs by way of the formulation of general epistemic criteria or methodology.

In contrast, *non-objectivism is the view that it is not rationally possible to arrive at an objective conclusion about the epistemic status of religious experience.* Perhaps the non-objectivist has fundamental doubts about the whole project of analytic epistemology. Another possibility is that he or she has more specific reasons to think that beliefs about the epistemic status of religious experience are paradigm-dependent, and both defenders and critics are inevitably arguing in a circle. So their conclusions cannot be objective.

If you are an objectivist, you can take a spectrum of positions:

1. *Strong skepticism*: there are good reasons to show that religious experiences are largely delusory.
2. *Weak skepticism*: there are good reasons to show that it is epistemically impermissible (even for people who have religious experiences) to treat religious experiences as having PFEF.
3. *Weak ARE*: there are no good reasons to show that it is epistemically impermissible to treat religious experiences as having PFEF (at least for people who have religious experiences).
4. *Modest ARE*: there are good reasons to show that it is epistemically permissible to treat religious experiences as having PFEF (at least for people who have religious experiences).
5. *Strong ARE*: there are good reasons to show that religious experiences have PFEF.

It is important to distinguish these positions, because a case may not be sufficient to establish a stronger position, but still be good enough for the weaker position. The strongest positions, like strong skepticism and strong ARE, are obviously quite difficult to establish. In this book, I try to argue for a strong ARE, and hopefully even if this case is not completely successful, it can still lend significant support to either weak or modest ARE.

### 1.2.2 Three Major Forms of Argument from Religious Experience

Defenders of ARE also adopt different strategies, and hence there are different forms of ARE. Readers should note that for reasons that will become clear, from now on Swinburne's Principle of Credulity (PC) will be renamed Principle of Critical Trust (PCT), and the kind of epistemology that takes

PCT as a fundamental principle will be called the Critical Trust Approach (CTA). I am glad that my terminology is at least accepted by Hick: "The term 'the critical trust approach' has been introduced by Kai-man Kwan (2003), and I use it in preference to the earlier 'principle of credulity'... and my own 'principle of rational credulity'" (Hick 2006, p. 210).

The Transcendental ARE can be formulated in this way:

TA1. Any justification from experience is possible only when the PCT is *presupposed*.
TA2. Hence the PCT should be applied to all kinds of experience.
TA3. Hence the PCT should be applied to RE, that is, it has PFEF.
TA4. Not all REs have been defeated, that is, shown to be delusory.
TA5. Therefore, it is ultima facie justified to believe in the veridicality of *some* REs.

In contrast, the Analogical ARE argues to the same conclusion using the analogy of RE with other commonly accepted types of experiences (e.g. SE) as premise. The Explanatory ARE takes REs as data, and then uses the inference to the best explanation (IBE) to support a religious worldview. It is important to distinguish between these forms, because some considerations (positive or negative) may be relevant for one form of ARE, but not the others. I will argue later that all three forms of AREs can be used in a mutually complementary fashion, but my main focus is on the Transcendental ARE, and the type of RE I want to defend is mainly (though not exclusively) theistic experience (TE).

### 1.2.3 Narrow Empiricism, Holistic Empiricism, and the Rainbow of Experiences

I suggest that when we consider the epistemic status of RE, we should also consider the whole spectrum of our experiences, which I call the rainbow of experiences. I divide them into seven major types:

1. Experience of self
   a. Experience of self as the basic subject—"I" (introspection, and so on)
   b. Experience of self as the existential subject—existential experience (e.g. quest for meaning and wholeness of human existence)
2. Sense experience (SE)—experiences mediated by the five senses, mainly about the natural world
3. Interpersonal experience (IPE)—experience of other persons
4. Religious experience (RE)
   a. Non-theistic RE—experience of the supernatural that is not explicitly the personal God
   b. Theistic experience (TE)—experience of a personal God
5. Moral Experience

6. Aesthetic experience
7. Intellectual experience (activities of reason, such as rational intuition)

Types 1 through 4 are the four basic types of experiential encounter: the encounter with one's self, the natural world, other selves, and the supernatural realm, respectively. Types 5–7 are the experiences about what the medievals call the transcendentals: Goodness, Beauty, and Truth, respectively. These seven types of experience (apart from the a priori intuitions) are all *noetic experience*: they are not just sensations or feelings, but have noetic contents or propositional contents about the world. Besides noetic experiences, we also have *two derived epistemic sources: memory and testimony*. The former is the testimony of one's own mind, and the latter is the testimony of others' words. Both sources are derived, in the sense that they cannot generate evidential force on their own; they only transmit the evidential force of other experiences.

Most critics of ARE are motivated by the conviction that REs cannot have PFEF because they are so unlike SEs. Often there is the implicit assumption that *SE is the only type of noetic experience that is also a basic source of justification*. This thesis is called narrow empiricism (sometimes exclusivist or radical empiricism). The narrow empiricists typically also accept memory as a derived source. Most of them accept intellectual intuition as a matter of pragmatic necessity, but they still hope to revalidate intuitions as a nonbasic source on the basis of SE (and memory), for example, reducing analytic truth to empirical truths about linguistic convention. So there are three possibilities when we consider a putative source of epistemic justification, S:

1. S is not a source of justification at all.
2. S is a source of justification and also a basic source of justification (BSJ), which can stand on its own. S does not require the validation of other basic sources.
3. S is a source of justification, but it is only a nonbasic source of justification (non-BSJ), which *requires* the validation of other basic sources.

Typically, foundationalists believe in some basic sources, but the classical foundationalists propose rather stringent criteria, like infallibility or universal consensus, as necessary conditions of a basic source. So they tend to accept only SEs as the basic source. As a result, not even IPE is considered a basic source. Since almost all of us find it hard to deny IPE altogether, so the foundationalists are forced to believe that IPE is a nonbasic source of justification. Indeed, the project of solving the "problem of other minds" is nothing but the attempt to validate IPE on the basis of SE alone. Now, when the deficiencies of the entire project of narrow empiricism have become clearer, some philosophers have proposed more open-minded epistemologies, for example, Alston's doxastic practice approach. In this book, I will advocate *holistic empiricism, which is the thesis that all seven types in the rainbow of experiences should be regarded as basic sources of justification.* (Holistic empiricism is also called pluralistic empiricism or integrated empiricism.) In other words, the PCT is applicable to them all, and we should give prima facie trust to the entire rainbow of experiences (to some extent). In the end, the beauty of this rainbow will lead us to a larger Being and more inclusive Truth.

### 1.3 Swinburne's Argument from Religious Experience and Epistemological Approach

Let us look at Swinburne's ARE (1979, chapter 13) in more detail. He proposes the Principle of Credulity as a fundamental principle:

(PC) If it seems (epistemically) to me that x is present, then probably x is present unless there are special considerations to the contrary.

The idea is that all experiences should be treated as innocent until proven guilty. Religious experiences should also be accorded PFEF, that is, the claims of REs should be trusted unless counterevidence can be brought forward. Swinburne argues that, apart from PC, we cannot provide any noncircular justification of either ordinary perception or memory. Then Swinburne formulates the following argument:

A) It seems (epistemically) to me that God is present.
B) There is no good reason to think either God is non-existent or not present; nor any good reason to think the experience unveridical.
C) Hence probably God is present.

Since the argument seems valid, there are mainly two kinds of responses open to the critics. The first is to challenge the validity of the PC, as do, for example, Rowe and Michael Martin. The second is to grant Swinburne's PC, but argue that (B) is false, that is, Swinburne has neglected some defeaters of the REs, as does, for example, Forgie.

We have to understand Swinburne's distinction between "epistemic seeming" and "comparative seeming." For him, "to use 'looks', etc. in the comparative use is to compare the way an object looks with the way other objects normally look" (Swinburne 1979, p. 246). So a coin may look elliptical (comparatively) to me, but on the basis of this experience I am inclined (more or less) strongly to believe that the coin is round. The former is how a thing seems comparatively, and the latter is how it seems epistemically. An "epistemic seeming" should be distinguished from a tentative judgment. When I describe my experience of a chair as an epistemic seeming that the chair is present, it does not mean I only tentatively hold to the judgment that there is a chair. On the contrary, it means that on the basis of my experience I am spontaneously and strongly inclined to believe that the chair is there. The "chair" stares me in the face, so to speak. The word "seeming" is only used because we want to have a description of the experience that does not commit one to the *actual existence* of the chair. Epistemic seemings are similar to Bonjour's "cognitively spontaneous beliefs": ordinary perceptual belief "simply occurs to me, 'strikes me,' in a manner which is both involuntary and quite coercive; such a belief is...*cognitively spontaneous*" (Bonjour 1985, p. 117).

Swinburne's initial formulation of PC covers only intentional experiences, defined as follows (the terminology here is mine rather than Swinburne's):

> A subject S has an *intentional experience*, E, of x if it seems (epistemically) to S that x is present and the concept of x is the concept of an object which is distinct from S and can exist independently of S; x is then called the *intentional object* of E.

However, Swinburne already thought that memory claims were covered by his PC. Since memory is not an intentional experience, presumably Swinburne by then already held to a form of PC that had a larger scope. Later Swinburne extends the PC to (almost) all kinds of matter: "other things being equal, it is rational to believe that things are as they seem to be" (Swinburne 1986, p. 292), including logical intuitions, epistemological intuitions, introspection, recognition of other minds, memory claims, perceptual experience, and intentional experience. (He will apply PC to moral or aesthetic claims, too, I think.) Swinburne explains as follows: "We find ourselves with *involuntary* inclinations to belief; in the absence of reasons against going along with such an inclination the rational man will do so" (italics mine). I suggest that the exact meaning and scope of the PC need to be spelled out in more detail (see Chapter 4).

The PC does not stand alone in Swinburne's epistemological approach. Swinburne also explicitly advocates the following principles:

1. The Principle of Testimony: other things being equal, others' experiences are likely to be as they report them to be.
2. The Principle of Simplicity: "in a given field, we take as most likely to be true the simplest theory which fits best with other theories of neighbouring fields to produce the simplest set of theories of the world."
3. Principle of Charity: other things being equal, we suppose that other men are like ourselves. (Swinburne 1986, pp. 13, 15)

The PC alone may look unduly egocentric. However, the Principle of Testimony shows that Swinburne is equally emphatic on trusting others' experiences. Second, Swinburne's approach is not an "anything goes" approach (the word "credulity" is somewhat misleading, though). It is recognized that epistemic seemings are fallible. The hope lies in our ability to sift and correct these initial or *presumptive data*. For example, an erroneous epistemic seeming can be corrected by other epistemic seemings. However, to do this we also need some rational principles to organize our data. For Swinburne, the supreme principle is the Principle of Simplicity (this will be explained later). So, within Swinburne's approach, he has his own way to sift the data and establish an orderly noetic structure. That is why I call this the "Critical Trust Approach" (CTA). In the following sections, I will look at some criticisms of the ARE, as well as the most recent development of the ARE. By listening to both critics and defenders, I hope to integrate their insights into my formulation of ARE.

## 1.4 Discontents with Arguments from Religious Experience

### 1.4.1 Non-Objectivism in Epistemology

Philosophers are still hotly debating the success or failure of AREs, but some people question the possibility of the entire project. For example, John Taber claims that "it is an illusion to think that one can stand back and judge the validity of RE 'objectively'" (Taber 1986, p. 57). I am an objectivist. This entire book is my reply to Taber's challenge, and it is better to let the readers judge the success of my project based on the arguments to be set forth. But just suppose the non-objectivist is correct that it is impossible to produce objective criteria to evaluate REs. What follows then? This conclusion in itself does not mean that trust in REs is unjustified. If there are no objective criteria to judge, we can pronounce REs neither veridical nor unveridical. So it seems at least *permissible* for people who have REs to trust them. Why not? So non-objectivism can be a roundabout way to establish the weak ARE. Like Kant, it is to abolish knowledge to make room for faith! This, perhaps, is enough for many defenders of ARE.

In any case, my objectivist attempt is a worthy one. For those who reject REs and deem acceptance of REs irrational often appeal to allegedly general criteria (e.g. we should only accept publicly verifiable experiences or unavoidable doxastic practices). In engaging with the critics in the same "game," I will argue against those restrictive criteria and suggest the plausibility of a more tolerant epistemology, the CTA. So I will focus my attention on critics of REs in the objectivist tradition.

### 1.4.2 A Sympathetic Critic of the Argument from Religious Experience

Gwen Griffith-Dickson (2005, 2007) is sympathetic to REs, but she has misgivings about the ARE, especially when it is based on allegedly universal principles. First, she complains that contemporary ARE "has had a somewhat obsessive focus on the idea of an Experience" as "a single event" divorced from the context of the experient's entire life (Griffith-Dickson 2005, p. 405).

Second, she has worries over the applicability of PC or the Principle of Testimony (PT) to experiences that are rich in meaning and demand skillful interpretation. "When the emphasis is on experience as what is interpreted, the PC and the PT become a little more complex to apply. Too much has been shoveled in under 'other things being equal'" (Griffith-Dickson 2005, p. 413). The problems are more acute in the context of ARE:

> PC and PT may hold when the experience in question is a simple matter of sense perception...But most spiritual experiences are...about one's inner experience, an insight, a feeling,...a commitment...one is talking about the interpretation of an event, its significance and meaning (Griffith-Dickson 2007, p. 687).

So she thinks the straightforward application of a general principle to REs is a little simplistic. (Her discontents reflect some leaning toward the hermeneutical orientation.)

She explains her misgivings about Swinburne's appeal to the PT in ARE: "our own experiences...have a testimony for us that we cannot do without...what they cannot do is to convince someone else—unless that someone trusts us and our judgement. Pace Swinburne,... 'testimony'...is not most at home in the context of 'proof'... 'proof' can be epistemically coercive.... Testimony, on the other hand, leaves the door open, and allows the listener to...form their own judgement" (Griffith-Dickson 2005, p. 429). She is not denying the significance of testimony altogether, but testimony should be used in "an individual, case-by-case judgement based on a relationship of trust" (Griffith-Dickson 2005, pp. 429–30).

Her advice is that we should "not view religious experiences as an analogy with sensory experiences or information-gathering in the sciences...religious experiences are more like experiences of a relationship than perception of a material object...Many personal experiences [experienced by us]...cannot be experienced by another exactly as we do. We can encourage others to have their versions of such experiences...but we must then recognize that their experiences would be unique and personal; and above all, subject also to the will of the other party whom one wishes to experience" (Griffith-Dickson 2007, p. 686).

Griffith-Dickson's criticisms are good reminders for the defenders of ARE. I would regard this as "friendly fire" from an ally, because she can be interpreted as a defender of *weak* ARE, too. In fact, she also has some inclination toward non-objectivism. She points out that many arguments of the skeptics or the defenders of religious experiences are ultimately based on their prior basic beliefs. So the argument from religious experience is like the dog chasing his tail. However, as I explain, non-objectivism can in fact lend support to weak ARE, and this may be the intention of Griffith-Dickson, as reflected in her great efforts in replying to the critics of RE. Her treatment of the alleged problem of interpretation in RE is one of the best I have ever seen. Apparently she is sympathetic to the claims of REs (at least the best cases), but not comfortable with objectivist or universalistic epistemology. She wants to emphasize the need for case-by-case judgments and hermeneutic insights. We should not claim to provide proof, but should engage in a dialogue with others instead. All these suggestions are not incompatible with the claim that we can justifiably *judge* some cases of RE to be reliable, after considering all the specific facts in their context.

I agree with Griffith-Dickson that the personal relationship model is a fruitful one for ARE. Perhaps both models of perception and personal encounter can be used at the same time. Complementarity of different models is common in physics when the reality is "elusive," for example, the particle-wave duality of light. In the framework of critical realism, the use of multiple models is not contradictory, but in fact necessary. It is because our models cannot be straightforwardly identified with the reality. We often need complementary models to reveal reality more adequately in its full complexity. I think this is the case with God. I also partially agree with Griffith-Dickson's claim that the likening of religious experiences to sensory perception "exacerbates…the philosophical problems… [and] the focus on 'experience' as 'experiences'—discrete and isolated events—threatens to distort our understanding of the religious or spiritual life" (Griffith-Dickson 2007, p. 689). I will propose a richer model of REs and try to put REs in the context of our uniquely human and spiritual existence.

Yes, we need to be sensitive when we apply the PCT or PT. Despite Griffith-Dickson's protest, many of her considerations can, indeed, be contained in the proviso clause of the PCT. My Critical Trust Approach does recognize that the application of PCT is not simple, and it requires a comprehensive assessment and sensitive consideration of all the defeaters. The subtleties and complexities of the epistemic context of an experience are, indeed, a mild defeater, because in our past experiences we find the possibility of a wrong judgment and incorrect interpretation more likely in this situation. So this will *diminish* the evidential force of that experience somewhat. So as far as the personal insights one gleans from a certain RE is concerned (e.g. one has a divine calling to go to Africa as a missionary), I agree with her that we cannot apply the PCT in a straightforward manner. But this is not contradictory to my CTA—it is only applying a second order critical principle (see Chapter 4).

Indeed the intention of ARE is not to endorse a blanket simplistic treatment of all REs, but to provide some support for the existence of God. So we can go with Alston's strategy to concentrate mainly on the most basic experiences of God, which do not involve idiosyncratic factors. The basic intimation that a transcendent personal God exists is the common import of all TEs (and coherent with many non-theistic REs). There is much less diversity of interpretation at this level, and the basic choice is either to accept it or to reject it. If the ARE is used at this level, the problems raised by Griffith-Dickson do not seem to be serious enough to merit a blanket rejection of all these experiences. This may not be her intention, either.

At times, Griffith-Dickson is on the verge of committing the *Super-Reliability Fallacy*, which is very common in the debate about ARE. The general form of this fallacy is as follows:

A.  A type of experience E1 is more reliable than another type of experience E2.
B1. Therefore, E2 as a whole is not reliable. OR:
B2. Therefore, E2 should not be regarded as a basic source of justification.

When applied to ARE, this fallacy is often manifested in the illicit inference from the fact that REs are less reliable than SEs to the conclusion that

REs are hence unreliable *tout court*. For example, Griffith-Dickson points out rightly that the "interpretation of a psychologically complex event is...*much more*...fallible than reporting sensory perceptions. It is easier to come up with...[a] distorted report...[It] can also be highly personal and have little meaning for another person" (Griffith-Dickson 2007, p. 687). Moreover, an "extraordinary event, unprecedented in our experience, may not have the 'right' pattern to match it in our minds. The subject may then fall back on similar experiences reported by others, or texts or ideas within familiar...traditions. But the pattern-match is only as good as the resources available to the individual; and here people may go wrong in labeling or categorizing their experience" (Griffith-Dickson 2007, p. 689). So she concludes, "all other things equal, people are credible witnesses to the fact that they experienced something...nevertheless, we have *better grounds* than usual for begging to differ on the...significance of" an RE (Griffith-Dickson 2007, p. 688; italics mine).

I in fact agree that REs suffer from more problems, and in general their evidential force is less than that of SEs. As emphasized above, the CTA allows for critical considerations that mitigate the original force of presumptive data. However, this does not mean they are unreliable or have completely no force at all. We cannot infer from the fact that a certain person (e.g. Lee Ka Shing, a billionaire in Hong Kong) is less wealthy than Bill Gates that he (Lee Ka Shing) is not rich at all.

However, Griffith-Dickson's final conclusion is somewhat ambivalent, and perhaps in the end she does not commit the Super-Reliability Fallacy. It is because she has a deep appreciation of the fact that problems of interpretation also occur in SEs, and more so in "special human experiences." So "if this [problem] applies to all experience that involves sensory input, it is not a problem uniquely for spirituality. In the dark, when anxious, one can mistake a rope for a snake just as one can mistake an inner voice for the voice of God when feeling distresses...Many other kinds of uncontroversial, but special human experiences would not survive the demands placed on religious experience to prove itself...On the other hand, it must be acknowledged that spiritual experiences pose these problems for us in a particular challenging way" (Griffith-Dickson 2007, p. 689). This conclusion is not entirely negative, and is consistent with my ARE, which only argues for a modest force of REs.

### 1.4.3 A Radical Critic of the Argument from Religious Experience

In the past decades, a group of Christian analytical philosophers has successfully revived the attention to traditional topics in philosophy of religion, such as natural theology. Keith Parsons is not at all happy with this development: this "return to...natural theology...seems to me a[n]...unfortunate turning back of the clock...These Christian philosophers would no doubt see their return to tradition...as just an escape from the dogmas of empiricism...I think it shows a failure to take to heart...what...empiricism and naturalism have achieved" (Parsons 1989, p. 8). Parsons emphasizes that the spirit of analytic philosophy is "liberation from dogma, mysticism, subjectivism, and muddle-headedness" (Parsons 1989, p. 12).

While it is fashionable in some circles to celebrate the death of foundationalism, Parsons extols the virtues of foundationalism. It has an indispensable critical function of eliminating the obviously irrational beliefs by providing us with universal criteria. "Unless we are to decide on a purely ad hoc basis which beliefs can and cannot be properly basic, we have to develop general criteria that will do the job" (Parsons 1989, p. 43).

Parsons then directs his fire onto Plantinga, whose assertion of the proper basicality of belief in God seems to flout the above requirements. (Although Plantinga has not explicitly formulated any ARE, some of his comments have been regarded by many as a weak defense of REs.) He asks, "The elimination of foundationalism may have gotten rid of unduly harsh restrictions on proper basicality, but...hasn't Plantinga thrown open the floodgates of superstition and irrationality?" (Parsons 1989, p. 45). His examples of superstition include Shirley MacLaine's claim to recall her past lives and the belief in the Great Pumpkin. The argument is that "if the existence of God is to be allowed as properly basic, then it would seem that just about any other sort of belief would have to be so allowed...To allow just anything to count as rational is to have no rationality at all...At least the foundationalist criteria have the virtue of eliminating much patent nonsense" (Parsons 1989, p. 49). His complaint is that Plantinga's principles "would inevitably lead to the Balkanization of the entire field...[So] theists must seek to establish *shared* principles of rationality with atheists" (Parsons 1989, p. 60).

I do not find Parsons's critique of Plantinga convincing, but still I intend to learn from the important questions he raises. First, I agree that Balkanization of epistemology is not a good thing, and the availability of shared principles of rationality is desirable *as far as it is feasible*. So in this book I will make an attempt to argue for some universal rational principles on the basis of widely shared intuitions, considerations of consistency and coherence, pragmatic effects, and so on. I do not expect to convince everyone, but I hope to reduce the degree of Balkanization by offering a plausible epistemology after the decline of classical foundationalism. Rational belief does require a critical attitude in which we do not blindly believe in purported truth claims, but try to test them by taking into account all relevant considerations.

It is interesting to reflect on the criticisms of both critics together. While Griffith-Dickson complains that the ARE is too universalistic and "simplistic," Parsons is worried about the loss of critical spirit and the lack of universal criteria. I intend to listen to both critics. So the way ahead is to formulate a kind of epistemology that can avoid the unnecessary restrictiveness of classical foundationalism (or narrow empiricism), but at the same time preserve the critical spirit. Moreover, the ARE needs to pay attention to the more subtle dimensions of human experience, and needs to be applied sensitively.

## 1.5  The Argument from Religious Experience in
## the Twenty-First Century

I review more recent developments below to show that the ARE is picking up momentum in the twenty-first century. Many scholars (not only from philosophy) now join forces in defending some form of ARE.

### 1.5.1  New Supporters of Arguments from Religious Experience

The Transcendental ARE has continued to find "converts" in the past decade or so. T. J. Mawson (2005) affirms the PCT as a fundamental principle and concludes that RE is some "evidence in favour of the religious outlook and against the physicalist" (Mawson 2005, p. 172). Stephen Layman also believes that "we ought to apply the Principle of Credulity to any form of experience" (Layman 2007, p. 45). Douglas Geivett is mainly concerned about the Analogical ARE. He thinks that "all salient analogies between sense perception and 'perception' of God are due to the subject-object presentational structure that they have in common" (Geivett 2003, p. 197). He is attracted to a generic PCT as well.

Another interesting development is the "coming out" of a trio of critical realists in support of the ARE. They consist of two sociologists (Margaret Archer and Douglas Porpora) and a philosopher (Andrew Collier). They all follow the lead of Roy Bhaskar's methodology of critical realism in natural science and social science. Recently, Bhaskar has shown a spiritual turn (Bhaskar 2000, 2002). Similarly, their book signifies another "spiritual turn in critical realism" (Archer, Collier, and Porpora 2004, p. 172) to a broadly Christian position. They affirm the PCT and apply it to RE (Archer, Collier, and Porpora 2004, p. 26). They are mainly influenced by Alston's *Perceiving God*.

They call themselves closet theists who have recently come out! Moreover, they are "all associated with the political left," which, they admit, is a "strange place perhaps from which to expect a defence of religion!...our religiosity is still regarded as something of an anomaly, at best a charming eccentricity.... it is an eccentricity that we often keep to ourselves. When we cease keeping it to ourselves, we suddenly find that there are a surprising number of us" (Archer, Collier, and Porpora 2004, p. 6). Of course their "coming out" is not easy because, as they point out, in academic circles, the atheist has occupied a privileged position. It seems to me that their decision is to some extent emboldened by the first-rate work of theistic philosophers like Alston and Swinburne. It is rather unusual for sociologists working in a secular environment to defend religious experience as they did.

There are still others who endorse some form of PCT: Stephen Evans and Zachary Manis (2009, p. 112), and Wystra (1990, p. 156). Robert Audi seems to be a qualified supporter of ARE. Although he does not have an explicitly affirmative conclusion, he defends ARE from some common objections (Audi 1998, pp. 272–3). In the end, he affirms that direct theistic knowledge is possible and may provide substantial justification for religious belief (Audi 1998, pp. 270, 274, 276). Audi does not propose a generic PCT, but he does think a kind of PCT can be applied to SE, introspection, memory, and rational intuition. He seems to agree that the PCT can be applied to some kind of seeing God in nature as an extension of perception.

### 1.5.2 Phenomenological Approach to Religious Experience

There are also defenders of ARE outside the tradition of analytic philosophy. Anthony Steinbock defends a phenomenological approach to RE that affirms the uniqueness and irreducibility of RE. Steinbock also argues for the broadening of the ideas of experience and evidence (Steinbock 2007, p. 1). I largely agree with his approach, but am worried about the isolation of each allegedly unique kind of experience. Wessel Stoker (2006) has also adopted a hermeneutical-phenomenological approach to defend a modest ARE, and he has published his work in Leuven (originally a Dutch edition). Perhaps the ARE is starting to have influence on the Continent, as shown by the fact that Stoker is heavily influenced by Alston.

### 1.5.3 New Analogical Arguments from Religious Experience

Past discussions of the Analogical ARE have focused on the comparison of SE and RE. I think these discussions are worthwhile, but there are also more fruitful ways to develop an Analogical ARE by comparing TE with other human experiences, like IPE, aesthetic experience, and so on. Garth Hallett has devoted a whole book to defending an analogical ARE by comparing an IPE about a mother to TE. He then argues that since, in important respects, belief in God does resemble his belief that this mother loved her child, which is rational, belief in God should also be deemed rational (Hallett 2000, pp. 19–20). Other authors, like John Cottingham, have appealed to the analogy of TE with aesthetic experience and textual understanding. Since I think the rainbow of experiences also has intrinsic force, analogies of TE with various types of experience (including SE) in complicated manners will help to defuse simplistic objections to TE (which often assume the exclusive reliability of SE) and provide enhancers of TEs.

### 1.5.4 New Explanatory Arguments from Religious Experience

Explanatory AREs are not the most popular form among the defenders of REs (an earlier example is Clark 1984). However, I think Philip Wiebe's impressive efforts have revived the prospect of explanatory ARE. The data he appeals to are the Christic visions (Wiebe 1997) and experiences of exorcism (Wiebe 2004). Methodologically speaking, Wiebe is more akin to the "tough-minded" empiricist. He has reservations about PCT, insisting on the guidance of more public experiences like SE. Most people who adopt his approach will *assume* the REs can be easily explained naturalistically, but Wiebe proceeds to study the empirical data in detail and comes to a surprising conclusion. Wiebe has collected many accounts of contemporary visions of Christ. He then tests various naturalistic and mentalistic explanations against the empirical data and finds them inadequate. So in conclusion, he states, the "claim that the transcendent is encountered in common experiences seems to me plausible primarily because of uncommon phenomena suggestive of transcendence" (Wiebe 1997, p. 215). I cannot go into the details of his arguments here, but I think he has provided an impressive case. Later, Wiebe extends the same procedure to the study of the experiences of exorcism and evil spirits. His conclusion is that "the evidence that is available suggests that the conjecture that evil spirits exist has some plausibility" (Wiebe 2004, p. 58).

I am aware that even defenders of RE are often suspicious of the appeal to visions and unusual REs, but I think we cannot dogmatically exclude the veridicality of *some* of these experiences. In my CTA, we need to be open to all experiences, but at the same time be careful about the less corroborated ones. However, as these unusual experiences are corroborated by more people, they should be taken more seriously. If a careful explanatory argument can be formulated about some of these unusual REs, then the overall case for ARE will be strengthened.

Another defense of an explanatory ARE comes from Block (2007). He mainly defends the validity of near death experiences (NDEs) and uses them as a confirmation of Jewish mysticism. For him "NDEs confirm...the ultimate truth of mysticism: everything is one and nothing exists outside this oneness. It is bonded by love and behind it all is what we call G-d" (Block 2007, p. 134).[2] He does not appeal to the PCT, but provides explanatory considerations that support the objectivity of NDEs. For example, a seventy-year old woman who had been blind since the age of eighteen "almost died due to a heart attack. After she was resuscitated, she told people about her NDE, and she "was able to describe in vivid detail what was happening around her as doctors resuscitated her...[S]he could even describe the colors [of the instruments]...[M]ost of these instruments weren't even thought of over fifty years ago when she could last see" (Block 2007, p. 140). His conclusion is that it is not only rational to accept the truth of NDEs, but actually irrational not to accept them in the light of all the evidence.

Another interesting line of argument offered by Block is his attempt to tie the mystical NDEs to the quest for the meaning of life: "the experience of the Light as attested to by all NDEers without exception conveys the ultimate experience which lifts the soul to such an elevated and rapturous state, that all who experience it have no doubt that this is the highest joy that any created being could attain and as such gives meaning to one's existence...the NDE...gives one a glimpse of the highest joy and happiness the soul can attain through love of G-d and the delight of basking in His radiance" (Block 2007, p. 184).

Since the assessment of explanatory considerations involves a careful study of all the details and the alternatives, I won't proclaim on the ultimate success of Block's explanatory ARE here. However, the combined efforts of Wiebe and Block show that explanatory AREs cannot be dismissed.

I find the approach to link up REs and the quest for meaning refreshing. Traditionally, analytic philosophers treat the ARE purely as an epistemic matter, and regard RE on a par with our experiences of tables and chairs, which are largely devoid of existential meaning. This misses the fact that REs are full of significance and can satisfy our existential quest for meaning. So if they are veridical, TEs not only reveal the existence of God, but also the true meaning of human existence. This point has epistemological implications. First, if TEs serve this purpose, then it leads us to expect other experiences, such as man's quest for meaning and love. We should expect the quest for meaning to be deep-rooted in human existence. If this is indeed the case, then TEs and existential experiences are coherent with one another and mutually supportive.

### 1.5.5 Arguments from Religious Experience and Postfoundationalist Epistemology

Grahame Miles (2007) also has a defense of ARE, and he also tries to articulate a new epistemological framework that can integrate science and religion. This seems to be a new trend, as manifested in Paul Moser's Volitional Theism. Moser not only defends some form of explanatory ARE, but also argues that we need to drastically rethink the epistemology of religion. Moser thinks that if we want to know God, we need to "let God be truly God…even in the area of human inquiry about God's reality" (Moser 2010, p. 28). Otherwise, we will commit the sin of cognitive idolatry.

Since God's purpose is to transform inquirers morally and volitionally, and to free us from selfishness, God needs to deal with our will, which can only be transformed by "the distinctive *power* of divine unselfish love…realized in a divine-human *interpersonal fellowship*" (Moser 2010, p. 118). There is a difference between spectator knowledge (which does not challenge the human will) and authoritative knowledge (which does), and we should expect authoritative evidence, rather than spectator evidence (Moser 2010, p. 42). If we respond to God's authoritative call to let ourselves be transformed by God, then our transformed personal lives will "*themselves* become evidence of God" (Moser 2010, p. 172).

I largely accept Moser's volitional theism, which is, in fact, congenial to my CTA. What he calls authoritative evidence is here called participatory evidence. The basic insight is that we should think about what is the most appropriate form of evidence for God if God is really there. Moser is also helpful in his emphasis on the idea of divine elusiveness; this shows that many disanalogies between TE and SE are not only explicable, but to be expected. Even if some entities are elusive, we can still have perfectly good evidence for their existence.

Stephen Evans argues that we can have an experience of God mediated by natural signs (e.g. sense of cosmic wonder, sense of moral obligation). In the end, he also adopts a kind of CTA. This kind of mediated TE is modeled on the Reidian account of perception: "sensations are not the primary objects of perceptual awareness but are 'natural signs' that make perceptual awareness [of external objects] possible" (Evans 2010, p. 29). The idea of mediated awareness of God has often been contested, but Evans provides an intelligible account of our mediated TEs and defends the plausibility of several theistic natural signs, which are in fact part of the rainbow of experiences.

Cottingham is advocating a kind of *participatory knowing.* The old empiricists pit cognition against participation because they believe personal involvement is inimical to the impassionate search for truth. Cottingham contends that in many cases of knowing, especially in more human forms of experience, proper knowing is founded on the right kind of personal involvement and inner reflection, and not on detached logical analysis. For example, he draws on Martha Nussbaum's idea of Love's Knowledge, which provides a "radical critique of the traditional rigid dichotomy between the supposedly antithetical faculties of reason and the passions...there are certain kinds of truth such that to try to grasp them purely intellectually is to avoid them" (Cottingham 2005, p. 10), for example, knowledge about love affairs.

Yet another example of participatory knowing is the process of self-discovery, for example, understanding one's own confused emotions: "Bringing to the surface the precise nature of our feelings, and the judgements and choices we make in the light of those feelings, is not a matter of identifying simple items like beliefs and desires, swimming around the transparent tank of consciousness. On the contrary, it often requires serious and systematic work to drag the relevant items into the light...distorted by all kinds of dark projections and shadows from the past" (Cottingham 2005, p. 63). I will defend participatory knowing in Chapter 3.

### 1.5.6 *Arguments from Religious Experience and Religious Pluralism*

The ARE is also accepted by people in various religious traditions. For example, Gellman and Block are both Jewish. Cafer S.Yaran, an Islamic philosopher, also shows support for the ARE (Yaran 2003, p. 22).

Paul Marshall (2005) has a recent study of the extrovertive mystical experience (EME). The major content of EME is the sense of unity between oneself and the whole word, and this experience occurs widely in various cultures and religious traditions (theistic or monistic). Marshall has rich discussions of the contents of EME and various theories of EME. He also provides an assessment of the more reductionist explanations of EME by means of pathology and neuroscience, but in the end comes down on Huxley's filtration theory (the inputs from the transcendent reality are always there, but normally filtered out by our brains). This theory permits a critical realist model of mystical experience that looks plausible (Marshall 2005, p. 240).

Marshall seems to assume some kind of PCT. He talks about "the evidence of mystical experience" (Marshall 2005, p. 259). Finally, he argues that the idealist explanation of EME is the best and is open to the theistic form of idealism: "A theistic explanation could trace luminosity, temporal inclusivity, omniscience, and love to the mystic's contact with the mind of God...Attaining union with the divine mind, the mystic experiences the world as God experiences it" (Marshall 2005, p. 274). Since his arguments throw doubt on naturalism and allow for theism as one of the most plausible solutions (alongside panentheism or pantheism), this book again contributes to the case for ARE.

I think the greatest challenge to the ARE is the conflict between different types of REs. Some critics argue further that there is, in principle, no way to resolve the conflict between REs, and this point seems to throw doubt on the entire realm of REs. I do not agree with this conclusion and will argue that the CTA provides a reasonable methodology to resolve conflicts between REs, and the PFEF of the rainbow of experiences is crucial in this process.

Moreover, critics have neglected the works of scholars like Michael Stoeber (1994) and Louis Dupre (1981), who have, in fact, suggested ways to resolve the conflicts and to integrate diverse types of mystical experiences. Stoeber (1994) made a notable effort to provide a theistic interpretation of the diverse religious experiences (unfortunately largely ignored by analytic philosophers), and an integration of monistic and theistic types of mysticism in particular. Stoeber's theory of theo-monism "secures a typology of mysticism that authenticates and harmonizes the various mystical experiences." Moreover, he argues that his theo-monism is more plausible than Sankara's monistic hierarchy, because while "Sankara's monistic hierarchy is unable to affirm or reinforce the authenticity of lower level theistic realizations in terms of higher level monistic realizations," theo-monism can provide "a pluralistic framework that secures the authenticity of monistic realizations" (Stoeber 1994, pp. 3–4). If impressive efforts like Stoeber's are taken into account, the force of the conflicting-experiences objection to ARE will be significantly reduced.

## 1.6  Arguments from Religious Experience in the Context of Human Existence

A new trend, which I wholly endorse, is to place the ARE in the context of the wider background of human existence and spiritual quest.

### 1.6.1  Brendan Sweetman, Gabriel Marcel, and Experience of Fidelity

The analytic philosopher Brendan Sweetman published a book in 2008 to defend Gabriel Marcel. He thinks that one weakness of Reformed epistemology's appeal to REs is that "such experiences do not seem all that common" (Sweetman 2008, p. 84). Instead, he appeals to Marcel's analysis of the experience of fidelity as unconditional commitment and then argues that existence of God is the best explanation for these commitments (see Chapter 12).

Sweetman believes that this type of argument is better than ARE "because the experiences he calls attention to and describes are ordinary experiences of human life, easily recognizable to many people" (Sweetman 2008, pp. 84–5). I find Sweetman's approach congenial, but he may have underestimated the force of the ARE. As I argue later, REs are sufficiently common to have appeal to a lot of people. Again, the ARE and the argument from human experiences are complementary, and Part B is an extended argument combining both.

### 1.6.2 *John Cottingham, Spiritual Dimension, and Religious Experience*

John Cottingham is also a defender of the modest ARE on the basis of a praxis-based approach in the context of the spiritual dimension of life. His is "an attempt at integration to show how a philosophical approach to religion needs to bring together the disparate areas of our human experience, emotional as well as intellectual, practical as well as theoretical, embracing the inner world of self-reflection as well as the outer world of empirical inquiry" (Cottingham 2005, p. x).

He defends the primacy of praxis and places RE in the context of other human experiences, like the experience of self-discovery. So religious understanding should not be modeled on SE or scientific explanation, but on a kind of spiritual growth, the escape from self-deception (Cottingham 2005, p. 71). Equipped with this understanding, he argues for the convergence of the psychoanalytic project and religious quest. I will also appeal to data from psychoanalysis and the existential quest, which are seldom discussed in analytic philosophy.

### 1.6.3 *Roger Scruton: Human Experiences and Transcendence*

In the past decade or so, Roger Scruton, a previously agnostic philosopher, has come to a defense of a religious worldview (Scruton 1996, 1998, 2009). Notably, he puts the emphasis on the study of human culture and human experiences, like aesthetic experience and moral experience, and argues for the plausibility of a theistic interpretation.

To begin with, Scruton defends the distinctiveness of human persons from animals. Only humans, and not animals, can do the following things: make choices; make judgments about the past and future, and engage in long-term planning; recognize the right of property and the duty to give away; engage in practical reasoning; have consciousness of injustice; have imagination and speculate about the possible, and even the impossible (Scruton 1996, pp. 60, 61, 65). The list can be extended *ad infinitum*...In short, only humans have a kind of spiritual existence and are blessed by the capacity for the rainbow of experiences. The intention of Scruton, I think, is to show that the categories of natural science are fundamentally inadequate regarding this unique kind of existence. The incongruity between human uniqueness and the categories of science also entails a gap between human subjectivity and the objectivity of the external world. This seems to reveal "our fallen state,...[i.e. the] gap between human longing and human satisfaction: the gap which comes from being not of this world, but only in it...it is our awareness of it that leads both to religious ritual and to the belief in a transcendental deity" (Scruton 1996, p. 89).

He then focuses on the "strangeness" of our interpersonal experience (IPE): "it is as though the world of objects were perforated by apertures, from each of which a subject peers, and through each of which we glimpse the 'transcendental' province of another's will" (Scruton 1996, p. 82). He then appeals to our experience of freedom and moral responsibility. The overall thrust is to show that they are intelligible only on the *imago dei* thesis:

> 'For Mercy has a human heart,
> Pity a human face.
> And Love the human form divine,
> And Peace, the human dress…'

Blake's words flow from the fount of reverence that springs in all of us, and which caused us not merely to cherish the works of unblemished nature, but to look on the human being as somehow exalted above them…an air of sacred prohibition surrounds humanity, since the "human form divine" is our only image of the subject (Scruton 1996, p. 119).

Scruton also argues that God is the only possible solution for the metaphysical predicament of the subject in the world of objects, and in particular REs like the experience of Holy Communion can help us overcome alienation (Scruton 1996, pp. 90–1). In the end, he affirms that "the experience of the sacred is therefore a revelation, a direct encounter with the divine" (Scruton 1996, p. 96). However, this defense is carried out not by formulating epistemic principles to evaluate these isolated experiences, but by exhibiting the meaning of these experiences in the larger context of human existence in the world.

In fact, Scruton also argues that our aesthetic experience, and even culture, finds fulfillment in religion. Scruton (1996, chapter 11) argues that music is a pointer to the eternal realm. Scruton (1998) has extensive discussions of art and culture, and comes to the conclusion that "culture is rooted in religion" (Scruton 1998, p. 129). Scruton (2009) further elaborates on similar arguments. In his several books, Scruton has provided an impressive defense of the argument from human spirit to a theistic worldview. This is also the approach I find fruitful and complementary to the more analytic type of ARE.

## 1.7 Conclusion

In this chapter, I have looked at the resurgence of the ARE in the late twentieth century. This resurgence has, in fact, gained momentum in the twenty-first century. Most of the works I discuss above were published between 1995 and 2010, and they provide a defense of ARE in its various forms. My inclination is to regard these efforts as mutually complementary. Of course, they need to be integrated into a coherent, cumulative ARE, and this is what I try to do in this book.

CHAPTER 2

# LUDWIG WITTGENSTEIN AND THE RAINBOW OF EXPERIENCES

*"Wisdom is grey." Life on the other hand and religion are full of colour.*
*—Wittgenstein*

*The problems of life are insoluble on the surface and can only be solved in depth.*
*—Wittgenstein*

Analytic philosophers do not talk much about the rainbow of experiences, and they are often suspicious of spiritual experiences. In this chapter I hope to show that spiritual experiences should be taken seriously, by means of a case study of a figure that many analytic philosophers can identify with—Wittgenstein.

## 2.1 Wittgenstein: Positivist or Mystic?

Wittgenstein was one of the most famous analytic philosophers in the twentieth century and inspired two important philosophical movements. In earlier days, his *Tractatus* made an impact on the Vienna Circle, whose members vigorously promoted the program of logical positivism, which rejected the legitimacy of metaphysics (including theology). However, Wittgenstein's later works inspired the development of ordinary language philosophy, the spirit of which seemed to contradict positivism. Wittgenstein's attitude toward religion also appeared to be enigmatic. On the one hand, some naturalists were delighted by Wittgenstein's "insight" that many philosophical sentences, especially in traditional metaphysics, were pseudo-sentences, devoid of factual significance. (Some of Wittgenstein's remarks were also used to attack the idea of the "soul.") On the other hand, despite Wittgenstein's lack of involvement in institutional religion, he seemed to have some kind of religious personality, and this was quite surprising to the early positivists.

Carnap met with Wittgenstein in 1927. However, it soon became apparent that Wittgenstein and the positivists had very different views and temperaments. In 1929, Wittgenstein indicated that he no longer wanted to meet with them. For Carnap, the major difference between Wittgenstein and himself was that "any idea which had the flavor of 'enlightenment' was repugnant to Wittgenstein" (Nieli 1987, p. 66). Carnap perceived "a strong inner conflict in Wittgenstein between his emotional life and his intellectual thinking. His intellect...had recognized that many statements in the field of religion and metaphysics did not, strictly speaking, say anything...but this result was extremely painful for him emotionally" (Nieli 1987, p. 67).

I think Carnap is right about the conflict within Wittgenstein, but I do not entirely agree with his diagnosis. Of course, since the positivists usually regard emotions as devoid of cognitive content and irrelevant to the quest for truth (if not obstacles), it is natural for Carnap to pit Wittgenstein's emotional life against his intellectual thinking. There is no doubt on which side Carnap's sympathy lies. However, I think it is wrong to regard Wittgenstein's emotions as "mere emotions"—they were, in fact, rooted in Wittgenstein's powerful spiritual and religious experiences, which suggested to him another kind of truth, which apparently conflicted with the thinking arrived at through his philosophical analysis. Wittgenstein tried to combine these two kinds of thinking in his *Tractatus*. Of course, this was a very difficult task, and Wittgenstein's remarks on the mystical have engendered bewilderment and numerous controversies. The positivists basically regard those remarks as some kind of joke (if not outright inconsistencies), but I think this is a serious misunderstanding. We cannot fully understand Wittgenstein's life and thought if we do not take seriously his spiritual and religious experiences.

## 2.2 Nieli's Interpretation of Wittgenstein

I agree there is some kind of conflict within Wittgenstein. However, Russell Nieli tries to argue that Wittgenstein is, in fact, consistently a mystic. This interpretation is apparently supported by Bertrand Russell's comments on Wittgenstein's *Tractatus* in his letter to Lady Ottoline Morrell on December 20, 1919: "I had felt in his book a flavor of mysticism, but was astonished when I found that he has become a complete mystic" (quoted by Nieli 1987, p. vi). Russell was surprised by Wittgenstein's devotion to authors such as Kierkegaard, Tolstoy, and Dostoevsky.

Nieli believes that"*Tractatus* had been fundamentally misunderstood by the logical positivists...Everything in the *Tractatus*...begins to fall into its proper place once the work is seen in its function as a ladder in the mystical ascent along the *via negativa*...the ethic upon which the *Tractatus* was built was a mystical or theocentric ethic"(Nieli 1987, pp. xi–xii). I find Nieli's interpretation of Wittgenstein as a consistent mystical theologian interesting, but it may have erred in another direction. It minimizes Wittgenstein's inclination to some kind of positivist thought, which is manifested in some of his writings. Nieli may also have too high an estimate of Wittgenstein's knowledge of the mystical tradition.

This seems to be a better interpretation: Wittgenstein's thinking is indeed torn in two directions. On the one hand, his philosophical analysis leads

him to reject the talk of the transcendent realm as "nonsense." On the other
hand, his spiritual and religious experiences *show* that this "nonsense" is
*apparently* real and existentially very important. So he said, "Don't, for
heaven's sake, be afraid of talking nonsense! But you must pay attention to
your nonsense" (Wittgenstein 1980, p. 56). I do not think he has come up
with a unitary scheme to combine these two strands of thinking. Some of his
remarks suggest that he does believe in the reality of the transcendent realm
and that he adopts some kind of *via negativa*. Other remarks suggest that,
while he holds on to the existential significance of the mystical, he adopts
a non-realist interpretation in the end. Perhaps he was drawn to different
solutions at different moments of his life.

I do not need to settle this issue here. It is enough to point out that
Wittgenstein has never consistently denied the reality of the mystical or
the transcendent. Wittgenstein affirmed the "longing for the transcendent,
because in so far as people think they can see the 'limits of human understanding', they believe of course that they can see beyond these...Perhaps
what is inexpressible (what I find mysterious and am not able to express) is
the background against which whatever I could express has its meaning"
(Wittgenstein 1980, pp. 15–16). This is confirmed by Wittgenstein's corre-
spondence with Ludwig Ficker: "The book [*Tractatus*]'s point is an ethical
one...My work consists of two parts: the one presented here plus all that I
have *not* written. And it is precisely this second part that is the important
one" (quoted from Keightley 1976, p. 23).

My major contention is that despite the severe constraints of Wittgenstein's
cognitive framework (whether hyper-mystical, extremely apophatic, or
positivist-scientist), he has had a lot of implicit religious experiences (e.g.
ethics as something supernatural, wonder at existence), and even some
direct experiences of God, such as consciousness of sin, sense of trust (absolute safety), and experience of salvation. It is really remarkable that these
experiences can occur against a very unfavorable cognitive background, for
example, Wittgenstein's strong distaste for organized religion and his antimetaphysical inclination.


### 2.3 Wittgenstein: Religious or Nonreligious?

Wittgenstein had a Catholic background, but at school he lost his faith.
However, some time later he seemed to recover a kind of private faith, which
somehow persisted to the end of his life. Although he never returned to
institutionalized religion, he did not bother to cut off the official ties either.
The recovery of faith happened during the First Word War. Wittgenstein
was mainly influenced by religious writers (and not the religious philosophers!). For example, he discovered Tolstoy's *The Gospel in Brief*:
"He read and reread it, and had it always with him, under fire and at all
times, and was known by the other soldiers as 'the one with the Gospels'"

(McGuinness 1988, p. 220). When he stayed in the prison camp at Monte Cassino, he read Dostoevsky a lot. As Anthony Kenny says, "At the front Wittgenstein showed conspicuous courage and was commended...he was also converted, by the reading of Tolstoy, to an intense though idiosyncratic Christianity. 'Perhaps the nearness of death', he wrote in his diary, 'will bring me the light of life. May God enlighten me. I am a worm, but through God I become a man. God be with me. Amen.'"(Kenny 2004, p. 201). Wittgenstein had even contemplated being a priest! In the end he decided to be a teacher, but this decision also had religious motivation: "I'd most like to be a priest, but when I'm a teacher I can read the Gospel with the children" (quoted from McGuinness 1988, p. 274).

Wittgenstein once said to O. C. Drury: "I am not a religious man but I cannot help seeing every problem from a religious point of view" (quoted from Rhees 1984, p. 94). This saying looks paradoxical, but becomes intelligible once we distinguish two kinds of religiosity: the existential-moral-aesthetic kind of religiosity, and the doctrinal-institutional aspects of religion. Wittgenstein was favorable to the former kind, while rejecting the latter kind. So was Wittgenstein religious or nonreligious? My answer is that although he was not a believer in orthodox or organized religion, he was a deeply religious person at heart. I doubt that a nonreligious person could utter a prayer like this: "May God enlighten me. I am a worm, but through God I become a man." Moreover, Wittgenstein had many experiences of God (mostly implicit) throughout his life that had lasting influence on him. The problem is that the contents of those experiences seemed to be "nonsense" from his cognitive point of view. So, intellectually, he could not wholeheartedly commit to the religious worldview, and he struggled over how to express these contents.

## 2.4 The Wonder of Existence

Although Wittgenstein did not believe in a cosmological deity, he did wonder at the cosmos. He said, "The mystical is not *how* the world is, but that it is" (*Tractatus* 6.44). Although we cannot say anything about what lies outside the world (if we do this, we can only produce "nonsense"), this "nonsense" is not unimportant, and it can be *shown* in some way: "the sense of the world must lie outside the world" (*Tractatus* 6.41).

Later, in Cambridge (1929), Wittgenstein delivered his "A Lecture on Ethics," and he again described an experience of "seeing the world as a miracle." He said, "When I have it I wonder at the existence of the world. And I am then inclined to use such phrases as 'how extraordinary that anything should exist'...the experience of wondering at the existence of the world...is the experience of seeing the world as a miracle" (Wittgenstein 1965, pp. 7–8, 11). He believed this was "exactly what people were referring to when they said that God created the world" (Wittgenstein 1965, pp. 9–10). Wittgenstein believed that "man has to

awaken to wonder...Science is a way of sending him to sleep again"
(Wittgenstein 1980, p. 5).

### 2.5 The Meaning of Life and the Existential Quest

In contrast with the positivists, who dismiss the quest for meaning as something curious, Wittgenstein had a passion for this question. He was concerned
with matters such as "birth, sickness, death, madness, catalepsy,...dreams"
(Wittgenstein 1980, p. 5), and he talked about the infinite torment of the
soul, loneliness, or isolation (Wittgenstein 1980, p. 53).

During the war, he volunteered for the post of artillery observer in an
advanced position: "Perhaps nearness to death will bring light into my life"
(quoted from McGuinness 1988, p. 240). For him, "A hero looks death in the
face, real death...Behaving honourably in a crisis...means rather being able
to look death itself in the eye" (Wittgenstein 1980, p. 50). So Wittgenstein's
passion for the question of life (to live an honorable life) made him even fear-
less of death. For him, this question was inextricably linked to the question
of God. On July 8, 1916, he wrote, "What do I know about God and the
purpose of life?...something about the world is problematic, which we call
its meaning" (Wittgenstein 1979, p. 74). Moreover, "to pray is to think that
life has a meaning...To believe in God means to see that life has a meaning"
(Wittgenstein 1979, p. 73). Why did Wittgenstein think that there is a connection between these two questions? First, the question of meaning seemed
to belong to the mystical, as well: Wittgenstein said, "Even if all possible scientific questions have been answered, the problems of life remain completely
untouched" (*Tractatus* 6.52). In *Tractatus*, this remark is embedded between
two explicit discussions of the mystical (6.45 and 6.522). In his *Notebooks*
(entry on May 25, 1915), his remark on the meaning of life follows this
comment on the mystical: "The urge to the mystical comes from the non-
satisfaction of our wishes by science" (Wittgenstein 1979, p. 51). No doubt
the quest for meaning was part of the mystical for Wittgenstein.[1]

Wittgenstein did have some kind of existential yearning: he felt that
"something about the world is problematic," but this problem of human
existence could not be satisfied by anything in this world. This question and
some other experiences force us to recognize our world as limited: "The
feeling of the world as a limited whole is the mystical feeling"(*Tractatus* 6.
45). Kenny also takes Wittgenstein's quest for meaning seriously: "Nothing
that one could say, whether as scientist or as philosopher, could state the
meaning of life. If life has a meaning, it is something which cannot be said
but which must show itself" (Kenny 2004, p. 209). Moreover, "To see the
meaning of life would be to have a conviction that life was worth living. By
contrast with a meaningless succession of disconnected episodes, a meaningful life would be one which constituted the fulfillment of a task...[But]
who sets the task?" For Wittgenstein, "God is the setter of the task and the
judge of its performance" (Kenny 2004, p. 210). For example, Wittgenstein

talked sympathetically of an author "seeing *his life as a work of art created by God*" (Wittgenstein 1980, p. 4; italics mine). He also said, "'of course, that's how it must be!' It is just as though you have *understood a creator's purpose*" (Wittgenstein 1980, p. 26; italics mine).

## 2.6 Existential Experience

Usually, the quest for meaning is accompanied by a keen self-consciousness and habits of self-reflection. No doubt this was also the case with Wittgenstein. As mentioned before, Wittgenstein once said, "I am a worm, but *through God I become a man.*" This expressed a strong sense of self-disgust (have you ever heard positivists confessing their own self-disgust?), and at the same time an experience of God which redeemed his sense of humanity. So far from having debasing effects, a theistic experience can, in fact, have a humanizing or personalizing effect!

Wittgenstein was deeply aware of the difficulty of honest self-reflection: "It is as impossible to view one's own character from outside." Similarly, a "man can see what he has, but not what he is" (Wittgenstein 1980, pp. 23, 49). The greatness of a person depends on his honest self-evaluation: "a man will never be great if he misjudges himself, if he throws dust in his own eyes." Unfortunately, it is very difficult to achieve greatness because "[n]othing is so difficult as not deceiving oneself" (Wittgenstein 1980, pp. 49, 34)!

As he gradually became famous, he was especially sensitive to the problem of vanity—in others and in his own soul (Wittgenstein 1980, p. 47). Then, in 1949, he admitted, "I thought when I gave up my professorship that I had at last got rid of my vanity. Now I find I am vain about the style in which I am able to write" (quoted from Rhees 1984, p. 175). This kind of ruthless honesty with oneself can be understood as a kind of religious aspiration toward the virtue of humility before God.

Indeed, his quest for honesty with himself led him to some kind of religious experience: "Understanding oneself properly is difficult...one may be acting in such and such a way out of genuine love, but equally well out of deceitfulness...only if I were able *to submerge myself in religion* could these doubts be stilled. Because only religion would have the power to destroy vanity and penetrate all the nooks and crannies" (Wittgenstein 1980, p. 48; italics mine).

## 2.7 Moral Experience

Wittgenstein took moral duty very seriously. He once said to Drury: "If it ever happens that you get mixed up in hand to hand fighting, you must just stand aside and let yourself be massacred" (quoted from Rhees 1984, p. 163). So in Wittgenstein's mind, the moral sense was so paramount that one could even sacrifice one's life for it! He placed stringent moral demands on himself. He went for confession in 1931 and wrote, "A confession must be part of the new life" (Wittgenstein 1980, p. 18). For him, confession reflected a desire to be utterly honest with himself. In 1937, he made a confession to Fania Pascal. Pascal asked him: "What is it? You want to be perfect?" Wittgenstein replied: "*Of course* I want to be perfect!" (quoted from Rhees 1984, p. 50). In general, Wittgenstein's ethical views were Kantian, and here we can see that he keenly felt the absolute force of the categorical imperative.

The desire for moral perfection and absolute honesty bespeak the call of transcendence in Wittgenstein's moral experiences, and he explicitly recognized this. In 1929, he said: "What is good is also divine. Queer as it sounds, that sums up my ethics. Only something supernatural can express the Supernatural" (Wittgenstein 1980, p. 3). In fact, earlier on in his Notebooks (entry on July 30, 1916), he wrote: "But this is really in some sense deeply mysterious! *It is clear* that ethics *cannot* be expressed!...Ethics is transcendental!" (Wittgenstein 1979, pp. 78–9). In any case, the "good is outside the space of facts" (Wittgenstein 1980, p. 3). Certainly Wittgenstein was not unaware of the many attempts to reduce the ethical to the natural, but nonetheless he affirmed that the good could not be reduced to naturalistic facts.

Wittgenstein clearly acknowledged the reality of the experiences of sin and salvation: "'consciousness of sin' is an actual occurrence, and so are despair and salvation through faith" (Wittgenstein 1980, p. 28). He also treated the judgment of God as a kind of reality. In a letter to Malcolm in 1940, he said: "May I not prove too much of a skunk when I shall be tried" (Malcolm 1993, p. 10). In 1951, he again wrote: "God may say to me: 'I am judging you out of your own mouth. Your own actions have made you shudder with disgust when you have seen other people do them'" (Wittgenstein 1980, p. 87). Wittgenstein had a sensitive conscience. Schopenhauer was judged by him to be "a crude mind" because "he never searches his conscience" (Wittgenstein 1980, p. 36). But for Wittgenstein, "conscience is the voice of God" (Wittgenstein 1979, p. 75).

## 2.8 Interpersonal Experience

Wittgenstein was sensitive to the depth dimension in life: "it is important...that someone may feel concerning certain people that their inner life will always be a mystery to him" (Wittgenstein 1980, p. 74). Wittgenstein acknowledged the sense of mystery in our encounter with other persons, and this reminds us of Buber and Marcel. As a result, Wittgenstein warned, "Don't play with what lies deep in another person!" (Wittgenstein 1980, p. 23). This also seems to reflect an Augustinian perspective, which emphasizes that a person is an abyss.

Moral experience is intertwined with interpersonal experience, which reveals to us a supreme value: love. Indeed, "If you already have a person's love no sacrifice can be too much to give for it" (Wittgenstein 1980, p. 42). Moreover, love is "man's greatest happiness" (Wittgenstein 1980, p. 77). Unfortunately, in human life, love is all too often replaced by indifference or even hate. As Wittgenstein reflected on this problem, he thought the root was our pride, which stops us from having a deep encounter with other persons: "Hate between men comes from our cutting ourselves off from each other. Because we don't want anyone else to look inside us, since it's not a pretty sight in there" (Wittgenstein 1980, p. 46).

This reflection led Wittgenstein to an appreciation of religion as a solution for the above problem: "Someone who in this way penitently opens his heart to God in confession lays it open for other men too. In doing this he loses the dignity that goes with his personal prestige and becomes like a child. That means without official position, dignity or disparity from others. A man can bare himself before others only out of a particular kind of love. A love which acknowledges, as it were, that we are all wicked children" (Wittgenstein 1980, p. 46). The above passage reflects Wittgenstein's own experience of confession (see below). It explains clearly how the experience of penitence before God was related to a new attitude of honesty in one's self, and to a childlike love for others. After all, in God's love, we are free to acknowledge "we are all wicked children," and this provides us a basis of solidarity in sin.

Wittgenstein also wondered at the phenomenon of faith in interpersonal experience: "Unshakable faith. (E.g., in a promise.) Is it any less certain than being convinced of a mathematical truth?" (Wittgenstein 1980, p. 73). Of course, the puzzle is that we can never support our absolute faith in others' promises with anything like a mathematical proof. Sometimes not even an empirical "proof" is available. For Marcel, this experience of fidelity opens up the possibility of an experience of a God who is the ground of our experience of fidelity to other persons (see Chapter 12). I am not sure Wittgenstein would go this far, but he no doubt saw an analogy between our faith in God and our faith in other persons. Before Plantinga wrote *God and Other Minds*, Wittgenstein had already made this comment: "If someone can believe in God with complete certainty, why not in Other Minds?"(Wittgenstein 1980, p. 73).

## 2.9 Aesthetic Experience

For some positivists, questions of scientific truth are almost like their ultimate concern. In contrast, Wittgenstein confessed, "I may find scientific questions interesting, but they never really grip me. Only conceptual and aesthetic questions do that" (Wittgenstein 1980, p. 79). Aesthetic experiences can teach us something apart from science: "People nowadays think that scientists exist to instruct them, poets, musicians, etc. to give them pleasure. The idea that these have something to teach them—that does not occur to them" (Wittgenstein 1980, p. 36). So Wittgenstein was also an opponent of narrow empiricism.

Indeed, when we read through Wittgenstein's *Culture and Value*, we find a lot of comments on different types of music, Shakespeare, and so on.

Wittgenstein's aesthetic experience also reflected his deep interest in the mystical or the eternal. For him, the work of the artist "is a way of capturing the world *sub specie aeterni*" (Wittgenstein 1980, p. 5). He wondered at the "infinite complexity" of the substance of music (Wittgenstein 1980, pp. 8–9). Aesthetic experience also has a depth dimension, which cannot be reduced to the physical. For example, "Tender expression in music...isn't to be characterized in terms of degrees of loudness or tempo. Any more than a tender facial expression can be described in terms of the distribution of matter in space. As a matter of fact it can't even be explained by reference to a paradigm, since there are countless ways in which the same piece may be played with genuine expression" (Wittgenstein 1980, p. 82). Similarly, "Architecture immortalizes and glorifies something. Hence there can be no architecture where there is nothing to glorify" (Wittgenstein 1980, p. 69). The language here (immortal glory) suggests something transcendent.

Aesthetic experience was related to Wittgenstein's wonder at existence: "art shows us the miracles of nature....We say: 'Just look at it opening out!'" (Wittgenstein 1980, p. 56). He was also impressed by the beauty of mathematics, which was analogous to the beauty of nature: "The mathematician (Pascal) who admires the beauty of a theorem in number theory; it's as though he were admiring a beautiful natural phenomenon. It's marvelous, he says, what wonderful properties numbers have. It's as though he were admiring the regularities in a kind of crystal" (Wittgenstein 1980, p. 41). Later, he again talked about "the beauty of mathematical demonstrations, as experienced by Pascal. Within that way of looking at the world these demonstrations did have beauty—not what superficial people call beauty" (Wittgenstein 1980, p. 79). Here Wittgenstein again emphasized the depth dimension of aesthetic experience—it was not something superficial. Wittgenstein did not develop this theme much further, but his comments remind us of discussions about "the unreasonable effectiveness of mathematics in the natural sciences" (this is the heading of chapter 17 in Wigner 1967) and the curious fact that the beauty of natural laws seems to be an indicator of truth. We will discuss these issues in Chapter 9.

## 2.10 Openness to Existential Religion

Wittgenstein had an openness toward various aspects of religion. He was touched by religious symbolism: "The symbolisms of Catholicism are wonderful beyond words...All religions are wonderful, even those of the most primitive tribes" (quoted by Rhees 1984, p. 123). He also positively commented on liturgy: "Yes, those prayers read as if they had been soaked in centuries of worship. When I was a prisoner of war in Italy we were compelled to attend Mass on Sundays. I was very glad of that compulsion" (quoted by Rhees 1984, p. 109). All these clearly show that Wittgenstein quite appreciated solemn religious practices, and it is likely that he had some religious experiences during these practices. Wittgenstein was no doubt deeply impressed by religious symbols and their beauty, and his religious experiences had often been mediated by aesthetic and existential experiences.

For Wittgenstein, experience of God was also mediated by actions: "Christianity is not a matter of saying a lot of prayers; in fact we are told not to do that. If you and I are to live religious lives, it mustn't be that we talk a lot about religion, but that our manner of life is different. It is my belief that only if you try to be helpful to other people will you in the end find your way to God" (quoted by Rhees 1984, p. 129). The Christian tradition has always insisted on the intrinsic connection of a genuine faith with concrete actions. It is in line with Wittgenstein's emphasis on the way to God through actions of kindness.

## 2.11 More Explicit Religious Experience

Despite insisting on the ineffability of the mystical, Wittgenstein sometimes used explicitly religious categories (and even recognizably Christian ones) to describe his experiences. In 1937, he explained his view on Christianity: "Christianity is not a doctrine; I mean, not a theory about what has happened and will happen with the human soul, but a description of an actual occurrence in human life. For 'consciousness of sin' is an actual occurrence, and so are despair and salvation through faith. Those who speak of these things (like Bunyan) are simply describing what has happened to them" (Wittgenstein 1980, p. 28). In 1944, he said: "People are religious to the extent that they believe themselves to be not so much *imperfect*, as *ill*. . . . Any half-way decent man will think himself extremely imperfect, but a religious man believes himself *wretched*" (Wittgenstein 1980, p. 45). Although these remarks seem to merely be observations of others' experiences, we have good reason to believe that Wittgenstein, personally, had a deep sense of sin or wretchedness, as manifested in his sense of being a worm. This experience was probably also related to his intense moral experiences, for example, his sensitive conscience and his desire to be perfect and absolutely honest.

Wittgenstein also had a deep sense of human anguish, and on this basis he could understand the idea of salvation. His description of the human situation was clearly spiritual and religious in tone: he talked about man's "infinite torment" or "ultimate torment," which happened when "a man feels lost." This drove him to search for "infinite help" (Wittgenstein 1980, pp. 45–6), that is, salvation from the infinite God, and this salvation was experienced as a gift (grace). "The Christian religion is only for . . . one who feels an infinite need . . . The whole planet cannot be in a greater anguish than a *single* soul. The Christian faith . . . is a man's refuge in this ultimate torment. Anyone in such torment who has the gift of opening his heart, rather than contracting it, accepts the means of salvation in his heart" (Wittgenstein 1980, p. 46). Indeed, Wittgenstein himself had some experience of "salvation through faith," although this experience seemed to be more sporadic. In 1937, he said: "Last year with God's help I pulled myself together and made a confession. This brought me into more settled waters, into a better relation with people, and to greater seriousness, but now it is as though I had spent all that" (quoted by Rhees 1984, pp. 191–2).

Another religious experience that seemed to give Wittgenstein strength was his "absolute safety" experience, which occurred for the first time around 1910–1911. When Wittgenstein was about twenty-one, he saw a play in Vienna by the Austrian dramatist Ludwig Anzengruber (Monk 1990, p. 51). "There was a scene in which a person whose life had been desperately miserable, and who thought himself about to die, suddenly felt himself to be spoken to in the words, 'Nothing can happen to you!' No matter what occurred in the world, no harm could come to *him*! Wittgenstein was greatly struck by this thought" (Malcolm 1993, p. 7).

In his "A Lecture on Ethics" (delivered when he was forty), Wittgenstein also talked about this experience: "I will mention another experience straight away which I also know and which others of you might be acquainted with: it is…the experience of feeling *absolutely* safe. I mean the state of mind in which one is inclined to say 'I am safe, nothing can injure me whatever happens'" (Wittgenstein 1965, p. 8). Some people have tried to disconnect Wittgenstein's mysticism from personal theism, but in his lecture, Wittgenstein went on to explicate this experience in terms of "feeling safe in the hands of God" (Wittgenstein 1965, p. 10). Together with Wittgenstein's deep sense of sin (which is absent from nature mysticism), it seems difficult to deny that Wittgenstein's religious experiences were basically theistic, rather than monistic. It can also be noted that, for Wittgenstein, this experience of being "absolutely safe" was connected with his moral experience and his inquiry into "what makes life worth living."

Of course, empirically speaking, talking about absolute safely is "nonsense." In our ordinary life, who dares to guarantee absolute safety? Nonetheless, for the psalmists who believe in the Everlasting Arm Underneath or the Rock of Ages, they do manifest a sense of *basic trust* in the world. Wittgenstein's experience of basic trust helped him to distinguish faith from superstition. In 1948, he wrote: "Religious faith and superstition are quite different. One of them results from fear and is a sort of false science. The other is trusting" (Wittgenstein 1980, p. 72).

Sometimes the deep religiosity of Wittgenstein is surprising even to me, as I discover he conceived of his whole life as a life for the glory and will of God: "I have had a letter from an old friend in Austria, a priest. In it he says he hopes my work will go well, if it should be God's will. Now that is all I want: if it should be God's will. Bach wrote on the title page of his *Orgelbuchlein*, 'To the glory of the most high God, and that my neighbour may be benefited thereby'. That is what I would have liked to say about my work" (quoted from Rhees 1984, pp. 181–2).

Since his work was mainly philosophical, we can say that Wittgenstein had done his philosophy for the glory of God. Indeed, in 1947, he said: "Is what I am doing really worth the effort? Yes, but only if a light shines on it from above. And if that happens—why should I concern myself that the fruits of my labours should not be stolen?" (Wittgenstein 1980, p. 57). I am not entirely certain that this "light from above" means divine enlightenment, but Wittgenstein also said, "God grant the philosopher insight into what lies in front of everyone's eyes" (Wittgenstein 1980, p. 63). Elsewhere, Wittgenstein even prayed for divine enlightenment in life: "How will I behave when it comes to shooting? I am not afraid of being shot but of not doing my duty properly. God give me strength! Amen!...Now I might have the opportunity to be a decent human being, because I am face to face with death. May the spirit enlighten me" (quoted from McGuinness 1988, p. 221).

### 2.12  Rejection of Metaphysical/Doctrinal/Institutional Religion

Despite Wittgenstein's powerful religious experiences, he rejected the metaphysical or doctrinal aspects of religion. He once advised Drury: "I would be afraid that you would try and give some sort of philosophical justification for Christian beliefs, as if some sort of proof was needed.... The symbolisms of Catholicism are wonderful beyond words. But any attempt to make it into a philosophical system is offensive" (quoted from Rhees 1984, p. 123). Dogma or institution was certainly not central in Wittgenstein's faith: "we have to live without the consolation of belonging to a church" (quoted from Rhees 1984, p. 129).

Wittgenstein adopted a non-realist existential interpretation of at least *some* doctrines of Christianity. The historical truth of Christianity is not important; what is significant is its existential significance for us. Wittgenstein also applies this perspective to the belief in resurrection (Wittgenstein 1980, pp. 32–3). So faith in God cannot be based on wisdom or rational proof. Only experiences can bring us to faith. In 1950, he said: "Life can educate one to a belief in God. And also *experiences* can do that...e.g., suffering of various kinds... Experiences...can force this concept on us" (Wittgenstein 1980, pp. 85–6).

Here Wittgenstein's viewpoint seemed to reflect his own experience. Certainly he was not convinced by philosophical arguments for God. However, his life experiences "force this concept [God, sin or salvation] on" him. The word "force" here not only indicates the forcefulness of those experiences but also, I suggest, shows that those religious experiences somehow needed to be *forced* into his mind, because his native cognitive environment was not hospitable to those experiences!

### 2.13  Conclusion: Wittgenstein and the Rainbow of Experiences

I am not suggesting that Wittgenstein was an orthodox Christian or consistent mystical theologian, but he did have some kind of religious belief. I know this interpretation is controversial, and even Putnam says, "he seems to me...to have aspired to but not achieved religious belief" (Putnam 1996, p. 169). The above discussions provide ample evidence to contradict this claim. Furthermore, Philip Shields has conducted a thorough study and come to a similar conclusion: "At the root of Wittgenstein's critique of metaphysics I found...the outline of a religious picture of the world—a picture that is broadly Judeo-Christian" (Shields 1993, p. x).

However, I find Shields, in attempting to reconcile Wittgenstein's critique of metaphysics with the Judeo-Christian picture of the world, has underestimated the inherent tension between these two elements. So scholars are right to find Wittgenstein's comments on the mystical puzzling, because these statements are, strictly speaking, ineffable nonsense within his framework (e.g. *Tractatus*). However, Wittgenstein continued to talk about it throughout his life. There is a real tension here, and my view is that this tension results from two independent sources of his thinking. One source was his philosophical analysis which, although not exactly identical to logical positivism, did incline him to an antimetaphysical and non-realist interpretation of religion. The other source was his spiritual and religious experiences, which suggested to him the reality of the transcendent realm.

This case study shows that spiritual and religious experiences are not entirely constrained by language or cognitive framework. Although Wittgenstein possessed a belief system that did not leave much room, if any, for spiritual and religious experiences, those experiences still forcefully occurred to him and burst through the crust of his antimetaphysical mindset. No doubt Wittgenstein struggled over this issue a lot, because in his own view, all his talk about ethics or religion was coming up against the boundaries of language. This struggle is a result of Wittgenstein's (unnecessary) acceptance of the vestiges of scientism (despite his own protest). If one is liberated from this straitjacket, then one is also free to acknowledge the intimations of transcendence in the rainbow of our experiences. As Nieli says, "Wittgenstein moves very near to an Augustinian-like understanding of God and man, but he is prevented from painting a more integrated picture because he is still, even in the 'lecture', committed too rigidly to the in/out framework of the *Tractatus*" (Nieli 1987, p. 148).

In any case, Wittgenstein's life suggests the reality and significance of this rainbow of experiences I talk about. As seen above, Wittgenstein has had powerful existential, interpersonal, moral, aesthetic, and religious experiences. It would be surprising to find an analytic philosopher talking about his experiences of feeling guilty, living (even doing philosophy) for the glory of God, absolute safety, absolute moral imperative, a deep sense of self, and so on. But these experiences will not go away just because analytic philosophers do not talk about them. I contend that all these spiritual and religious experiences are intrinsic to the human condition, and Wittgenstein was just a *person* who was open to these experiences. As he said, "Wisdom is grey. Life on the other hand and religion are full of colour"(Wittgenstein 1980, p. 62). For the narrow empiricists, their philosophy has "sent them to sleep" and their vision of the world is largely monochromatic, sensitive only to sense experience. On the other hand, Wittgenstein was experientially aware of the beautiful rainbow of experiences that makes our life colorful! Moreover, there is a depth dimension behind this rainbow (or, if you like, a transcendent realm beyond the end of the rainbow): "The problems of life are insoluble on the surface and can only be solved in depth" (Wittgenstein 1980, p. 74).

The depth dimension was mentioned especially when Wittgenstein talked about the experience of other persons. This depth dimension in persons is often symbolized by the spirit. Wittgenstein did believe in the human spirit (or the soul): "The earlier culture will become a heap of rubble and finally of ashes, but spirits will hover over the ashes" (Wittgenstein 1980, p. 3). He also marveled at the extravagance of the human mind or spirit: "If Freud's theory on the interpretation of dreams has anything in it, it shows how complicated is the way the human mind represents the facts in pictures. So complicated, so irregular is the way they are represented that we can barely call it representation any longer" (Wittgenstein 1980, p. 44). Jung would call these "representations" archetypes, and detect spiritual significance in them.

Anyway, Wittgenstein's articulation of his spiritual and religious experiences was all the more amazing because he lacked both the support of a believing community and a friendly conceptual framework. In the end, Wittgenstein affirmed that an honest faith was possible: "An honest religious thinker is like a tightrope walker. He almost looks as though he were walking on nothing but air. His support is the slenderest imaginable. And yet it really is possible to walk on it" (Wittgenstein 1980, p. 73). I agree with him that life experiences can educate one to a belief in God. In his life, what brought this about were moral, aesthetic, and interpersonal experiences of various sorts. Wittgenstein's honest exploration of his own soul also played an important part. Wittgenstein knew the depth in one's soul and in others' souls. These deep experiences forced him to acknowledge that these matters could not be handled by science, but only by religion—only God can reach such depth in the spirit. Moreover, Wittgenstein also had many explicit (and largely Christian) religious experiences, such as the experience of penitence, the experience of a love that acknowledges that we are all wicked children, and a sense of absolute safety. He even talked about submerging himself in religion!

So all these spiritual and religious experiences suggested to Wittgenstein a meaningful, coherent, and beautiful message, which he intuitively felt and received (sometimes). However, at other times Wittgenstein seemed to be of two minds: his epistemological framework prohibited him from wholeheartedly trusting this rainbow of experiences. The struggle is still with us. I use Wittgenstein to illustrate the richness and apparent reality of the rainbow of spiritual and religious experiences, and suggest that these experiences cannot be dismissed cavalierly. However, the questions remain: perhaps this rainbow of experience might be nothing but illusion, or only the projection of our feelings? I will try to address these critical questions in the remaining chapters.

# CHAPTER 3

# TOWARD HOLISTIC EMPIRICISM

## 3.1 A Holistic Theory of Sense Experience

Since SE will feature prominently throughout our discussions, it is necessary to analyze SE in more detail and see how it fits with my model. Let me first evaluate several theories of SE.

### 3.1.1 Theories of Sense Perception

#### 1. Sense Data Theory (SDT)

This theory contends that the things we really see in our SE are sense data, which are mind-dependent immaterial entities. The rest are our interpretations imposed on this experience of sense data. Since this theory is widely rejected, I will not go over those familiar objections. The particular defect of SDT I would emphasize is its inability to account for our cognitions of the physical world. It is because the sense-data language of color patches, for example is unable to capture the phenomenological content of our SE. Consider the Lyer-Müller illusion: how should we describe the content of this experience? Should we say that we sense a longer sense datum above a shorter sense datum? It may be part of the story, but it does not sound entirely adequate. Isn't it true that the following epistemic seeming is also part of the content of the experience: "it seems (epistemically) to me that the upper line is longer than the lower one?" This epistemic seeming is to be distinguished from the final belief of the perceiver—defeaters may already be available to him before the experience. But even in this case, the content of the experience still seems to embody the same epistemic seeming. This suggests that propositional content is essential to the analysis of SE.

#### 2. Pure Informational Theory (PIT)

According to this theory, any experience is exhaustively described by describing its propositional content. Qualia or sense data simply do not exist (Tye 1992). This position seems to swing to another extreme, but it seems plain to me that our experiences have a qualitative character. However, the denial of either PIT or Impure Informational Theory (IIT) is not strictly essential to my ARE since both theories deem epistemic seemings essential, and this is basically what I need.

### 3. *Impure Informational Theory (IIT)*

Sense data can be conceded to exist by this theory, but they are regarded to be entirely epiphenomenal to the cognitive process of perception. A recent defender of IIT is Jack Lyons: "what makes a belief a perceptual belief…is not a matter of the subject's contemporaneous nondoxastic experiences…Thus, even zombies…can have basic, justified, perceptual beliefs" (Lyons 2009, p. vii). He says clearly that "experience is irrelevant; it is process reliability that justifies our perceptual beliefs" (Lyons 2009, p. 14). According to IIT, the description of the experience of seeing a red, square book is like this: "It seems (epistemically) that I am seeing a book *and* I sense a square, red sense-datum." But the former does not depend on the latter in any sense. They are both produced by the same source, but two separate causal chains in the brain lead to two separate destinations, producing two independent products. Even if the latter chain malfunctions, it would not affect the former. This is supposed to happen in blindsight, where the description of this experience is: "It seems (epistemically) that there is light but I sense no luminous sense data."[1] Two questions can be raised here: first, the subject usually thinks he is only guessing. Isn't it an indicator that the mechanism of blindsight may not be identical to that of ordinary perception? Second, even if blindsight can occur in an elementary level, can this be extrapolated to more complicated SEs? For example, can there be a blind-painter? The IIT is far from being proved.[2]

### 4. *Fusion Theory (FT)*

I would contrast the Fusion Theory with the Addition Theory (AT). Both grant that SE has both propositional content and nonconceptual content. However, the FT tends to view them as organically related, while the AT sees no intrinsic connection between them: one is simply added onto another. I do not think the AT is correct, because there seems to be an organic relation between the qualitative contents of experiences and their noetic contents. They are not just conjoined more or less regularly. While pure sensing with no propositional content is conceivable, I doubt very much that it is the way we normally sense. In fact, the qualitative content and propositional content can be fused together in our experience to form *noetic-qualitative complexes* that function as integral units in our cognitive activity. First, the qualitative character of our experiences seems to depend partly on the concepts we bring to our experience. Consider this example: while I am reading a Chinese book, another Westerner who has absolutely no understanding of Chinese is also reading exactly the same book. Both of us see the same shapes in the same positions, but I suppose our experiences would feel very different indeed. Those shapes mediate a world of meaning to me, but the Westerner only sees some diagrams. The visual stimuli we receive should be roughly identical. So what makes the experiences so different is the difference between our conceptual frameworks.

A similar conclusion is reached by Christopher Peacocke in his analysis of SE: "nonconceptual content…cannot be explained except in part by reference to its relations to certain primitive conceptual contents. At the most basic level, conceptual and nonconceptual content must be elucidated simultaneously. The most basic elements of the scheme themselves form a *local holism*" (Peacocke 1992, p. 128; italics mine). Consider an extremely simple experience of sensing a red afterimage to the right of a green one. What would an experience be like if all conceptual contents are excised? Remember: even "to the right of" is a concept. In general, I think our visual field is permeated by some fundamental concepts that help to explain our experience of it as *a continuous field that is also spatially structured*. Otherwise, wouldn't it be better described as a blooming, buzzing confusion?

Second, nonconceptual content can embody information that is available for later "computations." This form of storing information also has an advantage: "The seer need not form any judgments about his visual experiences... At most the seer needs to be recognitionally sensitive to relevant features of his visual experiences" (Lowe 1992, p. 82). Consider any visual field and imagine how many propositional judgments are needed to exhaustively describe its characteristics! So FT seems most adequate to our SEs.

### 3.1.2 Mediated Immediacy

The terms "mediated immediacy" sound paradoxical. The key to unraveling this paradox is to note that "mediation" can be analyzed in several ways. The first sense can be called *"intentional immediacy"*—the mind is directed toward something in the world (if the experience is veridical) or to a merely intentional object, and the person is focally aware of that object. So the object is immediate to his mind, intentionally speaking.

However, this awareness can be mediated by some subsidiary awareness. This sense of mediation is best analyzed by Frank Jackson:

> x is a *mediate object of (visual) perception* (for S at t) iff S sees x at t, and there is a y such that (x~=y) and S sees x in virtue of seeing y. An *immediate object of perception* is one that is not mediate. (Jackson 1977, pp. 19–20)

So in this sense, no opaque physical object, as such, can be an immediate object of perception, for obviously we see such an object in virtue of seeing part of its surface. We can call this an *"experiential mediation."* So mediated immediacy means that an experience of X is an intentionally immediate perception of X, because the mind goes out right toward X in its intentionality, but this experience is mediated by another experience of Y. For example, my SE of a table is an intentionally immediate experience of a table, but it is experientially mediated by my seeing part of the table surface. So even simple SEs manifest this phenomenon of "mediated immediacy"!

There is another concept of *"computational" immediacy*. If an object of experience directly acts on the mind to produce the corresponding experience, then it is causally immediate to the mind. If the act is mediated by intervening "computations," then the experience is causally mediated by those "computations." An intentionally immediate cognitive state is still usually "computationally" mediated. It seems to me that the cognitive scientists have demonstrated this point beyond reasonable doubt. As Lyons says, "Helmholtz was certainly right in claiming that perception involves a kind of inference; that is, the causal processes that make ... perceptual beliefs possible are inferential processes. It does not follow from this, however, that perceptual beliefs are *epistemically* inferential" (Lyons 2009, p. 58).

### 3.1.3 Nested Epistemic Seemings

So even in our usual SEs, we can have different levels of epistemic seemings ESs nested within one another and embodied in the *same* experience. This is the main reason why experiences can be reinterpreted. Suppose I was walking inside Madame Tussaud's, and suddenly it (epistemically) seemed to me that I saw Steve Davis standing before me. Then a moment's reflection convinced me that this could not be Steve Davis. As I looked again, it then seemed to me that I saw a wax figure standing there. The questions are: Is there only one experience or two experiences? Does the example illustrate that my ordinary perception of people is mere interpretation?

My analysis would be as follows. First, I have had two different experiences, simply because the epistemic seemings embodied have changed. But the epistemic seemings that differ are the highest-level ones. Some lower-level epistemic seemings are nested within this highest-level one. So a fuller (tenseless) description of my earlier experience would be: "It seems to me (epistemically) that I am seeing Steve Davis, partly because it also seems (epistemically) that I am seeing a physical body that is very like Steve Davis's body, and partly because I am sensing Steve-Davis-ly, and it is because I sense a hair sense data, a face sense data, and so on."

However, when I realized that I had come to Madame Tussaud's, I changed my mind. I looked at it again and the experience changed: "It now seems (epistemically) that I am seeing a wax figure of Steve Davis because it seems (epistemically) that I am seeing a physical object that is very like Steve Davis's body, and it is partly because I am sensing Steve-Davis-ly, and it is because I sense a black-hair sense data, a face sense data, and so on." Notice that although the experiences' full descriptions conflict with one another, the lower-level description is *almost* identical. The upshot is that two experiences, which differ or even conflict at a higher level, can be very similar at a lower level of description. So the question whether there are two qualitatively different experiences or just one has no unambiguous answer. It depends on the level of description you have in mind.

### 3.1.4 Post-Experiential Reinterpretation

Clearly, epistemic seeming is defeasible and, in principle, open to reinterpretation. I call this process *post-experiential reinterpretation*:

1. The reinterpretation can take the form of a *further nesting*. Suppose I had the following experience: "Last night I saw a beautiful blonde." Later,

I received further information, which enabled me to identify this blonde as Mary. I then reinterpreted my earlier experience as: "So I have *actually* seen Mary." Although this intentional content was not represented in the original experience, my post-experiential reinterpretation means that I accept this description as true to the original experience. In general, background knowledge would enter into this process of reinterpretation.

2. In other cases, we may need to *scrap* the higher-level, ES because it is defeated by other ESs. For example, I had an experience of seeing Tom, but later found out that Tom has already died. I would redescribe my experience as seeing someone like Tom.

3. Sometimes both moves are needed: we scrap a higher-level ES and replace it by another ES at the same level, for example, in the wax-figure case.

4. In extreme cases, we are forced to scrap (almost) all ESs and retain the sense data description only. For example, in case of a hallucination, we would deny that the experience is directed to any outer reality at all.

The above discussions hinge on the distinction between *seeing that* and *seeing thing*. Jackson points out that "what constitutes perception of some material thing can occur without any appropriate interpretation occurring. I can see the headmaster without knowing that I am; I can see him even without realising that I am seeing a person—I may mistake him for a realistic dummy planted in a student rag" (Jackson 1977, p. 23). Now, this shows that the common usage of "seeing" is ambiguous. We can *actually* see something without *intentionally* seeing it. (It can be called a *seeing incognito*.) Jackson's contention is that if I see $D$ and $D=D'$, then I (actually) see $D'$, no matter whether I think I am seeing $D'$ or not.

So whether we *actually* see something may not be easy to decide sometimes. As an approximation, we can take Lowe's definition: "One *sees* an object...if and only if one's visual experience is directly causally dependent on certain properties of that object in such a fashion that one is thereby enabled (with the aid of certain background knowledge, maybe) to form a reliable judgment as to what those properties are" (Lowe 1992, p. 79).

The above account makes clear that ESs are influenced by our background knowledge, beliefs, and the constitution of our cognitive apparatus. In more common terms, every SE is theory laden. Perhaps one may resist this move and think that no matter how mistaken our higher-level ESs can be in our SEs, at least we can be sure that we have confronted *some* physical thing. But I suggest our ordinary realist interpretation of experience *could* be scrapped as well. Suppose at this moment, while you are reading this passage, a voice suddenly arises irresistibly in your brain/mind: "I am the so-called 'evil superscientist' and it pleases me to tell you that you are only a brain in MY vat! I know you will not believe just now, because you are convinced by the Wittgensteinians that this position is incoherent. Anyway, I will convince you. Now I am going to disconnect your brain from the current program while maintaining your consciousness and memory. So you will feel a 'blackout' for 10 seconds. Then I will insert another perceptual input program and you'll have an experience of 'playing football.' Then 10 seconds empty input. Then you'll experience 'talking to your dead grandfather.'" The voice then stops and the predicted experiences happen to you exactly as you are told. If this kind of experience *repeatedly* happens to you, would you still cling to your realist interpretation of ordinary experiences? I doubt it. So the "brain in a vat" hypothesis is not empirically vacuous. It can possibly be verified by our experience. All our *experiences* in themselves are perfectly compatible with this possibility. To reject this possibility as a rational alternative, we seem to need some a priori epistemic principles. To this question now we turn.

### 3.1.5 *The Principles of Experiential Evaluation*

If the above account is correct, many thorny epistemological issues inevitably pop up. If the high-level ESs are defeasible, what justifies our acceptance of them in the first place? What should be our epistemic starting points?

#### 1. *Bottom-Up Approach*

Let us consider this principle:

> Every higher-level ES[3] has to be (inferentially) justified by the lower-level ES, together with our background knowledge.

This is the kind of principle we often use when we want to challenge other people's experiential claim. For example, if one claims to see a ghost, we might counter that he only sees a ghostly shape, and his interpretation that the shape is a ghost needs to be justified. We may then argue that the interpretation cannot be justified, because there is no way to infer from that ghostly shape to the ghost. However, the issue here is whether this principle can be the *first* principle in epistemology. Indeed it cannot. First, it threatens an infinite regress. Second, we have to ask whence our background knowledge comes from. I assume that this can't come from a priori intuitions. Then it is clear that any principle of experiential evaluation that depends on our background knowledge can't be a first principle. Background *knowledge* is only possible after we have settled the question of how we should evaluate our experiences, and then build it up from the experiences we deem trustworthy. So the above principle has to be replaced by another one that acknowledges some self-justified level of ES with respect to which every other level is to be justified:

There is a foundational level of ES (the truth of) which is self-justified. All other levels of ES have to be ultimately justified with respect to the foundational level.

This is a form of foundationalism whose defects are familiar. The problem I want to emphasize here is the justifiability of the realist interpretation of our experiences. If we do not accept the PCT, then ESs about the physical world themselves cannot constitute the self-justified foundational level. The next lower level is the phenomenological description, and it is notoriously difficult to justify the realist level with respect to this level. (Consider again the above skeptical possibility.) So the Bottom-Up Approach would probably lead to skepticism.

Jack Lyons also rejects the Bottom-Up Approach, and his analysis is similar to my idea of nested epistemic seemings. For example, in our experience of a coffee cup, he points to the coexistence of two levels of belief:

1. There is a coffee cup in front of me.
2. There is in front of me a squat, upright, partly hollowed out cylinder with a curved vertical handle on its side.

He admits that if pressed, we could defend (1) by appealing to (2). If the Bottom-Up Approach is correct, this would make (1) nonbasic. But his "view is that both beliefs are basic, in fact that both are perceptual beliefs...[One may be] tempted to...conclude that (1) is based at least in part on (2) and is therefore nonbasic," but this inference is incorrect. "The fact that I could appeal to $p$ in defending $q$ shows at most that the belief that $p$ bolsters my justification for $q$, not that the former is necessary for the prima facie justification of the latter" (Lyons 2009, p. 99).

Lyons uses face recognition to illustrate his point. Suppose we see a person and believe he is Mr. Smith. Can we justify this belief on the basis of our lower-level perception of a list of facial features, plus the fact that no one else can satisfy that description? Lyons doubts that "any collection of low level beliefs about nose shape, skin tone...would come anywhere near singling out a unique individual...This is true despite the fact that we can and sometimes do cite such low-level features in defending our perceptual beliefs. So it is not the case that if I can cite my belief that $p$ in defending my belief that $q$ then the former must make a positive and substantial contribution to the prima facie justification of the latter" (Lyons 2009, pp. 99–100). Normally, we directly form beliefs about other people's identities; "it is only victims of serious brain damage who actually form beliefs in [an inferential way]. Prosopagnosics...can't use their face recognition systems to do so, and this is why they are so singularly bad at it" (Lyons 2009, p. 100).

### 2. Top-Down Approach (the CTA)

Now consider the possibility of beginning from the top: the whole experience, including its highest-level ES. Of course, it is only the starting point, having only PFEF. Perhaps much of the higher levels are to be trimmed off. But what are the resources to help us do this "trimming"? Earlier I mentioned the fact that an ES can be defeated by *background knowledge*. Now isn't it clear that background knowledge consists mainly of our other experiences, accepted as they are? So the process of experiential evaluation can be described as follows:

1. Accept our experiences as they are as a starting point.
2. Take into consideration the whole gamut of our experiences and then trim off the higher-level ESs that we have reason to discard, for example, being inconsistent with other ESs or the knowledge that is solidly grounded on many other ESs.

The first shows our *trust* and the second shows that this trust is a *critical* one. Isn't it exactly the way of the Critical Trust Approach? So the PCT, in contrast with the Bottom-Up Approach, can be seen to be a more plausible first principle of experiential evaluation.

### 3. Optimal Level of ES

Some may object that the above alternatives do not exhaust the options: we can start somewhere in the middle, which we can regard as the optimal level of ES. For example, when we see a tree *as a tree*, this is the level in which we can rest (at least initially). To argue that this ES should be justified with respect to the experience of the tree sense data is to *under-interpret* the experience. It is this *unreasonable* doubt that itself needs to be justified. Nevertheless, to see the tree as the manifestation of the tree spirit (which can be common in an animistic culture) is to *over-interpret* the experience. This *interpretation*, even given spontaneously in experience, needs to be justified with respect to the optimal level. Doubt here is amply warranted. In contrast, the Top-Down Approach is faulted for its gullibilism.

The example sounds plausible. However, is the above approach adequate as an account of our *first* principles? No, because the word "optimal" only draws our attention to a category, but it does not *tell* us what constitutes this optimal level and how we arrive at it. The example given earlier is convincing only in a modern, secularized society, and it presupposes the worldview of this society. It assumes that we know a lot of things about the world and our perceptual capacities. This approach also fails to tell us what the optimal levels of ES are in the case of, for example, moral experience, when we ourselves do not agree. I guess most people who want to take this approach will suggest the physical level of description as the optimal level. But consider these examples from our rainbow of experiences:

1. A son seems to see genuine concern in the eyes of his mother.
2. A Jewish victim seems to have experienced horrendous evil in the Nazis' acts which he suffered.
3. We seem to hear beautiful music when listening to Beethoven's symphony.

These *common experiences* all contain descriptions that transcend the physical level, and hence they *have to* be justified with respect to what we experience at the physical level, according to the theory we are considering. This immediately leads to the intractable problems of other minds, moral realism, and aesthetic realism. Besides being counterintuitive and dismissive of the phenomenological content of those experiences, the whole procedure begs a lot of questions. (Part B will be devoted to this problem.) If we just assert a certain level (e.g. the physical level) to be optimal without adequate justification, it is hard to escape the charge of arbitrariness. It is also hard to justify why doubt is condemned on one side of *this* level, while it is encouraged on the other side.

While this approach suffers from methodological infirmities, the CTA can actually embody its insights. The CTA is free to admit that in matters of experiential evaluation, we do have some idea of the optimal level of ES. However, the determination of this level is itself parasitic upon the adoption of the PCT and other rational principles in the CTA. The process of evaluation, while guided ultimately by the CTA, does not need to begin from scratch every time. While we take the experiences as they are initially, the course of *our* experiences would suggest to us that some level of ESs are not very reliable. *The optimal level is the highest level of ES which has withstood this whole process of critical sifting.* The animistic interpretation of ordinary objects is subject to initial doubt because this has not withstood the critical sifting of the past centuries. The sense-data description is not regarded as the optimal level not because it has been falsified, but because it is not the *highest* level which remains unscathed. This shows that in positing the optimal level, there is an implicit "bias" toward the higher level. This can only be explained by the Top-Down Approach. Apart from this, I can't see how we can dogmatically condemn the doubt of the phenomenalists as unreasonable. So the CTA agrees that there are under-interpretive and overinterpretive experiences with regard to an optimal level of ES, but these distinctions are *derived* from the first principles of the CTA.

## 3.2  A Holistic Model of Experiences

### 3.2.1  *Toward a Broader Concept of Experience*

Although phrases like moral and aesthetic experiences are not uncommon in ordinary life, in philosophy they are not taken seriously. For the exclusivist empiricists, "experience" is often equated with sense experience (SE), and "empirical support" is identified with "confirmation by *sensory* experience," which, until recently, has been regarded as straightforward and unproblematic. However, it is an impoverished concept of experience, which is not true to our life-world. This neither faithfully captures the ordinary meaning of "experience" nor phenomenologically rings true.

Let us be faithful to *our* experiences and describe *our experienced world, the Lebenswelt.* Isn't it a world that consists of truths and errors, kindness and evil, joys and sorrows, love and hatred, beauty and ugliness, creativity and dullness, comedies and tragedies, saints and villains, heroes and cowards, freedom and slavery, gods and devils, and so forth? What kinds of experiences do we have? Sensory, moral, aesthetic, religious, intellectual, interpersonal, and so on. It seems perverse to banish all our rich experiences from the philosophical discussion by the empiricist hijacking of the words "experience," "empirical," and so on. I maintain that a correct phenomenological description of our experiences would make it meaningful to speak of "experiencing an objective external world," "experiencing our hunger *causing* us to eat," "experiencing others' kindness," and so on. As our earlier discussions show, the elements of interpretation are incorporated in our experiences from the very beginning. It is futile to seek the interpretation-free given, even in SE.

### 3.2.2 Typology of Experience

When I insist on the unity of our diverse experiences, what I reject is a *qualitative difference in terms of epistemic virtue* between SE and other experiences. Different types of experiences do fall into rough types. Now by what principles do we group token noetic experiences together as one type? I suggest two main criteria:

1. Phenomenology: what kind of sensations or feelings are involved in this kind of experience?
2. Ontology: what kinds of thing, processes, or properties are typically supposed to be involved in the objects of experience?

I think that the ontological criterion should take primacy over the phenomenological criterion. For example, SE is the most clearly demarcated kind of experience. However, if the phenomenological criterion is primary, SE is not actually one type, but a collection of many types: visual, auditory, tactile, olfactory, gustatory, and so on. It seems better to see SE as an epistemological unity, and this unity is explained by the common ontology shared by all these experiences: they all have physical objects as objects of experience. Of course, within this type, we can further distinguish subtypes that have different phenomenologies, for example, visual experience. The other problem is that if we define SE as the experience that is mediated by sensory content or sensations, then experience of ghosts, witches, angels, visions of Holy Mary, and so on should also be counted as SEs. Also, it would be difficult to distinguish aesthetic experience from SE. So this way of classification does not seem to serve the epistemological task well. So in this book, I mean "SE" mainly by an experience of a physical thing or event. Sensations or sense data would come in as the *qualitative character* of SE.

Similarly, I would define an *interpersonal experience* as an experience of other persons. Obviously, it also consists of many kinds of experience, phenomenologically speaking. It is mediated by SE, but it is regarded as a distinct type, because the ontology of persons is not obviously reducible to the ontology of physical objects. Surely, we need our eyes and ears to perceive a person in normal cases. However, a body is seen as a person and the sounds are heard as meaningful communication or expression. Behavior is more than mere movement: they are movements which are experienced as actions, reactions, expressions, and so on. All these experiences can be integrated into one coherent conceptual framework, Folk Psychology (Churchland) or Intentional Stance (Dennett). Of course, this type of experience also has some characteristic phenomenology, for example, feelings of warmth, love, hatred, and so on.

Earlier I proposed a sevenfold classification of experience. Here I elaborate a little bit:

1. Experience of self: This is a noetic experience that yields epistemic seemings about the subject himself. It includes experience of action, introspection, and experience of self-discovery, as well as existential experiences, such as the quest for meaning and wholeness, or depth experiences like hope or despair. Although we often emphasize the emotional nature of existential experiences, they do seem to embody some vague epistemic seemings about the general human and cosmic situation in relation to oneself (cf. Quentin Smith's metaphysics of feeling).

2. Intentional experience: This is a noetic experience in which the subject seems to encounter some *external* object that can exist independently. SE, interpersonal experience, and RE are the three most common types of intentional experience in which people encounter physical things, persons, and supernatural beings.

3. Experience of the Transcendentals: Moral experience, aesthetic experience, and intellectual experience are, respectively, the search for Goodness, Beauty, and Truth. Each of these three realms is typically characterized by the application of a distinct set of *predicates*. Aesthetic experience consists of the application of predicates such as "beautiful," "ugly," and "sublime" to a contingent state of affairs or an event. Whereas the unity of a type of intentional experience consists of the fact that many experiences are of *the same kind of thing*, the unity of aesthetic experiences consists of the fact that many things can be characterized by *the same set of predicates*. Note how many different sorts of things can be called beautiful: a face, a sculpture, a novel, a character, a scenery, a sonata, a drama, and so on.

Similarly, moral experiences consist of the application of moral predicates like "good," "wrong," "cruel," and so on to diverse kinds of thing, for example, persons, actions, and states of affairs. For intellectual experience, the distinct set of *predicates* contains concepts like necessary, possible, likely, justified, and so on. These can also be applied to many realms of inquiry.

4. Memory: This is a noetic experience that embodies epistemic seemings about a past contingent state of affairs. As for the content, it can be about the self, the world, or any state of affairs.

Some observations are in order here. First, the distinctions between the above kinds are not hard and fast. They are often tied together, and the boundaries between kinds are sometimes fuzzy. Moral experience is inextricably involved with interpersonal experience, while aesthetic experience merges imperceptibly with SE. Furthermore, I would argue that experience of self and intentional experience are correlated with one another. So inner reality and external reality are the two poles of noetic experience, and both the first-person perspective and third-person perspective are irreducible. Memory depends on the first two types of noetic experience for the source of content, but as our experiences constantly recede to the past, memory is essential for our access to those experiences. Experience of change in turn depends on both memory and current experiences. I would also argue that it presupposes some form of experience of self. Second, the listing out of so many types of noetic experience here should make us wary of imposing a unitary model of noetic experience on our experiences (beyond the very general principles of CTA). Many empiricists are often doing a priori epistemology instead. I insist that we should be open-minded about what kinds of experience we actually have and what their structures are, and the way to answer these questions is to *attend to our experiences.*

## 3.3 A Holistic Model of Experiential Knowing

Narrow empiricists have emphasized the discontinuity between SE and other types of experience. However, I contend that various types of experience in fact have a common structure and can be located in a continuum. Earlier I defended a holistic theory of SE. I now extend that into a holistic model of experiential knowing that is applicable to diverse types of experiences. My holistic model is in stark contrast to the model of narrow empiricism, which is exclusive and reductionistic. My method is broadly phenomenological, and I contend my model can do more justice to *our human experiences.*

### 3.3.1 Human Beings as Holistic Beings

First let me note the three dimensions of human experience:

1. Noetic dimension: Experiences in general yield judgments about reality by embodying "epistemic seemings." Apart from those experiences that mainly have a qualitative character, for example, sensing an afterimage, propositional content is never totally absent from an experience,[4] and experience is fundamentally intentional in structure.
2. Qualitative dimension: Experiences also have an essentially qualitative character that is not reducible to the noetic dimension. There is something concerning what it is like to have a certain experience. For example, SEs have characteristic sensations, and moral experiences are also connected with emotions. I would regard both sensory and affective contents, though having different character and functions, as belonging to the nonconceptual or qualitative dimension of experience.
3. Volitional or conative dimension: Experiences are usually correlated with the self as *subject*, but it is important to remember that, in many experiences, the self experiences himself as an active, purposeful *agent*, effecting changes in himself and the outside world. For example, we have experiences of action, choice, deliberation, speaking, and so on in which the will is essentially involved.

These three dimensions of experience are generally intertwined. In particular, the noetic dimension is intricately related to the qualitative and volitional dimensions.

### 3.3.2 Feeling Perception: Integration of Noetic and Qualitative Dimensions

Most of the time, our conceptual descriptions cannot really exhaust the qualitative content introspectively available to us: how can we use language to express the exact shade of red we see, or all the meaning inherent in a very intimate relationship? So all experiences are *to some extent* ineffable. Qualitative contents can also play a role in our cognitions. Consider the following three conditions:

1. Sensations have a determinate character, which is accessible to the mind, and the sensations *as nonconceptual contents* can be memorized and recalled.
2. The character of those sensations exhibits a sort of functional dependence on external reality.
3. The mind/brain can cognitively operate on those nonconceptual contents to yield propositional contents.

If these conditions are satisfied, then it can be seen that information can be implicitly stored in the sensations. This information can be retrieved later and turned into propositional content. I think we have clear empirical evidence for (1). When we recall a past scene, we often do this by evoking some sort of mental image. For example, I often recall whether I have locked my bicycle by evoking the image of the actions I performed when I left the bicycle. Our judgments about the past can then be mediated by a mental image and its qualitative contents. In this process, we do not seem to run through a list of propositions about the past and then find the one we need. Rather the "propositions" are stored in *the image* in an "analogue" form, and when we "process" it, we can arrive at some *new* beliefs about the past. This illustrates (3). As for (2), I can only say that this is a fundamental assumption that is hard to justify on grounds that do not presuppose this.

What kinds of noetic-qualitative complexes there are is an empirical question. All major kinds of noetic experience seem to have their own kinds of noetic-qualitative complexes. Consider moral and interpersonal experiences, which are often saturated with emotions. I certainly hold that emotions have irreducible qualitative contents, that is, emotions are not *merely* implicit judgments. However, the individuation of emotions and their descriptions seem to be implicitly tied to some judgments. For example, gratitude is an emotion that has characteristic qualitative contents. The implicit judgment that someone else has done something *good* for you seems to be embedded in it. Imagine that you discover that the "favor" done for you is actually performed with ulterior motives. Your gratitude would automatically turn into anger or disappointment! Do we only have a causal relation here? But this is to presuppose that "feelings of gratitude" can be individuated and described *apart from* the implicit judgment. I can hardly think of any way of doing this. So it seems plausible to think of "feelings of gratitude" as a noetic-qualitative complex in which nonconceptual contents and noetic contents form a local holism.

Second, it is arguable that emotions can play a role in our noetic experiences about other persons and their moral properties. For example, Douglas Sloan suggests that we can have "feeling perception": "It is emotional reason that is our capacity to apprehend objective values.... Feeling opens and discovers the world of qualities...Feeling as an organ of perception is, likewise, crucial to our coming to know other persons.... In the other's words, gestures, expressions, the form and aspect of their bearing and presence, we sense in a more immediately feeling way their inner reality. Our capacity to enter into intimate, knowing communion with another also depends mightily on the degree of our sensitivities and our felt inner reality" (Sloan 1983, pp. 160–1).

Hearing this sort of stuff, some narrow empiricists may want to cry "mystery!" Yet if it is a mystery, it is one attested widely. Even Konrad Lorenz, not known for his predilection for religion or mystery, emphasizes the reality of value perceptions and the feeling perception of, say, injustice: "The murderer or the ruthless terrorist elicits feelings of horror and deep indignation...the feeling a normal human has for what is lawful and right is anchored in an innate, heritable program" (Lorenz 1988, p. 104). Sloan also says, "A narrow reason by itself is poverty stricken; it can know only an empty shell of a world, and can sustain only a starved and cramped personal life" (Sloan 1983, pp. 160–1). His judgment on "narrow reason" (not on the people) may seem harsh, but what can we say to a person who is incapable of horror and indignation even in front of grave injustice like the Tiananmen Square massacre? But wouldn't the narrow empiricist commit to the position that these feelings are *nothing but* feelings?

Sloan claims that feeling perception is important in our IPE and moral experience. I think this is true to the phenomenology of these experiences (see Chapters 12–13). There has also been a new trend in recent decades for philosophers to recognize the cognitive roles of emotions, and this is an important discovery in the post-foundationalist context. For example, Catherine Elgin agrees that "emotions play a variety of cognitive roles, not all of them derived from or dependent on beliefs or propositions they embed...My aim is not to anesthetize emotion but to sensitize cognition—to show that the understanding we achieve is not indifferent to emotion but that understanding is none the less objective for that" (Elgin 1996, p. 147). It is because "emotion need not distort perception or derail reason. Emotions often heighten awareness, redirect attention, and sensitize their subjects to factors that had previously eluded them...Absent specific reasons to distrust them, *cognitive deliverances of emotion are initially tenable*" (Elgin 1996, p. 150; italics mine). So Elgin contends that emotional perception has PFEF. The mathematical physicist Roger Penrose also recognizes that "we conscious beings gain benefit from any circumstance where we can directly 'feel' things; and *this*...is just what a purely computational system can never achieve" (Penrose 1995, p. 399).

Of course, presumptive data can be defeated, and from our experience we do know that emotions can also mislead us. But it just means hallucinatory emotional "perceptions" are more common than hallucinatory sense "perceptions." It does not mean that they are cognitively irrelevant. But as in other realms, what we need is to criticize and test our emotional or feeling perceptions and formulate second-order critical principles, for example, emotional perception of people who are narrow-minded and lacking in self-knowledge tend to be unreliable. Ulterior motives and subconscious conflicts may also explain mistakes in feeling perceptions. We should also seek those who are enhanced by consensus. So in various ways, we need to train our emotions as well, and learn to discriminate between those feelings that are appropriate to the occasion or situation and those that are not. We know that the development of emotional sensitivity depends a lot on interaction with emotionally mature persons. This cannot be reduced to a mechanical process, but, in accordance with *the kataphysical principle*, it is fitting that personal qualities are developed in more personal ways. The kataphysical principle basically means that the way to know a type of thing has to be appropriate to the nature of that type of thing. So we should expect, rather than be surprised, by the fact that knowing persons is rather different from knowing inanimate things.

The above model for SE can be extended to explain why "feeling perception" is possible. If emotions also functionally depend on the reality encountered or the state of affairs apprehended, then they can mediate perceptions of reality. The function may not be quantitative and mathematical; it may be more qualitative, for example, a sort of emotion roughly correlates with a sort of situation. So feeling can be said to be "the appropriate adjustment of the whole person to the reality which confronts him in a specific situation" (Ward 1974, p. 26). For example, emotions of fear can be related to situations of danger; emotions of desire to perceptions of value; emotions of love and gratitude to experience of grace and favor; feelings of reverence to noble qualities in another person, and so on.

Just as the nonconceptual contents of SE can be operated on later to provide new information, our emotional content of experiences can also continue to shape our noetic framework. While I acknowledge the inseparability of propositional content from the qualitative contents, I do not believe that everything is determined by propositional content, either. If no experience can precede an already existent linguistic framework, as though we could only experience what our language had already predetermined for us, then we have to deny that an infant can have experiences. It is also mysterious how the small child who has not yet learned how to speak can ever come to have an intelligible experience of the world, or to acquire a language. According to Merleau Ponty's phenomenological study of perception, "the differentiation between self and otherness, then self and object, and finally, self and other subjects, have to be phenomenally acquired before we are capable of making the distinctions which language presupposes...language can only be learnt after unmediated practice in the world, and it gains its meaning from its relation to this same independent reality" (Archer, Collier, and Porpora 2004, p. 68). So I uphold the possibility of a largely prelinguistic experience of the world, which can have an impact on us and lead to the development of new concepts. So "our reactions to the situations in which we find ourselves can have an inner richness and emotional complexity which is able to suggest new developments and refinements of our present linguistic resources. And especially in the field of religion, our language often stammers and blunders in trying to express something...new combinations of words do sometimes fall into place, and when they do they are often able to clarify our unexpressed feelings and reactions" (Ward 1974, p. 33).

The implications of feeling perception for ARE is quite obvious, and Ward has tried to spell it out. There is a common suspicion about REs that is based on their emotional nature. Some theorists propose that REs are initially nothing but mere emotions; they become religious only because the experient later imposes a layer of religious interpretation on the emotions. However, if emotions can play a cognitive role in noetic experiences, and are inseparable from noetic content, then the presence of emotions in RE is not a good reason to deny their validity. Ward's comments also point out the shortcomings of radical constructivism, which are often applied to aesthetic experience or RE. Our model, however, shows that experiences are always ineffable to some extent, but at the same time the possibility of articulation is always there—I call this *limited and provisional ineffability*.

When we have intimate experiences of another person, we often feel hard-pressed when we try to tell others our *judgments* about that person. However, an experienced counselor would know that those judgments can be drawn out by asking the subject to articulate his feelings about that person and reflect on the implications. This sort of process also happens in aesthetic experience, experience of self-discovery, and RE. So the factor of ineffability is common to all types of noetic experience, and need not be a debilitating factor. It is likely that there are always some elements of our experience that cannot be expressed by words, but it is also the case that we can always forge new words to describe our experiences. The degree of ineffability is always relative to the kind of language we have, but language is always on the move, too.

Since scientistic empiricists will no doubt have reservations about the idea of "feeling perception," it is important to point out that recent studies of science have shown that even emotions have a cognitive role to play in scientific and rational thinking. Since this is such a big topic, here I can only summarize the findings of some authors who have studied this problem extensively. For example, Paul Thagard believes that current research in cognitive science is increasingly challenging the view that emotions and reason are antagonistic to each other: "emotions such as curiosity, interest and wonder play a crucial role in the pursuit of scientific ideas.... Even in the third context, justification, emotions are a crucial part of the process of recognizing a theory as one that deserves to be accepted. Good theories are acknowledged for their beauty and elegance, which are aesthetic values that are accompanied by emotional reactions" (Thagard 2002, p. 236). Watson's discovery of the double helix is a good illustration. Watson wrote, "a structure this pretty just had to exist" (cited in Thagard 2002, p. 243). The conclusion is that since there "is abundant evidence from psychology and neuroscience that cognitive and emotional processes are intimately intertwined.... we cannot insist that a person's thinking should be emotion-free when it is biologically impossible for people to think that way" (Thagard 2002, p. 249).

One basic objection to feeling perception is that it is vague and not rule-based, and hence inferior to rational reflection, which is rule-based (e.g. canons of deductive or inductive reasoning). However, this alleged superiority of rational reflection over feeling is exaggerated. As Christopher Hookway points out, our rational judgment (either doubting some argument or affirming some inference) often presupposes an implicit awareness of too many standards or items that we cannot fully articulate. Rules of reasoning are not sufficient, and in the end we depend on a *feel* for the whole situation. This feeling judgment helps us detect a "pattern of salience in our evidential set...[O]therwise we are stuck in the unending process of considering more and more factors...[A]s Quine has insisted, epistemic reflection is generally very shallow...[T]he goodness of an inductive argument (or an explanation) is more easily *felt* than articulated, [and] we generally cannot *say* what makes such an argument a good one" (Hookway 2002, p. 254).

The narrow empiricists think that emotional detachment may help us make objective epistemic evaluations. Studies by Damasio have shown that damage to the areas of the brain involved in the production of emotions will instead impair subjects' abilities to make rational decisions. These people are obsessives who are unable to leave a problem behind, forever checking facts, and so never come to a decisive judgment. The conclusion is that "emotionally charged evaluation frees us from the need to carry out some enormously complicated assessments of the relevant evidence and information...[It helps us to be] sensitive to information that is not even available to conscious reflection.... [So] effective epistemic evaluation could turn out to be impossible without...appropriate emotional responses" (Hookway 2002, p. 257). Indeed, "patterns of salience that are provided by emotions can function as 'a *source* of reasons', as something that comes '*before* reasons'" (Hookway 2002, p. 260). If so, the dichotomy between emotion and reason is misguided. Polanyi long ago emphasized the importance of personal knowledge and intellectual passions, and it is interesting to see that recent cognitive science seems to lend support to his ideas.

Del Ratzsch has made an important study of this problem and applies it to the problem of religion. His paper contains a wealth of detail. He cites Wilkinson approvingly, "How do we then choose between alternative scientific hypotheses when we have used up all our scientific criteria?

We are, of course, left face to face with ourselves. The only remaining criterion is what seems right to us...in the deepest seat of human feeling... [I]n science, we sift and exhaust the evidence and then choose because we feel. Man's essential humanity must become, at this stage, not integrated with, but a replacement for, science until new data come along to permit the taking up again of the scientific method" (cited in Ratzsch 2009, p. 229). In the end, he accepts a PCT in the area of rational understanding and judgment: "Identification of sense-making, or intelligibility, presents itself to us experientially as a particular *feel*, a particular *seeming*...we cannot get behind or underneath this experience to examine its credentials. Any evaluation of its credentials would have to employ resources and procedures whose justification would ultimately track back at least in part to that experiential dimension itself—the support for those credentials would have to strike us as themselves making sense. As with our other faculties of cognition, at some point and in some circumstances it must simply become a human brute given of the process" (Ratzsch 2009, p. 220).

The implication for religion is that "if feels (or intuitions or emotions or the like) really do constitute the bedrock of science itself, one cannot demonstrate any substandard rationality of religious belief merely by citing emotion, subjective experience, interpretation, etc. as constituting components of religious belief—unless one is willing to see scientific rationality sink alongside it" (Ratzsch 2009, pp. 242–3). The convergence of emotion and reason also suggests that a more holistic knowing is possible: "An inescapably unified science/religion picture will arise out of the unity of the traditionally disparate aspects of human personhood itself, the unity of the multi-hued ingredients of rationality itself, and the unity of scientific and religious truth within the cosmos itself. Given that a single, unitary cognitive terrain underlies all our cognitive procedures—including both science and religion—the same fundamental structures and processes of rationality are of necessity imposed on, or better, partially constitutive of, both science and religion" (Ratzsch 2009, p. 243).

My conclusion is that the noetic dimension of experience is inextricably involved with the qualitative dimension. Tacit, inchoate feeling perceptions can come before articulate perceptions and beliefs. This kind of perception will be called *oblique perception*. Similarly, some human experiences contain inchoate intimations of the transcendent realm that may take time and efforts to spell out. These will be called *implicit REs* or *proto-REs*.

### 3.3.3 Participatory Knowing: Integration of Noetic and Volitional Dimensions

It is customary to oppose the noetic dimension to the volitional dimension of experience, but I think the two are actually intricately interrelated. Our everyday actions, though not explicitly noetic, are implicitly guided by our beliefs about the world. When we open the door, we are implicitly affirming or judging that there is a door. On the other hand, some SEs seem to be purely noetic and devoid of any volitional element, for example, seeing a chair. Yet it should be clear that everybody has to *learn* to see a chair as chair. Learning is active, and it is achieved through many practical actions: witness how a child plays with a chair by climbing on it, rocking it, and so on. So even such a passive experience is built on the foundation of our many past active experiences, which are fuelled by our will to trust and explore reality. SEs come effortlessly for mature human beings, but this is a wonderful achievement built upon our lifelong participation in and interaction with the reality around us.

The interaction of these two dimensions is clearer in those experiences like listening, which is neither wholly active nor wholly passive. (The more familiar you are with the language or the subject, the more passive you can be.) There is such a thing as a *will-to-listen*, as well as hearing without listening. People who are not willing to listen not uncommonly end up misinterpreting others. In general, "will is called into play...as the active openness of the whole person to the influx of new meaning and new perception.... As an activity of sustained, attentive awareness, will takes its proper place in thinking as a striving toward participation in reality" (Sloan 1983, p. 167). The prominence of the role of will in IPE, moral experience, and aesthetic experience accounts for a larger degree of variability in these areas, but this is not a good reason to discredit these experiences.

In many types of experience, proper cognition is inseparable from the will to participate in reality. At least we need some kind of openness, that is, the absence of the will to refuse to participate. This condition is amply attested in our IPE, especially in intimate relationships. In SE, the degree of activity in our experiences dwindles with the degree of our familiarity with the object of experience. We need not make volitional exertion afresh every time when we experience an object. But this attitude is only appropriate to an I-It relationship, not to an I-Thou relationship. It is because, in most cases, there is nothing new to grasp about a table or chair, but a Thou may have a depth that requires our constant attention and effort in order to grasp the meaning of the relationship with it. That is why Marcel talks about *creative* fidelity. If one stops paying attention to the other, and ceases to make oneself available, then the relationship will become ossified. We need a will to create the relationship afresh every day. All these examples show that in some types of knowing, detached knowing is not the best way. Instead, we need a kind of participatory knowing. We need a will to participate to begin with, and the knowledge will be deepened as we intimately interact with the reality in which we participate. This model seems particularly apt for IPE and TE.

People like Polanyi have emphasized that we can know more than we can tell, that is, much knowing is tacit. This claim baffles those epistemologists who think that knowing has to be propositional. It should be noted that the paradigm Polanyi uses is mainly know-how activity, like riding a bicycle. How do we learn to do it? Not by formulating propositions and memorizing them, but by repeated *attempts* to ride on it and *feel* the way to do it. This kind of process is what Polanyi calls "dwelling in one's experience," in which volitional and emotional elements feature prominently. Some people dismiss

Polanyi by positing a distinction between knowing-how and knowing-that, and say that Polanyi's model of tacit "knowing" applies to the former only. They may also refuse to acknowledge it as proper knowing. However, this distinction tends to be overdrawn. Knowing-how and knowing-that again seem to be two poles of a continuum. (This thesis is extensively argued in Polanyi's *Personal Knowledge.*)

For example, consider how a blind person can dwell in his stick to find his way. It is effectively an extension of his experiential capacity, namely, his tactile perceptual capacity. Consider how a doctor learns to read a radiograph or to diagnose a disease. These cases, as convincingly argued by Polanyi, exhibit many features similar to a knowing-how. The doctor has to *attend* to the detailed pieces of information and then arrive at a judgment without knowing exactly how he has done it. We can also consider Newman's emphasis on informal inference and illative sense. These activities, from riding a bicycle to informal inference, yield more and more explicit propositional judgments. Yet it seems that some degree of personal participation or dwelling in is required in all of them, the greatest in riding a bicycle, and the least in informal inference.

It seems this sort of "dwelling in" or participatory knowing basically consists of these two things:

1. An active and persistent will to participate in reality by attending to all the cues one possesses, and a willingness to be transformed by the reality.
2. The capacity to utilize noetic-qualitative complexes and to synthesize them by feeling one's way through, for example. utilizing the kinaesthetic sensations due to the stick to arrive at judgments about the world.

So Polanyi's account of tacit or personal knowing fits well with my account above, and it further illustrates how the three dimensions of experience interact dynamically in our knowing. Polanyi himself sees religious implications in his idea of participatory knowing. Recently John Cottingham has effectively applied the model of participatory knowing to RE, and he contends that in many cases of knowing, especially in more human forms of experience, proper knowing is founded on the right kind of personal involvement and inner reflection, and not on detached logical analysis (see Chapter 1).

Another important point about participatory knowing is that it is affected by the moral and spiritual conditions of the knower: the "assumption that truth or reality ought to be accessible irrespective of the character and state of mind of the aspirant to truth... may be correct enough in the case of inquiring into truths within meteorology... [but] there is no reason to accept it when we are dealing with... truths about how a poem or symphony may be appreciated, or how a loving relationship may be achieved and fostered. In these latter areas, the impartial application of a mechanical technique is precisely the wrong approach: the truth yields itself only to those who are already to some extent in a state of receptivity and trust"

(Cottingham 2005, p. 139). So similarly, we come to know God not by detached arguments, but by a spiritual praxis. So belief in God is a result of trust and involvement in a living community of faith, not of intellectual analysis.

Religion is not simply a matter of blind faith, even when it is not subject to a proof by SE or science. The believer often has what Pascal calls the reasons of the heart: the occasional glimpses of Transcendent Reality mediated by experiences of overwhelming goodness and beauty, or of the spiritual transformations wrought in our lives by religious practice, or the sense of meaning we possess in a life in God. Austin Farrer contends that this is also empirical confirmation, "as empirical as the matter allows." To test the reality of God, we can devote ourselves to his will, and obtain "empirical verification...in so far as we find 'life' or 'blessing' in the process, through God's uniting us with his will" (Farrer 1967, p. 57).

Critics may object that it is not scientific at all, but Farrer points out that "God does not stand alongside us or on a level with us, nor do we become aware of him through any external collision...He is related to us...as the will which underlies our existence...To look for God by the methods we use for examining nature would not be scientific, it would be silly...it is not scientific to look for a note of music through a microscope. How can we have experimental knowledge of the will behind our will? Only by opening our will to it, or sinking our will in it; there is no other conceivable way...Then his will takes effect in ours and we know it; not that we manipulate him, but that he possesses us" (Farrer 1966, pp. 106–7).

The idea is that if there is a God, a participatory knowing by immersing oneself in the love of God, and letting oneself be transformed by Him, is the most appropriate way to know Him. (This is also the argument of Moser 2010.) One must be willing to act and step forward into a process of inner transformation. This may be an arduous process, developing over a long period of time. So far the holistic model of experiential knowing opens up the space for feeling perception and participatory knowing of God. If this model is accepted, rather than some outdated foundationalist models, many objections to ARE will automatically fall to the ground. However, participatory knowledge is not opposed to reason. This book is an attempt to show that reason can serve as a confirmation of participatory knowledge in many ways.

### 3.3.4 *Diverse Experiences in a Unitary Life*

In the framework of narrow empiricism, SE is placed in a unique position, which other types cannot reach. The above discussions show that this model falsifies our experiences. Instead, SE is located in various kinds of continuums, together with other types of experience. For example, various experiences form a continuum between the poles of the purely noetic and the purely qualitative. Moreover, different types of experience fall on the line of continuum between the poles of activity and passivity. The structure of SE is basically similar to many types of experience.

### 3.3.5 Biographical Unity

It is also important that the diverse kinds of experience belong to a single self. Bertocci wrote: "Whatever else personal existence is, as lived, it consists in a unity of activities—sensory, memorial, perceptual, reasoning, emotive, volitional, moral, and appreciative (aesthetic and religious)...It is an irreducible, active matrix, a complex unity of activities defined by their capacity to undergo or enjoy qualitative 'contents'" (Bertocci 1970, p. 212). The experiences are found as a variegated unity, and there is a "seamless stitching of the parts into a unity," and an "awareness of the interpenetrating texture of activities and of contents at any one point." Moreover, this unity is "owned"; "this active, throbbing fact of unity is *my* unity" (Bertocci 1970, p. 212). It is an experiential fact that all these diverse experiences occur to a single self. They do not just occur to him separately, but they interpenetrate and fuse with one another in such a way that a *unitary biography* of a self is constituted by them. We will find out later, in Part B, that the self is not just a cognitive machine, but is also a spiritual being oriented to the quest for Meaning, Community, Truth, Goodness, Beauty, and ultimately God.

## 3.4 Conclusion

Let me summarize the implications of the discussion so far. SE is often extolled above all other experiences because it is regarded as the paradigm of a noetic experience, uncontaminated by emotional and volitional elements. For example, aesthetic and moral experiences are sometimes dismissed as nothing but feelings; RE as nothing but wish fulfillment. However, I have tried to show that it is a mistake to pit the noetic dimension against the qualitative and volitional dimensions. The latter dimensions are intricately involved with the former and are sometimes integral parts of our knowing.

Furthermore, I have argued that the unity of all our experiences is grounded in a biographical unity that is more than merely a Kantian transcendental postulate. It is also implicitly experienced as another pole of our noetic experiences. If it is true, then it is a mistake to take SE *in isolation* as the paradigmatic cognitive experience: cognitive experiences are inseparable from the cognizing subject and its self-awareness. Introspection and self-awareness are often impugned because they do not conform to the model of SE. Now, if the two types of experience are already united in our actual perceptions of the world, then SE in isolation is only an abstraction from the whole. How can we then use it alone to judge the whole? Narrow empiricism can now be seen to be increasingly implausible: what can be the grounds for completely isolating the cognitive dimension from the other dimensions and for isolating SE from the other types of experience? The onus is clearly on the narrow empiricist.

# CHAPTER 4

# THE CRITICAL TRUST APPROACH

The Critical Trust Approach (CTA) is a comparatively new epistemology. Although some of its elements have been contained in various epistemological proposals, the way they are integrated here is my personal attempt to formulate a more adequate epistemology in the post-foundationalist context. Before defending it, CTA needs to be carefully explained and elaborated.

## 4.1  Basic Issues in Epistemology

### *4.1.1  Concept of Justification*

Obviously the concept "justification" is crucial to my thesis. Unfortunately, the explication of this concept is controversial, and we have the great debate between internalism and externalism. Externalists claim that what justifies a subject's belief is some *fact external to the subject*, for example, causal or nomological connection. Internalists reject this and assert that what justifies a belief must be internal to the subject *in some way*. Some internalists think that a belief can only be justified with respect to other beliefs of the same subject. Generally, they would tend to a coherentist position, as, for example, Bonjour does. It should be obvious that the PCT would commit to a more "lenient" internalism. It claims that an experiential state or an epistemic seeming, which is not identical to the subject's belief, can also justify a belief. Nevertheless, it is still a kind of internalism, because epistemic seeming is an internal state of the subject that is introspectively accessible to him. I can only briefly explain here why I hold to an internalist, rather than an externalist, position about *justification*. (I will not assume internalism about *knowledge*.)

I will largely follow Alston's internalist externalism (Alston 1984). The position is roughly as follows: for me to have a belief *P* that is justified, I need to have adequate grounds for *P*. The grounds need to be potentially accessible to me, but that they are adequate as reliable indicators of the truth of *P* need not be accessible to me. Some internalists have imposed the more stringent requirement of meta-awareness, namely, that to be justified in accepting a belief, one must not only recognize that one has good grounds according to some theoretical criteria, but one must also have a meta-justification of those criteria. It seems that the externalists have correctly argued that this meta-awareness requirement will lead to skepticism. So I will eschew the meta-awareness requirement.

Reliabilism asserts that a belief is justified if it *is* produced by a reliable doxastic process. The problem is that if external considerations alone determine the justifiedness of a belief, then a belief can *in fact* be justified, while we have no inkling whatsoever as to whether it is justified. What is the point of *saying* that it is justified? For the person who has this belief, he can't *show* its justifiedness, that is, its being reliably produced, to a skeptic; neither can he adjust his belief or way of forming belief according to this consideration. And the observer can evaluate this belief only by reference to his *beliefs* about the reliability of that belief. If reliabilism is correct, what matters more is not whether a belief is justified, but whether we can *show* that it is justified. So perhaps reliabilism is hinting at one sense of "justified," the evaluative sense from the third-person viewpoint.

Jack Lyons is a reliabilist who defends the claim that "justification is primarily a matter of reliability rather than evidence," and he admits that facts about reliability are often inaccessible to us. Nevertheless, he issues this reliabilist injunction: "The overarching injunction is just to use the most reliable process available" (Lyons 2009, p. 175). I find this rather interesting. It is not clear how we can obey this injunction if we do not know what "the most reliable process available" is. So in practice, the actions of the reliabilist are not directly guided by this reliabilist injunction; they are determined by what *we believe* to be the most reliable process. Obviously, if Lyons tells the primitive tribes to obey this injunction, they will be happy to comply by continuing their practices of divination and consulting the witch doctors!

Michael Bergmann (2008) has argued against internalism on the grounds that in the end we cannot avoid some degree of "accident" in our knowing, but to avoid this has been the major motivation for internalism. For Bergmann, a strong awareness of what justifies the belief is an awareness that involves conceiving of the justifier as relevant in some way to the belief's justification or truth. This is similar to meta-awareness, and I agree that this requirement is unrealistic. However, Bergmann continues, if the internalist accepts a weak awareness only, then it cannot satisfy the internalist intuition that a belief be justified from the perspective of the subject. His conclusion is that such a weak form of internalism seems to offer no real advantage over externalism.

Bergmann's arguments are plausible, but not directly relevant here. My own preference for internalism is not based on the ambition to have a transparent grasp of our cognition and its ultimate grounds. To require this is contrary to the spirit of trust I advocate. Instead, it is the intuition that in the contexts that most obviously demand "justification" (e.g. debates over a controversial belief, internal struggles over what one should believe), an appeal to something entirely external is basically useless. For example, Swinburne does not deny there is something to externalism, but it's just that "only justification of an 'internalist' kind can be of any use to a person in deciding how to act" (Swinburne 2001, p. v). What is required is, in William Lycan's words, a doxastic decision procedure (DDP): a "recipe that real people could look up in a book and act on as practical advice in forming their beliefs...A perfectly good normative theory of justified belief may be correct...and yet be quite useless as a DDP, owing to a subject's inability to tell from within his...first-person-present epistemic situation whether or not the conditions laid down by the normative theory of justification are satisfied" (Lycan 1988, p. 131). So perhaps I can grant that externalism is a good normative theory of justification in some sense, but not a theory of justification most relevant to the debate over ARE, which should provide a DDP (which I intend my CTA to do).

I hope that enough has been said to show that modest internalism about justification makes sense. Fortunately, it seems to me, although my arguments here assume (a lenient form of) internalism, the gist of them can be adopted by an externalist and expressed in other terms. An externalist could reject the PCT, but this does not hinder him from formulating a structurally similar argument. Suppose we grant reliabilism. How can we then decide whether claims of REs are justified? They are justified if they are *in fact* reliably produced. So the theist and the atheist will each bring in their prior beliefs and come to the conclusion that claims of REs are justified or unjustified, respectively. Reliabilism will not improve the stalemate one bit.

Lyons basically agrees with Swinburne that experience is a kind of epistemic seeming (what he calls the "perceptual output"), and accepts a form of PCT in SE: "this perceptual output sense of 'looks' is epistemically significant. You are justified in believing that Joe's here because the face looks...like Joe to you." He even formulates a "Looks Principle": "our perceptual beliefs are epistemically justified, at least in part, because of how things look, sound, taste, smell, or feel to us" (Lyons 2009, pp. 107–8).

However, his Looks Principle is not grounded on a fundamental principle of PCT. To simplify a bit, his theory is that a belief is justified if it is a basic belief produced by a reliable process. A "basic belief is one that is the result of the noninferential operation of a primal system, an inferentially opaque cognitive system that has resulted from an interplay of learning and innate constraints" (Lyons 2009, p. ix). He also argues that our ordinary perceptual beliefs are basic beliefs produced by our perceptual systems. However, there is still a gap between his theory of justification and his Looks Principle, which is only entailed by his epistemology *plus his belief that our perceptual systems are in fact reliable*. Otherwise, even if they are basic, they are still not justified. But why believe that our perceptual systems are, in fact, reliable? Obviously, apart from our prior trust in our perceptual systems, it is impossible to prove the reliability of our perceptual systems. However, since Lyons is a naturalistic epistemologist, he is not too worried abut circularity. Well, he is not exactly against religious belief. He even claims that his epistemology is more God-friendly than Plantinga's!

He is also open to the Theory of Mind (TOM) explanation of the origin of belief in God. So in the end, his judgment is that although belief in God may not be basic, it is pretty close (Lyons 2009, pp. 161–2). So on his theory, it is still possible that belief in God is a basic belief, but everything turns on the empirical studies of cognitive science on our belief-formation systems. However, for the theists, the obvious question is that if the naturalist can simply help himself to the assumption of the reliability of SEs, why can't they have a similar assumption about the TEs? Why should he be held hostage to empirical studies?

The above considerations of reliability drive us to ponder how we can evaluate any complete epistemic practice. At some point, we find that we can no longer give noncircular reasons for its reliability. Alston argues that this is the case with both perceptual practice and Christian practice. The only question we can further ask is whether there are adequate reasons for supposing that this practice is unreliable. If not, the practice can be regarded as weakly justified in a normative sense, $J_{nw}$. Alston suggests that "if we are to have any chance of acquiring knowledge, we must simply go along with our natural reactions of *trust* with respect to at least some basic sources of belief, provided we lack sufficient reason for regarding them as unreliable. . . . we must be content with being $J_{nw}$. And if some, why not all?" (Alston 1983, p. 119; italics mine). The spirit here is surprisingly similar to that of the PCT. This convergence suggests that if we probe deeper into considerations of reliability, we may get a result close to that obtained by applying the PCT.

### 4.1.2 Prima Facie Reason

Now I need to explain more clearly what is meant by a *prima facie* justification. First, a belief is self-justified (to some extent) for a subject if its justification does not *wholly* derive from other beliefs of the subject. Of course, a self-justified belief *could* also be inferentially justified by other beliefs. Here is one definition:

> A belief is *prima facie justified* for a person S if and only if . . . it is necessarily true that if S holds the belief and has no reason for thinking he should not then he is justified in holding the belief. (Pollock 1986, p. 29)

A belief can be justified by being inferred from a set of prima facie justified beliefs. This process can be called *prima facie reasoning*, or *defeasible reasoning*, because the inferential justification provided by prima facie reasoning can be defeated. Suppose a certain prima facie justified belief, $B$, is used to infer $B^*$. Obviously, one way to defeat this justification is to find reasons for thinking that $B$ is false. Such reasons are called *rebutting defeaters* in Pollock's terms. The other way to defeat the above prima facie reasoning is to undercut the evidential connection between $B$ and $B^*$. This can be achieved if we have reasons to think that even if $B$ is true, it would not raise the probability of $B^*$ at all. These reasons then serve as an *undercutting defeater*.

## 4.2  The Spirit of the Critical Trust Approach

The general rationales for the CTA can be characterized by several themes:

1. The Priority of Trust over Doubt
2. The Superiority of Pluralistic Empiricism over Exclusivist Empiricism
3. Impartiality toward Our Experience*s*
4. Unity in Diversity

### *4.2.1  The Priority of Trust over Doubt*

We have seen that the atheists' main worry about belief in God (like Parsons's) is the opening of the floodgates of superstition and irrationality. This certainly reflects a spirit of criticism and doubt, which are central themes in modern epistemology. However, doubt is neither necessary nor natural. For example, in the Chinese intellectual traditions, skeptical doubt has never been prominent. (It may even be unintelligible to many Chinese.) In contrast, emphasis is placed on *Xin* (trust) as a virtue of the gentleman, the morally mature person. Excessive doubt toward the claims of others will probably be regarded as inappropriate, or even impolite. So we need to understand the specific historical background of the primacy of doubt in the West. Of course, the story usually begins with Descartes's quest for certainty. In a time of drastic changes and upheaval, Descartes resolved to doubt everything that could be doubted, including commonsense beliefs, traditions, and religion. He adopted this method of doubt in order to find an indubitable foundation upon which the human cognitive edifice could be securely built.

He accepted a principle of doubt. As explained by Polanyi, "[i]t has been taken for granted...that the acceptance of unproven beliefs was the broad road to darkness, while truth was approached by the straight and narrow path of doubt...It trusts that the uprooting of all voluntary components of belief will leave behind unassailed a residue of knowledge that is completely determined by the objective evidence. Critical thought trusted this method unconditionally for avoiding error and establishing truth" (Polanyi 1958, p. 269).

Another related development is the hermeneutics of suspicion developed by Feuerbach, Marx, Nietzsche, and Freud. "What unites them...is...*the deliberate attempt to expose the self-deceptions involved in hiding our actual operative motives from ourselves, individually or collectively*" (Westphal 1993, p. 13; italics in original). The scope for the hermeneutics of suspicion is very wide: it can be applied in spheres of political economy, bourgeois morality, psycho-sexual development, religion, and so on. In fact, suspicion is contagious, and it has a tendency to spread from one field to another. Once the image of the rational autonomous individual is gone, and the dark unconscious with its seething libido is seen to be calling the shot, what is there to stop the suspicion from spreading to other kinds of belief, political or scientific or whatever? The image of the human being as portrayed by the masters of suspicion cannot but create doubts about human beliefs. In the long run, it also leads to Nietzsche's genealogy, Foucault's understanding of power/truth, the Derridean project of deconstruction, and so on. So the intensification of the hermeneutics of suspicion finally results in the demise of meaning and truth, and it is now fashionable for scholars to write obituaries for epistemology. The roots of many postmodern claims are still epistemological: the demise of foundationalism or the impossibility of metaphysics is the unarticulated common assumption of many postmodern thinkers.

Since doubts are so powerful, perhaps doubt can't be defeated except by itself. We may hope that the acid of doubt will be applied to itself in such a way that we begin being suspicious of suspicion, doubting doubt, relativizing relativism, and being skeptical of skepticism. As Polanyi suggests, we should turn the critical attitude to the principle of doubt itself (Polanyi 1958, p. 272). The first thing to do is to note, with William James, that a failure in knowing can be manifested in two ways. Believing a false or unjustified belief is only *one* form. Advocates of the principle of doubt regards "gullibilism" as a mortal epistemological sin. Doubt and critical acumen are regarded as epistemological or even moral virtues. The idea seems to be that we should try our best to avoid having false beliefs. However, this seems to ignore another kind of epistemic failure, namely, failure to believe the truth. Being overcritical is also a defect. Gullibilism is not the only devil to be exorcised. We should also beware of the dangers of dogmatic skepticism, and Polanyi offers a good example. "We may regard this sceptical movement as altogether reasonable and be unaware of its fiduciary character until we are confronted with its blunders…[For example,] scientific scepticism…brushed aside all the instances of hypnotic phenomena…even in the face of systematic demonstrations of hypnosis by Mesmer and his successors" (Polanyi 1958, p. 274). No doubt the critical spirit can also lead us to errors.

We can even argue for the priority of trust over doubt. First, a failure to trust when we should is not only foolish, but also detrimental to oneself or others, or to the interpersonal relationship. Without trust, we could hardly survive, and doubt is out of the question. If a child adopts a habitual critical attitude, he may never grow up! He can never answer all the critical questions he can ask if he embarks on this project. Second, doubt and criticism seem to presuppose a certain existing framework. We need the relevant concepts and knowledge to ask the right questions and to give criticisms. Doubt never occurs in a complete vacuum. The artificiality of the Cartesian method of doubt is often noted: "someone who really believed that he knew nothing would not even know how to begin on a course of radical doubt; for he would have no conception of what his task might be, of what it would be to settle his doubts and to acquire well-founded beliefs" (MacIntyre 1980, pp. 59–60).

Popper is famous for his critical rationalism, and some critical rationalists, such as Hans Albert, are very critical of religion. Interestingly, Popper also upholds our prima facie trust in traditions. After all, rationalism itself is a tradition. Moreover, the critical attitude has to work on something: "we cannot start afresh...we must stand on the shoulders of our predecessors. We must carry on a certain tradition...you need something with which to start. If you have nothing to alter and to change, you can never get anywhere" (Popper 1969, pp. 129–30). Popper points to a fallibilist conception of epistemology. Though we can only start with fallible beliefs or theories (or for Popper, even myths), we can *criticize and falsify* them and then invent better theories. In this way, we may still gain knowledge.

All in all, these criticisms converge toward the idea that the dependence of doubt on trust is inescapable. A completely presupposition-less doubt seems unrealistic.[1] As Wittgenstein says, "If you tried to doubt everything you would not get as far as doubting anything. The game of doubting itself presupposes certainty" (Wittgenstein 1969, paragraph 18e). It is possible to adopt a wide-ranging principle of trust as the basis of epistemology, and it is worthwhile to explore this kind of approach, especially in view of the inadequacies of approaches that are built on the principle of doubt. However, the Critical Trust Approach needs to give a due place to criticism and doubt.

The PCT is a general, first-order principle. By applying it, we usually get some second-order *critical* principles. For example, the Principle of Testimony tells us to give initial trust to others' words. However, it does not forbid us from formulating a second-order principle to the effect that a certain type of person and a certain sort of statement are not to be trusted. Indeed, the only grounds for this kind of principle may only be derivable when we adopt the first-order principle. I have no intention of saying that trust should be unlimited. An attitude of initial trust may be defeated. CTA can be regarded as a kind of post-critical philosophy (Polanyi), but *post*-critical philosophy is not *un*-critical. It just insists that the principles of criticism and suspicion are *second-level* principles that are derived from *first principles* of trust. In this way, it reconciles two indispensable poles of epistemology: trust and criticism.

So we have to start somewhere, but where, exactly? The metaphor of Neurath's ship is helpful. He likens our body of knowledge to a boat at sea. Repairs must be made afloat, and though no part is untouchable, we must stand on some in order to replace or repair others. Not every part can go at once. Experience is the only channel for us to get in touch with reality. If we do not trust the deliverances of our experiences, it would be impossible for us to gain knowledge of reality. So the CTA suggests that an attitude of *prima facie trust* toward our experience is wise and inescapable.

### 4.2.2 *The Superiority of Pluralistic (Holistic) Empiricism over Exclusivist Empiricism*

I will be contented with staking out my claims clearly in this section, and provide the more detailed arguments in the next few chapters. The CTA is also empirical in spirit. However, it objects to the kind of narrow empiricism prevalent in modern Western philosophy and advises us to attend to the richness of our experience.[2] It believes that to posit a *qualitative* difference between SE and other kinds of noetic experiences is not sustainable after the downfall of foundationalism. It objects to the narrow empiricists' reductionist project, which is prima facie implausible, and the eliminative project, which is impracticable. So narrow empiricism is a kind of intellectual imperialism.

For the pluralistic empiricism (or holistic empiricism), the "complaint against many modern empiricists is that they are not empirical enough. So often they set arbitrary limits to human experience and thus themselves exclude mystery *a priori*. It is only when experience is taken into account in its full dimensions that we can have an adequate basis for philosophizing; and it will be my contention...that the most rigorous analysis of our experience confronts us with mystery as its depth: mystery that is illuminated...by the distinctive mystery of the Christian revelation" (Clifford 1971, p. 33). Clifford's talk of mystery may sound alarming, because the exclusivist empiricists often have an aversion to mystery, and they tend to classify everything that cannot fit into their naturalistic worldview as mystery. The emphasis on mystery here should not be equated with obscurantism. Instead, the contention is that exactly as we pursue the *greatest degree of intelligibility* in the context of the rainbow of experiences, we are confronted with a depth dimension with seems to call for belief in transcendence. (There is even a mysterious dimension of our experience of the natural world—see Chapter 9.) There will be an extended argument for this contention in Part B.

### 4.2.3 Impartiality toward Our Experiences

The pluralistic empiricist tries to be impartial toward our diverse experiences. So often only knowledge by sensory experience is thought to be unproblematic, while all other modes of cognition are suspected, for example, a priori intuition and moral intuition. However, knowledge by senses is not as unproblematic as we used to think and also, in some sense, mysterious. In the end, skepticism about SE can only be replied to with a basic, prima facie trust. We have to ask why the same attitude of trust cannot be adopted with regard to other experiences? Why can't we accept pluralistic sources of justification? In fact, there is already internal plurality within sense experience (five senses together with kinesthetic sensation and gustatory sensations, etc.). There is also plurality among sense experience, memory, introspection, and reason—the four basic sources of justification most commonly recognized—and these four sources are very different.

The chauvinistic attitude of traditional empiricism toward other kinds of experience is unwarranted. The CTA contends that we have to shake off the shackles of a narrow empiricism and recover a more realistic notion of "experience" that is actually part of our *Lebenswelt*. Some analytical philosophers have come to see that. For example, Bonjour says, "the relevant notion of experience should not be restricted to sense experience in a

narrow sense, but should rather be understood to include any sort of cognitive factor or element which...provides...information, *input*, concerning the specific character of the actual world as opposed to other possible
worlds. Thus...introspection, memory, and nonsensory forms of input like
clairvoyance and telepathy (if these should exist) count as varieties of experience and the knowledge derived therefrom as *a posteriori*" (Bonjour 1985,
p. 192).[3]

Of course, equality in starting point does not guarantee equal outcome;
different types of experience do differ in epistemic strengths. I agree that,
in the end, sensory experience does possess some properties to a unique
degree that make it more trustworthy. However, it does not follow that SE is
qualitatively different from all other kinds of experience. It is illegitimate for
narrow empiricism to make this assumption as our *epistemological starting
point*. In the end, the pluralistic empiricist also wants to fit the deliverances
of our experiences into a unitary worldview, and acknowledges the need to
unite different kinds of experience. This will lead to intellectual integration. So the pluralistic empiricist is at the same time the holistic empiricist.
Moreover, the acceptance of other types of experience (e.g. moral, religious,
and spiritual experiences) provides us more resources in the quest for personal wholeness.

### 4.2.4  Unity in Diversity

Some critics of the ARE may be sympathetic to the claims of religious experience. However, they think it is not fruitful to subsume religious experience together with other experiences (e.g. sense experience) under the same
framework. Taber thinks that the efforts of defenders of religious experience
(e.g. Wainwright) to emphasize the similarities of religious experience with
ordinary experiences are mistaken: "For the whole thrust of the mystic's
endeavour is to open up a new faculty, precisely to see (perceive) what most
others cannot see" (Taber 1986, p. 53). So too much similarity or agreement
could even be seen as a kind of invalidation! Of course, the critics are also
mistaken to judge "religious experience...by the standard of the given experience of the world. Yet the import of religious experience is often to call
into question the given experience of the world" (Taber 1986, p. 55).

The emphasis on the uniqueness of religious experience serves to remind us
of the dangers of reductionism or epistemic chauvinism that often attempts
a complete assimilation of religious experience to sense experience. This is a
kind of imperialism that is forgetful about the intrinsic plurality of human
experiences and sources of justification. However, while I agree that respect-
ing plurality should be our starting point, we should also beware of the dangers of a fragmented epistemology or incoherent worldview. It is possible
that when we try to ward off imperialism, we posit unnecessary discontinui-
ties between religious experience and other types of experience. We should
also distinguish different types of religious experience here. Taber says,
"the import of religious experience is often to call into question the given

experience of the world" (Taber 1986, p. 55). I think it is true to say this for a radical kind of monistic mystical experience, but for theistic experience it is another story. Theistic experience will only challenge naturalism or scientism, but not our ordinary experiences. I will argue that theistic experience is coherent with most other types of ordinary experiences.

However, the proliferation of "unique" and autonomous types of experience does indeed raise legitimate epistemological concerns.[4] The specter of gullibilism or relativism looms large. To avoid these problems, we should also note that plurality at one level in itself does not exclude unity at another level. So the CTA agrees with the importance of a common epistemological framework by virtue of which diverse types of experience can be brought together somehow (while at the same time not negating their legitimate differences). This is achieved by the combination of the PCT and the kataphysical principle, which acknowledges that each type of experience has its uniqueness. The PCT and other principles in the CTA are only very general methodological principles. After applying these principles in a certain realm of experience, we gradually come to understand the basic characteristics of the nature of reality in that realm. Then, and only then, can we formulate second-order critical principles or second-order principles of enhancement. In this way, the integrity of that realm is respected, although the CTA does aspire to a unified methodology. So religious experience can be judged by criteria that are common to all types of experience, for example, PCT or the Principle of Simplicity, but given our understanding of religious reality, we won't insist on the kind of manipulation or experiments possible in the realm of SE. So we can maintain a balance of plurality and unity in the CTA. In the following section, I try to delineate in more detail the structure of this kind of post-critical epistemology.

## 4.3 Different Formulations of the PCT

A PCT can be formulated in diverse ways: descriptive, normative, or prescriptive. In this book, I am primarily concerned with the normative version of PCT about the source of epistemic justification: "All other things being equal, it is *justified* to believe that things are the way they seem." However, there are some ambiguities which need to be clarified.

### 4.3.1 The Scope of PCT

Let the content of the bracket following PCT denote the scope of this PCT. So PCT(SE) and PCT(TE) mean a PCT that is supposed to be applicable to SE and TE, respectively. Summarizing various proposals, the scope of the PCT can be formulated in four major ways:

1. Localized versions, like PCT(SE), PCT(moral experience), and so on.
2. PC(intentional experience): it covers an encounter with something external to oneself (SE, IPE, and RE). Moral and aesthetic judgments

(or perhaps also memory) are not covered (Yandell 1984, p. 6). This is Yandell's formulation: "If it seems to one that one experiences **x**, then one who claims that there is no **x** ... has ... some evidence contrary to the claim, to overcome" (Yandell 1984, p. 31). Swinburne's earlier formulation (1979) is similar.

3. PCT(noetic experience): "noetic experience" is defined as follows:

   A subject S has a *noetic experience* E iff it seems (epistemically) to S that a certain contingent state of affairs A obtains or obtained. Let $p$ be the proposition that A obtains or obtained. E can be described as the epistemic seeming that $p$ and $p$ is neither logically contradictory nor necessarily true; $p$ is then called the propositional content of E.

Noetic experience excludes a priori intuitions about necessary truths, but includes the rest of the rainbow of experiences and also the two derived sources of memory and testimony.

4. PCT(epistemic seeming) or a wider PC: it covers all spontaneous beliefs or epistemic seemings, including noetic experiences and a priori intuitions. Lycan's PCT seems to have a wide scope: "Accept at the outset each of those things that seem to be true" (Lycan 1988, p. 165). Swinburne's later formulation (1986) is also a wider PCT, as is Michael Huemer's Phenomenal Conservatism: "If it seems to *S* as if *P*, then *S* thereby has at least prima facie justification for believing that *P*" (Huemer 2001, p. 99), which is intended to be "a general principle of foundational justification" applicable "to all other kinds of knowledge" (Huemer 2001, p. 102).

The four versions of PCT listed above have increasing breadth. Each version is included in the latter version, but not vice versa. Strictly speaking, the ARE only needs the localized version PCT(RE). Nevertheless, the wider principles may be needed to motivate support for PCT(RE). For example, in studying the analogy between SE and TE, we may find PCT (intentional experience) plausible. I will argue for a PCT with a wider scope because I think at least aesthetic experience and moral experience merit prima facie trust. Although there may be no independent realm of "moral objects" or "floating beauty," *wicked* deeds, *good* persons, *beautiful* sceneries, and so on are integral parts of our experienced world. Moreover, prima facie trust in memory is crucial to my case, but memory is not an intentional experience. I intend the PCT to also cover memory, introspection, and experiences of other persons. They are so closely interwoven with our ordinary perceptual experience that it would be ludicrous to apply the PCT to the latter, but not to the former.

In the wider PC, prima facie trust is further extended to the realm of necessary or analytic truths: logical, semantic, epistemological intuitions. It is possible to accept PCT(noetic experience), but not the wider one. However, I think intellectual experience is, indeed, an integral part of our epistemic practice, which is interrelated with various kinds of experience. In this thesis I try to argue for the wider PCT, but readers are reminded that some narrower versions of PCT are sufficient for the ARE.

### 4.3.2 The Force of the PCT

There is a recurrent problem regarding Swinburne's approach: the force of his PCT. Gutting doesn't object to the application of the PCT to RE, but he wants to restrict its force. He thinks that Swinburne takes "*prima facie*" evidence to mean that "the evidence of the experience is by itself decisive unless there is some overriding consideration in our background knowledge. But this claim is too strong" (Gutting 1982, p. 148). His idea is that "an of-**X** experience in general provides *prima facie* evidence of **X**'s existence only in the sense of supplying some (but not sufficient) support for the claim that **X** exists. For belief in the claim to be warranted, the solitary of-**X** experience requires supplementation by additional corroborating experiences.... In cases of kinds of objects of which we have frequently had veridical experiences, we can of course rightly believe that they exist, without further corroboration beyond our seeming to see them. But this is because we have good inductive reason to expect that the further corroborations will be forthcoming. With relatively unfamiliar objects...this sort of inductive reason is not available; and warranted assent must await further corroboration" (Gutting 1982, p. 149).

He gives an example of an experience of apparition. He suggests that even if we can't find cogent defeaters of this isolated experience, such an experience, though not completely without force, still can't be deemed veridical. He then draws the conclusion that "we should think of an individual of-God experience as providing significant but not sufficient evidence for God's existence, needing to be included in a cumulative body of diverse evidence that can warrant the claim that God exists" (Gutting 1982, pp. 149–50).

This criticism seems correct.[5] The strength of the PFEF accorded by the PCT is not decisive in all the cases, and that may not be fixed and uniform either. In the end, the assessment of claims of any experience has to depend on complicated considerations of theories, alternative explanations, fit with other experiences, and so on. Swinburne does not give sufficient attention to these matters, and at times he exaggerates the force of the PCT, for example, when he implies that "an experience of Poseidon is good evidence for Poseidon" (Swinburne 1979, p. 254). What follows is my proposed refinement of Swinburne's epistemological approach.

First, let us distinguish a Token PCT that applies to every token experience, and a Type PCT that applies to a *type* of experience. Second, we should recognize that justification comes in degrees. Token PCT may have three different degrees of force:

1. *Weak Token PCT*: Every token experience provides at least *some degree of justification* for the embodied epistemic seeming.
2. *Moderate Token PCT*: Every token experience provides at least *prima facie justification* for the embodied epistemic seeming.
3. *Strong Token PCT*: Every token experience provides at least *incorrigible justification* for the embodied epistemic seeming.

Remember that a belief that has prima facie justification is one in which it is necessarily rational or justified to believe if there are no defeaters available. If an experience provides only *some* justification for the corresponding experiential claim, it only means that the claim is more worthy of belief than before, but it may still not suffice for prima facie justification. Also note that these three PCTs are not mutually exclusive. In fact, the Strong PCT entails the other two, but not vice versa. The Strong PCT is obviously false, because only a few token experiences can satisfy its condition, for example, experience of intense pain. The critics' point is that numerous odd and idiosyncratic experiences (e.g. experience of apparition) are counterexamples to the Moderate PCT. For example, perhaps we do not have the defeaters to prove the isolated experience of apparition delusory, but our intuition is that, even in this scenario, it is not *necessarily* rational to believe in the apparition. This contradicts the Moderate PCT. Suppose this counterexample is valid.[6] What follows?

We may reject the Moderate Token PCT, but still defend the Weak Token PCT. It seems implausible to deny that isolated token experiences cannot provide at least *some* justification. I think the case is similar in SE. Is it true that every token SE by itself will confer prima facie justification? I don't think so (Gutting seems to agree). Suppose we have a single recalcitrant experimental datum, while all others lie on a straight line. Suppose we can't explain away this anomaly and provide the defeaters. It still seems rational to opt for a simple experimental law and to reject the anomalous experimental datum. This would not be justified if the Moderate Token PCT is right. Hence it seems that although an odd experience provides some justification, this justification can be overcome if the adoption of this experience would reduce to a significant degree the coherence of the theory that is based on other more coherent experiences. Lycan has a similar view: the initial weight of spontaneous beliefs are only minimal and they can be overridden by "almost anything: new input, noncoherence with other beliefs in a minimal way, slight explanatory advantage to be gained elsewhere, or whatever. The justification conferred on a spontaneous belief by the Principle of Credulity is flickering and feeble" (Lycan 1988, pp. 166–7).

Nevertheless, such tokens of SE still have *some* evidential force: it is only *overridden* by coherence considerations. That is why such "odd" SEs can become falsifiers when the defeaters are defeated in turn. For example, the isolated anomaly of Mercury's perihelion was defeated by the coherence of the Newton's Mechanics. When the latter was in turn defeated by Relativistic Mechanics, the earlier datum becomes important evidence. This is hardly explainable if it *had never possessed any evidential force*. So "oddness" is not an intrinsic character of the experience: this status is contingent and mutable. Suppose all humans now start to have experiences of apparitions regularly. Isn't it now the case that the earlier experience is no longer odd and merits serious consideration? All these suggest that the Weak Token PCT is still needed. Otherwise, it is also difficult to account for the evidential force of the *first* experience of a completely novel phenomenon in science, for example, a new elementary particle or electro-magnetic effects.

Perhaps it may be objected that my account of SE can't be correct, because in practice we don't check the coherence of a token SE with another. Each token seems able to provide prima facie justification on its own, for example, a transient sighting of a bird in the sky by one person. I think that it is the case only because we have *taken for granted* the fact that all our token SEs actually form a coherent type and reinforce one another in almost all of our life experiences. Hence it is true that every single SE can then confer prima facie justification, but it is only so considered as a token *of a well-established type of experience.*

### 4.3.3 The Type PCT

If even one token experience can confer some justification, then it seems to follow that if a token coheres with many other tokens, that is, it falls within a type of experience, this should confer a higher degree of justification. Here we accept the coherentist idea that justification can be accumulated. So the following seems to be plausible:

Moderate Type PCT:

> Every experience which belongs to a well-established type of experience pro-vides prima facie justification for the embodied epistemic seeming.

When we can identify an experience as belonging to a well-established type, this has several implications:

a. Shared Experiences: This experience is not altogether idiosyncratic. Similar experience occurs repeatedly and is shared by a substantial amount of people, preferably across cultures and eras.
b. Common Ontology: The tokens of the type have to largely cohere with one another before they can be grouped into a kind. Namely, the group of tokens does not have massive internal contradictions. They also need to share a common ontology such that different tokens can be mapped onto that ontology, exhibiting different sorts of epistemic relations among themselves (e.g. mutual support, explanatory dependence).
c. Conceptual Coherence: To enable mutual communication of the experi-ences, which is the prerequisite of our identification of a type of non-solip-sistic experience, the experiences have to be *to some extent* describable. It also requires a conceptual framework that is not obviously incoherent.

The degree of PFJ provided by a type of experience varies with the degree to which each type is established. When a type of experience exhibits a significant degree of *intra-coherence*, I call it a well-established type. It is possible that a collection of token experiences, while conflicting with one another, does exhibit some coherence at a lower level of description. I would call that a *loose type* of experience. The factors contributing to the degree of *intra-coherence* of a type of experience are summarized below:

The Criteria of Intra-coherence

The degree of intra-coherence of a type of experience *E* will increase with the following factors, ceteris paribus:

a. the number of people sharing *E*,
b. the frequency of occurrence of *E* to an individual,
c. the variability of the situations in which *E* occurs,
d. the explanatory coherence between the tokens of *E*, and
e. the conceptual coherence of *E*'s ontological framework.

Another question can also be raised: "Why don't we just uphold the Type PCT and discard all those 'odd' and isolated experiences?" The suggestion is that we can dispense with the Token PCT altogether. However, it won't do, because I think the Type PCT requires the Token PCT. If we deny the latter, it is very difficult to see how we can establish the former. If a token experience in general does not provide any degree of epistemic justification, it is difficult to see how a type can do so. Consider the role of SEs in the justification of scientific theories. Popper thinks that observations are all theory-laden, and hence the so-called foundation is only a swamp. The scientific enterprise is likened to a structure of piles driven down into a swamp, and to what depth we drive those piles is a matter of decision. So in the end, we can only take the consensus of the scientists as final concerning what observations are acceptable.

Here we can note a common criticism of Popper: "If no single SE can confer *any* degree of justification at all, neither the consensus can." This seems plausible. Furthermore, before we can decide what experiences form a well-established type, we need to trust *some* token experience or other. So the Token PCT seems indispensable.

### 4.3.4 Reply to Some Objections

It is important to make the above distinctions, strong, because not every formulation is equally defensible. Sometimes a quick dismissal of the PCT is due to inadequate appreciation of the distinction between the Weak Token PCT and Moderate Type PCT. For example, T. A. Roberts presses a UFO objection to Swinburne: "On this very generous interpretation of the PC, that some objects in the sky appeared to be extra-terrestrial to some would be evidence that they were. This is clearly taking credulity too far!" (Roberts 1989, p. 85). This objection does not have much force in my refined framework. This is because it cannot yet be said that experiences of UFOs constitute a well-established subtype of experience. So the application of Weak Token PCT to them only yields some justification, which is likely to be overridden by coherence considerations. Moreover, sightings of UFOs belong to the realm of SE and hence are subject to the second-order critical principles generated from our past SEs. From our own understanding of SE, we know that it is difficult to conclude from afar about the nature of distant objects in the sky. There can also be alternative explanations of these experiences, such as people mistaking balloons, airplanes, and some really unidentified objects as flying saucers, or there are psychological explanations for their reports, and so on. These moves are by no means contrary to my *Critical* Trust Approach.

Richard Gale also objects to Swinburne: "the unrestricted version of PC is not acceptable. A person's nonperceptual epistemic seemings are notoriously subject to all kinds of irrationalities. The best that can be said for a nonperceptual epistemic seeming that a proposition *p* is true is that it increases *p*'s probability...but this watered down version of PC is too weak" for Swinburne's ARE (Gale 2005, p. 428). First, Gale seems to have underestimated the PFEF of nonperceptual epistemic seemings. Second, this supposed dilemma is solved by my distinctions here. Gale seems to grant the Weak Token PCT, and he is right that this alone is not sufficient for the ARE (though it cannot be said to be without force altogether). But in this book, I also argue for the Type PCT and give reasons why this is applicable to TE (if not RE as a whole).

## 4.4 The Structure of the Critical Trust Approach

The two basic components of CTA are the critical spirit and the attitude of trust. They need to be kept in a healthy tension. This is similar to Thomas Kuhn's emphasis on a kind of *essential tension* between tradition and innovation in science (this phrase is the name of one of Kuhn's books).

### 4.4.1 Data Gleaning–Trust

The data for the CTA are *all* our experiences. In accordance with the Top-Down Approach, the original incorporated epistemic seeming of a given experience is taken as the epistemological starting point and accorded PFJ. These *presumptive data* are defeasible. The basic principles are the weak Token PCT and moderate Type PCT.

### 4.4.2 Data Sifting and Epistemic Ascent—Critical Trust

#### 1. Ground-Level Sifting

Presumptive data can be defeated. Unfortunately, typically the defeater itself is also defeasible, and there can be defeater-defeater as well as defeater-defeater-defeater and so on. Suppose we have a defeater *D* of an originally prima facie justified belief *B*. Presumably *D* only has PFJ. Why can't we use the original belief to defeat the defeater instead? Bonjour has summarized Rescher's suggestion:

> the basic idea is to first segregate the total set of data or presumptions into maximal consistent subsets and then choose among these subsets....one might then

choose among the maximal consistent subsets on the basis of the plausibility of
their members. (Bonjour 1985, p. 224)

The idea is that we have to bring in coherence considerations to determine the weight of each presumptive datum. Once a presumptive datum
coheres with many other presumptive data, its weight would be increased,
and it could serve to defeat another less weighty presumptive datum. A presumptive datum that conflicts with many other presumptive datum is then
defeated. In general, we can formulate this methodological rule:

The Rule of Ground-Level Sifting

It is justified to choose the consistent subset of our presumptive data that
has maximal weight.

## 2. Explanatory Ascent and Feedback Sifting

The data of experience need to be ordered and made more intelligible. So
the data of SE, when subjected to the search for order and intelligibility,
yield the scientific framework. However, the framework itself can have a
feedback effect on the initial data. Some presumptive data of SE may be
rejected due to theoretical reasons (e.g. the Principle of Simplicity). This can
be captured by the following principle:

The Principle of Epistemic Defeat

> We should not believe that things are as they seem to be in cases when such a
> belief is in conflict with the simplest theory compatible with a vast number of
> data obtained by supposing in a vast number of other cases that things are as
> they seem to be.

Moser understands the PCT as a form of naïve realism and objects: "Our
best science...can present subtle evidence independent of (some) commonsense beliefs...that challenges a commonsense belief resting on a principle
of credulity" (Moser 2010, p. 207). This seems to be a misunderstanding,
because my CTA of course allows for this kind of challenge. This kind of
feedback sifting would be regarded as the rational search for intellectual
economy. In general, it is rational to believe in the theory that best explains
our diverse presumptive data. It is the so-called *inference to the best explanation (IBE)*. When the presumptive data conflict, and the best explanation cannot comprehend all the data, our best explanatory theory can serve
as defeater of those "recalcitrant" data. That is also why a worldview can
affect our feedback sifting, because it is supposed to be an explanation of *all*
our presumptive data.

Actually, ground-level sifting and feedback sifting are not clearly demarcated levels. It is because experiences rarely directly conflict. For example,
suppose I see the table and you don't. Our experiences won't conflict unless
we assume that if the table is there, both of us should see it. So in employ-
ing the Rule of Ground-Level Sifting, some "theoretical" considerations are
inevitable. Nevertheless, the rough distinction is still useful.

### 3. Second-Order Critical Principle

When we trust the majority of our presumptive data, those data may suggest to us that some types of presumptive data are not altogether reliable. For example, those presumptive data are found to be grossly inconsistent, or they are contradicted by other well-established data. In such cases, we can formulate second-order critical principles. They are *second-order* principles because the justification of these principles depend on our basic trust of our presumptive data by and large, which is prescribed by the first-order PCT. For example, our experiences may tell us that drunk people are prone to having hallucinations. So we can form this second-order critical principle: "Bizarre perceptual claims of drunk people are not to be trusted." Of course, without the first-order basic trust, we cannot establish the grounds for this principle; nor can we find out who the drunk people are! These principles are, in fact, crystallized out of repeated applications of our Principle of Epistemic Defeat.

### 4. The Kataphysical Principle (from the Greek kata physin, "according to its own nature")

The ways of knowing and the systems of sifting (e.g. the Second-Order Critical Principles) may be different in different types of experience, and they should be built up in accordance with the nature of the reality experienced. We should respect the uniqueness of each type of experience. This principle has been espoused by T. F. Torrance, and dubbed by Alister McGrath "the kataphysical principle" (McGrath 2004, p. 165). Moser also appeals to a similar principle: "we should let our understanding of evidence, and thus of knowledge, regarding a subject matter … be guided by the nature of the subject matter and the actual corresponding features of our evidence regarding that subject matter" (Moser 2010, pp. 37–8).

This principle is even operating within SE, since the modalities of SE also have different natures. So we would not use the eye to test the taste of something or use the ear to hear a color. In science, every measuring instrument is constructed according to our understanding of the thing we want to measure. So we would not use the thermometer to measure the weight of something or use the galvanometer to measure the length. To insist on using an inappropriate instrument to measure something is stupidity. To insist that the reality that cannot be measured by one's favorite instruments is therefore nonexistent is dogmatism. Of course, if we cannot have any experience at all of an alleged type of reality, then nothing further can be said. However, if we do have experiences of some reality, then it is better to pay attention to the nature of that kind of reality as revealed by our experiences, and then use the most appropriate way to interact with that reality in accordance with our understanding. This is the attitude we should adopt to the diverse experiences in the rainbow of experiences. We cannot treat a person as an inanimate object, nor should we subject aesthetic judgments to scientific experiments.

### 5. Consensus and Testimony

Our data consist of personal experiences, as well as testimonies. The Principle of Testimony, which will be assumed here, dictates that others' testimonies are also presumptive data, for one. We can formulate this as follows.

The Principle of Consensus:

When an epistemic seeming is consensually corroborated, it is justified to a much higher degree.

However, any consensus has to be *discovered* by each individual. Consensus is not in any sense given directly, *as if each of us can determine whether there is a consensus or not apart from one's experience.* Moreover, my principle does not entail that when an experience is not, or even cannot be, consensually corroborated, it should then be doubted. The latter position (*consensus empiricism*) would amount to a reverse of PCT. But, of course, even a consensus can be defeated by a stronger conflicting consensus.

### 4.4.3 *The Need for Both Foundation and Coherence*

The above pattern of reasoning is similar to Susan Haack's foundherentism, and her crossword puzzle metaphor is helpful (Haack 1994, p. 736). In short, an entry is much more likely to be correct if it not only corresponds to the clue given, but also coheres with other entries, which in turn correspond to their clues. We can formulate the following principle to capture this idea.

The Principle of Epistemic Enhancement

> When an epistemic seeming is coherent with other epistemic seemings, and its truth is coherent with or even suggested by the simplest theory that can explain many other epistemic seemings, then its degree of justification will be considerably enhanced.

So apart from defeaters, a presumptive datum may also have *enhancers*—those considerations that enhance its PFEF. The Principle of Consensus is just a special case of the Principle of Epistemic Enhancement. So the CTA needs to appeal to both a foundation and coherence. Without some foundation (albeit weak), the process of justification cannot get off the ground. Without coherence, we can hardly build a decent cognitive edifice on the foundation.

### 4.4.4 *Comparison and Conflict*

We can evaluate a type of experience by its coherence with other types of experience, *Inter-Coherence*:

A type of experience $E_1$ is coherent with another type $E_2$ if:

a. the ontology of $E_1$ is consistent with $E_2$, and
b. one type helps to explain the nature, possibility, veridicality, and so on of the other type of experience, or

c. the realization of the ontology of one type receives inferential support from the other type, or

d. they are analogous in some respects, for example, phenomenology, structure.

I call a doxastic system a *worldview* if it is meant to incorporate all the phenomena into its scope and unify them by explaining the whole lot with reference to a few fundamental principles. The weight of a type of experience would also be affected by its *worldview coherence*: the degree of ease with which this type of experience can be accommodated within a coherent worldview with high explanatory power. But, of course, the explanatory power of a worldview is, in turn, determined by its capability to explain *all* experiential phenomena, and the well-established types in particular. So a worldview's adequacy is determined by both its *empirical adequacy* and *theoretical adequacy*. This is just the application of the Principle of Epistemic Enhancement to a larger context. It is obvious that the possession of the above kinds of coherence to a higher degree would make a type of experience better established.

Principle of Comparison:

A type of experience $E_1$ is better established than $E_2$ if

a. ceteris paribus, $E_1$ has a higher degree of intra-coherence than $E_2$, or
b. ceteris paribus, $E_1$ has a higher degree of inter-coherence than $E_2$, or
c. ceteris paribus, $E_1$ has a higher degree of worldview coherence than $E_2$.
d. The validity of $E_2$ presupposes the validity of $E_1$, but not vice versa.

This principle of comparison seems to imply the following principle:

Principle of Conflict Resolution:
If type $E_1$ conflicts with type $E_2$, and $E_1$ is better established than $E_2$, then $E_1$ can serve as a defeater of $E_2$.

If either (a), (b), or (c) of the Principle of Comparison is fulfilled, $E_1$ would, in general, be better justified than $E_2$. So in case of conflict, it is rational to reject the latter. If (d) is fulfilled, it is impossible to reject $E_1$ without rejecting $E_2$, but possible the other way round. The latter is obviously the rational option.

Now we can arrive at a criterion of "ultima facie justification." When a belief is ultima facie justified, it is more reasonable to believe it than to suspend belief.

Criterion of Ultima Facie Justification:

A token experience is ultima facie justified if the following hold:
a. it belongs to a well-established type $E$,
b. $E$ is not defeated by other types of experience,

    c.  it is not defeated by other token experiences of the same type,

    d.  it is not defeated by other token experiences of other well-established types, and

    e.  it is not inferentially defeated, that is, no solid theoretical considerations and cogent arguments show that it is not justified.

This criterion is actually entailed by our earlier principles. If (a) is fulfilled, that experience is covered by the Type PCT, and hence prima facie justified. If a prima facie justified belief is not defeated, it is necessarily justified. If conditions (b) to (e) are further fulfilled, no defeaters are available, and hence that experience is ultima facie justified.

### 4.4.5 Cognitive Adjustment

When a prima facie justified belief is defeated, what kind of cognitive adjustment should we make to our original cognitive structure? An experiential claim can be false in different ways and to different extents. Suppose I thought I saw John on a street in London last Monday, but this was contradicted by many reliable witnesses. I ought to retract my claim. Consider these possibilities: (a) I might be hallucinating, or (b) I actually saw someone who looks very like John. The second is at a higher level of epistemic seeming than the first. *All other things being equal*, we should reinterpret the original experience so as to preserve as much truth in the original experience as possible. So (b) is rationally preferable. We can formulate the following.

Principle of Conservation:

> When an experience is defeated, it is rational to salvage as much noetic content as possible from that epistemic seeming, that is, to retain the highest undefeated level of epistemic seeming embedded in that experience.

### 4.4.6 Kinds of Coherence

Coherence is a very vague word. To make my following argument clearer, I try to outline several kinds of coherence.

#### 1. Theoretical Coherence

This is the kind of coherence that can be achieved between several propositions, or between a proposition and a theory, or between theories. There can be three levels of theoretical coherence:

    a. *Compatibility*: this is the minimal degree of coherence, that is, the fact that the several propositions (or theories) being considered can be simultaneously true. Incompatibility should be avoided at all costs.

    b. *Congruence*: this is a sort of coherence that is more than mere compatibility. Lack of it is easier to discern: incongruity. Two things may not be incompatible but, nevertheless, they do not fit well with one another. For example, consider the following propositions:

P1. The only real phenomena are physical phenomena.
P2. Mental phenomena are real.

Dualists tend to think that (P1) and (P2) are incompatible, but the identity theorists disagree. However, even if they can defend the compatibility between (P1) and (P2), these two propositions still seem incongruous. The physical phenomena and the mental phenomena still seem to possess radically different properties, and the respective descriptions of them employ radically different concepts and categories. So the set of (P1) and (P2) still lacks level II coherence—congruence.

c. *Consilience*: this can be more positively characterized as the mutual support between several propositions. Consider the following:

P3. Jane was dead and John was reported to be just beside the corpse.
P4. John's hand was holding a knife that was stained with blood.
P5. John was crazy for Jane, but Jane repeatedly refused him.

Now, these propositions are obviously compatible and congruent, but the kind of coherence manifested here seems to be more than that. They seem to point to the same conclusion:

P6. John has murdered Jane.

In light of this conclusion, they also reinforce the credibility of one another. I call this kind of coherence consilience. The individual propositions can be likened to the threads of a rope or the legs of a table. Just as the threads are conisilient after being woven into a single rope, and the legs enable one another to stand by being connected to a common surface, it seems that propositions are consilient by being incorporated into a simple theory or hypothesis. In the above case, (P3) through (P5) may possess some initial credibility. (P6) is the simplest hypothesis that explains (P3) and (P4), while (P5) provides the motivation of the murder and, in a sense, explains (P6). It is in virtue of these coherence relationships that (P6) is vindicated by an inference to the best explanation. But it also seems to be the case that the availability of (P6) shows the consilience of (P3) through (P5), and in this way reinforces the credibility of each.

Well-accredited scientific theories usually show this kind of consilience. For example, Newtonian mechanics incorporate facts about motion on earth, planetary motions, tides, velocity of sound, and so on into a single theory. These heretofore unconnected facts then manifest a kind of consilience that renders the whole theory worthy of rational assent. In such a case when mathematical methods are applicable, this kind of consilience can approach a kind of "bootstrap" (Glymour's bootstrap theory of confirmation). However, this does not seem to be a necessity. Nonmathematical consilience can also be very convincing, for example, that manifested by the theory of plate tectonics (cf. McMullin in Leplin 1984). Aronson's theory of confirmation also seems to emphasize similar features. He argues that scientific explanation, confirmation, and so on should best be construed as the process of mapping diverse empirical phenomena onto a common ontology. This account can be regarded as a special case of my informal account of consilience.

### 2. Experiential Coherence

Not only propositions can cohere or fail to do so; kinds of experience can as well. First, we demarcate a kind of experience by the kind of coherence shown by the token experiences of this kind. For example, tokens of visual experience possess similar phenomenal features, and they usually deliver stable perceptual beliefs. In this way we group together all those tokens into a single kind of experience. Considered in this way, visual experience and auditory experience are very different, because they possess different phenomenology. That's why they can be demarcated from one another. However, they can also be grouped together under the rubric of "ordinary perceptual experience," because in our actual experiences they express a high degree of coherence. The diverse kinds of visual experience, auditory experience, tactile experience, olfactory experience, and so on can be mapped onto a common ontology of material objects. So these experiences express a sort of experiential consilience. Such experiences can also fuse together and form a *single unitary experience*. For example, when I am driving a car, my seeing of it, my hearing of the engine noises, my feeling of the car's motions and so on, can be fused into a single experience. I would call this kind of phenomenon *experiential fusion*. It would be very inconvenient indeed if human beings did not possess this kind of capacity.

Now, the above kind of experiential consilience and experiential fusion seem to be the highest kind of experiential coherence achievable by us. There can be a lesser kind of coherence between kinds of experience. For example, they can be merely compatible and congruent. Also they can be *analogous* in their structure, characteristics, and so on.

CHAPTER 5

# A POST-FOUNDATIONALIST ARGUMENT FROM RELIGIOUS EXPERIENCE

Developments in the past half century have been decidedly against traditional types of empiricism or foundationalism. Parsons has complained that the theistic philosophers have turned back the clock. It seems to me some critics of ARE have indeed turned back the clock, ignoring the more recent developments in philosophy that make foundationalism an essentially contestable position.

## 5.1  The Decline of Traditional Foundationalism and Stock Objections to Religious Experience

Traditional foundationalists are motivated by the quest for some indubitable foundation (the given), which is free from interpretation or open to public confirmation. Although this foundationalist quest has already been widely regarded as mistaken, many objections to the argument from religious experience still reflect this longing. The ARE is usually dismissed on the basis of objections such as the following.

### 5.1.1  Stock Objections

1. The Logical Gap Objection: Critics such as Antony Flew admit that religious experiences often produce subjective certitude in the subjects. However, there is a logical gap between the psychological data and the ontological claim of the religious experiences. To bridge the gap, we need independent certification of the religious belief: "How and when would we be justified in making inferences from the facts of the occurrence of religious experience, considered as a purely psychological phenomenon, to conclusions about the supposed objective religious truths?" (Flew 1966, p. 129).[1]

2. The Theory-Ladenness Objection: The religious experiences are heavily (or even entirely) shaped by the conceptual framework of the experients. Hence they are not useful as evidence for ontological claims. Indeed, a recent critic, Graham Oppy, thinks that since "cases of revelation and selective ('private') religious experiences" are "rarely reported by those who are not already religious believers—or by those who are not embedded in a

community in which there is considerable religious fervour…there are good reasons for non-believers to suspect that there is pollution by prior theory in these cases" (Oppy 2006, p. 350, n. 4).

3. The Privacy Objection: "mystical experiences are private, like halluci-nations, illusions, and dreams, and that like these 'nonveridical' experiences, religious experience is really of no noetic significance at all" (Edwards 1972, p. 318).

### 5.1.2 Evaluation of the Logical Gap Objection

First, we should note that the logical gap objection to religious experiences basically conforms to the structure of the general skeptical argument. This can be seen from Gutting's parody of Flew's question: "How and when would we be justified in making inferences from the facts of the occurrence of experiences of material objects, considered as a purely psychological phe-nomenon, to conclusions about the supposed objective truths about material objects?" (Gutting 1982, p. 147).

The certitude/certainty distinction applies to almost all kinds of experi-ence, including SE. If the certitude/certainty distinction *in itself* threatens religious experiences, it will also threaten sense experience. Why, then, is the logical gap not damaging in other cases? This confirms Alston's charge that critics of religious experiences often adopt a double standard:

> The objections…involve unfavorable epistemic comparisons between mystical perception and sense perception;…they either condemn the former for features it shares with the latter (double standard) or unwarrantedly require the former to exhibit features of the latter (imperialism). (Alston 1991, p. 255)

### 5.1.3 Evaluation of the Theory-Ladenness Objection

Even ordinary perception is theory-laden, and a similar problem plagues scientific realism. The positivists have searched hard for the rock-bottom "given" that is interpretation-free. However, the development of modern philosophy and, especially, contemporary philosophy of science bespeak the downfall of this project. For example, Nancy Cartwright writes:

> We can be mistaken about even the most mundane claims about sensible prop-erties, and…their defense will rest on a complicated and sophisticated network of general claims about how sensations are caused, what kinds of things can go wrong in the process, and what kinds of things can and cannot be legitimately adduced as interferences. (Cartwright 1993, p. 259)

It is widely recognized that modern psychology confirms the idea that interpretation "is absolutely essential to there occurring a perceptual experi-ence at all…. We are not passive recipients of ready-made representations of our environment; rather, stimuli from that environment must be processed by various interpretive mechanisms before they can have any significance for us" (Davis 1989, p. 149). Ralph Baergen, after surveying the empirical study, concludes that the "psychological evidence shows that the operation of the human visual system certainly is influenced by beliefs, assumptions, expectations, and so on." Moreover, "the processing involved is, to some extent, top-down...our beliefs, expectations, and so on influence our visual presentations, and not merely their interpretation" (Baergen 1993, p. 16).

That means even our sensations are "polluted." Let us examine Oppy's claim that in the case of religious experiences, there is likely to be "pollution by prior theory." This allegation involves at least two claims. First, believers' prior theory has significant influence on the content of their RE. Second, this influence tends to "pollute" the experience, rendering it unveridical. The former claim is not implausible in light of the above considerations. It is not likely that RE can be the sole exception to a general rule about our experiences. However, there is also substantial evidence that prior theory does not *entirely* determine the content of TE:

> many people have experiences which are highly individualistic...some...feel the arms of God wrapped around them; others sense Jesus' love gradually coming into their body from head to toe or from toe to head;...many experience Jesus or God in ways not clearly derived from Scripture or from reports in the church or elsewhere...at one time they have a fairly standard experience of Jesus and at another have an Eastern form of experience (we may think of Joy, who first of all had a Nirvana-type experience, which then developed into an experience in which she felt herself to be a participant with Jesus on the cross, sensing the meaning of his death. (Wall 1995, p. 302)

I will give more counterexamples to Oppy's claim in Chapter 16. In any case, the most we can say is that the interpretation of RE is fallible, and we cannot conclude that they are cognitively worthless. The more important point is that the influence of a prior conceptual framework in experience is not necessarily cognitively debilitating. In fact, after pointing out the top-down way of processing in the human visual system, Baergen goes on to say that it is "the top-down aspects of vision which allow us, for example, to recognize objects under poor viewing conditions or when only a small part of them is visible...certain forms of agnosia arise when our knowledge about objects is prevented from influencing perceptual processing" (Baergen 1993, p. 16).

In other words, prior theory does not necessarily pollute. It is, in fact, *necessary* for our perception, which can effectively reveal the world to us. Griffith-Dickson presses the question: "Does one say that the humiliation a rape victim fees in the attack is just 'her interpretation' of the event, distinct from the physical sensations, or is it an integral part of it?" (Griffith-Dickson 2005, p. 400). This question highlights the dubious assumption that the less interpretation in an experience, the better it is. As the phenomenon of agnosia in vision shows, it is just as possible to miss the genuine significance of an experience through under-interpretation as it is through overinterpretation. Experience only becomes "knowledge" when our basic experiences of the world are transformed by "quite elaborate theoretical interpretations." After all, the "commonsense *physical objects dispersed in space* conceptual scheme is inculcated in a thousand subtle and not so subtle ways in the course of socialization. Does this imply that we are not proceeding rationally in forming perceptual beliefs in the standard way?" (Griffith-Dickson 2005, p. 402).

### 5.1.4 Evaluation of the Privacy Objection

In what sense is a sense experience public? My *experience* of a chair occurs essentially in my mind—it is every bit as private as other experiences in this aspect. I cannot directly experience how you experience the chair and vice versa. What makes a sense experience public is that verbal reports of different persons can be compared. However, reports of people having religious experiences can also be compared. Experiences of God are present in almost all ages, all places, and all cultures. The reports, to a considerable extent, match. The experience also develops in a continuous tradition. So in these aspects, religious experience is also public. As Rem Edwards emphasizes,

> the experience of the Holy seems to be very much *unlike* dreams and hallucinations. Extremely large numbers of people from extremely diverse cultural backgrounds claim to experience the Holy One, and there is a significant amount of transcultural agreement about what the experienced object is like. This is not the case with the objects of hallucinations—most hallucinators do not see pink elephants...*Pink elephant* is simply a convenient symbolic abbreviation for the immense variety of weird entities encountered by people having hallucinations. (Edwards 1972, pp. 320–1)

### 5.1.5 Vestiges of Traditional Foundationalism

The force of many stock objections to religious experience depends upon the traditional foundationalist framework. Although "a narrowly empiricist and foundationalist position is rarely found now outside discussions of religious experience," the philosopher of religion comes up time and again against this outdated assumption (Davis 1989, p. 143).

Unfortunately, what Davis says is still true of some recent discussions. For example, James Harris's severe critique of the ARE basically follows the foundationalists' line of attack. He thinks that when a subject S has a RE, "it is not reasonable to attribute to S the power of determining that x is God who is seeming to appear rather than a near-god, an intelligent alien from some distant galaxy, or Satan" (Harris 2002, p. 153). However, it is also not clear that when S has a SE, it is reasonable to attribute to S the power of determining that x is a physical object that is seeming to appear, rather than an alien super-scientist or Satan manipulating his brain/mind. Ex hypothesi, phenomenologically indistinguishable experiences can be produced by a physical object, an alien super-scientist, or Satan. How can S determine which is the case on the basis of his experience alone? An appeal to further experiences will not help, because similar problems plague those experiences.

The decline of foundationalism does not mean an automatic victory for the ARE. However, the critics should make sure their case is not based on problematic epistemological positions. Of course, the defenders also need to defend their epistemological framework. This book is such an attempt.

## 5.2 The Major Options: Theism, Naturalism, and Monism

In the face of the ARE, there are only several major options. Naturalism will obviously reject the ARE. For those who are sympathetic with the ARE, they can either be theists and monists, who believe the nature of the Ultimate Reality to be personal or impersonal, respectively. I explicate my understanding of these three major options below.

### 5.2.1 Theism: Immanent Transcendence

Some theists will emphasize the transcendence of God to such a degree that God and the world seem wholly discontinuous and separated. This is widely criticized as a form of metaphysical dualism. In this book I will avoid dualism and advocate the model of immanent transcendence. A proper understanding of the transcendent God would require His immanence as well. Since the world is radically contingent upon the sustaining activity of God moment by moment, God's energy or activity has to be present at the core of all beings—human or otherwise. So a Deist God won't do. As Schilling says, "God is conceived as the dynamic personal love who is the ultimate ground of all being and becoming." Hence "he might be known in personal communion...and sensitive participation in experiences like...depth, dependence, meaning, responsible action, and hope" (Schilling 1974, p. 181).

Especially in Christianity, there are the theological resources of creation and incarnation. Although God is transcendent, at the same time man is made in the image of God. This is inconsistent with any claim that God is *absolutely* unlike humanity in *all* aspects. At least we should say that human nature, at least in its unfallen state, is a better key to the divine than other inanimate objects. The God revealed in Jesus Christ also shows that human life is the locus of the divine. If we hold to the Chalcedonian Christology, then we can even talk about the hypostatic union of divinity and humanity in Christ. This is not a God who has no real relation to history and creatures.

Transcendence basically means *a qualitative difference* between God and man, but it is a misunderstanding to think this entails a *separation* between God and man. Chalcedonian Christology is exactly an attempt to insist on both "no confusion" and "no separation." So a transcendent God is not necessarily a supreme being over against man, existing in and by himself. Divine transcendence does not refer to another realm that is totally separate from the "secular" realm. Rather, divine transcendence is the ground for everything, and also the reason everything exists. The image of God is not a static entity. It means a relationship to God in which we are called to become an image of God, to grow in the likeness of God. This is a dynamic process that gives human existence a telos. Knowing it or not, every human being is driven, or even tormented, by this dynamic. Since God is Perfect Beauty, Goodness, and Truth, the call from God is also a call from Beauty, Goodness, and Truth. This is the source of human spirituality, which is also the reason culture exists.

So in my model, religious experience need not be a miraculous intervention from a totally distinct order. "It is simply a penetration of the finite and partially spontaneous by That Which brought it into being and from Which it derives not only its origin but also whatever degree of spontaneity it possesses, and it is thus the reinforcement and heightening of a life already there by a fresh current of life from the original Source; this influx of life being rendered possible by a certain purity and receptive disposition on the part of the spontaneous agent" (Bouquet 1976, pp. 63–4).

According to Gregory Baum, true humanity and divine transcendence are inseparable: "Man comes to be through a process, in which God is redemptively involved. Every man, through the dynamics of his action, is carried forward to a crucial option in regard to life, in which he *either* opens himself to the infinite and thus enters into his true humanity *or* locks himself into his finite house and in this way undoes the foundation of his humanity.... the supernatural is present to human life as the possibility of man"s true humanity" (Baum 1971, p. 124). So God moves us from within and addresses us from without. God is present in the listening and responding by which men constitute themselves as subjects. That is why the transcendent God is at the same time immanent in human experiences.

We also need to emphasize the importance of human freedom. God does not want to compel us; he desires a spontaneous human response. As Pascal points out, God purposely orders his self-revelation so that he can be found by those who seek him, while remaining hidden to those who do not. So there are various intimations of transcendence in our experiences, and oblique perception of God is also possible in "secular" contexts, but these can be ignored or suppressed. In short, God's revelation in our experiences has to respect the nature of a truly personal and interpersonal communion, which is impossible unless people are free to make decisions and to respond in accordance with their perceived values. If this is true, then it accounts for the ambiguity of the human experiences as pointers to God. So I expect readers to disagree with me regarding whether some experiences can be an implicit experience of God and so on. That is the reason I need to amass a variety of pointers and produce quite a few concrete examples in this book. It is natural that some people are more sympathetic to the experience of contingency, while others are more impressed by the depth dimension of the I-Thou encounter, and yet others only feel the force of aesthetic experiences, and so forth. I hope the overall case will at least impress most of us with *some* peculiar feature of human existence. If the implicit presence of

God in those experiences is not obvious, it is also far from obvious that the human being is nothing but a random product of naturalistic evolution in a naturalistic universe. I think the cumulative case makes the religious interpretation more plausible, but this is a matter that the readers need to judge for themselves.

### 5.2.2 Naturalism

It may look easy to define naturalism, but in fact there is also a controversy here. For Michael Rea, "Naturalism is not a philosophical thesis, but a research program. The program consists of a disposition...to treat the methods of science and those methods alone as basic sources of evidence" (Rea 2005, p. 344). However, Stewart Goetz criticizes Rea and argues that a more natural understanding of naturalism should think of it as primarily a philosophical thesis (Goetz 2010). His arguments look plausible to me, but I suspect both sides of this controversy may be correct!

It is interesting to see how a self-confessed naturalist, John Herman Randall, defines "naturalism" in an essay entitled "The Nature of Naturalism." Randall seems to give support to Rea: "naturalism can be defined as the continuity of analysis—as the application of...'scientific methods' to...every field...There is no 'realm' to which the methods for dealing with Nature cannot be extended" (Randall 1944, p. 358). But at the same time he also gives support to Goetz, because he says that "naturalism...can be defined negatively as the refusal to take 'nature'...as a term of distinction...[It is] opposed to all dualisms between Nature and another realm of being...[e.g.] the Supernatural...'Nature' serves rather as the all-inclusive category" (Randall 1944, p. 357). Apparently for Randall, naturalism is both a methodological disposition (commitment to the universal and unrestricted application of scientific method), and a philosophical thesis (Nature is all there is) that entails the denial of the Supernatural. So it seems that for many naturalists, naturalism involves both methodological and metaphysical commitments—the dichotomy is unnecessary.

In this book, naturalism is primarily defined as a metaphysical worldview that accepts Nature as the all-inclusive category and rejects the Supernatural in any form. However, it is also understood that the naturalists will typically accept a form of scientistic empiricism, and their understanding of the natural is governed by the results of contemporary natural science. Moreover, the theory of evolution is deemed as essential to the naturalistic worldview, because it is "the only game in town" that can provide a naturalistic account of life and human existence.

### 5.2.3 Monism

In fact, all major worldviews will provide some kind of unity for the entire world. The unity is grounded in God for theists, and in the basic physical laws for the naturalists. However, typically they believe that many things are also distinct in this unitary world. In contrast, the monistic conception wants to go further and affirm that, ultimately, there is only the One, the Absolute, or the Infinite Whole. This One is all-inclusive. So the finite has no integrity of its own. Our belief in the separation of the finite from the Whole only reflects a kind of estrangement, a "fall" from some kind of primordial union between everything previously enjoyed. Everything gains significance as part of the whole in which it participates, and it unconsciously longs to return.

Keith Yandell's definition of pantheism is also helpful: "pantheism is a radical type of monism, holding both that there is, strictly, only one thing, however many and diverse its interlocking elements, and one fundamental kind of thing...such distinctions as soul and body, concrete and abstract, and immaterial and material, seen as identifications of kinds of things such that anything belonging to one kind cannot belong to the other, are rejected" (Yandell 2006, p. 202).

## 5.3 A Cumulative Argument from Religious Experience

My ARE will be divided into two stages. In the first stage, I will argue that the loose type of religious experience helps to provide some reasons for believing in the transcendent realm. In the second stage, I will further argue that considering all the evidence together, there are good reasons to think the transcendent realm is ultimately more personal than impersonal in nature. Some defenders of ARE stop at the first stage (Davis 1997, pp. 136–7). I propose that the advancement of the ARE from the first to second stage is not impossible. However, even the second stage of ARE is only an argument for generic theism, and not for a particular form of theism. TEs across cultures (Jewish, Islamic, Christian, Hindu, or Chinese) will be included among the data.

### 5.3.1 Stage One Argument from Religious Experience to the Transcendent Realm

We have defined a RE as any experience of a supernatural object, and suggest that the Weak Token PCT applies to every token RE. Michael Martin, in reply, groups all the experiences of Kali, Virgin Mary, angels, ghosts, fairies, God, Brahman, and so on into a single type, and then argues that the application of the PCT to every token of this group would lead to inner tensions and unpalatable consequences—a bloated ontology. This objection appears to be convincing at first sight, but is ultimately based on a misunderstanding of CTA.

First, the degree of conflicts has been greatly exaggerated. In any case, any alleged conflict needs to be argued for. For example, the existence of angels or spirits and the existence of God are not incompatible. Many traditional religions, in fact, accept a variety of spiritual beings in the supernatural realm. Just as we accept a variety of physical objects, there is in principle no difficulty in accepting a variety of spiritual beings, *as long as there is good evidence*. So the defender of ARE can keep an open mind and look at the problems case by case. Concerning fairies, we may question whether we really have enough serious witnesses to the existence of fairies (in distinction from just legends about fairies). However, concerning evil spirits, if the argument put forth by Wiebe (2004) is correct, then the case looks better.

Second, since the force of the Weak Token PCT can be overridden by coherence and explanatory considerations, and the CTA also has second-order critical principles, there is no necessity for accepting the veridicality of each and every RE. Certainly we can refuse to trust some REs because there are available defeaters (like abnormal conditions of sleep deprivation or excitation by drugs). In still some other cases, we can have a slight reinterpretation to avoid the conflicts, while preserving much of the original PFEF of those REs. For example, in India there is a pantheon of deities, which contradict the ultimate status of Braham. Hindu thinkers contend that it is a misunderstanding to characterize Hinduism as polytheism, because those deities may be just some sort of spiritual beings under the supreme authority of Brahman, or they may simply be mythological expressions of different aspects of Brahman. There are conflicts in every realm of experience, and people adopt various kinds of rational strategies to resolve them. There is no reason similar strategies cannot be adopted here.

I think in the end some kind of conflict is unavoidable, and this is mainly the conflict between the experience of the Ultimate as personal, versus the experience of the Ultimate as impersonal. Even here various kinds of strategy (e.g., reinterpretation) are still available to mitigate the problem. I also agree that just by looking at the REs, it is difficult to formulate a highly specific ontology of the supernatural. Hence RE forms only a loose type. However, if we look at a lower level of description, we do find some degree of coherence of the REs; that is, they all point to *some* kind of supernatural or transcendent realm, and there is some Ultimate that is crucial for human wholeness and fulfillment, leaving open whether this Ultimate is more personal than impersonal, or vice versa.

### 5.3.2 *Stage Two Argument for Theistic Experience via the Type PCT*

However, when we focus on *theistic experience* (TE), the experience of God, a perfect being who is better described as personal than impersonal, the picture is different. I contend that theistic experience, a subtype of RE, is indeed a well-established type in its own right, and the argument for it would be more promising. We can formulate the following argument for theistic experience:

1. Type PCT is correct.
2. Theistic experience is a well-established type of experience.

3. It seems (epistemically) to $S$ that God exists on the basis of a TE, $E$.
4. The theistic experience, $E$, is not defeated.
   Therefore,
5. $S$ is justified in believing that God exists.

The argument seems valid. Premise (3) just states the fact of TEs. If premise (2) is correct, then the conditions in the antecedent clause of Type PCT
are satisfied. So if Type PCT is correct (premise 1), then it follows that $S$
has prima facie justification for belief in God. Further, grant the truth of
premise (4), and it means $S$ is not faced with defeaters. Hence $S$'s belief in
God is sufficiently justified. The crucial premises are (1), (2), and (4). A
large portion of Part A is an extended argument for (1). (2) will be defended
in Chapter 17. The defense of (4) will be distributed in various chapters,
Chapters 4, 16, and 17 in particular.

### 5.3.3 Supportive Argument from the Rainbow of Experiences

Since most alleged defeaters at most possess prima facie force, the extended
argument for the coherence between TE and the rainbow of experiences
in Part B will provide enhancers that can serve as defeaters for the alleged
defeaters, in both stages of my ARE. I argue that the rainbow of experiences as a whole strongly points to the spiritual nature of human existence,
and the apparent incongruity between naturalism and the intrinsic force
of the rainbow of experiences is sufficient to disprove the alleged superiority of naturalism. This may not dislodge naturalism immediately, but it
should remind us that naturalism itself needs to face the tribunal of *all* our
experiences, and not only SEs. Moreover, as our study of the rainbow of
experiences shows, our human experiences do point in the direction of some
transcendent realm. So the low-level epistemic seeming of the REs is significantly enhanced by the rainbow of experiences. This provides significant
support for Stage One of the ARE.

Moreover, as I develop my arguments in Part B, I also highlight how various aspects of this rainbow not only provide support for the transcendent
realm, but are also strong witnesses to the existence of a personal God. I
also argue that they do not quite cohere well with the monistic worldview.
So when theism faces the challenge of monistic experience in Stage Two, our
human experiences as a whole provide resources to resolve the conflict in the
theistic direction. Since this Rainbow Argument is not common in analytic
philosophy, I clarify and delineate the structure of this argument below. The
arguments in Part B can be divided into three steps:

### 1. Preliminary Analysis of Human experiences

The first step is to make clear the data available. Various resources will be drawn
upon, for example, common experiences, the depth psychologists, existentialists, transcendental Thomists. No claim is made that all these experiences are

*universal.* Some are nearly universal, for example, moral experience. Others may not be so, for example, peak experiences. But all of them seem to be sufficiently shared by a substantial portion of people and sufficiently recurrent that they can't be dismissed as just freaks. *If* they also fit into a larger picture, then their significance would be further vindicated. It is admitted that such experiences are more theory-laden than ordinary perceptual experiences. However, this cautionary note is not a sufficient reason to completely ignore the import of such experiences. In Part A I argue that the Weak Token PCT should also be applied to these types of experience. However, they are only presumptive data, which need to be critically evaluated.

Some types are better established than others. For example, the intrinsic force of IPE is well-nigh impossible to deny. I think experience of self and rational intuition are also difficult to deny, though some philosophers try to do that. The status of moral and aesthetic experiences are more controversial. In the relevant chapters, I also give more arguments for the applicability of PCT to them. In any case, I admit the fallibility of these presumptive data, and I will try to stick to those that seem to be sufficiently widespread to merit at least serious considerations.

Especially in the case of existential experience, the critics are likely to retort, "Aren't all these alleged 'data' irremediably *subjective?*" They just tell us how some people *feel* and can never tell us *how things are.* Let us, however, listen to Casserley's protest:

> The essence of existentialism is to insist that our own intimate experience of existence in the world (our experience of the reality of our freedom and of the way in which life again and again frustrates our freedom, our experience of hope and fear and unquenchable spiritual need, our experience of life and its inescapable fragility and impermanence as it confronts the necessity of death, our experience of love and its disappointment and disillusions) is the most vivid kind of experience of reality which we enjoy and that it constitutes the proper and necessary point of departure in philosophy. (Casserley 1955, p. 87)

This approach seems justified to me. It is at least defensible, because the contrary assumption, that human subjectivity can never us tell us anything about the objective world, seems to beg the question as well.

In my approach, the force of the data of existential experience varies a lot. For example, the experiences of freedom seem to be well-established presumptive data that should be accorded significant prima facie force. Of course, these presumptive data can be defeated by reasonable arguments to the effect that the concept of freewill is incoherent. Revisionary accounts like compatibilism are also possible. The CTA tries to navigate between the extremes of dogmatic intuitionism and narrow empiricism. I have never been impressed by the dismissive attitude toward our experience of freedom. Many arguments against free will seem to beg the question. Sometimes it is argued that an experience of freedom is plainly impossible: how can a person know that his decision is *not determined* by the antecedent causes? This argument seems to rely on a narrow model of experience that has been heavily criticized before. Of course, we can also ask why SEs can tell us that the objects of subjective experiences can exist independently of the experiences, and the answer is also difficult to come by.

In contrast, the quest of meaning does not deliver any clear epistemic seemings about the world. However, even in this case, such human experiences can still serve as metaphysical data that we need to take into account. Whether the above experiences are cognitive or not, "that these experiences occur" is a *fact* and it demands a decent explanation as to why these experiences *can* and *do* occur. For example, even if the quest for meaning and wholeness is ultimately a confused and futile project, *the existence of this project still needs to be explained.* Questions such as the following need to be asked: "Why do we come to have such a strong urge for meaning?" "Why can human beings with such peculiar cravings evolve?"

## 2. Evaluation of Experiential Coherence

It will also be argued that theism shows a greater degree of experiential coherence with a broad range of human experiences. They are, in many respects, analogous. They can also be mapped onto a common ontology, and in this way rendered more intelligible and consilient. Furthermore, experiential fusion of TE with many other human experiences is possible. On the other hand, naturalism seems to be experientially incongruous with many human experiences.

## 3. Evaluation of Theoretical Coherence

Building on the basis of the better-established data from various kinds of human experience, I will evaluate the coherence of theism. The coherence of the naturalistic interpretation of REs with human experiences is often evaluated as a foil. I argue that the human experiences considered are consilient with a theistic interpretation of REs. On the other hand, those human experiences are at least incongruous with the naturalistic worldview, because they show that human existence is a sort of spiritual existence. Gelven's *Spirit and Existence* is a book-length defense of the autonomy of the spiritual. He convincingly argues that the way human beings exist is very different from the way a material object exists. The former is characterized by an autonomous set of categories, for example, radiance, worship, redemption, importance, suffering, rapture, humor, and adventure. (The meaning of the "spiritual" is primarily defined by these predicates. In this book I do not touch on the debate between materialism and substance dualism.) It is difficult to see how we can house these predicates in the naturalistic world.

When I compare the coherence of theism and naturalism with our human experiences in Part B, I mainly contrast the theistic hypothesis ($H_t$) with the naturalistic hypothesis ($H_n$):

> $H_t$ Man is ultimately created by God from the "dust," but also in His image with the purpose that he would freely choose to have personal communion with God and other human beings.
> $H_n$ Man is *entirely* the physical product of naturalistic evolution.[2]

Given an experiential data $e_i$, I will adopt Bayes' Theorem and evaluate $P(e_i/H_t)$ and $P(e_i/H_n)$. If the former is greater than the latter, it would be taken to mean that theism is confirmed by $e_i$ relative to naturalism. I am aware of the various problems associated with the employment of Bayes' Theorem, for example, the assignment of prior probability. If one rejects the formal apparatus, he can still treat that as a short form for what I intend to say.

Note that $H_t$ is not only a bare theism, but also a sort of personalistic theism. The divine purpose of achieving personal communion is taken as part of the hypothesis. Of course, it complicates the hypothesis a little bit, and the latter clause specifying the divine purpose could be separated as an auxiliary hypothesis. However, my way of formulation can highlight an overriding purpose, which would prove to have much explanatory power later. It can be argued, of course, that this is implied by the original hypothesis, and is not an ad hoc accretion, because God is the ground of the very nature of man, *imago dei*.

Note that the conclusion I claim in each chapter is relatively modest. I do not claim to have a rebuttal of naturalism, but only that this and that piece of evidence (e.g. the experience of absolute moral obligation) is more coherent with theism than with naturalism. To make a stronger claim, I need to deal with many more arguments. However, I hope the cumulative effect of many relatively weak claims will add up to a plausible argument.

CHAPTER 6

CRITIQUE OF NARROW EMPIRICISM

In this chapter I will give more reasons Narrow Empiricism is wanting.

### 6.1 Two Types of Narrow Empiricism

Actually, "empiricism" does not stand for a uniform position. There are two main strands of empiricism: *classical empiricism*, which mainly understands experience in terms of sensations, sense data, or appearance beliefs, and *scientistic empiricism*, which understands experience in terms of publicly reproducible or shared SEs or observations. Classical empiricism emphasizes the first person perspective and tends to view sensations (or "ideas," "impressions") as units of experience (mainly defended by the British empiricists, such as Locke and Hume). This analysis of experience tends to be atomistic: the continuous stream of experience is broken down into spatiotemporal particulars. With such an analysis of experience, even our ordinary perceptual experience is thrown into doubt: from such atomistic data we can reconstruct by logical methods neither "the external world" nor "causal connections" in the world, not to mention such an entity as a "self" or "person." When its logic fully unfolds, it would most likely land on a Berkeleyan idealism or Humean skepticism. Although its starting point sounds very commonsensical, its implications are deeply skeptical and solipsistic.

Scientistic empiricism views experience from a predominantly third-person perspective. So it is not the quality or phenomenal properties of experience that are emphasized. Rather, the emphasis is heavily put on the publicly ascertainable experiential *claims* concerning the physical objects. Coupled with this emphasis is the standard of scientific explanation, which admits only the quantitative. By mathematicizing those experiential claims and seeking further explanations, theoretical entities (such as quarks or superstrings) are postulated, which are regarded as the *really real* things, the building blocks of everything else.

Here we can see that these two positions, though they have often been equated, are, in fact, in tension. According to classical empiricism, the really real things are the sensations, and mind-independent physical objects cannot be directly experienced, not to mention quarks and black holes. So they must be fictions (Berkeley) or at best theoretical constructions (Ayer

1973, chapter V). According to scientistic empiricism, however, properties of objects that do not figure in the explanatory structure of science cannot be real, for example, colors. So they must be projections of the mind—the redness of the rose is actually in our minds, and not in the rose. At first, scientistic empiricism is quite conciliatory toward the mental world. However, for those naturalists who are impressed by the achievement of science, to admit the fundamental reality of the mental world is to accept that there are two radically different kinds of things that are really real. This "dualism" greatly offends their theoretical sensibility, and hence they have an urge to do away with the mental world entirely (eliminativism) or to reduce the mental to the physical (reductionism). Of course, there are also other ways to blend them together. In recent years, it seems that scientistic empiricism has become the more dominant strand.

Let us define these two positions more clearly, spelling out their exclusivist nature. I also assume they can provisionally accept reason as a basic source of justification (BSJ), but usually it is emphasized that reason alone can only provide justification for analytic truths, and can't tell us what contingent states of affairs obtain. So SE is still the *sole* source of justification for our empirical beliefs.

Classical Empiricism (CE)

1. The only basic sources of justification are reason and SE, where SE is understood in terms of the given, that is, the sense data or the introspective knowledge of appearance.
2. A belief is justified if and only if it is either directly justified or inferentially justified by the basic sources of justification.

Scientistic Empiricism (ScE)

1. The only basic sources of justification are reason and SE, where SE is understood as that which yields publicly checkable observation statements (about physical objects).
2. A belief is justified if and only if it is either directly justified or inferentially justified by the basic sources of justification.

## 6.2 Implications of Narrow Empiricism

Narrow empiricism maintains that only SE *is* a BSJ. So narrow empiricism posits a *qualitative* gap between SE and other types of noetic experiences. Now, there must be some rational grounds for this move, for example, differences between SE and other types. Naturally, for example, we should posit a larger gap when there are larger differences. Since the narrow empiricist posits a *qualitative* gap between a BSJ that can stand its own, and other sources that *have to* be validated by the BSJ, we should expect there to be a *qualitative* difference between SE and other kinds of experiences,

*epistemically speaking.* To sum up, narrow empiricism seems committed to
the following theses:

1. Demarcation Thesis

SE can be clearly demarcated, *epistemically speaking*, from other types of noetic
experience. Namely, there is at least one relevant *epistemic* property of SE which
is not possessed by all other types of noetic experience.

2. Self-Sufficiency Thesis

SE should be *epistemically* self-sufficient: by and large the justification of claims
of SE does not depend on other types of noetic experience.

3. Reducibility/Dispensability Thesis

Every type of noetic experience apart from SE is either justificatorily reducible
to SE or cognitively dispensable.

### 6.3 Narrow Empiricism and Our *Lebenswelt*

The spirit of narrow empiricism has largely shaped the modern world. Both
versions of empiricism are deeply destructive of our commonsense picture.
For example, both moral responsibility and free will are presupposed in our
*Lebenswelt*, but they are hard to prove on the basis of SE. So the scientific
"world of regular, morally neutral, magically un-manipulable fact...pre-
supposed by science, is in fact not at all self-evident....historically it is a
great oddity. It is separated from...worlds in which men have lived by a
profound chasm" (Gellner 1974, p. 180).

The chasm, however, only slowly reveals itself. People in the past by and
large still accepted ideas of value, responsibility, and so on. However, it
now seems that even the self with a free will is an awkward thing in both
empiricist frameworks. Humeans report their failure to find any self in their
sensations. The naturalists object that it is impossible for a free agent to
exist. Without the self, it is difficult to say to what we can ascribe moral
responsibility. So moral responsibility must be a confused notion, and it is
better to excise it from our conceptual repertoire.[1]

The consequences of this approach are deeply counterintuitive. Many
people think that any approach that leads to such consequences should be
rejected unless really compelling reasons can be given for the approach.
However, the empiricists deem their opponents' "intuitions" simply as
deeply embedded cultural prejudices. Since the consequences of narrow
empiricism are far-reaching, we need to examine it critically. To begin with,
let us remember that in Chapter 3 we argued that the movement toward
a broader concept of experience phenomenologically rings true when we
try to be faithful to *our* experiences in *the Lebenswelt*. We also argue
that epistemically speaking, SE lies in a continuum with other kinds of

experiences, rather than in its own kingdom. The following is an elaboration of these lines of argument.

## 6.4 Self-Referential Inconsistency of Narrow Empiricism

As it stands, I think there is a strong reason to reject narrow empiricism: in either version, it is self-referentially incoherent. The following argument is closely parallel to Plantinga's argument against classical foundationalism (Plantinga 1983, p. 60). Consider the statements of CE and ScE. Assume they are true *and* justified. Then they are either directly justified or inferentially justified. But they are not directly justified: neither by the direct deliverance of SE (understood in either way) nor by reason. Further, it is extremely difficult to see how they can be inferentially justified by deliverances of SE and reason. So they cannot be justified, and a contradiction arises. The initial assumption must be wrong. So both must either be false or unjustified. In either case, we have no reason whatsoever to believe in them. One possible reply is to affirm that either the CE or ScE is an analytic truth. However, I can't see that there is any reason to think that their denial would result in a logical contradiction; nor does the denial violate any semantic convention.

Perhaps the defender of ScE may claim that epistemology is a branch of psychology that is grounded in SE and science. Hopefully, psychological research would, in the end, vindicate the truth of ScE. This is the way of naturalized epistemology. However, even if we allow the intelligibility of a naturalized epistemology, the above claim is still an unsubstantiated one: nobody has yet shown how psychology can decide the criteria of justification, let alone shown that the result would come out in favor of the ScE. Until then, it is eminently rational to reject ScE. Recently, Moser has also argued for the self-defeating nature of core scientism (Moser 2010, pp. 76ff).

Putnam's discussion of the conceptions of rationality also points in the same direction. Putnam calls "any conception according to which there are institutionalized norms which define what is and what is not rationally acceptable a *criterial* conception of rationality" (Putnam 1981, p. 110). (Those norms for Putnam are mainly those which insist on observational and experimental testing.) He then argues, "no philosophical position of any importance can be verified in the conclusive and culturally recognized way I have described. In short, if it is true that only statements that can be criterially verified can be rationally acceptable, that statement itself cannot be rationally acceptable. If there is such a thing as rationality at all—and we commit ourselves to believing in *some* notion of rationality by engaging in the activities of *speaking* and *arguing*—then it is self-refuting to *argue* for the position that it is identical with or properly contained in what the institutionalized norms of the culture determine to be instances of it. For no such argument can be certified to be correct, or even probably correct, by those norms alone" (Putnam 1981, p. 111). For example, the theory that observational and experimental testing are essential for the justification of any theory itself cannot be supported by observational and experimental testing.

Putnam's discussion of "what is rationally acceptable" parallels our discussion of "what is justified." Putnam's argument enables us to see that the major problem of all narrow conceptions of justification is that epistemology is a very high-order cognitive activity whereby we reflect on our knowing and the criteria for justification. This activity seems to presuppose a sort of rationality and justification that can't be narrowly circumscribed. Any notion of rationality or justification has to allow for the rational or justifiable formulation of that notion itself. It is doubtful whether exclusivist empiricism, after excluding so many cognitive resources, can do that.

## 6.5  Evaluation of the Reducibility/Dispensability Thesis

This thesis asserts that every type of noetic experience apart from SE is either justificatorily reducible to SE or cognitively dispensable. The semblance of plausibility of this thesis, I think, derives from the fact that SE is indeed foundational to *several* other types of experience, for example, interpersonal experience, moral and aesthetic experiences. The latter experiences are mediated by SE by and large. However, it does not mean that they are then *reducible* to SE. Nor should this imply that those experiences have to be defended with respect to SE. We have already criticized this Bottom-Up Approach in chapters 3 and 5.

Let us examine in more detail the implication of this Reducibility/Dispensability Thesis. For example, moral experience is regarded by many narrow empiricists as irreducible because basic moral predicates can't be analyzed into naturalistic terms (is-ought gap or fact-value dichotomy). So the narrow empiricist just dispenses with moral experience as cognitively irrelevant. He may resort to an *error theory* or try to propose non-cognitivist interpretations of moral experience, for example, emotivism, projectivism. True, there are narrow empiricists who are moral cognitivists, but their position is often hinged on their belief (or hope) that moral predicates can be naturalistically analyzed. A consistent narrow empiricist will treat *every* other kind of noetic experience in this way.

So in the past centuries, empiricist and naturalistic philosophers have been engaged in a great industry to reduce various kinds of experience to SE. Not only moral experience, but also apparently the ontologies assumed in IPE, aesthetic experience, or intellectual experience (e.g. personhood, the aesthetic and the sublime, necessary truths) go beyond that of physical objects and properties. It is also difficult to see how the justifiability of these experiences can be derived from SEs *alone*. The more scientistic empiricists also attempt projects like non-reductionist physicalism (the use of the concept of supervenience, for example, to accommodate the mental), naturalistic moral realism or quasi-realism, the conventionalist explanation of a prior truths, naturalized epistemology (treating philosophy itself as a kind of science—often depending on a Quinean framework), and so on. So far this reductionist project has encountered seemingly intractable problems of other minds, naturalistic analysis of self-identity, and so on.

It is widely held that this reductionist project is not a success, at least not yet. Many philosophers think that this project often looks contrived and not very coherent. They also feel that the procrustean bed of empiricism unavoidably leads to distortions of other kinds of experience, or unnecessarily tortuous explanations. Of course, a full-scale justification for the above claims is impossible here. I just point out that for those who have this sort of discontent with the reductionist project, they can't help wonder whether this empiricist straitjacket is really needed, and whether too much has been lost. Part B will further substantiate the grounds for discontent.

In fact, many narrow empiricists agree that the reductionist project is not successful. So they are greatly tempted to dispense with those experiences that are found irreducible. For example, one radical project of this kind is Eliminative Materialism (the Churchland couple), which aims to replace the entire realm of the mental (folk psychology) by the scientific description. To note the prima facie implausibility of this move, we again need to remind ourselves of the *intrinsic force* of numerous kinds of experience we have. Many are not dependent on SE at all, for example, experience of self, introspection, memory. Not one of these three seems to be dispensable. Can we really dispense with our self-identities or introspection?

It is possible for the narrow empiricists to reject the intuitions above. So how can we settle this clash of intuitions? Perhaps the non-reductionists can further point out that many noetic experiences are *practically* indispensable (e.g. IPE), and claims to dismiss them are often contradicted by narrow empiricists' practice. For example, many naturalistic philosophers' official position would commit them to the view that moral properties or their self-identities are nothing more than human projections or social constructions. However, quite often their practices show that they are paying only lip service to their doctrines, because they still talk and behave as if there are genuine moral properties and their selves are concrete, determinate entities. This is not only an ad hominem argument. This shows that those beliefs and their corresponding experiences are so fundamental in our practices that they are indispensable relative to those practices. Part B of this book touches on many of these topics.

Of course, we can only judge the dispensability or indispensability of a thing *relative to some purposes*. So if a narrow empiricist is "tough" enough, he can bite the bullet and dispense with all practices and intuitions in tension with his doctrine. Ultimately we need to look at our own experiences carefully, and check different positions with our experiences. If more and more types of noetic experiences are shown to be irreducible to SE, then the eliminative strategy will be increasingly costly (the bullet to bite becomes larger and larger). Isn't it grossly implausible to claim that all our noetic experiences apart from SE are gigantic delusions or inner projections? In any case, narrow empiricism has never proved its dogma, and it is hard to see that there are good theoretical and practical motivations to pursue this costly project.


## 6.6 Evaluation of the Self-Sufficiency Thesis

The validation of SE is intimately involved with the validity of other kinds of experience:

### 1. *Experience of Self and Introspection*

Empiricists have not been sympathetic with the notion of "self," not to mention "the experience of self." But actually, this notion seems to be presupposed by every experience. What is a perception that is possessed by no one? What accounts for the unity of a person's experiences? These are the questions that drive Kant to the conclusion that the self has to be postulated in order to account for the transcendental unity of apperception. Hume's argument presupposes that the self, if real, has to be experienced as other physical objects are experienced. But we have to ask, "Why does every experience have to be modeled upon an experience of the external physical world?"

If we are truly empirical in spirit and attend to our experiences, it does seem that in every experience of a person, there is an inchoate and unthematic awareness that this experience is *his*. William Barrett says, "we have a direct awareness or intuition of our own minds: When we are conscious of anything, we are also conscious that we are conscious...If the word 'empiricism' means an openness and fidelity to experience, then we should not close the gates arbitrarily against any mode of awareness" (Barrett 1987, p. 42).

Suppose the above is wrong. Then I have to first identify a "floating" experience, and only subsequently attribute this experience to myself. But what can be the grounds for this self-attribution? Can I do that by more perceptions of the outer world? This only complicates the problem, because again I have to identify these perceptions as mine. Otherwise it is not clear how they can be relevant to *my* problem. Perhaps another answer can be: "By recognizing the close relation of this experience with other experiences, for example, relations of continuity and coherence." To avoid circularity, the "other experiences" mentioned above cannot mean "other experiences of *mine*." So what are those relevant experiences with which the relation counts? Are they experiences related to the same body? But what about a thought out of the blue? We just have no way to check its relatedness to a certain body. The suggestion that we have to first examine the content of a thought and then its relation with other thoughts before we decide "who possesses this thought?" seems extremely implausible.

Perhaps the "I," like the "average man" is just a logical construct out of a mass of separate perceptions? But what is this "construct"? Is it a concept, an abstract identity, which is also "floating," that is, belonging to no one? This seems contrary to our experience. "I" has to be a concept possessed by someone. A "self" is not *merely a postulate*. In our everyday experiences, the self disclosed in our *activities* is a *concrete* self who can effect changes in the outside world. It is hard to see how an abstract idea, as such, can have these causal powers. The self is also presupposed in our looking for our selves: "The self is uncapturable...in any sensory experience....Hume is like a man who goes outside his house and looks through the window to see if he is at home....He stands outside the self and looks for it as some kind of sensory datum, forgetting that he himself has launched the search and is involved in it throughout" (Barrett 1987, p. 46).

## 2. Interpersonal Experience

Consider a broadly Wittgensteinian reply to skepticism. It is argued that the skeptics ask us to entertain the possibility of solipsism, but the latter is not really a coherent possibility. This is supposed to be demonstrated by the Private Language Argument, which shows that the use of language already entails the realm of the public. Hence the "possibility" of a solipsistic soul entertaining radical doubt about the public realm, which includes ordinary physical objects and other persons, is only apparent. No language can coherently express this. There are some insights in this type of argument, but it is not sufficient to dispel the skeptical fog. Let us grant that solipsism is incoherent. This does not mean the end of skepticism because skepticism can be formulated without presupposing the possibility of solipsism (see Chapter 12).

However, the above discussions still point in the right direction. Perhaps it is part of the concept (loosely construed) of an *ordinary* physical object that it is a *public* object. An ordinary physical object is that sort of object that can be confirmed by others' observations. However, to validate this, we have to have reliable access to others' observations. This is only possible by hearing others' testimony, which belongs to the realm of interpersonal experience. So the justification of SE also depends on the general reliability of interpersonal experience. Access to other minds is as indispensable to our cognitive enterprise as our access to physical objects. The acute skeptical problem only occurs from the perspective of the narrow empiricist, which denies that interpersonal experience, though mediated by SE, is another basic source of justification.

## 3. Memory

The justificatory dependence of SE on memory, personal and factual, is too apparent to need elaboration. Without our basic trust in memory, what we can get from even an infallible SE is only and always a vanishing point. Narrow empiricists seldom reject memory simply because it seems indispensable. At the same time they often insist that for REs to have PFEF, they have to closely resemble SE. However, memory does not closely resemble SE either. So again there seems to be some kind of double standard.

*4. Rational Intuition*

SE presupposes some analytic truths that can only be grasped by reason. For example, "No two physical objects can occupy the same place," or "the same physical object cannot occupy two different places at the same time." Such truths are important for reidentification of a physical object. Michael Rea argues that there is a special problem for the naturalist (who is basically a scientistic empiricist). It is because "the methods of science alone provide no justification for accepting realism about material objects (RMO)—the thesis that there exist material objects with intrinsic modal properties...[Therefore] naturalists cannot rationally accept RMO" (Rea 2005, p. 344). (Modal properties cannot be discovered by science.) He is aware that the naturalist may help himself to the faculty of rational intuition, but he points out that this move is problematic within the naturalistic worldview: "it is hard to see how evolutionary processes could select for cognitive faculties in which the bare appearance of necessity is a generally reliable indicator of genuine necessity...We have no reason to think that evolutionary processes could give rise to creatures that have reliable rational intuitions and, apparently, good reason to think that they could not" (Rea 2002, pp. 193–4). Rea is also open to the possibility that the problem is less intractable in a theistic worldview. In short, narrow empiricism has the problem of handling intellectual experience (see Chapter 15).

## 6.7 Conclusion

The evaluation of the Demarcation Thesis is trickier. An alternative model of experience has been presented in Chapter 3. The possible replies to this case are discussed in Chapter 7. If the above arguments are correct, both the Reducibility/Dispensability Thesis and the Self-Sufficiency Thesis are mistaken. This is sufficient to warrant the rejection of narrow empiricism.

# ARGUMENTS FOR THE PRINCIPLE OF CRITICAL TRUST

The Principle of Critical Trust (PCT) is the foundation of my ARE, but it is also controversial, although gaining in popularity. In earlier chapters, I provided some motivation for accepting PCT. In this chapter, I further explore various arguments that can be given for PCT

## 7.1 Different Ways to Defend the PCT

### 1. The Argument from Intuition

Swinburne says the PCT "seems to me, and I hope to my readers, intuitively right in most ordinary cases...to take the way things seem to be as the way they are" (Swinburne 1979, p. 254). So the PCT as a general principle receives inductive support from these intuitions about particular cases. Alternatively, we can go with George Wall, who says that "we just grasp PC to be a rational principle...It is an appeal to the experience of grasping the positive epistemic status of PC and noting that PC 'stands on its own two feet,' is OK just by itself" (Wall 1995, p. 19). Wall warns that further attempts to justify PC will quickly land us in circularity or an infinite regress. I agree that we should not insist that PC have independent justification, but it does not follow that the PCT *cannot* be vindicated on other grounds. In our weak foundationalist framework, we don't legislate that basic beliefs cannot receive further inferential justification from another source.

### 2. The Argument from Conformity with Actual Epistemic Practice

Swinburne also seems to suggest that the PCT is a principle that we in fact employ. He is calling to our attention something implicit in our epistemic practice. So, in accordance with the metaphor of Neurath's boat, unless we have reasons to accept something better, it is rational to go along with what we have now. This argument is relevant when we consider some competitors to CTA, such as explanatory foundationalism. Even if the two approaches have no conclusive arguments against one another, we can still argue that the CTA conforms better to our actual practice, and hence has an extra merit (see next chapter).

### 3. The Argument from Practical Living

While the above argument focuses on our epistemic practice, John Hick argues that the PCT is implicit in our whole life: "The implicit principle by which we all live, then, is critical trust. We could not live on any other basis...Critical trust, then, is part of our working definition of sanity" (Hick 2006, p. 130).

### 4. The Argument from Pragmatic Utility

Rescher uses his methodological pragmatism to provide justification for a principle similar to PCT. He argues for "a presumption of positivity that pivots on adopting the stance that in rational problem solving a presumption stands on the side of the most positive alternative...the most useful and productive for problem solving" (Rescher 1995, p. 90). So you can make free use of the epistemic resources you have in hand until something discernibly better comes along, and here an attitude of *open-minded conservatism* is called for—this attitude is similar to my idea of critical trust.

In contrast, "the dogmatically negativistic approach 'allow no presumptions—accept nothing until and unless it has been established evidentially' is a frustratingly sterile policy that does not permit the process of cognitive problem solving to get off the ground" (Rescher 1995, p. 102).

### 5. The Argument from Practical Rationality and Impartiality

Alston argues that we cannot provide any noncircular proof for any of our socially established doxastic practices. How should we proceed then? There are basically three options:

a. *accept*, prima facie, the doxastic practices
b. *suspend* our acceptance of the doxastic practices
c. *replace* the current doxastic practices with some others

It is "eminently reasonable for us to go along with our very strong, and perhaps even irresistible, inclination to form beliefs in these ways" (Alston 1993, p. 126). If this is true, then the suspension option (b) is either impossible or extremely costly. This point is especially weighty given Alston's opinions that many of our beliefs are involuntary: we just "cannot help...believe many other things" (Alston 1993, p. 127). So the acceptance option (a) is in, and (b) out.

Furthermore, "If we could adopt some basic way of forming beliefs about the physical environment other than SP [sensory practice], or some basic way of forming beliefs about the past other than memory...why should we?...It is not as if we would be in a better position to provide an epistemically noncircular support for the reliability of these newcomers" (Alston 1993, p. 125). The point is that the replacement option (c) cannot put us in a better epistemic situation, and of course it involves further costs. So (c) is inferior to (a). The conclusion is that there is no "reasonable alternative to practicing the ones with which we are intimately familiar" (Alston 1993, p. 126) from the viewpoint of practical rationality.

Alston is aware of the possibility that we may "take our stand on one or more of these [doxastic practices], and hold the others subject to judgment on that basis," but this approach is "vulnerable to a charge of *undue partiality*" (Alston 1993, p. 126; italics mine). I'll unpack this line of argument below.

## 7.2 The Impartiality Argument for the Principle of Critical Trust

### 7.2.1 *The Impartiality Argument: The Outline*

T1. *Impartiality Thesis*

> If we adopt a certain epistemological attitude toward a certain type of experience, we should adopt the same attitude toward other types of experience when we can find no epistemologically relevant distinction.

T2. *Applicability Thesis*

> The Type PCT should be applied as a *fundamental* principle to at least some types of our experience. (Note that "Type PCT" here actually means a principle identical to my generalized Type PCT, except that its scope is unspecified.)

T3. *Seamless Web Thesis*

> We can find no clearcut distinctions within the whole web of our experience that are epistemologically relevant *with respect to the applicability of the Type PCT*.

Therefore,
T4. The Type PCT should be applied as a fundamental principle to all types of experience.

The argument seems valid. Let us look at the credibility of the premises.

### 7.2.2 *Impartiality Thesis*

(T1) is intuitively very plausible, and is also the implication of the general principle of impartiality: "Treat similar cases similarly unless the relevant differences are shown." If we let go of this principle, then we are effectively abandoning any rationality in various kinds of discourse, for example, legal reasoning, personal judgment of scientists, literary criticism, social sciences, philosophy. These consequences seem too costly. If we reject the Principle of Impartiality in epistemology, then we can just choose to treat different token experiences in arbitrary ways. It would also be difficult to justify how we can treat a *type* of experience, say sense perception, as an epistemological unit. Certainly there are differences between every two individual percep-tions, and it is hardly possible to *show* that each of these is not epistemo-logically relevant. If we have to discuss whether *each* perceptual claim is credible and which attitude we should adopt to *this* or *that*, epistemology would hardly be possible!

### 7.2.3 Applicability Thesis

Some critics contend that we can justify claims of experience without appeal-ing to the PCT. We'll consider the cases of SE and memory.

#### 1. Application of the Type PCT to Sense Experience

Alston (1991, 1993) has extensively and convincingly argued for the thesis that we cannot noncircularly show the reliability of SE. To avoid repeating his points all over again, I offer only brief discussions and put my focus more on memory below. It may be argued that our belief in the general reliability of SE is justified by inductive evidence. But it is not hard to see that in gathering this inductive evidence, we cannot avoid the use of memory. So in the end, to "jus-tify" ordinary perception inductively, we have to rely on the prima facie reli-ability of memory. But, of course, memory claims can be prima facie reliable as data about the world only if our past perceptions were prima facie reliable. We are trapped in a circle if we deny PCT's status as a fundamental principle.

#### 2. Application of the Type PCT to Memory

It is clear that our memory is fallible. How can we safeguard from mistakes and distinguish real memory from false ones or even imagination? Some philosophers have suggested the reliable memory claims have intrinsic char-acteristics that are accessible to us, for example, vividness of the images associated or degree of conviction. However, after a long exploration in his book on memory, Von Leyden concludes, "since a false memory claim is as a rule qualitatively indistinguishable from a correct one, no memory experi-ence alone can make it certain that what is alleged to be remembered really occurred" (Von Leyden 1961, pp. 115–16).

Since reliance on memory is almost *ubiquitous* in formation of our beliefs *at every moment*, it is extremely difficult to see how there can be noncircular justification of memory. Consider the suggestion that the general reliability of one's memory is to be established by our perceptual experiences. However, unless we take the reliability of memory for granted, it is well-nigh impossible to gather sufficient empirical evidence for memory. This is because our experi-ences almost all happened in the past. Without our basic trust in memory, what we can get from an even infallible SE is only and always a vanishing point.

Suppose we attempt to justify memory by some a priori argument. Further, suppose we have a valid proof that needs several pages to be written out. When you come to the end and believe that the conclusion is proved, how is this justified? Not directly by the steps, because we can't hold all of them together in our minds and see their connections all at once; but it is by *memory* that you have checked all the connections and found them convincing. So memory would also be vital in this piece of reasoning (and any other reasoning). So either way (empirical or a priori), it is extremely difficult to see how there can be noncircular justification of memory.

Some philosophers suggested we can check our memories with documents and archaeological evidence, for example, Hamlyn (1970). Gutting has also written, "it is not clear that memory claims admit of no justification apart from an appeal to the PC. A memory claim might...be supported by its coherence with an immense body of other memory claims and present experiences" (Gutting 1982, p. 187). However, if we do not already trust our memory of the meaning of the words, how can we be sure that we have interpreted the documents (which we use to check our memory) correctly? Moreover, what is the basis of my belief that the documents are reliable? Their reliability cannot be read off directly. Here we again need some inductive evidence from the past, *which we can remember*, to support it. So this kind of check is also, in the end, circular. Gutting is correct that a memory claim is supported by coherence considerations, but the problem is twofold. First, how can we be sure that we correctly remember the past coherence? Second, coherence alone cannot generate justification, but coherence between presumptive data can provide an enhancer. So Gutting's observation does not repudiate the CTA, but is presupposing it.

In the case of our memory beliefs, the appeal to the PCT as a fundamental principle seems inescapable. I have surveyed quite a few authors, and found that all of them reach similar conclusions. For example, Russell claims that "the past occurrence is itself a premiss for my knowledge" (Russell 1948, p. 205). Other authors concur: "in the last analysis...we cannot...validate our memories further than by...assuming that the sufficient conditions of remembering are in fact very often fulfilled" (Von Leyden 1961, p. 119). Ginet also thinks we "should trust...the direct perceptual deliverance of one's memory" (Ginet 1975, p. 202). Most critics of PCT who want to deny the Applicability Thesis have tried to do so in the case of SE. Their case will never be complete if they cannot show how we can justify our memory claims noncircularly.

### 3. Explanatory Foundationalism

Explanatory foundationalism wants to deny that the PCT is a fundamental principle by suggesting that the hypothesis of the external world can be justified as the best explanation of our SEs (interpreted as appearance beliefs such as "it appears to me that a table is there"). Alston (1993) has already criticized many versions of explanatory foundationalism, for example, those of Alan Goldman and Slote. Here I want to discuss the attempt by Jonathan Vogel.

Vogel considers the isomorphic skeptical hypothesis (ISH), which is, in a way, parasitic upon the *real world hypothesis (RWH)*. "The relationships among causes and effects according to the ISH match those of the RWH. To that extent, it seems, the explanations provided by the one are no better or worse than the explanations provided by the other" (Vogel 2005, p. 75).

For example, if our experiences are produced by the computer of a mad neuroscientist, then different portions of the computer disk can be supposed to occupy the explanatory roles we normally assign to familiar objects. This is called the *computer skeptical hypothesis (CSH)*. This kind of improved skeptical hypothesis apparently can do as good or as bad a job as the RWH does. However, he contends that necessary truths, such as "two distinct objects can't be in the same place at the same time," in the RWH has some explanatory power, but ISH has to guarantee that by invoking "an extra empirical regularity," say, one written down in the computer program of the super-scientist. So the ISH is shown to be inferior by its "lack of simplicity" (Vogel 2005, p. 77).

I doubt whether this really works. We can ague that the ISH just needs a computer and a brain, whereas RWH needs a myriad of separate objects. Hence the former scheme is much more economical. Vogel is aware of this point, but then he goes on to assert that "it is far from clear that, all by itself, positing fewer entities is a theoretical virtue" (Vogel 1998, p. 355). Well, it seems to me quite clear that when we consider our practice of IBE, a theory that posits fewer entities is indeed simpler than another theory that posits more. A detective will not posit ten murderers to explain a dead body when one will do. Astronomers will not posit ten more planets to explain the deviation of Uranus's orbit from Newton's theory if just one (Neptune) will do, and so on.[1]

So in terms of simplicity, it is by no means clear that the RWH will win over skeptical competitors. To make a successful epistemic *ascent* possible, the Principle of Simplicity alone is not enough, because its basic inclination is to trim things *down*. In the Simplicity Contest, the theory that nothing exists will surely become the champion, and the theory that nothing but a mind or brain exists will likely be the runner-up. In our ordinary application of IBE, we have already used the PCT side by side with the Principle of Simplicity.

In any case, there are some general problems with explanatory foundationalism that even Vogel's version cannot overcome. First, the basic trust in memory seems quite inescapable. The common data for the competing hypotheses like RWH or CSH are the *continued coherence* of our experiences. But this datum we can only know through our memory. Indeed, the presupposition of memory in almost all attempts to vindicate SE's reliability is quite obvious. Or perhaps we can try to provide a coherentist justification for memory, or even an IBE for the reliability of memory? Bonjour clearly points out the problems:

> the issue arises of how…the memory beliefs upon which any access to the fact of *continued* coherence must rely are themselves to be justified. Many philosophers have offered coherence theories of the justification of memory beliefs, but such an account seems clearly to be involved in vicious circularity if the only reason for thinking that coherentist justification is conducive to truth, and so that the memory beliefs in particular are true, relies on the existence of coherence over time and so on those very memory beliefs themselves…there is no

noncircular way for a coherentist to appeal to sustained or long-run coherence. (Bonjour 1999, p. 130)

Second, we have argued that memory is also vital in reasoning. So *the explanatory argument for RWH* also needs to depend on the memory belief that the argument has proceeded correctly. I will also argue that the alleged superiority of explanatory power of the Real World Hypothesis is, in fact, *irrelevant* to the applicability of PCT to SEs (see the next chapter).

### 7.2.4 Seamless Web Thesis

Suppose the critic wants to reject (T3). The basic strategy is to acknowledge SE and memory as the only BSJs. All other kinds of experience are then non-BSJs that must be justified by the deliverances of the BSJs. However, how do we justify this kind of "discrimination," which apparently violates the principle of impartiality? Perhaps we may claim that the BSJs *alone* are infallible, incorrigible, or uncontaminated by theory. But then it is doubtful that any *type* of experiential claim can aspire to this status, not even SE and memory. We may claim the BSJs *alone* are public. But to know a type of experience is public, we need to first know that it is shared by many people, and they agree quite a lot. But we can't know that unless we *presuppose* PCT (SE and memory).

Some may claim that the BSJs *alone* are the *most* reliable, and SE and memory are the only candidates here. However, once it is admitted that the difference between the various kinds of experience is only a matter of degree, is it still plausible to cling to the *qualitative* distinction between the BSJs and the non-BSJs? Admittedly SE and memory are more reliable, but this judgment is only possibly arrived at when we give initial trust to our various kinds of experience. Furthermore, given two kinds of experiences, $E1$ and $E2$, is it plausible to demand that $E2$ *has to be validated by $E1$ before it has force* if $E1$ is *only more reliable* than $E2$? Suppose a mutant species of human beings (X-men) start to emerge among us, and they possessed a kind of super-perception, which is much more reliable than our perception. They may insist *only their* super-perception is a BSJ, and that our perception needs to be validated by their super-perception before it can be trusted. Would it be a reasonable requirement? No!

(T3) asserts that we can find no relevant distinction between the various kinds of experience with respect to the applicability of the PCT. Although this is hard to *prove conclusively*, the discussions above suggest it may be well-nigh impossible to defeat (T3) once we accept (T2). If we grant (T2), then we are conceding that the Type PCT should be applied as a *fundamental* principle to, say, our sense experience as epistemic seeming, and *on this ground alone*. That means we accept SE for no other reason than that it seems to us to be true. Then, when we consider experiences in other areas, the only relevant point seems to be whether they are also epistemic seemings. The other factors are just irrelevant. So (T3) follows.

## 7.3  Alternatives to the Principle of Critical Trust

The above presentation of the impartiality argument is only a sketch. Of course, there are many challenges. I deal with the more prominent ones below.

### 7.3.1  Paul Moser's Explanatory Foundationalism

I have criticized Vogel's argument above. Paul Moser has adopted a similar approach. He thinks that the foundation for our knowing is the non-conceptual content of experience, and our sensory beliefs can be justified by the fact that they are the best (non-epistemic) explanation of these non-conceptual contents. Then other beliefs are justified in turn by being the best explanation of these sensory beliefs. Moser is a believer in the Given: "I take conceptual experiences to be simply additive. They essentially have a nonconceptual attention-attraction component *and* a conceptual component. But there seems to be no reason to think that the nonconceptual component, including its nonconceptual object, is essentially a function of the relevant conceptual component" (Moser 1989, pp. 87–8). He suggests that "one's subjective nonconceptual contents can make a proposition, $P$, evidentially probable to some extent for one in virtue of those contents' *being explained for one* by $P$ in the sense that $P$ is an essential part of an explanation for one why those contents exist" (Moser 1989, pp. 91–2).

We might wonder if this project can defeat skepticism. Here Moser "accomplishes" this task by producing the trick of forbidding a "gratuitous entity." A "gratuitous entity relative to explained subjective nonconceptual contents $C$ is an item posited by an explanation of $C$ that is not itself *represented* in $C$ by means of any corresponding feature." Suppose I now experience an apparent blue book. The Cartesian demon is exorcised because the "demon is *not* represented in my experience by means of any of its own features, whereas a blue book is" (Moser 1989, pp. 97–8; italics mine).

I, in fact, do not need to show that Moser is wrong, because he is also a defender of ARE. He contends that "humanly experienced acquaintance with God's call … is best explained, relative to all available evidence, by the proposition that God has actually intervened in that person's experience" (Moser 2010, p. 150).

So Moser, in fact, agrees with me that TEs can be prima facie evidence for God, but he wants to establish this via an IBE. I agree that this explanatory argument needs to be taken seriously: "genuine character transformation toward God's unselfish love does not admit of convenient dismissal, because it bears directly on who one really is, or has become, including the morally relevant kind of person one actually is, or has become. Such transformation, in any case, cuts too deeply against our natural selfish tendencies to qualify as just a self-help ploy. As a result, it arguably offers a kind of firm nonpropositional evidence that resists quick dismissal and offers a basis for theistic belief" (Moser 2010, p. 137). However, whether we can establish the theistic explanation of life-transforming TEs as the best explanation is less clear. Moser has another move that makes his argument much more persuasive: appeal to the semantic understanding of "truth indicator": "Suppose that we form the settled semantic intention to use 'truth indicator' and 'epistemic reason' as follows: a visual experience...of an *apparent* book in a situation with no accessible opposing evidence is a (fallible) truth indicator and thus an epistemic reason for a visual belief that an actual book exists...may serve as ultimate, even if revisable, truth markers for ascriptions of an epistemic reason" (Moser 2010, p. 189). He contends that "it is *part of what we mean* by 'epistemic reason'...we now may shift the burden of argument to the skeptic" (Moser 2010, p. 190). This is basically the same move proposed by him in 1989. So if we grant that this move of Moser to defeat the skeptic is successful, then we can use the same move to argue that God is the best explanation of our TEs.

However, I still have reservations about Moser's arguments. Let us remember that Moser, for the sake of the purity of the Given, insists that the conceptual content is just added to the nonconceptual content. So what, actually, is meant by Moser's description of some *nonconceptual content* as "experience of an apparent blue book"? It cannot refer to the epistemic seeming that one is apparently seeing a blue book. To do so would be introducing conceptual elements. Perhaps it refers to the complex of sensations or the qualitative character of the experience that *is* typically caused by the presence of a blue book. But this way of interpretation would already presuppose some empirical facts about the world: that there are books and they typically cause such and such...This hardly serves Moser's intention to defeat skepticism. So perhaps it refers to the complex of sensations that *we believe* to be typically caused by a blue book. If we take seriously Moser's "additive view," then this description of the nonconceptual content is just a conceptual tag and not an *intrinsic* description. It is because the nonconceptual content has determinate character independent of any conceptual elements.

It is hard to see how "the blue book" is *represented* by the nonconceptual content of "an apparent blue book." This is only an illusion created by our language. Now suppose there is a skeptic who is convinced by a priori arguments that the evil demon exists. He then believes that all our perceptions are only ingenious deceptions. As a result, he decides to call the nonconceptual content "blue-book-deception-by-demon." (If Moser is correct, this would not change the independently determinate nonconceptual content a bit!) For him, the Cartesian demon is not *gratuitous* at all! So Moser's way to mark out the "gratuitous entities" already betrays his basic trust in our *natural* way to conceptualize the nonconceptual contents of our experience. In his system, this trust has no further source that can justify it. So it seems better to grant PCT as a fundamental principle.

### 7.3.2 *Explanationism and PCT*

Many contemporary philosophers regard the argument to the best explanation as fundamental in epistemology. Let us call this approach explanationism. Does it succeed in avoiding the PCT or the like? Let us first consider
how Lycan is forced by his explanationism to accept a version of PCT.
Lycan believes that a belief is justified by its being the best explanation
of all the data. However, the problem immediately arises concerning the
status of the data to be explained. Are the descriptions of them justified
or not? If they are not, how can an explanatory hypothesis be justified
with respect to them? If they are, then they are either self-justified to some
extent or not at all. If they are not self-justified to any degree, then how are
they justified? Because they are explained by the "best" explanation? That
would be viciously circular. Because they can best explain other data? An
infinite regress threatens. So in the end we would arrive at some data that
are self-justified. (Probably they are not infallible: they are only prima facie
justified.)

For this reason Lycan formulates his Principle of Credulity: "Accept at the
outset each of those things that seem to be true" (Lycan 1988, pp. 165–6).
This justifies our spontaneous beliefs, which help to get our explanatory
enterprise off the ground. The general idea is that the explanatory edifice
needs some ground level data. If a person chooses some spontaneous beliefs
as data, but rejects others, isn't it incumbent on him to justify this arbitrary
move?

Second, there are general reasons to expect that explanationism cannot
avoid the appeal to some form of PCT. Why do we think this or that is a
good explanation? How can we show that seeking a good explanation is
truth-conducive? These are not matters easily settled by empirical facts. For
example, Ian Hacking objects: "Nor is *the* explanation of a phenomenon
one of the ingredients of the universe, as if the Author of Nature had written
down various things in the Book of the World... and also the explanation of
events. Explanations are relative to human interests." Moreover, "there are
times when we feel a great gain in understanding by the organization of new
explanatory hypothesis. But that feeling is not a ground for supposing that
the hypothesis is true" (Hacking 1983, p. 53). So it seems to me that explanationism is relying on some fundamental a priori intuitions. It has often
been pointed out that whether a hypothesis is a good explanation depends
on many criteria that are not clearly truth-related, for example, simplicity.
Why is a simpler hypothesis more likely to be true? Furthermore, to compare rival explanations would need a lot of judgments. Why do we think
our judgments can ever lead us closer to the truth? To justify these sorts
of beliefs, a PCT(intuition) and PCT(rational judgment) may be needed.
Otherwise, it is hard to justify those intuitions by further empirical knowledge, which, according to explanationism, has to be justified by the *application of some explanatory principles* on some foundational beliefs. Hence
the Applicability Thesis is still unavoidable.

James McAllister (1996) is an attempt to solve this problem by the use of "aesthetic induction." McAllister is an empiricist who wants to make sense of the (somewhat surprising) appeal to aesthetic judgments (including simplicity) in science. He argues that the connection between truth-conducivenss and the aesthetic properties of scientific theories is not an a priori matter. Instead, this connection, if it exists, is discovered in the history of scientific practice by induction: "a scientific community's aesthetic preferences are reached by an induction over the empirical track record of theories: a community attaches to each property of theories a degree of aesthetic value proportional to the degree of empirical success of the theories that have exhibited that property" (McAllister 1996, p. 4). For example, if we find out from the past track record that the simplicity of a theory is reliably correlated with empirical adequacy, then this is a good empirical reason for believing that the Principle of Simplicity can lead us to truth.

McAllister's idea is interesting, but I doubt this has really solved the problem. The first problem is that he seems to have assumed the connection between the truth of a theory and its empirical adequacy, but this is an assumption that needs support. Usually the realists try to bridge the gap by an IBE based on the empirical success of science, but this is contested by many prominent philosophers of science, for example, Van Fraassen. The main point is that a successful aesthetic induction can, at most, establish a general connection of, say, simplicity with empirical success, and not truth. Perhaps McAllister cannot prove that much without already assuming the principle of simplicity. Suppose, in the past, that simplicity of a theory has invariably been correlated with empirical success, but there are various ways to interpret these data. We may suppose the principle of simplicity will work at all times. However, we may equally suppose the principle will work only before 2050, and not after, or perhaps the principle will only work when the theories are proposed by people shorter than four meters, and so on. So the aesthetic induction cannot avoid Goodman's paradox of the grue, and the problem of curve-fitting on a higher level. Why should we choose the first hypothesis instead of the more contrived ones? Because of its simplicity! So we have reasons to believe that the principle of simplicity cannot be inferred inductively from past evidence, because induction itself seems to presuppose it.

So it seems that explanationism without the PCT does not deliver the promises. The PCT again seems unavoidable.

### 7.3.3 Preliminary Attempts to Demarcate Basic Sources from Nonbasic Sources

To accept the applicability of the PCT to a type of experience is to accept it as a BSJ. The most common way to block the impartiality argument is to challenge (T3), the Seamless Web Thesis, by giving some criteria of a BSJ in such a way that SE and memory will be vindicated as BSJs, but REs will not.

In other words, the critic only accepts some localized versions of PCT and refuses to accept the generalized one. We have to ask, "What is the reason for this differential treatment?" Perhaps he can just say it is *purely* his decision, and he needs no reason for this. This amounts to a flat denial of the Impartiality Thesis, and I have argued that it would have grave epistemic consequences.

Suppose the critic is going to argue for his criteria. We need to remember that one implication of the distinction between BSJs and non-BSJs is that the nonbasic experiential claims *must* be justified with respect to the BSJs. This is assuming the epistemic superiority of the former over the latter, and the epistemic dependence of the latter on the former. To avoid dogmatism, the criteria for BSJs have to be well motivated by epistemic reasons that make intelligible why we should trust one rather than the other. Let us consider several suggestions:

a. "The BSJs *alone* are infallible or incorrigible."

If this is the case, then it is a more than sufficient justification for according prima facie validity to the BSJs. But even if it is the case, it is not clear why a fallible kind of experience has to be validated by the infallible kind. Why can't we have two independently valid kinds of experiences, one infallible and one fallible? Similarly, we might have two independently valid kinds of reasoning, one infallible and one fallible. The refusal to accept this possibility underlies the attempts at a deductive justification of induction or, when it fails, the rejection of induction (Popper, Watkins).

However, this criterion will immediately disqualify SE and memory as BSJs. It is also doubtful that any *type* of experiential claim can aspire to this status. Then the class of BSJ may turn out to be an empty set! Even if we allow the class of appearance statements to be infallible or incorrigible, the class of BSJ would still be too small for solving the problem of epistemic ascent.

b. "The BSJs *alone* are pure—that is, uncontaminated by theory."

Again, this characterization may suffice for the distinction, but it is again doubtful any *type* of experiential claim can fulfill this role. It seems to be widely recognized that all experiences are theory-laden. At least both SE and memory are theory-laden.

c. "The BSJs *alone* are the most reliable."

Perhaps the critic will concede the above, but still insist that SE and memory are more secure than other experiences, and hence we should still begin there. For example, Gellner admits that experience is never pure, but he thinks "there are very marked and narrow limits to the extent to which it can be corrupted, and hence a reverence for experience makes an enormous and salutary difference" (Gellner 1974, p. 206). Here "experience" means SE alone. As for the other kinds of experience in our *Lebenswelt*, Gellner thinks that they are problematical and need to be revalidated by SE and science.

I think his claim is not very compelling. When he admits that experience is never pure, the difference between the various kinds of experience is only a matter of degree. Is it still plausible to cling to the *qualitative* distinction between the SEs and other experiences? Admittedly, SE and memory are more reliable, but this judgment is only arrived at when we give initial trust to our experience. Hence this distinction still cannot undercut the argument here.

I raised this question before: given two kinds of experiences, E1 and E2, is it plausible to demand that *E2 has to be validated by E1 before it has independent force* if E1 is *only more reliable* than E2? My X-men analogy suggests a negative answer. In this situation, it is reasonable to demand that E2 be compatible with E1, but it is another matter to insist that the validity of E2 should be *derived* from E1. To argue this way is to again commit the Super-Reliability Fallacy. We can liken our belief system to a table. Perhaps SE is the central and strongest leg, but it does not mean that the other, thinner legs do not bear weight at all.

### 7.3.4 Consensus Empiricism

Try this criterion: "The BSJs *alone* can produce consensus and public statements." For example, Michael Goulder claims that "we only think it rational to trust our this-worldly experience normally when there are ... public ... and visible signs to bear it out" (Goulder and Hick 1983, p. 50). However, it is by no means easy to say what, exactly, is a public claim. Let me try this definition: "A public statement is one on which all (competent) speakers of a language give the same verdict when given the same concurrent stimulation."[2] There are several problems. The above criterion seems to exclude memory claims, because in many cases memory claims are essentially private and not open to public checks, for example, memory of events that happened when one is alone or memory of past mental events. It is also difficult to make sense of "same concurrent stimulation" in the context of checking of a memory claim.

Second, how do we find out which is a BSJ? Obviously we need to find out:

a.  who are the speakers of a language?
b.  who are the *competent* speakers?
c.  what are the verdicts of these competent speakers?
d.  whether those speakers are given "the same concurrent stimulation"?

So such an innocent-looking definition actually assumes an awful lot of things. Such a distinction is idle if we cannot make the distinction in practice. But it seems we can't do that unless we *presuppose* PCT(SE and memory), and our capacities of identifying "speakers," "verdicts," and perceptual situations. So this distinction, even if it is unproblematic, cannot be accessible to us apart from a basic trust in SE and memory. However, the public checkability aspect can be justifiably ascertained *after* we accept the PCT, and in this way, the validity of SE is enhanced. This accounts for our emphasis on consensus, while rejecting its fundamentality: consensus seems to be neither a sufficient condition nor a necessary condition for justified belief. However, consensus does count toward the positive epistemic status of an experiential claim, and this is captured by my Principle of Consensus. What is disastrous is to claim that consensus *alone* justifies.

### 7.3.5 *The Criterion of Unavoidability*

John Schellenberg has argued that religious practices should not be taken as innocent until proven guilty. His basic argument is that if we are investigators of truth, we would only grant PFEF to an alleged epistemic source when we *have to* (Schellenberg 2007, p. 170). Later he argues that "the *only* way" to get started is to accept the "most basic and unavoidable" ones (Schellenberg 2007, p. 171).

I find it difficult to assess Schellenberg's argument, because he has not really tried to explicate the meaning of unavoidability or necessity he has in mind. Let us first discuss "necessity" (his "have to")—of course logical necessity or nomic necessity are not intended here. It may mean some kind of necessity in view of some purpose. But what are these purposes? Suppose he wants to claim that a source is a BSJ only if it is necessary for the defeat of global skepticism—he once raises the point that to defeat global skepticism we do not need to grant a global PCT. However, to defeat global skepticism, trust in introspection alone is enough. It may lead to solipsism, but this is still not global skepticism.

Try this: "A source is a BSJ only if it is necessary for biological survival." Well, no experience in itself is necessary for survival. In fact, vegetative existence is also possible for human beings. Schellenberg, of course, will reply that the aim of biological survival is too low for human beings. So at least we are aiming at a meaningful human existence. But once the question of meaning is raised, the ambiguity of Schellenberg's criterion is aggravated, because people profoundly disagree on what is a meaningful life. Perhaps Schellenberg will argue that, despite these disagreements, no one can lead a meaningful life apart from a trust in SE and memory. This at most shows that all of us need to accept SE and memory, but it cannot show that TEs should be excluded. In fact, many people who have strong TEs typically think that a relationship with God is crucial for a meaningful human existence. So at least for them they *have to* trust their TEs. So on this understanding of Schellenberg's criterion, it is rational *for them* to do so.

A more likely interpretation of Schellenberg's intended meaning of "have to" is "psychological necessity," namely, people find that they have to believe something under some kind of psychological compulsion. Schellenberg's list of BSJs includes SE, introspection, memory, and rational intuition, which provide us a certain basic picture of the world. Schellenberg then emphasizes that "we find ourselves unable to *not* form beliefs" in this way (Schellenberg 2007, p. 172). Yes, but remember that all epistemic seemings are spontaneous inclinations to believe something. The inclination varies in degrees, but for all strong experiences in whatever realm (moral experience, aesthetic experience, or RE), the experient will find himself unable to *not* form beliefs in those ways, while others can do that. So psychological necessity is person-relative. It seems obvious that for many believers who have powerful REs all through their lives, it is necessary for them to trust them, psychologically speaking. To deny their intimate experiences and their apparently real relationship with their Savior and Lord is psychologically impossible for them. So Schellenberg's argument against the PFEF of REs cannot be successful for all—which seems to be his intention. Another suggestion is that one can only trust his experience if that kind of experience is psychologically necessary, not only for oneself, but *for all others*. His criterion of unavoidability is transformed into the requirement of universality. But this is a strange demand indeed. Why should I deny my own experiences just because some others do not have similar experiences?

Wessel Stoker has considered a similar argument against the application of PCT to TE: "That our trust in our memory cannot be proved is not a problem because memory, like sense perception, is part of our lives. We do not need to give any reasons for it, for we simply take part in the practice of perceiving or remembering. Does that also obtain for faith in God?...in our Western society we can deny faith in God without ceasing to function as human beings." But then he goes on to say: "That is different for the oral cultures of Africa. There religion is so bound up with society as a whole that denying the religion is at the same time denying one's own existence" (Stoker 2006, p. 212). The idea is that, although the argument under consideration has force in the modern Western society, it may not apply to other cultures. Now this acknowledges the limitation of the kind of consideration adduced by Schellenberg. But Stoker's reply does not go far enough. Why suppose everyone in Western society can or needs to agree on the question of whether faith in God is essential to our function as human beings? Obviously the answer to this question depends very much on how we understand what the proper function of a human being is, and the people who have strong REs typically have a different view from that of secular people. So his answer is begging the question against the religious people.

## 7.4 General Difficulties for the Critics

I want to further adduce general considerations for the Seamless Web Thesis. For simplicity's sake, we consider only SE and TE in the following argument. Usually people who dispute the application of the PCT to TEs would suggest that the PCT is only applicable when a certain set of conditions C is satisfied. Then he claims that C obtains in the case of SE, but not in that of TE. So they argue that, though the PCT can apply to SEs, it does not actually apply to TEs. However, we have to distinguish two claims:

1. PCT is applicable *if* SC obtains (SC as sufficient condition).
2. PCT is applicable *only if* NC obtains (NC as necessary condition).

The critic can use (2) in this argument:

2. PCT is applicable only if NC obtains.
\*. NC does not obtain in the case of TEs.
3. So PCT is not applicable to TEs.

The above argument seeks to find the necessary condition NC for applicability of PCT. If this search is successful and NC is shown not to obtain in TE, then my argument would be effectively *rebutted*. Now the obvious problem is how we can establish (2), except by fiat or stipulative definition. I cannot see any easy way to establish (2) at all.

However, there is another way to *undercut* my argument. Suppose the following argument can be formulated:

1. PCT is applicable *if SC obtains*.
#. SC obtains for sensory experience.
4. So PCT is applicable to sensory experience.

The idea is that perhaps we can justify the applicability of PCT to SE by finding some sufficient condition SC. But it can't be argued that since SC does not obtain for TE, PCT is inapplicable to TE. It is because SC is only the sufficient condition and not necessarily also the necessary condition for the applicability of PCT. For example, consider conditions such as universality, checkability, and so on. We can grant that these are sufficient conditions for PCT to be applicable. Yet if they are not claimed as necessary conditions, there is no reason lack of them shows that PCT is not applicable. Now "eating arsenic" is sufficient for death, but a man can still die of other causes, for example, suffocation. So the above argument can't rebut my argument directly. However, this can refute (T1) by showing that the PCT is not a fundamental principle: it can be inferred from the obtaining of SC. But then the problem is how we can *justifiably believe* that (1) and (#) are true. Remember, we cannot assume PCT in justifying (1) and (#) because it is the basic trust that is being considered. How it can be done is not easily conceivable. For any likely candidate for SC, for example, universality or checkability, both (1) and (#) seem unknowable if we do not assume the PCT.

The above discussion's key idea is simple: since the application of PCT means a *basic* (or unconditional) trust, it is difficult to show that the epistemological distinctions between types of experience that are often *derived* are relevant to this basic trust.

Perhaps enough has been said to make (T2) sound plausible. Anyway, the burden is equally on the critic who rejects the PCT to *show* what the relevant distinction is. If the above reflections are on the right track, there are general reasons to believe that the critics of the Transcendental ARE cannot show this distinction in a non-question-begging way. Suppose we get a stalemate: neither side can agree on the NC for the application of PCT, and neither side has neutral reasons to convince the other. Even in this situation, the prospect for a weak ARE is not bad at all, especially in our post-foundationalist context.

## 7.5 Conclusion

In this and the previous chapters I have argued for both the Weak Token PCT and the Moderate Type PCT. I agree with Swinburne's conclusion: "the PC is a very fundamental principle for the interpretation of experience…Initial credulity is the only attitude a rational man can take—there is no half-way house" (Swinburne 1979, pp. 275–6). Since we are trying to decide a "fundamental" principle of rationality, no single argument can carry the weight. The best we can do is to construct a whole case weaving diverse considerations together in favor of the PCT. In the next chapter, I will further explain the advantages of the CTA, relative to other kinds of epistemology. Then in Part B, I will defend the application of Type PCT to several types of experience in some detail. If we find that, in realm after realm of experience, a kind of principle akin to the PCT should be (or has been) invoked, then it provides strong "inductive" evidence for the PCT as a fundamental general principle. Any attempt to formulate a PCT specifically to exclude REs is ad hoc and unconvincing if no sufficient reason can be given for this move.

# CHAPTER 8

# THE CRITICAL TRUST APPROACH AND OTHER EPISTEMOLOGIES

I think it is important to situate the PCT within an epistemological frame-work like CTA. Even if we cannot directly prove the PCT, it is still possible to find it plausible if it is entailed by an epistemological framework (CTA or others), which is superior to (or at least not inferior to) other epistemo-logical frameworks. In this sense, we can mount a comparative epistemo-logical argument for PCT. The full defense of this claim, of course, cannot be done here. I just try, below, to indicate how this case might be argued. In any case, the following discussions will help us clarify the similarities and dissimilarities between CTA and different kinds of epistemologies. The common complaint about the CTA is that it is too lenient, leading to gull-ibilism. However, when we situate the CTA within the entire spectrum of contemporary epistemologies, we find that there are positions that are more lenient than the CTA, for example, coherentism, negative coherentism, and non-foundationalism. So perhaps CTA has already struck the balance.

## 8.1 Critical Trust Approach and Explanatory Foundationalism

Even if the explanatory foundationalist can produce a successful argument that shows that the Real World Hypothesis is the best explanation of our experiences, it cannot really explain the greater appeal of external world realism. First, the whole approach of explanatory foundationalism is psy-chologically unrealistic and unappealing. Typically, ordinary people won't feel that their perceptual beliefs are the products of any kind of inference, not to mention complicated arguments that appeal to abstract criteria of explanation. We can distinguish two questions:

1. Does something like Vogel's Real World Hypothesis (RWH) have the greatest explanatory power in comparison with other skeptical hypotheses?
2. Suppose we are justified in believing the RWH. Does its justification derive solely from its superior explanatory power?

I have argued for a negative answer to the first question. If this is correct, then explanatory foundationalism simply fails. For the sake of argument, suppose the positive answer to the first question is correct. It still does not automatically entail a positive answer to the second question. First, even if a successful argument for explanatory foundationalism *could* be used to justify our ordinary perceptual beliefs, as a matter of fact it is not available to most people. Pollock has argued persuasively that appearance beliefs can't form the foundation level of cognition (Pollock 1986, chapter 2) simply because we don't usually have beliefs such as "I am appearing to redly," not to mention the problem of grasping the whole corpus of appearance beliefs about all our experiences. Furthermore, many people simply do not have the capacity to understand as complicated a theory as Vogel's argument against skepticism. So if explanatory foundationalism is the only route to epistemic salvation, then I am afraid the vast majority of people are still lost, and many of them are predestined to be lost forever.

Second, the success of explanatory foundationalism does not entail the falsity of the PCT. It is possible that while our perceptual beliefs possess some degree of intrinsic justification (as the PCT says), at the same time they *could* be justified by an explanatory argument, and hence receive epistemic enhancement. Suppose this is false, namely, perceptual beliefs derive their justification solely from their superior explanatory power, and possess no intrinsic justification. It follows that we should immediately accept the skeptical hypothesis were we to discover that some skeptical hypothesis indeed provides the best explanation of all our experiences. (We cannot completely discount this possibility, because IBE is fallible and essentially open.) I think this consequence is implausible and counterintuitive.

Just suppose Vogel were to discover a Superior Skeptical Hypothesis (SSH) that can provide the best explanation of all our data according to the epistemic principles he accepts. What would he do? I *guess* he would not accept skepticism, and suspend his belief in the external world for a moment. He may try to revise his epistemic principles, or spend nights to come up with a better defense of the Real World Hypothesis. Even if these attempts to defeat the SSH fail, he would shelve the problem and continue to trust in his sense experience and memory. Whether Vogel will really do that is only a matter of guessing, but I suppose the vast majority of ordinary people will do that (in fact, most students who have sat in an introduction to philosophy class do not feel able to rebut either the Cartesian Demon Hypothesis, or the Brain-in-a-Vat Hypothesis, or the Matrix Hypothesis, but they trust their experiences all the same). If their experiences never have independent weight, and derive their epistemic force entirely from the relatively superior explanatory power of the RWH, then their reactions would be utterly irrational. This is implausible. Even if we think that some of them are, indeed, justified in accepting the SSH, we would not want to say that they have nothing to overcome initially. In other words, even if the SSH were to win in the explanatory game, it would at most be a defeater of our experiences, which already have some degree of PFJ. That means that the PCT has been presupposed.

*The conclusion is that the success of an explanatory argument for RWH, even realized, in itself does not entail the falsity of the PCT.* Since it is widely believed that some form of explanatory foundationalism is already the best bet for those who want to provide external justification for our experiences, so it appears more clearly that the PCT is unavoidable.

## 8.2 Critical Trust Approach and the Selective Trust Approach (STA)

### 8.2.1 General Problems

My critic might argue that we just need a plurality of fundamental, localized PCTs, instead of a global one. I call this a Selective Trust Approach (STA). The idea is that we only have *fundamental* trust in several types of experience, but refuse this trust to others. The former ones are treated as innocent until proven guilty, but the latter ones are treated as guilty until proven innocent. If the proponent of STA can provide some criteria to justify this disparity of treatment, then his distinction can be justified in principle. But this strategy is facing a lot of difficulties (see Chapter 7). Suppose the proponent just says this is his choice. This is certainly arbitrary, but the proponent can bite the bullet and say that this is still a logically possible position. The critic may remain unrepentant in his initial skepticism toward REs. He may also evince other reasons to show that his resulting worldview is superior, even if his epistemological stance is far from satisfactory. For example, he can say that although he cannot provide a clear criterion to justify his disparity of treatment, his position is at least safer and is consonant with the *Selector Thesis*, which also has intuitive support.

*Selector Thesis*: The Type PCT should not be applied as a fundamental principle to all types of experience. We should be selective in our trust.

The above thesis seems plausible to philosophers of the empiricist bent (e.g. Keith Parsons). The prima facie case for it is the intuition that some experiences are very suspicious and ought to be rejected. There is also the fear that its denial would open the floodgate to all sorts of nonsense, and hence gullibilism.

I want to criticize this move from a broader perspective. First, this pluralistic scheme is very untidy. It should be observed that all those localized PCTs are structurally identical. Each of them might be a *fundamental* principle, but in this way we are positing several fundamental principles that have no further justification or explanation. It seems that we should not proliferate fundamental principles beyond necessity. So it is more natural to see them as corollaries of a single principle in different domains. This epistemological scheme would be much simpler and tidier. If one insists that we shouldn't commit too much, then why shouldn't we formulate a localized PCT that is also temporally restricted, for example, "if it is before 2050 a.d., then PCT(SE) is true"? This is hardly plausible.

Second, all those experiences can be subsumed under a unitary description in terms of epistemic seemings. Insofar as those types of experience can't admit of any unitary description, it is more plausible to view each localized PCT as an *independent* fundamental principle. Now that this description is available, it is quite implausible to draw an arbitrary boundary between these sources and other sources. Suppose the PCT(SE) is a rational principle, and our question is: is it fundamental? If it is fundamental, then when the PCT is applicable to a SE, it is in virtue of the fact that it is a *sense experience*. Since SE is also a sort of epistemic seeming, another explanation is that the PCT is applicable in this case in virtue of the fact that it is a sort of epistemic seeming. If we adopt the latter explanation, then we should positively expect that the same principle would apply to memory, since it is also a kind of epistemic seeming. This seems to be the case. If the PCT(SE) is applicable in virtue of an experience being SE, then since memory is not SE, there is no reason to think the PCT should also be applied to memory. So the latter explanation is more powerful than the former one.

Third, suppose we grant STA. This does not mean the end of the defense of TE. The defender can suggest that PCT(TE) is *yet another fundamental principle*. What can the proponent of STA say to exclude this principle from the set of fundamental principles? In view of the various structural parallels and analogies, the burden of proof seems to be on those who want to exclude this principle. This claim will be strengthened if we can show that the localized PCT is also applicable to other types of experiences and epistemic capacities, which are in many ways similar to TEs. I will argue for this in Part B. The point remains that the critic's "differential treatment" toward different kinds of experiences looks arbitrary. If no possible reason is forthcoming, it is reasonable to suspect him of bias and particularism.

### 8.2.2 Robert Audi

Let me explore these problems further by interacting with some defenders of STA. Robert Audi's case is interesting because he appears to occupy some kind of middle ground between the CTA and the STA. He grants four BSJs, and applies a form of PCT to perception, memory, introspection, and rational intuition. But concerning whether there are other BSJs, he is somewhat ambivalent: "I doubt that any general argument shows that there can be no other basic sources... But it is not clear that there are other basic sources, particularly considering how broad the notion of perception is. Perception is not necessarily tied to the five senses. It could occur through other causally sensitive modality associated with the right sorts of experiential responses... I leave open the possibility of other basic sources" (Audi 2001, p. 18).

So far it seems that Audi is open to a kind of general PCT. However, he goes on to say, "There is... no reason to think that any other sources *play the same role* in the notion of justification that operates in the standard descriptive and critical practices of normal adults. It appears that the four standard sources of justification *are the only sources* of it which do not need to earn their justificational credentials, as extrasensory perception presumably would, by correlation with one or another kind of ground already taken to generate justification" (Audi 2001, pp. 18–19; italics mine). It seems that although Audi is in some sense open to BSJs other than those four "standard" sources, in the end he favors a kind of STA that restricts the BSJs to four.

Given this kind of STA, it might seem that Audi would not accept TE as a BSJ, but in fact we are not sure. This is because he adheres to a broad notion of perception that is not necessarily tied to the five senses: "It could occur through other causally sensitive modality associated with the right sorts of experiential responses." Given this concept of perception, Audi admits that Alston has made "a rigorous case that there can be a perceptual source of this kind" (i.e. perception of God) (Audi 2001, p. 237, n. 11). I think Audi is correct. So his kind of STA need not be inimical to our case for TE. In fact, we earlier discussed his sympathetic assessment of the ARE.

### 8.2.3 Nicholas Everitt

Everitt also seems to adopt a kind of STA. He believes in the importance of SE, memory, introspection, and reasoning power, but he wants to emphasize the disanalogy between these standard sources and religious experience. The major difference is that whereas all the standard sources are not optional, but in fact essential for survival, MP [mystical practice] is entirely optional: "It is possible to lead a long, healthy and flourishing life without participating in MP at all. And those who do participate in MP are not noticeably more successful by such criteria than those who do not." So the standard sources are likely to be reliable, and "this is some reason, though admittedly not a strong one, for thinking that MP is not a practice which connects with any real mind-independent reality" (Everitt 2004, p. 167).

It is likely that the above line of argument is one Everitt would like to push, but to his credit, he is self-critical enough to point out that the reason is not a strong one. Everitt is aware that there can be counterexamples to the presupposition of the above criticism, namely, everything mind-independent is crucial for an organism's survival and flourishing. "For example, if a strange sensory deficit had left humans unable to detect moonbeams, it seems unlikely that anyone's well-being would be seriously affected. And yet moonbeams are clearly mind-independent objects" (Everitt 2004, p. 167). Moreover, no theistic religions have ever suggested that theistic experience is essential for earthly survival, and this is to be expected, even assuming theism. Does anyone suggests that anyone without a theistic experience will be struck dead directly by God, or that he will be inflicted with some kind of deadly disease? In that situation, perhaps everyone would believe in God, but it is not a genuinely free choice.

I think he has not properly argued for the thesis that the standard sources are really essential for survival either—bacteria or plants don't have any, but seem to survive quite well! Survival only depends on our behavior. Reasoning and introspection don't really matter as long as the behavior is appropriate. Nor do bacteria or plants need any kind of conscious perception or memory. For materialists, the sufficient explanation for our behavior lies in our brain states: our beliefs or conscious experiences are just irrelevant. Plantinga has plausibly argued that, given naturalism and evolution, the reliability of our cognitive faculties cannot be said to be probable. According to modern science, our SE in fact gives us a lot of false beliefs. But that does not seem to affect our survival. In the end, the alleged disanalogy can prove neither the reliability of the standard sources (on the pain of circular reasoning), nor the unreliability of theistic experience. So it is dubious to use this as a reason to deny the status of BSJ to TE (see also Chapter 9).

### 8.2.4 Super-Reliability Fallacy

I think both Audi and Everitt have committed the super-reliability fallacy. It is perhaps true that there is "no reason to think that any other sources *play the same role* in the notion of justification that operates in the standard descriptive and critical practices of normal adults" as the standard sources. However, if in the end this is only a difference in degrees, then it is quite arbitrary for Audi to refuse the status of BSJ to other sources. Audi has not produced any independent proof of those four standard sources, and he lays down those four principles directly. Audi is sure that it is eminently reasonable to believe in PCT(SE), and says, "It also seems to me that my justification in holding such an epistemic principle is a priori" (Audi 2001, p. 192). Presumably, he will say the same thing about PCT(memory), PCT(introspection), and PCT(intuition). Notice that PFJ has been accorded to such a diversity of epistemic sources by an a priori process. It seems Swinburne and Wall are quite reasonable in saying that their justification in holding the PCT(epistemic seeming) is a priori. They can argue that their intuition is not incompatible with Audi's four different intuitions, and is, in fact, the root intuition underlying those four restricted intuitions. After all, if we are doing things in the a priori way, then empirical details are not crucial. What is common to all those four cases is just that they are all epistemic seemings, and this seems to be the crucial factor for our intuition that they have PFJ.

For Everitt, because he has a narrow concept of perception, his STA has an additional problem of accommodating interpersonal experience, moral and aesthetic experience. They seem to be prevalent in adults' lives as well, and I think they are also BSJs. The foundational role of testimony is also neglected. As Plantinga points out: "Reid is surely right in thinking that the beliefs we form by way of credulity or testimony are typically held in the basic way, not by way of inductive or abductive evidence from other things I believe" (Plantinga 1993, p. 79). He concludes that testimony is an independent source of warrant. So Audi's list of standard sources is not, in fact, as self-contained as it seems initially. He has not really given strong reasons for the claim that the four standard sources do not need to earn their justificational credentials, but the others have to.

Audi does try to give a case for the collective negative autonomy of the set of standard sources: "there is some reason to think that where a belief is justified in virtue of all four sources supporting it, its justification is defeasible only through considerations arising from at least one of those very sources. If we make the plausible but by no means self-evident assumption that defeat of justification can come only from what confers...justification, and if we add the (controversial) assumption that all justification of belief derives wholly from the four standard sources, we may conclude that those sources are (justificationally) self-sufficient. I make neither assumption, but I would suggest that in fact these sources may be self-sufficient" (Audi 2001, p. 23). I think Audi is correct to say that what is supported by the whole set in fact is not likely to be corrected by an outside source. However, this does not entail that there are no other basic sources of justification. It is enough to say that, even if there are other basic sources, they will not be as well established as these four sources. This seems to be the case and compatible with my CTA. Consider this analogy. The shares of a company called Epistemic Justification are distributed in this way: there are four major shareholders, who each possesses 15 percent of the shares, and ten minor shareholders, who each possesses 4 percent of the shares. If all four major shareholders agree on a certain decision, it is true that no others can overturn this decision. But it does not follow that the minor shareholders have no say at all. If all minor shareholders unite together and further secure the support of one major shareholder, then they can decide the fate of Epistemic Justification.

My conclusion is that neither Audi nor Everett have given us good reasons to believe in a closed form of STA.

## 8.3  Critical Trust Approach and Naturalized Epistemology

If we proceed by way of fundamental epistemic principles, then it is likely that STA will suffer from double standard or arbitrariness. However, some philosophers want to proceed by way of their favorite worldview instead, for example, naturalism. They think traditional epistemology does not yield fruits, and the way to decide what is knowledge is to use our best knowledge (which is SE and science). In this way, they may come to ascertain that there are only four standard sources that are BSJs, but the others are non-BSJs. This is roughly how the STA might be established by a kind of naturalized epistemology.

Some responses are in order here. First, the advocates of this position flatly admit the circularity of their project. In this case, the theist seems to have the same right to assume his worldview, theism, and then proceed to determine what is the scope of knowledge. Naturally, theistic experience will also be vindicated. Moreover, we have reasons to believe that the theistic circle is more coherent than the naturalistic one, and the former provides better explanations of the reliability of the four standard sources.

In fact, both introspection and intuition look quite problematic in a naturalistic worldview, and some hard-line naturalists suggest that if these two things can't be explained by naturalism, then we can just eliminate them. Many agree that the mind has the power to grasp infallibly at least some of his own mental states, but in analogy with other empirical processes that are all fallible (even if extremely reliable), this sort of infallibility seems mysterious or even magical.

The power of reason to grasp necessary truths by intuition is another thing that looks magical. Devitt thinks that "the whole idea of the *a priori* seems deeply obscure…mysterious" (Devitt 2005, pp. 105–6). In response, Bonjour rightly points out that "Devitt asks how finding something to be intuitively necessary can constitute a reason for thinking that it is true…There is (obviously) no non-circular way to establish that such insights are genuine, but there is equally no cogent way to argue that they are not…To reject all such insights is to reject the capacity of human intelligence to have good reasons for believing anything beyond the narrow deliverances of direct experience" (Bonjour 2005, pp. 120–1). This is a forthright assertion of the PCT(intuition). The above debate is a good illustration of the common strategy of the naturalist. Things that cannot be accounted for in the naturalistic worldview (such as mind, introspection, intuition, or TE) will be labeled as odd, mysterious, magical, and occult. But for those who would like to accept introspection and intuition as BSJ, this only shows the incoherence or tension between the naturalistic worldview and these epistemic sources.

Furthermore, even empirical knowledge, from the skeptic's perspective, is odd. Devitt acknowledges that empirical knowledge is also mysterious in a sense: "we do not have a serious theory that covers even the easiest examples of empirical knowledge" (Devitt 2005, p. 107). I am not as sanguine as Devitt about the prospect of a solely naturalistic explanation of even empirical knowledge (see Chapter 9). In contrast, the reliability assumption is best made sense of in a theistic framework. Even Audi admits that "perhaps Descartes was right in thinking that the only deductive path from justification to truth about the external world is theistic" (Audi 1988, p. 15).

My basic reservation is about Devitt's one-sided path from the naturalistic worldview to the kinds of knowledge regarded as possible. There should be a bidirectional feedback here. After all, we can only determine the nature of the world on the basis of what we know. Bonjour is right in insisting on our a priori knowledge. If the naturalistic worldview cannot accommodate it, so much the worse for naturalism. Perhaps we can just be contented with the possibility of a priori knowledge, and go without any further explanations. However, the apparent mystery of both mind (introspection) and intuition in the naturalistic worldview does suggest the mind's transcendent capacity. But given theism, it is not really mysterious. If the human mind is made in the image of the Divine Mind, who knows all the necessary truths, then some human capacity for knowing necessary truths is to be expected. So in the end, theism provides the better explanation for our BSJs, and the mutual support of CTA and theism makes the whole system more coherent. The CTA seems better than the naturalistic version of STA.

## 8.4 Critical Trust Approach and Coherentism

Most critics of ARE complain that it leads to gullibilism and that Alston's approach is not foundationalist enough. However, there is also the complaint from the other direction: "leading accounts of religious experience...go against the grain of current epistemology and its attempts to explain the acquisition and legitimation of knowledge in nonfoundationalist terms" (Grube 1995, p. 37). Grube thinks that the CTA is still too foundationalist and suggests coherentism as a better choice.

As far as the ARE is concerned, we can just say that the justification of the belief in God does not seem particularly difficult in the coherentist framework. However, is it really true that coherentism is more promising than the kind of weak foundationalism I am defending? Not necessarily. There are a lot of problems with coherentism. Positive coherentism denies that there can be a foundation for our epistemic system. Every belief depends on at least some support from some other beliefs one holds in order to be justified. Usually it is stated that a belief is justified by its "coherence" with the believer's entire belief system. The problem is that if all the beliefs of one's belief set have no independent evidential force, it's doubtful that mere coherence with these beliefs could generate justification.

It is also revealing that a former defender of coherentism, Bonjour, has now abandoned it. He admits, "While it is very plausible that coherence or something like it is *one* important ingredient in empirical justification, it is initially *very* implausible that it is the whole story...probably no one has ever seriously advocated a *pure* coherence theory of empirical justification" (Bonjour 1999, p. 122). To Bonjour, "coherentism seemed a project worth attempting, albeit one that clearly faced pretty long odds from the very beginning. Now, however, it seems to me time to concede that it has not succeeded and almost certainly cannot succeed" (Bonjour 1999, p. 129). We earlier explained why Bonjour thinks that the coherence theory, in the end, cannot avoid vicious circularity.

We can also point out that the PCT and coherentism are compatible. The CTA can be regarded as a type of weak foundationalism that eschews incorrigibility and extends the foundational set to all epistemic seemings. However, the CTA does require these initially credible epistemic seemings to be reinforced by coherence considerations.

So coherence has an important role to play in CTA. However, it has to be emphasized that coherence considerations only become important after we have applied the PCT. Consider Alvin Goldman's comment: "coherence is not the highest standard of justificational rightness but a derivable, subsidiary, standard...Coherence enters the picture only because coherence considerations are generally helpful in promoting true belief. *On the assumption that prior beliefs are largely true*, new prospective beliefs should be examined for consistency with prior beliefs" (Goldman 1986, p. 100; italics mine). So, arguably, it is the PCT that explains the attractive force of coherentism. In considering coherentism, we are prone to consider coherence with our beliefs that we do regard as having PFJ. Perhaps coherentism appears to be plausible because we have already surreptitiously brought in the PCT.

Moreover, the line of demarcation between weak foundationalism and coherentism may not be hard and fast. For example, Catherine Z. Elgin's proposal of an imperfect procedural epistemology has a spirit akin to mine. In fact, she says that whether her sort of holism is a coherence theory is not clear: "Using Bonjour's (1985) categories, it might be classified as a very weak foundationalism or as a coherence theory. Deliverances derive their initial tenability from their status as deliverances...something other than coherence is involved. But...there are no intrinsically privileged kinds of deliverances. The account does not insist that there is something epistemically special about perception or introspection or analyticity. It simply says that the fact that a consideration presents itself as true gives it a modest measure of tenability. Second, even that small measure of tenability is easily lost" (Elgin 2005, p. 166).

Elgin's epistemology is quite similar to mine, but hers is more inclusive than mine. She endorses my Token PCT (weak form) and extends it further to all "deliverances"—unfortunately, the concept here is not entirely clear. My major difference with her is that I give priority to better-established noetic experiences like perception, memory, and TE. We may also argue that her system is too lenient (cf. Van Cleve's criticisms). In fact, the coherentists have always been troubled by the objection that a coherent system can still be completely isolated from the real world. To address this concern, Bonjour (1985) has argued that we need to introduce the observation requirement (which gives some special place to observations—cognitively spontaneous beliefs, which are analogous with epistemic seemings) in his coherentist framework. Elgin is perhaps also moving in this direction.

So it seems that the CTA has a merit by clearly specifying the contact point with the external world. It is even plausible to argue that the inclusion of PCT in a coherentist framework makes it less vulnerable to objection, and hence its coherence is enhanced. In any case, if Elgin's more lenient system is adopted, the ARE may be even easier to justify.

## 8.5 Critical Trust Approach and Negative Coherentism

Negative coherentism takes all beliefs to have PFJ. If "one holds a belief, one is automatically justified in doing so unless he has a reason for thinking he should not" (Pollock 1986, p. 72). Pollock goes on to give two criticisms, but

I do not need to settle the debate here. I just point out that although the PCT is similar to negative coherentism, it does not regard every belief as having PFJ. Some beliefs are justified only if an inferential justification is available. The ground-level data, so to speak, consist of only epistemic seemings, or cognitively spontaneous belief, which convey a sense of reality. Again, I don't need to belabor the point that if negative coherentism is adopted instead of mine, the ARE is really easy to justify (just try to believe it).

## 8.6 Conclusion

The above discussions indicate that the CTA avoids the major problems of various epistemological approaches, while incorporating some of their insights. Hence the CTA has much to recommend it as an epistemological approach. To summarize:

1. It avoids a self-stultifying skeptical approach from the start.
2. It extends the unreasonably narrow set of foundational beliefs usually allowed by traditional foundationalists.
3. It eschews the unrealistic incorrigibility requirement and recognizes that the initial dataset has only PFJ. The model of prima facie reasoning is eminently close to what we actually adopt to *guide* our reasoning.
4. It allows a suitable place for coherence in epistemic justification.
5. Considerations of reliability converge on a similar principle.
6. It is not as lenient as positions like negative coherentism, which are arguably too uncritical.

If the above arguments are correct, then even if my argument for the PCT is not entirely convincing, it still does not follow that we are not justified in believing the PCT. As long as we have reasons to judge that the CTA is not worse than other approaches, and the CTA can withstand objections, theists have as much right to choose CTA as STA or other alternatives. The ARE within the framework of CTA, then, can still provide some kind of justification for belief in God (though weaker). If the critics want to defeat Transcendental ARE completely, they can't be content with showing that CTA is not necessarily compelling for all rational people. They also need to show that STA (or some more restrictive framework) is superior to CTA. Of course, the above extremely sketchy discussions can't be said to have fully established such conclusions—nothing less than a massive epistemological work could. But I hope to have indicated the initial plausibility of such a case.

PART B

CRITICAL TRUST, THE RAINBOW OF
EXPERIENCES, AND GOD

CHAPTER 9

# EXPERIENCE OF THE NATURAL WORLD, CRITICAL TRUST, AND GOD

## 9.1 Sense Experience and the Natural World

### 9.1.1 *Science as the Vindication of Narrow Empiricism?*

The prestige of science is often used to buttress narrow empiricism. Of course, it is clearly circular to use SE to justify science and then use science to justify SE. However, it might be thought to be significant that the reliability of SE can be nicely incorporated into a coherent scientific (perhaps *scientistic*) worldview in such a way that the resulting worldview and its epistemological principles mutually support one another. At times, this circle formed by the deliverances of SE and the scientific theories seems to be such a self-sufficient and closed one that all else outside this circle is automatically discounted or thrown in doubt. For example, Gellner asserts that

> science...is discontinuous with the notions of everyday life, and...science manifestly has much greater cognitive power...[So] we are not too sure of the status of anything within this ordinary world...science, may re-validate it—or not. In the meantime, we continue to live in the ordinary world...but...with a certain amount of *distrust*. (Gellner 1974, p. 198; my emphasis)

I argue below that a careful examination of the wonder of SE and our experience of the natural world does not support Gellner's contention.

### 9.1.2 *The Wonder and Fragility of Sense Experience*

SEs generate spontaneous and non-inferential epistemic seemings that are imbued with a sense of reality. Yet SE is far from infallible. As explained before, CTA allows for feedback sifting and, interestingly, the fallibility of SE is strikingly demonstrated by the systematic probing of our SEs in science. So we have the scientific distinction between primary and secondary qualities, the Copernican theory of astronomy, and the current theory of elementary articles. Critics of RE often emphasize the numerous conflicts among REs, and hence their fallibility. However, this problem is not unique to REs. By and large, scientific and philosophic criticisms of sense experience have discredited more and more the presumptive data provided by SE. For example, matter seems to our senses to be an extended, continuous substance; but science tells us that it is made up of discrete protons and electrons. It provides a defeater of our common lumpish conception of matter. The scientific data, together with some plausible philosophic criticism, may also defeat *all* statements made about colors on the basis of sense experience.

As we argue, the model of mediated immediacy applies to ordinary SE. In one sense, the mind cannot wrap itself about its objects. Some mediating instrument—our mind/brain—is needed, but the computations are done with such lightning speed that the sensory act seems to be simple, unitary, and direct. Now, we know that our perceptual system builds up its own objects on the occasion of external stimuli and in accordance with principles immanent within itself. But how do we know the computations are done correctly? We can only trust. Critics of RE often look at aesthetic experience or RE as a projection of the human mind, but now it seems that the natural world is also a projection of the human mind. We cannot check whether this projection is objective, apart from first trusting it. But assuming the basic trust, when we look at our sense organs as cognitive machines, their ingenuity strikes us as wonderful. For example, David Marr's work on vision implies that the brain seems to have some a priori principles which guide its processing of the stimuli, and it seems to do the job perfectly well.

At the same time, the world of senses, considered as qualitative contents, is also a wonder. Cheryl Forbes tries to convey this sense of wonder in theistic language. (Atheists can ignore the references to God first and pay attention to the facts about our SE alone.) Forbes says, "God is enormously inventive. He took a few basic shapes, one and two-dimensional figures, and made the most of them—triangles, squares, rectangles, straight lines, parabolas, circles...Then God added light and color...There are just a few basic colors from which the almost limitless array of tints and shades come. Without light, shapes and colors would be meaningless.... God has provided people who have captured light on canvas, Turner and Monet, for example; the shimmer and gleam evoke a poignancy that cannot be satisfied until we see Light itself" (Forbes 1986, pp. 165–6).

He is the "God of texture as well.... rough, smooth, slippery, crinkled, soft, nubly.... God also added scent to his creation. The earth itself, warmed by the sun, has a rich musky odor. The plants, vegetation, trees, and shrubs it nourishes...also have their own particular scent,...[e.g.] a whiff of the sweet alyssum" (Forbes 1986, p. 166). Moreover, "the sounds of God are miracles in themselves...[e.g.] birds...many species must learn the songs anew every year...[There are also the] squirrels and chipmunks who play the continuo, woodpeckers who sit on drums, frogs on tuba and double bassoon, crickets working the violin, ducks and geese on trumpet, crows on trombone—all playing together harmoniously but without a visible conductor...We have the privilege of a free concert day after day...These concerts are acts of worship by God's creatures" (Forbes 1986, p. 167).

These are just basic facts about our senses, but when we ponder over them, we see that our sense experience is itself mysterious. For example, why should our brain be able to produce our high-tech color vision? The senses are just delightful, rich, and also extravagant. If Lyons is right that a zombie can also have adequate sensory knowledge, then all these experiences, together with their qualitative contents, are unnecessary. So why should evolution produce them? The mystery here is the wonderful adaptability of our SE for aesthetic enjoyment of the world.

### 9.1.3 The Mystery of the Natural World

The more we seem to reach to the depth of matter, the more it seems that the world picture provided by sense experience is largely phenomenal and cannot be equated to the deep metaphysical truth about the natural world. Even scientists are forced to talk about the mystery of the natural world, as more and more exotic features of the quantum world are revealed. For example: "How is it that the mere counterfactual *possibility* of something happening—a thing which does *not* actually happen—can have a decisive influence upon what actually *does* happen?" (Penrose 1995, p. 419). This is not to deny the PFEF of SE, nor to deny the apparent reliability of SEs on some level of description. However, we need to keep in mind the limitations of sense experience as revealed by modern science when we compare SE with RE.

For example, both friends and critics of RE want to emphasize that human language is intrinsically inadequate for representing the ineffable reality of God. This is quite right, but it seems equally true to say that human language is intrinsically inadequate for representing the ineffable reality of the natural world. Does our SE have direct access to the essence of the physical world? Can we say that our scientific language is a *literal* description of the physical world? It seems, in both realms, we need to struggle with human language, which is basically a use of symbols. For example, George Lakoff thinks that cognitive science has shown that "thought is *largely unconscious, embodied, and metaphorical*...Where the old view saw thought as literal and consistent—a proper topic for logic—in the new view, thought is literal only in part. So-called 'abstract thought' is largely metaphorical" (Lakoff 2003, pp. 50–1). If we really think hard about questions regarding the nature of matter or energy, we may realize that the physical world seems equally mysterious and ineffable (to some extent). For example, what exactly is electric charge? Is this some physical stuff or just some dispositions? As Penrose points out, "questions about reality at its deepest levels such as 'what is an electron?' or 'why does space have just three dimensions?'" could even cause "embarrassment" for scientists (Penrose 2007, p. 1028).

The above problem is compounded by the fact that consciousness somehow emerges from matter (according to naturalism). As Penrose admits, "We simply do not know the nature of matter and the laws that govern it, to an extent that we shall need in order to understand what kind of organization it is, in the physical world, which gives rise to conscious beings...the more deeply we examine the nature of matter, the more elusive, mysterious, and mathematical, matter itself appears to be." Without minimizing the mystery of divine reality, the holistic empiricist wants to point out that humans indeed live in a world of mysteries—physical, personal, moral, aesthetic, and divine. We need to recognize this common cognitive situation of humans in order to avoid unfair comparison of SE and RE.

## 9.2  Fusion of Experience of the Natural World with Religious/Theistic Experience

### 9.2.1  Sense of Cosmic Wonder

In Chapter 5, we discussed Wittgenstein's wonder at existence.[1] This experience is more widespread than we think. William James believes that "it is only familiarity that blunts it. Not only that anything should be, but that this very thing should be, is mysterious" (James 1916, pp. 39–40). Heidegger points out that this wonder at existence can arise in various situations: "In great desperation, for instance, when all weight tends to disappear from things and all meaning is obscured, then this question arises... In heart-felt joy this question is there because here all things are transformed and stand around us as newly born in such a way that they may almost be conceived as not being... The question is present in boredom where... a hard-ended ordinariness spreads a desolation in which we are indifferent to whether the being is or is not, and thus again the peculiar question begins to sound: why is there being at all and not rather a nothing?" (cited in Nichols 1991, p. 84).

As in the case of Wittgenstein, this experience of wonder is not entirely constrained by prior beliefs. It can happen to nonbelievers, such as J. J. C. Smart. As Evans points out, although Smart dismisses the cosmological argument, he "cannot quite let go of the experience that drives such arguments, and wonders if there is room in his naturalistic world view for 'genuine mysticism.' Such mysticism is one that Smart says he 'feels' with the question 'why is there anything as all?' even though it seems impossible that the question should ever have an answer... He finds himself still uneasy, wondering whether the feeling is one that he ought to 'cherish' or one 'to be explained psychologically'" (Evans 2010, p. 72).[2]

Another example is Paul Williams, the Buddhist scholar who was also a practicing Buddhist. Nevertheless, this sense of wonder continues to haunt him: "for me the question 'why is there something rather than nothing?' has become a bit like what Zen Buddhists call a koan. It is a constant niggling question that has worried and goaded me (often, I think, against my will) into a different level of understanding, a different vision, of the world and our place in it" (Williams 2002, p. 30). In the end, this experience and some other factors led him back to the Catholic faith.

This experience is also a noetic-qualitative complex. There are the unique feelings of wonder, awe, unsettlement, and so on in this kind of experience. The noetic content is vague, and often it may be nothing more than an inchoate sense that the natural world is contingent and not self-sufficient, and that something transcendent may lie beyond it. At other times, after being steeped in the sense of contingency, there may emerge a strong intuition that something like God, the Necessary Being, *must* exist. For Evans, cosmic wonder is a theistic natural sign that mediates a "perception of the createdness of the natural world" (Evans 2010, p. 63). So in my terms, this can also be a proto-RE or even an implicit TE. I call it the experience of contingency.

I suspect that skeptics may charge that this experience is "odd." However, when we see that some of the sharpest intellects in the twentieth century (Wittgenstein, Heidegger, James, etc.) and even some of the staunchest atheists cherish this experience, isn't it rash to dismiss the experience out of hand? It is only odd in the naturalistic world, but quite natural in the theistic world. So the dismissal of these "odd" experiences is not neutral, but a paradigm-bound decision. As the "odd" experiences continue to accumulate (as will be shown throughout Part B), it is the naturalistic paradigm that needs to be questioned. Of course, for those who are totally immersed in the practical life of a technological society, the sense of wonder may diminish almost to the point of nonexistence. Nevertheless, Evans argues, "we must also consider the possibility that the concerns of 'real life' may be ones that immerse us in the relative and the superficial, concerns that lessen our ability to perceive what is really deep and profound about our lives and our world" (Evans 2010, p. 64). It is, indeed, a wonder that we can wonder about the world. There is not the slightest reason why the process of naturalistic evolution should throw up such a being as us.

### 9.2.2 *Experience of Design*

The sense of wonder, if coupled with a prior atheistic faith, may generate a sense of absurdity. However, it need not be, because our experience of the natural world also has positive aspects that suggest that the world is not absurd. For example, Lewis Thomas, a distinguished physician, seems to be a nonbeliever, but he "cannot make...peace with the randomness doctrine." This is not wishful thinking, but is based on his in-depth interaction with the natural world in science: "I do not know a place like this place is absurd, when it contains, in front of our eyes, so many billions of different forms of life, each one in its way absolutely perfect, all linked together to form what would surely seem to an outsider a huge spherical organism" (cited in Evans 2010, pp. 98–9). I call this the experience of design. I do regard the design *argument* as a powerful argument, but this is another big topic that cannot be dealt with in this book. However, even the greatest critic of the design argument, Hume, suggests the design of the world need not be an inferential belief, but a kind of sensation forced on us when we contemplate the wonder of the world.

The experience of design may only be a proto-RE, but in some cases it is fused with an explicit TE. James N. BeMiller, a scientist of the Whistler

Center for Carbohydrate Research in Purdue University, says, "I marvel at the beautifully ordered complexity and diversity of the universe as we know and understand it (from subatomic particles to complex, living, thinking organisms). When I contemplate the many, many marvels of nature (for example, how one of the enzymes involved in starch biosynthesis in both leaves and nonphotosynthetic storage tissue has the same catalytic unit in both tissues but different regulatory units because of different functions of the starch), I must conclude that God—the all-powerful, our Creator—is the greatest scientist of all" (Anderson 1998, p. 44).

### 9.2.3  Experience of Natural Beauty

The natural world can mediate a sense of transcendence in various ways. Consider the religious experience of Paul Hawker, in which the sense of natural beauty is most paramount. Once he was standing on the edge of the precipice: "It was as if I was standing on the clouds themselves, an angel in heaven. I watched the setting sun cast colors onto my clouds—pinks, then golds with purples out on the far edges. It was so beautiful I held my breath so as to capture the consummate peace of this exquisite moment... There was no great voice, no burning bush, but internally something 'clicked'. I had a deep, clear sense... that all before me had been created, and that this creation somehow accommodated me... A warm feeling grew inside me, a knowing that I was enjoyed as much as I was enjoying the moment" (Hawker 2000, p. 20).

   However, at that time he was not "religious" at all, and so there was no conceptual framework for him to use to understand or express this experience. He kept this experience to myself. For Hawker, this was not only a momentary experience, because the sense of support has remained for years as a glowing coal deeply embedded in his soul. His mountain experiences were very much like, but even better than, sex! It was because, as he says, "nothing else had ever made me feel so alive, so good, so complete, so integrated, so whole" (Hawker 2000, p. 27). So his RE fulfills his existential quest for meaning and gives him a sense of wholeness.

### 9.2.4  Scientific Experience and Religious Experience: The Case of Albert Einstein

Below, let us analyze the scientific experience of Einstein (1879–1955) in relation to the rainbow of experiences.

#### 1. Scientific Research and Cosmic Religious Feeling

Despite Einstein's negative views on organized religion, he did not reject religion as such. He probably returned to deep religiosity in the 1930s. He even believed that religion and science had complementary roles to play, as his famous aphorism showed: "Religion without science is blind. Science without religion is lame." For him, the essence of religion was a cosmic religious feeling: "The individual feels the nothingness of human desires and aims and the sublimity and marvellous order which reveal themselves both in nature and in the world of thought. He looks upon individual existence as a sort of prison and wants to experience the universe as a single significant whole" (Einstein 1949, p. 26). This is akin to nature mysticism. Interestingly, Einstein believed that this kind of cosmic religious feeling could have a positive interaction with our scientific experience. On the one hand, science can engender this feeling. In fact, "it is the *most important* function of art and science to awaken this feeling and keep it alive in those who are capable of it" (Einstein 1949, p. 27; italics mine).

Moreover, "cosmic religious feeling is the strongest and noblest incitement to scientific research. Only those who realize the immense efforts and, above all, the devotion that pioneer work in theoretical science demands, can grasp the strength of the emotion out of which alone such work, remote as it is from the immediate realities of life, can issue. What a deep conviction of the *rationality of the universe* and what a yearning to understand, were it but a feeble reflection of *the mind revealed in this world*, Kepler and Newton must have had to enable them to spend years of solitary labour in disentangling the principles of celestial mechanics!...Only one who has devoted his life to similar ends can have a vivid realization of what has inspired these men and given them the strength to remain true to their purpose in spite of countless failures. It is cosmic religious feeling that gives a man strength of this sort" (Einstein 1949, p. 28; italics mine).

Kepler's and Newton's achievements fascinated Einstein. Today we take their work for granted, but Einstein correctly pointed out that Newton's discovery was a kind of miracle, because the problem of "finding out the operative forces" in the universe was so immense: "To a mind less bold than Newton's it must have seemed hopeless, considering the immeasurable multifarity of the effects which the bodies of a universe seem to produce upon each other" (Einstein 1993, pp. 78–9). So why did they succeed? It was partly because their faith in cosmic order and the high value they placed on the discovery of this order, both inspired by their religious faith, provided the impetus for and sustained their scientific research. Einstein's comments on the pioneers of modern science have been confirmed by recent historical studies of the origin of modern science, which demolish the myth that modern science and religion have been locked in a fatal combat ever since the beginning of the scientific revolution. Here Einstein was also talking about his own scientific experience: his driving force was also to know the mind of God. As he told Buber: "what we strive for is just to draw His lines after Him...I want to know how God created this world...I want to know His thoughts, the rest are details" (cited in Clark 1973, p. 33.)

I also want to note that the emphasis of Einstein was on the unity of the rational order of the universe (which is the "reflection of the mind revealed in this world"), instead of on some kind of metaphysical unity. So Einstein was not a monist. Similarly, the following quote shows that the cause of the scientist's rapture is the manifestation of superior intelligence in the world: "You will hardly find one among the profounder sort of scientific minds without a peculiar religious feeling of his own ... His religious feeling takes the form of a rapturous amazement at the harmony of natural law, which reveals an intelligence of such superiority" (Einstein 1949, p. 28).

## *2. Personal or Impersonal God*

Einstein was very fond of mentioning "God." However, there is a debate on what exactly Einstein's God refers to. On the one hand, in Einstein's mind, God must be the foundation of the unifying order of physical reality and its mathematical simplicity. This naturally suggests a personal God with immense intelligence. In fact, Einstein talks about the "humble attitude of mind towards the grandeur of reason incarnate in existence" (Einstein 1950, pp. 32–3).

On the other hand, Einstein urged religion "to give up the doctrine of a personal God" and promote "emancipation from the shackles of personal hopes and desires."[3] However, when we look carefully at his criticisms, what he in fact rejected were the ideas of divine intervention in nature, and a religion based on fear and superstition. He denied that he was an atheist, and rejected the Freudian attack on God, because he thought belief in the personal God was at least better than the atheistic alternative (Goldman 1997, p. 5). Given his unambiguous affirmation of a God having reason and intelligence (these concepts are difficult to comprehend apart from a Mind), perhaps the most reasonable conclusion is that, although Einstein did not accept the full package of the personal God, his God was minimally personal (at least not impersonal).

## *3. The Intelligibility of the World*

Einstein's reflection on the scientific enterprise also generated a sense of wonder. Although Einstein was very much against miracles, as violations of the natural order, he thought the intelligibility of the natural order itself was a miracle: the comprehensibility of the world was itself incomprehensible. Einstein mentioned this point in his letter to Solovine on January 1, 1951 (Einstein 1956, p. 102). Solovine's Machist reply to Einstein provoked another letter on March 30, 1952: "You find it surprising that I think of the comprehensibility of the world ... as a miracle or an eternal mystery. But surely, a priori, one should expect the world to be chaotic, not to be grasped by thought in any way ... the 'miracle' ... becomes more and more evident as our knowledge develops ... here is the weak point of ... atheists ... Curiously, we have to be resigned to recognizing the 'miracle' without having any legitimate way of getting any further. I have to add the last point explicitly, lest you think that weakened by age I have fallen into the hands of the priest" (Einstein 1956, p. 115).

So although Einstein instinctively felt that this problem showed the "weak point" of atheism, he did not want to draw an explicitly religious conclusion. But, of course, the comprehensibility of the world is only a miracle in a naturalistic world. If we assume theism, then this is something to be expected, and in fact this is exactly the pioneers' "deep conviction of the rationality of the universe," that Einstein himself refers to. The argument from intelligibility will be explored later.

For Einstein, scientific discovery was not a mechanistic process (Einstein 1949, p. 36). He was a scientific genius exactly because he could blend to an extraordinary degree those highly distilled powers of intellect, intuition, and imagination that are rarely combined in one mind. His discovery was heavily guided by considerations of beauty, the invariable, absolute, geometrical beauty of nature in particular. The starting point of his two theories of relativity "was not a positivist aggravation with experimental incongruities, but a burning desire to safeguard the beauty of nature and of laws which reflected that beauty...The simple beauty of Maxwell's equations was safeguarded by according to them the utmost generality, which in turn imposed a most specific singularity, the invariable constancy of the speed of light" (Jaki 1978, p. 188).

For Einstein, "genuine scientific knowledge about the cosmos was not sensory evidence, but a cosmic leap beyond the sensory. The scientific reliability of that leap filled him with the greatest wonder" (Jaki 1978, p. 192). His case also manifests the marvelous inventiveness of the human mind. The merging of aesthetic factors (beauty and symmetry) and philosophical insights with empirical considerations in scientific theorizing shows that aesthetic experience, intellectual experience, and scientific experience are closely linked, again manifesting the coherence of the rainbow of experiences.

### 4. Einstein's Religious Experiences

No doubt Einstein had some religious experiences, mainly in the forms of nature mysticism (but not the monistic type), experience of design, and aesthetic-TE. "The fairest thing we can experience is the mysterious. It is the fundamental emotion which stands at the cradle of true art and true science. He who knows it not and can no longer wonder, no longer feel amazement, is as good as dead, a snuffed-out candle. It was the experience of mystery...A knowledge of the existence of something we cannot penetrate, of the manifestations of the profoundest reason and the most radiant beauty...in this sense, and in this sense alone, I am a deeply religious man" (Einstein 1949, p. 5).

When Einstein encountered nature through his sense experiences and scientific pursuits, he was struck by feelings and experiences of wonder, mystery, beauty, sublimity, and intelligibility. The experience was at the same time intellectual, aesthetic, and religious. It seems that when Einstein explored the depth of the natural world, he saw the convergence of Truth and Beauty, and this suggested a Mysterious Source of all things. This was perhaps an implicit experience of God as Incarnate Reason, which was never presented as an inference. Einstein talked about the sense of the religious (and not a religious belief) that depended on the experience of grasping the intricate world order. He mentioned feelings of awe. Those atheists who did not have this kind of experience were likened to people who "cannot hear the music of the spheres" (Goldman 1997, p. 5). All these are clearly experiential categories.

Einstein's unorthodox attitudes toward traditional religion help to show that his religious experiences were not constructed out of his prior religious indoctrination. They seemed to be a spontaneous response to the wonderful world he encountered through his scientific study. In fact, he often tried to dissociate himself from the idea of personal God, but apparently in the end he found the idea of God unavoidable.

### 5. Conclusion: Einstein and Spiritual Existence

Einstein himself was not an enemy of religion. Not only do religion and science not conflict, "religious feeling" in fact also goes hand in hand with "the profounder sort of scientific minds!" This picture seems very different from that portrayed by the atheist scientist Richard Dawkins.

At the turn of this millennium, Einstein was chosen by *Time* to be the Person of the Century: "As the century's greatest thinker, as an immigrant who fled from oppression to freedom, as a political idealist, he best embodies what historians will regard as significant about the twentieth century. And as a philosopher with faith both in science and in the beauty of God's handiwork, he personifies the legacy that has been bequeathed to the next century" (Issacson 1999, p. 20). Einstein was familiar with the rainbow of experiences in his own life, and he advocated "a reverence for everything spiritual" (Einstein 1949, p. 91). Indeed, Einstein, as one of the most eminent scientists in human history, was a witness to the spiritual nature of human beings, rather than to narrow empiricism. He understood and respected the human search for meaning (Goldman 1997, pp. 109–10). For Einstein, what should guide our lives are not utilitarian ends (such as ease and happiness), but the transcendentals: "The ideals which have lighted me on my way and time after time given me new courage to face life cheerfully, have been Truth, Goodness, and Beauty" (Einstein 1949, p. 2).

He admitted that science was insufficient to guide our lives, because it could not satisfy the whole soul! (Goldman 1997, p. 108). The basic problem was that "science...cannot create ends and, even less, instill them in human beings; science, at most, can supply the means by which to attain certain ends. But the ends themselves are conceived by personalities with lofty ethical ideals" (Einstein 1993, p. 2). It seems that Einstein was, indeed sensitive to the rainbow of experiences. It is pretty ironic that, as a scientist, Einstein's attitude is so different from those narrow empiricists who dismiss our experiences of subjectivity, morality, and the transcendent—all in the name of science!

### 9.2.5 *The Witness of Other Scientists*

The vivid experiences of other famous scientists show that Einstein is not alone. For example, we can listen to Heisenberg:

> When one reduces experimental results to formalized expressions...one has a feeling of having oneself invented these formulae...However, when one stumbles upon these very simple, great connections which are finally fixed into an axiomatic system the whole thing appears in a different light. Then our inner eye is suddenly opened to a connection which has always been there—also without us—and which is quite obviously not created by man. (quoted by Pedersen 1989, p. 133)

Here we find scientists having a feeling of awe and wonder before the beautiful and intelligible natural order, which is disclosed in the scientific experience. There is a sense that we are facing a mystery, a *Numen* that fascinates us. There is also the sense that "Reality is self-communicative, and scientific rationality is not a purely human product" (Pedersen 1989, p. 134). There is also the feeling that science is a *gift*, but

> To receive something as a gift must be the prerogative of personal beings. To recognise a part of the outcome of science as a gift is, therefore, to admit that our relationship with nature has at least one feature in common with personal relationships, and that the knowing subject is more intimately connected with the known object than the metaphor of "finding" is able to convey. (Pedersen 1989, pp. 134–5)

There seems to be deeper dimensions of the scientific experience, which sometimes amount to an ecstatic experience or a mystical insight.

### 9.2.6 *Convergence of Beauty and Intelligibility*

I think the most important aspect of the depth dimension of scientific experience is the convergence of beauty and intelligibility. As the theoretical physicist Paul Davies says: "In some cases, when the road ahead may be unclear, mathematical beauty and elegance guide the way. It is something the physicist feels intuitively, a sort of irrational faith that nature prefers the beautiful to the ugly. So far this belief has been a reliable and powerful travelling companion" (Davies 1984, p. 53).

Examples include the "undoubted beauty of Euclidean geometry...[the] extraordinary elegance of Newtonian dynamics, with its deep and beautiful underlying symplecitc geometry structure... [t]he mathematical form of Maxwell's electromagnetism...[the] supreme mathematical beauty of Einstein's general relativity...the extraordinary mathematical elegance of quantum-mechanical spin, of Dirac's relativistic wave equation, and of the path-integral formalism of QFT as developed by Feynman" (Penrose 2007, p. 1038).

So apparently "Beauty and Truth are intertwined, the beauty of a physical theory acting as a guide to its correctness in relation to the Physical World" (Penrose 2007, p. 1029). The implications of this convergence of beauty and truth will be explored below.

## 9.3  Coherence of Experience of the Natural World with Theistic Experience

### 9.3.1  The Reliability of Sense Experience

We have mentioned the a priori principles inbuilt into our brains. Can evolution provide an adequate explanation for this? True, correct perception would help survival, but is this a reason for us to *expect* the evolution of such intricate processing machinery equipped with correct a priori principles? I argue below that the evolutionary explanation is possible, but not a strong one.

It is interesting that, far from using Darwinism to support the reliability of SE, some people think that Darwinism may tend to throw doubt on it. Even committed evolutionary naturalist Patricia Churchland says, "There is a fatal tendency to think of the brain as essentially in the fact-finding business... [However,] looked at from an evolutionary point of view, the principal function of nervous systems is to get the body parts where they should be in order that the organism may survive... truth, whatever that is, definitely takes the hindmost" (cited in Fodor 1998, p. 191). Plantinga has also made an evolutionary argument against naturalism, which is widely discussed (Kvanvig 1996). Jerry Fodor has provided a critique of both Churchland and Plantinga, and argues that evolutionary theory does not throw doubt on SE or science (Fodor 1998, p. 190).

I do not intend to defend Plantinga's argument here. I want to argue for the more modest claim that the reliability of SE is more coherent with theism than naturalism. Here we can note that Fodor's position is that evolution is basically *neutral* about the reliability of our beliefs on the whole: "It is... the adaptivity of the beliefs, and not their truth per se, that evolution cares about... the fact that evolution chose us isn't, in and of itself, a reason for thinking that we're true believers. There is... no Darwinian reason for thinking that we're true believers. Or that we aren't... Darwin isn't in the epistemology business, and evolution doesn't care whether most of our beliefs are true... it just doesn't give a damn" (Fodor 1998, p. 201). In fact, Fodor has general doubts about whether Darwinian natural selection can satisfactorily explain the mind: "I'm not actually an adaptationist about the mind; I doubt... that Darwinism is true of the phylogeny of cognition... our kinds of minds are quite likely 'hopeful monsters,' which is why there are so few of them" (Fodor 1998, p. 190). However, none of these shakes Fodor's faith in scientism.

For the orthodox Darwinists, the appeal to hopeful monsters (which is fundamentally an appeal to gigantic good luck), of course, is hopeless. So Fodor's position lends support to my claim that even if the evolutionary explanation of the reliability of SE is possible, it does not give us a reason to expect it. On the other hand, the reliability of SE is to be expected if theism is true. In itself, this point is not too strong, but it can be added to the other points, which are more forceful. Anyway, we need to remember that it is a fallacy to argue from "Darwinism doesn't imply that most of our beliefs are false" to "it's therefore likely that most of our beliefs are true." Unfortunately, many Darwinists seem to presuppose this fallacious inference.

The basic weakness of evolutionary explanations of cognition stems from the fact that the Darwinist process cannot distinguish true believers from false believers, as long as both have adaptive behavior. So the Darwinists *always* need a further premise: given the behavioral success of some beliefs, it is much more likely that they are generally true than generally false. This premise has various degrees of plausibility, depending on the type of beliefs under consideration. For SEs about daily life, this premise is perhaps not obviously implausible (but can still be challenged by arguments). For other beliefs, such as necessary truths and mathematics, this premise will be less plausible or even wildly implausible. I'll come to the latter point below. Edward Stein compares natural selection to a porous filter because "selection cannot distinguish between knowledge and mere useful opinion…selection as a filter…is too porous to precipitate only true theories" (Stein 1990, p. 122).

The above point can be brought out by distinguishing these two claims:

1. The possession of generally reliable sense organs is a sufficient condition for adaptivity.

2. The possession of generally reliable sense organs is a necessary condition for adaptivity.

In general, it is difficult to establish a claim like (2), because there are so many ways to survive and to adapt to the environment. In particular, we can point to the existence of innumerable species of plants to refute (2). So it is a fallacy to infer from (1) to (2). But something close to (2) is needed for a strong evolutionary explanation of the reliability of SE.

So "we cannot conclude that the origin of scientific methodology lies in its adaptive value to the human species…. The most we can conclude, on biological grounds, is that the features in question are not positively maladaptive…we need some independent means of determining which patterns are or are not adaptive—independent of whether or not they tend to survive" (Bradie 1990, p. 36). But there are general difficulties for us to do that: "The evolutionary history of the mind and its abilities is too little understood for any view to take independent comfort from the support of Darwinian lines of reasoning…. Reconstructing phylogenies is hard enough when the evidence is physical" (Bradie 1990, p. 37).

### 9.3.2 The Beauty of the Natural World

#### 1. The Argument from Natural Beauty

F. R. Tennant (1956) formulates an aesthetic argument for theism that has been defended by Swinburne (1979) and Mark Wynn (1999). This is not supposed to be a proof. For example, Swinburne only claims that it is an inductive argument that raises the probability of theism. It is enough for our purpose to show that natural beauty on the whole is more coherent with theism than with naturalism.

Tennant avoids the discussions about human art works and focuses on the saturation of Nature with beauty. In contrast, man's productions (other than professed works of art) are aesthetically vile. Theism seems to be an obvious explanation of this fact: nature is expected to be beautiful if it is the work of the Divine Mind, and more particularly of a mind attuned to aesthetic kinds of fulfillment. So natural beauty is some evidence for theism.

Tennant anticipates an obvious rejoinder: the denial of the objectivity of aesthetic judgment. However, he claims that this controversial question is irrelevant to his argument: "For the doctrine that aesthetic value is constituted by feeling does not imply that the feeling is not objectively evoked, as if we could see beauty when and where we chose...Thus diverse theories as to the constitution of beauty may be said to have in common the implication that the ontal world is ultimately responsible for the evocation of aesthetic thrills and sentiments" (Tennant 1956, pp. 89–90). The idea is that even if aesthetic judgment is by nature subjective, for example, constituted by a form of human sensibility, we still need to explain the fact that various aspects of nature, though not objectively beautiful in themselves, can still evoke the proper aesthetic feelings from our human sensibility.

Let me distinguish four different world scenarios:

W1.   Aesthetic sensibility exists in the world, and the world is judged by that kind of aesthetic sensibility to be saturated with beauty.
W2.   Nothing like aesthetic sensibility exists in the world.
W3.   Aesthetic sensibility exists in the world, and the world is judged by that kind of aesthetic sensibility to be largely devoid of beauty.
W4.   Aesthetic sensibility exists in the world, and the world is judged by that kind of aesthetic sensibility to be largely ugly.

There is no assumption that aesthetic properties objectively belong to the world, though it is not denied, either. Both Tennant and Swinburne think that obviously W1 is a correct description of our actual world. Let us suppose this is right. Then the obvious question is why should W1 obtain, when all four world scenarios are possible.

Especially in the naturalistic world, objective aesthetic values are not likely to exist, and hence they cannot have causal effects on the world. It is *conceivable* that somehow W1 obtains, but there is no particular reason that this should happen, because W2 and W3 are equally likely, if not more likely. In a naturalistic world, nothing much depends on which scenario obtains as far as survival is concerned. Suppose genuine aesthetic sensibility, which admits of rational discussions, is confined to the human species alone. Then W2 was the correct description of our world before the emergence of human beings. Aesthetic sensibility seems to be an accident that is largely epiphenomenal or redundant. Just remember the fact that millions of biological species (in fact, all except one) manage to survive pretty well without the blessing of aesthetic sensibility. So any evolutionary explanation that ties biological survival to aesthetic sensibility too strongly needs to explain another fact: the overwhelming majority of the biological organisms manage to go without the alleged survival advantage conferred by aesthetic sensibility completely. So it is most likely that aesthetic sensibility is a spandrel.

If evolutionists admit that aesthetic sensibility is a spandrel, say, the by-product of a beneficial mutation, then they should also admit they cannot predict the particular shape of this spandrel. Let us compare the existing world to a lock with a definite structure. Then the emergent key of aesthetic sensibility may fit the lock or not. Since the shape of the lock has been fixed before the appearance of the key, and the key is supposed to be generated by a random process (with absolutely no idea what the lock is like at all), it is quite improbable that such a key will fit the lock. After all, it stands to reason that there are vastly many more ways the key will not fit the lock than there are ways the key will fit the lock. So W3 seems more likely than W1.

It may look as if W4 should be less likely than the other scenarios, because living in an ugly world makes one's survival very unpleasant. But we cannot be sure of this judgment because the evolutionary psychologists have an impressive track record of creative theorizing. Suppose W4 were the actual world. Do you really think that it would be beyond the capacity of an E. O. Wilson or Robert Wright in W4 to produce an evolutionary explanation of the ugliness of that world? I guess not. I can imagine Wilson in W4 writing a book called *Biophobia*, which produces a selectionist explanation such as this: since the human species finds ugliness everywhere, it poses a challenge and provokes a desire to refashion our world into a beautiful world. This, in turn, will stimulate the development of our rational power and technology. Of course, if this explanation fails, there is always the possibility of a spandrel "explanation." After all, we have to live in this world, and hence sooner or later we have to get used to the ugliness that surrounds us. Once the feeling of discomfort is reduced to a tolerable level, I cannot see any substantial disadvantage incurred here, since this is not likely to affect our reproductive activities. Anyway, even if the experience of ugliness incurs a slight disadvantage, it is always possible that this will be more than compensated by the positive effects of the beneficial mutation that is supposed to produce the spandrel of aesthetic sensibility in the first place.

If you object that this is a just-so story without empirical corroboration, and hence has little intrinsic credibility, then you are objecting to one basic game rule of evolutionary psychology. I am, in fact, sympathetic to this objection, but I do not want to assume this at this stage of the argument.

The reason is that without rejecting the current practice of evolutionary psychology and disputing the evolutionary explanations currently offered for W1, I can still argue for my favored conclusion. My strategy is to assume the success of the naturalistic project of evolutionary psychology. Then I argue that exactly because it is successful (maybe too successful), all scenarios from W1 to W4 are equally likely, and hence evolutionary naturalism does not lead us to expect one over the others.

So my conclusion is that, from the naturalistic perspective, there is no particular reason that W1 should obtain rather than W2 to W4. However, the theist has much more reason to expect W1, rather than the others. So the obtaining of W1 is better explained by theism than by naturalism. In Swinburne's words, "God has reason, apparently overriding reason, for making, not merely any orderly world...but a beautiful world...also...he would seem to have overriding reason not to make a basically ugly world beyond the powers of creatures to improve...A priori, however, there is no particular reason for expecting a basically beautiful rather than a basically ugly world. In consequence, if the world is beautiful, that fact would be evidence for God's existence" (Swinburne 1979, p. 150). This seems to be a plausible argument.

## 2. The Hypothesis of Biophilia

Currently one of most popular naturalistic explanations of aesthetic experience is offered by E. O. Wilson in his book *Biophilia*, which argues that our felt affinity for the natural environment is explicable in terms of the role such an environment played in our evolution. For example, Robert Hinde notes that not only aesthetic experience, but also "mystical experiences are often triggered by natural beauty," and that "people prefer natural to artificial landscapes." His explanation is that "the appeal of some natural landscapes...is due to mechanisms developed early in the evolution of our species...Among landscapes, savannah is particularly attractive...Savannah was almost certainly the environment of early human evolution, and certain characteristic features of savannah would have provided conditions conducive to survival, such as vantage points and hiding places" (Hinde 1999, pp. 187–8).

Plausible as it sounds, this theory of biophilia, in fact, can only explain severely limited aspects of our aesthetic experience, and has been sharply criticized by Wynn and O'Hear (2008). Let us first list out various things we find beautiful in the natural world:

B1. The beauty of the basic natural laws.
B2. The beauty of the microscopic structure of a physical thing that can only be revealed under the microscope, for example, snowflakes, the double helix of DNA molecules.
B3. The beauty of the visible forms of animals and plants.
B4. The beauty of the visible forms of things that we can come into contact with, for example, mountains, savannah.

B5. The beauty of the visible forms of things that we cannot come into contact with, for example, the starry sky, the rainbow.

B6. The beauty of the visible forms of things that are too large or too distant for us to perceive in ordinary situations, for example, the blue planet earth as seen from a satellite, the Andromeda as seen by the telescope.

It is obvious that the biophilia hypothesis is basically inapplicable to B1, B2, B5, and B6. These counterexamples are enough to demonstrate its fundamental inadequacy. The only realms to which it may be applicable are B3 and B4. Critics may challenge that aesthetic experiences such as B5 may be biologically useful. For instance, the beauty of the starry heaven will induce an interest in the stars, which has been useful for purposes of gauging the approach of dawn. This response is weak because "it does not identify...clearly a vital connection between some feature of the world and our prospects of survival" (Wynn 1999, p. 32). I would add that the interest in the movement of the stars is more a scientific interest, than an aesthetic interest. It is quite conceivable that a Kepler or Tycho can maintain a keen scientific interest in the movement of the stars with a view to finding out their underlying patterns without the slightest aesthetic appreciation of the starry sky.

Consider aesthetic experiences such as B3. It might be suggested that we find cockroaches ugly because this will cause us to hate them and to exterminate them. This may be beneficial for our survival. However, it is difficult to see how the beauty or ugliness of flowers, for example, are in any obvious sense related to our survival. Moreover, we in fact find some dangerous predators of human beings beautiful, for example, lions and tigers (we even love to wear their skins!).

Consider aesthetic experiences such as B4. It has to be pointed out that some dangerous places, such as a desert, may also possess sublime beauty. Lakes are beautiful and look peaceful, but we can drown in them if we do not stay away. Isn't it more fitting for lakes to repel us so that we are kept safe? As Wynn points out: "we have a tendency to value aesthetically landscapes which are basically hostile to human well-being, or at any rate far removed qualitatively from the savannah type of natural environment...our appreciation of them [desert and ice landscapes] is not easily related to any drive for self-preservation" (Wynn 1999, p. 32). My feeling is that all these discussions seem largely irrelevant, because it is difficult to believe that the degree of survival-conduciveness is the key to the treasure house of aesthetic experiences!

In any case, evolutionary psychology's biological approach to aesthetic experience has not met with any consensus. Many critics point out that this biological approach is fundamentally flawed, because it has ignored the cultural influence on our aesthetic judgments and the human capacity for creativity. Charles Jencks once attended a lecture by Wilson, and he afterwards wrote a satirical response. His conclusion is that "all periods hunt for new beauty; all art at least partly focuses on the expressive plane...There will always be a key part of the expressive language that is emergent, new, novel...and it will never be reducible to hard or soft-wiring within *Homo sapiens*. Every good artist has known this truth: that creativity concerns moves made within the language of art, independent of the neurocircuitry that responds to it...we must acknowledge the deep truth of emergence and limited creativity...we can never reduce behavior to nature, nurture or their combination" (Jencks 2000, pp. 52–3).

In view of all these criticisms, Wynn's conclusion seems to be sound: "Tennant's argument remains, in large part, cogent...evolutionary mechanisms seem to offer at most a partial explanation of...our aesthetic appreciation of the natural would" (Wynn 1999, p. 33).

### 9.3.3 The Argument from Intelligibility

Let us consider why the world is intelligible. Wigner talks of the existence of science as a puzzle: "Surely, our science was not necessary to assure man's survival in the Darwinian sense. No other animal has developed a science even vaguely similar to ours—it is not needed for survival" (cited in Elvee 1982, p. 123). Furthermore, the development of science, in particular physics, is miraculous:

> every step in its development shows that the preceding theory was valid only approximately, and valid approximately only under certain conditions. Newton's theory is valid with a high accuracy if only gravitational forces play a role, all pre-quantum theories are valid only for macroscopic bodies and for these only under certain conditions. It is *lucky* that such special conditions exist under which simplified approximate theories present a wonderfully good approximation.... General relativity would not have been invented, not even by Einstein, had the original theory of gravitation not existed.... it was a wonderful *gift* to be provided with situations in which the laws of nature in very simplified form were excellent approximations. (in Elvee 1982, p.124; italics mine)

In a similar vein, Benjamin Wilker and Jonathan Witt argue that we cannot take the periodic table for granted, but without something like this, the development of chemistry is basically impossible: "The periodic table itself is a masterpiece of order, precision and intellectual beauty, and order that appears designed for both life and discovery...in the way the order of the elements has wrung from great scientific minds their best efforts and only then yielded up its secrets, the genius of the elements would seem also to have had in mind not merely life, but specifically the development of human genius" (Wilker and Witt 2006, p. 27). So one condition for the intelligibility of the world is the specific forms they take.

Moreover, our intellectual capacity, which is another condition for the intelligibility of the world, is also surprising. Putnam has pointed out the prima facie implausibility of evolutionary explanations of our intellectual abilities:

> our intellectual abilities were, according to evolutionists, essentially as they are today...According to the current scientific view, all this latent intelligence (for

learning calculus and physics) was the result of natural selection.... We are, on this view, computing machines programmed by blind evolution—computing machines programmed by a fool! For evolution *is* a fool as far as knowing about calculus, or proving theorems, or making up physical theories, or inventing telephones is concerned.... selection pressure would naturally weed out members of the different humanoid species who could not learn to hunt deer, use stone axes and spears...But there was no selection pressure for being able to make up scientific theories—that was not something *any* member of the several humanoid species did *then*. So that a device molded by selection pressure to do the one thing should be able to do the other is quite a miracle—exactly as if we set a fool (who knew about hunting with stone axes and spears) to program a computer and he programmed it so that it could *also* discover the theory of relativity. (Putnam 1990, pp. 158–9)

Perhaps evolutionists can appeal to Stephen Jay Gould's famous idea of spandrels. Gould himself believes that "if any organ is...replete with spandrels the human brain must be our finest candidate...the nonadaptationist principle of spandrels may still dominate human nature...Many, if not most, universal behaviors are probably spandrels, often coopted later in human history for important secondary functions. The human brain is the most complicated device for reasoning and calculating, and for expressing emotion...most of our mental properties and potentials may be spandrels—that is, nonadaptive side consequences of building a device with such structural complexity" (Gould 2000, p. 124).

However, Putnam is critical of this kind of appeal to "concomitant variation": "Nature—which imposed the constraints on how neural connections could be manufactured and installed—does not even have the pseudo-'intelligence' that selection pressure does;...nature has no *ends*, and does not simulate having any.... So it is as if selection pressure—the fool that programmed us—had to operate subject to constraints imposed by a *moron*. And it just happened that the moron imposed such lucky constraints that the only way the fool could program us involved making us intelligent enough to do mathematics, discover general relativity, and so on!...'concomitant variation' is just a fancy name for *coincidence*" (Putnam 1990, p. 159). It seems to me that "spandrel" is another fancy name that has gained respectability.

Steven Mithen has tried to explain how the capacity for scientific thinking has developed in the evolutionary history. He argues that our ancestors needed to employ the key elements of scientific thinking for their survival. These elements are detailed and extensive observation of the natural world; the generation of hypotheses that have the potential for falsification; a concern with causation; the use of tools to extend human perception and cognition, tools which may be no more complex than a pencil and paper (or calculator, computer, telescope, or microscope); the use of metaphor and analogy to facilitate scientific thought and to aid communication (Mithen 2002, p. 24).

I think this argument is woefully inadequate, because it has only scratched the surface of the problem. What he talks about are very elementary or low-level cognitive tasks, and it is relatively easy for us to envisage how they evolved. The progress he surveys is also minimal when compared to the achievements of modern science in recent centuries! With only those capacities, it is very likely to expect very meager output from our science. It is hard to believe that what suffices for farming (one of the evolutionary contexts that Mithen appeals to) will inevitably lead to modern science. Many deep factors that make possible the development of modern science are not even mentioned, for example, our penchant for the deep explanations, the mysterious capacity for mathematics. In some sense, intelligence certainly has survival value, but this point in itself is not a satisfactory enough explanation of science:

> intelligence, in the sense of the ability to use language, manipulate tools, and so on, is not enough to enable a species to do science. It also has to have the right set of *prejudices*.... Suppose we have evolved...a firm prejudice against the unobservable.... Then we...could hunt deer...and so forth...Such a race...would not develop geometry, beyond the Egyptian level of practical land measurement, because the notion of a straight line with no thickness at all, or the notion of a point with no dimension at all, would make no sense to it. It would never speculate about atoms swarming in the void...it would never develop physics or mathematics! (Putnam 1990, p. 161)

Perhaps it is all a matter of good luck? But this is not true to the achievement of modern science: "Maybe what happens is that we just test one scientific hypothesis after another until by trial and error we come to the right one.... indeed, the history of science does not support the view that it was all trial and error...There does not seem to be anything common to all the good theories that scientists succeeded in producing except this: each was suggested by some line of thinking that seemed *reasonable*...Science is arrived at by...plausible reasoning that is often subjective, often controversial, but that, nevertheless, comes up with truths and approximate truths far more often than any trial-and error procedure could be expected to do" (Putnam 1990, p. 161).

Eugene Wigner, after surveying the development of modern physics, is deeply impressed by "the two miracles of the existence of laws of nature and of the human mind's capacity to divine them" (Wigner 1967, pp. 229–30). It is because "physics...would not be possible without a constant recurrence of miracles...[It is] surprising how readily the wonderful gift contained in the empirical law of epistemology was taken for granted. The ability of the human mind to form a string of 1000 conclusions and still remain 'right,' which was mentioned before, is a similar gift" (Wigner 1967, pp. 232–3). His conclusion is that "fundamentally, we do not know why our theories work so well...The miracle of the appropriateness of the language of mathematics for the formulation of the laws of physics is a wonderful gift which we neither understand nor deserve" (Wigner 1967, p. 237). Is the attribution of all these "miracles" to luck really plausible?

In addition to, Putnam's emphasis on our explanatory "prejudices" and plausible reasoning, let us contemplate the role of mathematics. In the realm of theoretical physics, the mathematical systems we use are so obviously human constructions (they are not determined by inputs from the world) that it is surprising that they seem to work so well. This prompts the remark about this "unreasonable effectiveness of mathematics" by a Nobel laureate, Eugene Wigner. Isn't it surprising that the evolutionary process did throw up human beings with such apparently useless (in the primitive jungles) capacities?

Michael Ruse (2003), a staunch evolutionary naturalist, tries to provide some answers to these puzzling questions. He believes that much of our cognitive machinery consists of innate dispositions: the "rules of mathematics and logic, the basic beliefs about causality and the like, the epistemic values...at some level are ingrained in our biology" (Ruse 2003, pp. 121–2). Of course, the general evolutionary strategy is to tie our cognitive capacity to survival. Quine has done that concerning induction: "Creatures inveterately wrong in their inductions have a pathetic but praiseworthy tendency to die before reproducing their kind" (Quine 1969, p. 126).

Ruse has tried to apply the same strategy to our mathematical and logical reasoning: "an intelligent primate that could see that three oranges were more than two oranges, or that thought that where two tigers were seen to enter a cave and but one emerged was a place of danger, or that simplicity is a virtue when a lion approaches, was ahead of a primate that did and thought none of these things. The proto-human who saw beaten down grass and blood stains and heard growls and who yet said, 'Tigers, just a theory not a fact', was less biologically fit than the proto-human who started running" (Ruse 2003, pp. 123–4).

But of course, the problem is how to traverse the almost *infinite* gap between the elementary capacity for counting oranges and tigers to mathematics that deal with the infinite or the infinitesimal (like transfinite arithmetic or calculus), not to mention Reimannian Geometry and the like. As J. W. Smith points out: "evolutionary considerations do not show that the world must be so mathematically accessible that its secrets can be reaped in a great and rich harvest which presumably contemporary mathematical physics has yielded. The world must encapsulate 'learnable' patterns...but this fact is consistent only with a very crude and basic mathematical accessibility of the world" (Smith 1988, p. 188). In fact, Ruse is aware of the limitations of the explanation he gives. He knows that it at most explains "the basic tools for building science," and the problem still remains of why, from these humble beginnings, the most sophisticated edifices of science can be built up. He himself raises these questions: how can biology lead to such insights as Fermat's Last Theorem, let alone its proof? "Why is it that one can peer so far into the mysteries of nature, given the rather crude principles that selection throws up? How can elementary principles of reasoning lead to higher mathematics...or to the understanding of the largest and smallest elements of possible experience?" (Ruse 2003, p. 130).

The best answer he comes up with is this: "it is generally not a good policy to assume that because we find something implausible natural selection will be likewise handicapped...science is built up from humble beginnings with initially simple tools, and you are stuck with this fact whether or not you think that it points to bigger things" (Ruse 2003, pp. 123–4). This is puzzling, but it is "simply something that the Darwinian has to accept as a given" (Ruse 2003, p. 130). In the end, he admits that mathematical beliefs are not necessary for survival at all: "whether on Andromeda, say, things would all be the same as here on earth seems to be speculative... Not that the Andromedans would have 2+2=5,...but that they might not think in such mathematical terms at all...I do not think that the Darwinian can throw much light on some of the ultimate metaphysical questions" (Ruse 2003, p. 132). I think we do not need to consider such a distant place as the Andromeda. Plenty of biological organisms on earth illustrate the same point. Ruse's discussions suggest, and he effectively admits above, that evolution cannot answer the question about the intelligibility of the world. Ruse seems open to the possibility of a religious explanation, and admits "perhaps religion can say something useful here." But he does not develop the point.

Now suppose our mathematical reasoning is grounded biologically in some kind of epigenetic rule or algorithm that was selected for by evolution. However, Penrose says: "there can have been no selective advantage to our remote ancestors for an ability to reason about very abstractly defined infinite sets, and infinite sets of infinite sets, etc. Those ancestors were concerned with...such things as the...design of mammoth traps" (Penrose 1995, p. 148).

The power of this algorithm to solve *unforeseen problems* is just astounding: "The algorithm would have to have encompassed...the potential for making precise discriminations, distinguishing valid from invalid arguments in all the, then, yet-to-be-discovered areas of mathematical activity that nowadays occupy the pages of mathematical research journals." The basic problem is: "How could the blind processes of natural selection, geared only to promote the survival of our remote ancestors, have been able to 'foresee' that such-and-such an unknowably sound computational procedure would be able to resolve obscure mathematical issues that had no relevance whatsoever to those survival issues?" (Penrose 1995, pp. 149–50).

Furthermore, it is even more surprising that considerations of elegance and beauty in mathematics work quite well. The most impressive example is Einstein's general relativity, which, according to Roger Penrose, shows the deep underlying unity between mathematics and the workings of the world: "When Einstein's theory was first put forward, there was really no need for it on observational grounds...In the early years after Einstein's theory was put forward, there were only a few effects that supported it, and the increase in precision over Newton's scheme was marginal...now, nearly 80 years after the theory was first produced, its overall precision has grown to something like ten million times greater. Einstein was not just 'noticing patterns' in the behaviour of physical objects. He was uncovering a profound mathematical substructure that was already hidden" (Penrose 1995, p. 415).

Even the atheist Nicholas Maxwell wonders at the mysterious problem of the unreasonable effectiveness of mathematics: "One especially mysterious feature of scientific discovery is the way in which mathematical ideas, developed, it would seem, independently of theoretical physics, nevertheless subsequently turn out to be exactly what is needed in order to delineate some aspect of physical phenomena. Thus Menaechmus, in 350 BC, invents the idea of conic sections…[e.g.] the circle, the hyperbola, the ellipse, and the parabola. Over 1,000 years later, Kepler discovers that the planets move in ellipses round the sun, while Galileo discovers that terrestrial projectiles move along parabolas. Again, Gauss and Riemann, in the nineteenth century, develop the idea of curved non-Euclidean or Riemannian space. Yet again, the mathematician David Hilbert develops the idea of 'Hilbert space', a 'space' of functions, a purely mathematical notion. Subsequently, it turns out that it is just this that is needed in order to formulate quantum theory. It almost seems that the minds of mathematicians and the nature of physical reality are mysteriously in harmony with one another" (Maxwell 1998, p. 74).

Penrose also dwells on this mystery: "More remarkable is the subtlety of the mathematics that seems to be involved in Nature's laws, and the habit that such mathematics seems to have in finding applications in areas far removed from its original purpose…[e.g.] calculus of Newton and Leibniz" (Penrose 2007, p. 1016). So "despite our distance from our intended goal, we have come to a remarkably impressive understanding of the operations of the universe at the deepest levels that we know" (Penrose 2007, p. 1034). But when we look back, we find that the magic of mathematics has played an indispensable role in this "miraculous" road to reality.

The theoretical physicist Polkinghorne argues that this surprising fact "finds coherent explanation in terms of natural theology" (Polkinghorne 1991, p. 28). Maxwell recognizes that theism can provide an answer: "if God exists, we can understand why the physical universe is comprehensible to us" (Maxwell 1998, p. 206). In the end, Maxwell is not a theist, because of the problem of evil, but his discussions suggest that the argument from intelligibility has independent force.

Putnam's "view is that the success of science cannot be anything but a puzzle as long as we view concepts and objects as radically independent" (Putnam 1990, p. 162). Putnam's solution is to assert that reality is partly constituted by *our* concepts. This seems counterintuitive. The theist seems able to offer a more natural explanation of this puzzle: the rapport of the mind with nature is due to the fact that both were derived from the same source, the Prime Reason, that is, God. This accounts for the surprising intelligibility of the world, while at the same time saves the strong realist intuition that reality is independent of *our* concepts. On the other hand, it can also accommodate the antirealist insight that reality and concepts are not ultimately separable: but the concepts in question are those of God, rather than ours.

### 9.3.4 The Multiple Convergence of Truth, Beauty, and Intelligibility

Let us summarize the data:

$e_1$  Our SE is reliable.
$e_2$  Our SE is adaptable for the enjoyment of aesthetic experience.
$e_3$  The natural world is beautiful at many levels.
$e_4$  The beauty of natural laws is one important truth-indicator.
$e_5$  Our cognitive capacities and dispositions are adaptable for significant scientific discovery of the truths of the natural world.
$e_6$  The form of the natural laws is adaptable for our scientific discovery.

I want to emphasize that the above data, from the naturalistic perspective, are independent of one another. Evolutionary naturalism perhaps has some reason (however slight) to expect $e_1$, but beyond that, to put it mildly, the natural world wonderfully exceeds all reasonable expectations. The beauty of the world, and our aesthetic experience of it, seem something extraneous to our survival. Moreover, our senses seem wonderfully equipped for aesthetic experience beyond expectation from the very beginning. A black-white vision can provide discriminative information relevant to our survival and the high-tech color vision that we possess is not necessary at all, not to mention the qualitative aspects of our SE. The beauty at the level of natural law and the beauty of physical forms in nature (microscopic and macroscopic) are also independent. There is no particular reason the laws have to be beautiful or elegant. The convergence of Truth and Beauty in our world is, itself, a mystery.

Another mystery is the convergence of cosmic rationality and human rationality. Even if humans have reliable sense organs or some elementary capacity for counting, there is no reason to expect that organisms that emerge from the struggle for survival in primitive jungles, or whatever evolutionary context, will develop sophisticated capacities for mathematics, logic, plausible reasoning, and a penchant for depth explanation. Moreover, even if humans do develop these capacities and dispositions accidentally, the universe has to "cooperate"—the natural laws may be too deep or complicated for us to grasp. But contrarily, the laws are not only intelligible to us, but, as Wigner suggests, the form of the basic laws is such that it can be approximated in successive stages by simpler laws, which are much easier for us to discover. So the deep truth of the natural world seems adaptable for our science before we emerge on the scene. All these, I suggest, are conundrums in the naturalistic world. The problem is aggravated by the "miraculous" coordination of several realms.

Roger Penrose has a keen awareness of the magnitude of the problems here, although he does not adopt the theistic solution. He considers these three worlds: the world of our consciousness, the physical world, and the Platonic world of mathematical forms. The mystery is manifold: first, the "mystery of why such precise and profoundly mathematical laws play such an important role in the behaviour of the physical world. Somehow the very world of physical reality seems almost mysteriously to emerge out of the Platonic world of mathematics." The second mystery is "how it is that perceiving beings can arise from out of the physical world. How is it that subtly organized material objects can mysteriously conjure up mental entities from out of its material substance?...[There is also the] mystery of how it is that mentality is able seemingly to 'create' mathematical concepts out of some kind of mental model. These apparently vague, unreliable, and often inappropriate mental tools...appear nevertheless mysteriously able...to conjure up abstract mathematical forms" (Penrose 1995, pp. 413–4).

In a later book, Penrose continues to contemplate these mysteries: "Why...each of three worlds—Plationic-mathematical, physical, and mental—has its own kind of reality and where each is (deeply and mysteriously) founded in the one that precedes it...where each seems to be able to encompass the succeeding one in its entirety, while itself seeming to depend only upon a small part of its predecessor"? (Penrose 2007, p. 1029).

Penrose believes that there is a deeper truth: "No doubt there are not really three worlds but *one*, the true nature of which we do not even glimpse at present" (Penrose 1995, p. 420). My proposal is that to solve the problem of coordination, we need to have a unitary source that has access to all three worlds and also the power to shape the natural world and the mental world. It seems that only God can do that. Moreover, the convergence of Truth and Beauty, and the convergence of cosmic rationality and human rationality, are to be expected on theism. In light of $H_t$, it can be seen to be part of God's purpose: our relationship with him is partly realized by rational pursuit of an understanding of this created world and our aesthetic enjoyment of the world as a wonderful gift from God. All the pieces of data and their coordination can be explained. Hence, it seems to me $P(e_1.e_2 \ldots e_6/H_t)$ is greater than $P(e_1.e_2 \ldots e_6/H_n)$, and these data relatively confirm theism.

## 9.4 Conclusion

Narrow empiricists believe that SE and science are on their side. In this chapter, I pointed out that from the intrinsic features of SE to the deliverances of SE about the natural world, we are everywhere confronted by "mystery," which also seems to point to a transcendent realm. SE is, in fact, the friend of the CTA.

# CHAPTER 10

# EXPERIENCE OF SELF, CRITICAL TRUST, AND GOD

## 10.1 Introduction: Do I Have a Self?

Nothing seems more certain to us than the fact that we exist, that is, our selves exist. The father of modern philosophy, Descartes, makes the existence of the self (*cogito*) the foundation of his philosophy. Many philosophers are self-enthusiasts. For example, J. B. Pratt says: "We know *that* the self is, and we know *what* it is by observing what it does. And this we know because every theory of the inner life which fails to recognize a knower and actor does violence to the facts of experience" (Pratt 1937, pp. 311–12). However, there is a great controversy among philosophers about the reality of the self. Especially among analytic philosophers of mind or cognitive scientists, the voice of the naturalists who want to deconstruct the self seems to be dominant. Similarly, scholars in Continental philosophy are celebrating with the postmodern gurus like Foucault about the death of Self. Of course, it is already anticipated by Nietzsche: "'The doer' is merely a fiction added to the deed—the deed is everything... our entire science still lies under the misleading influence of language and has not disposed of that little changeling, the 'subject'" (quoted in Sorabji 2006, p. 18).

Here I am mainly concerned about two challenges by narrow empiricists. First, they think that the self is extremely elusive, unobservable and, in the end, nowhere to be found. Second, they believe that the "self" cannot be integrated with our current scientific understanding of the world, and seems to be the leftover of ancient superstition.

### 10.1.1 The Humean Argument from Experience

For Hume, "self or person is not any one impression, but that to which our several impressions and ideas are supposed to have a reference. If any impression gives rise to the idea of self, that impression must continue invariably the same, through the whole course of our lives; since life is supposed to exist after that manner. But there is no impression constant and invariable." He further claimed, "For my part, when I enter most intimately into what I call *myself*, I always stumble on some particular perception or other, of heat or cold, light or shade, love or hatred, pain or pleasure. I never can catch *myself* without a perception, and never can observe any thing but the perception.... I may venture to affirm of the rest of mankind, that they are nothing but a bundle or collection of different perceptions, which succeed each other with an inconceivably rapidity, and are in a perpetual flux and movement" (in Perry 1975, pp. 161–2). Many think Hume has established that a self, even if it exists, is experientially inaccessible.

### 10.1.2 *The Naturalists' Arguments from Science*

The naturalists are prone to reject the "illusion" of self, especially when the self is interpreted as an immaterial ego or immortal soul—these and related ideas are just too spooky to accept. Owen Flanagan thinks "that the self is a construct, a model...The illusion is that there are two things: on one side, a self, an ego, an 'I,' that organizes experience, originates action, and accounts for our unchanging identity as persons and, on the other side, the stream of experience...The better view is that what there is, and all there is, is the stream of experience." So the relentless conclusion is that "We are egoless"—although Flanagan admits, "This, of course, sounds crazy" (Flanagan 1992, pp. 177–8).

By "self" I mean an enduring subject of experience, something that has a certain experience or mental state with a capacity for first-person Perspective (FPP). The self as a basic subject needs to be distinguished from the self as an existential subject—an "I" in search of coherence, value, and meaning in life (see the next chapter). I do not intend to argue for a very specific understanding of the self here. For those who agree that there are selves, some think they must be immaterial substances, while others think they are necessarily embodied subjects (Richard Sorabji), or constituted by (but not reducible to) the physical body (Lynne Baker). My aim here is limited: to argue that there is good experiential evidence for the existence of the self as a basic subject.

## 10.2  Is the Self Experientially Inaccessible?

We can properly speak of experiences of selves and the fact that this type of experience is actually closely connected with other kinds of experience, including sense experience. What do I mean by an "experience of self"? It means nothing other than the epistemic seemings that one has about oneself. As a matter of fact, I have a large number of spontaneous epistemic seemings about myself, for example, "It (epistemically) seems to me that I am depressed," "It (epistemically) seems to me that I am thinking about my mother." It seems that nothing can be more banal than the fact that we have experiences of selves.

### 10.2.1 *Evaluating Hume's Criticisms*

The meaning of "experiential accessibility" varies in different accounts of "experience." On Hume's view, experience is nothing but a set of discrete, atomistic sense impressions. So when Hume says that the self is experientially inaccessible, it means only that he can't find a constant sense impression that can correspond to his self. I, indeed, think this is correct, but given the same understanding of experience, it is also doubtful whether tables or chairs are experientially accessible. There is also no single, constant sense impression that can be identified with, say, a table. So Hume's phenomenalist approach to experience itself faces general difficulties. In Part A, I argued that we can understand an experience as a spontaneous epistemic seeming, and so far I only contend that we have experiences of selves in this sense. Nothing in Hume's arguments seems to threaten my contention. Indeed if we look at Hume's passage, it seems obvious that despite his failure to find a sense impression *of* self, he continues to have epistemic seemings about his *self*. If he doesn't, it would be difficult to make sense of how he can go about doing what he intends to do.

This problem is brought out nicely by Chisholm: "How can he say that he doesn't find himself—if he is correct in saying that he finds himself to be stumbling...on certain things and not to be stumbling on certain other things?" (Chisholm 1969, p. 10). "What Hume found, then, was not merely the particular perceptions, but also the fact that *he* found those perceptions as well as the fact that *he* failed to find certain other things. And these are findings with respect to himself" (Chisholm 1969, pp. 11–12). We have to ask why Hume, who professed not to believe in the existence of his own self, reported his "discovery" in the way he did? The natural explanation is that Hume did have spontaneous epistemic seemings about and continuous awareness of himself during his "unsuccessful" search for himself.

Clack, a critic of Chisholm, argues that "If Hume 'finds' himself in any sense it is not as something *observed* but as something *presupposed*. The (necessary) inclusion of 'I' in Hume's account of his situation when he tries to locate the self within experience does not entail he is, all the while, observing this I...Hume's use of 'I' is...testimony to the primitive, fundamental role in our language of the first-person pronoun" (Clack 1973, p. 341). Clack's sharp distinction between presupposing something and observing something in experience seems sustainable only in a broadly phenomenalistic analysis of experience, and it cannot plausibly be drawn given Chisholm's more propositional interpretation of acquaintance. As William James, one of the major self-antirealists, admits: "each of us spontaneously considers that by 'I,' he means something always the same" (quoted in Flanagan 1992, p. 184). This is consonant with our experience of the self.

### 10.2.2 Does the "Self" Come from a Misunderstanding of Language?

Some charge that the self-realists must have been misled by the language. For example, Harre has claimed that it is the "lack of sophistication that leads some to take entity-like self-talk seriously as metaphysics. It is, though, a sophisticated lack of sophistication, since it is just the error of assuming that every substantive *must* refer to a substance that Wittgenstein spent the second half of his life trying to eradicate" (Harre 1993, p. 4; italics mine). Let us suppose Wittgenstein has been successful. This would mean that "I" *might* not refer to a substance or a thing at all. However, this does not entail that "I" *does not* actually refer. On the contrary, the linguistic evidence clearly points to the referential use of "I": "If we consider the logical powers of the first-person statements and the role played by the first-person pronoun in communication, nothing seems clearer than that in all first-person statements, including 'avowals,' the word 'I' functions as a singular term...Statements expressed by the sentence 'I feel pain' have it in common with those expressed by sentences like...'Jones feels pain' that they contradict the proposition 'Nobody feels pain' and entail the proposition 'Someone feels pain'" (Shoemaker 1984, p. 6). Since "I" is meant to refer, and apparently people have no problem in using this term, there is a strong presumption for believing that it does refer successfully. So we need strong arguments, instead of bare assertion, to defeat this presumption.

Furthermore, two other kinds of considerations reinforce this presumption. First, many people have what Foster calls "intuitions about ownership": "mental items can only occur as the token-states or activities of subjects, and that this ontological dependence on subjects forms part of our fundamental understanding of their nature" (Foster 1991, p. 212). Jonathan Glover also recognizes that "to speak of experiences which no one has may be...like talking of a grin without a face" (Glover 1988, p. 50). If this intuition is correct, then we can't have experiences without a subject. Since it is also evidently true that I have some experiences, "I" must refer to the subject, myself, who has those experiences.

Of course, some philosophers explicitly deny the intuitions about ownership. For example, Hume and Ayer think experiences are essentially impersonal particulars. However, intuitions about ownership seem sufficiently strong and widely shared (by philosophers of many schools) to merit serious considerations, and hence they should not be dismissed without counterevidence. Furthermore, there are some experiences that are not like phenomenal objects at all. For example, an experience of pain "is not to be ultimately represented as the presentation of a pain-quale...The subject is aware of the pain, but he is aware of it as an episode of sensing or feeling...as the qualitative mode of the sensory act...rather than as its object" (Foster 1991, p. 218).

There is also the need to "relativize" thought: "to mark the difference between what is part of this stream of consciousness and what is part of another. For this, we need to go beyond 'It is thought' to 'It is thought here.' But...'here' is totally figurative, and it is hard to see what sort of 'location' can be given except by reference to the person who has the thought: the kind of location normally indicated by 'I'" (Glover 1988, p. 51). I have some discussion of this problem in Chapter 6.

Apart from the above a priori and conceptual considerations, it can also be argued that the self or the subject is needed to make sense of our *actual* experiences, no matter whether experiences without a subject are conceptually possible. We have experiences of learning and understanding, for example, when reading through a philosophical treatise attentively and grasping its developing themes and arguments. It doesn't seem true to describe this process as merely a collection of essentially discrete experiences. Isn't it much more adequate to say that *I* have gone through a series of experiences, each one building on the earlier ones and contributing to the later ones? Consider the experiences of deliberation and making a decision. Isn't it an experience of a subject agonizing over the question of what *he* should do? It does not make much sense to say that an impersonal experience is pondering over its future action. Similarly, it seems that the experiences of promise, hope, humiliation, and worry can hardly be made sense of apart from someone who promises, hopes, is humiliated, and worries. The proponent of impersonal experience asserts that talk of a subject having an experience can easily be translated into talk of the relation between discrete experiences. If we take into account the richness of our experiences, we can see that the above assertion is gravely in need of substantiation. Perhaps with ingenuity the job could be done (probably by postulating complex relations between experiences). But why should we accept this kind of account, even if it were available? Isn't it much more plausible to say that the data of our experiences reveal to each of us a single and continuous self? Experiences of self do have PFEF.

## 10.3 Experience of Self and Sense Experience

I also think that experience of self and SE are actually intertwined:

### 1. Analysis of Sensory Perception

Consider the phenomenal character of SE. How should we analyze it? The more traditional approach is the act-object model: SE is conceived as the perceiving of mental objects, such as sense-data or arrays of colours. The other model is the adverbial analysis of SE. This account rejects the existence of mental objects. It alleges that it is a fallacy to infer from "I am aware of a red appearance" to "there is an appearance which is red." Rather "being-aware-of-a-red-appearance" is a unitary state, a way of experiencing that cannot be further analyzed into components. So in the former example, the experience is preferably described as "I am appeared to redly." On either account, SE is intimately connected with the experience of self.

Suppose the act-object model is correct. Then unless we adopt an impersonal account of qualia, sense-data, and so on, we can't help postulating a sensory act as well, but the act would in turn require a subject to perform it. Indeed, Foster argues that to view a visual array of colors as a *phenomenal* object is to imply that there is "something *to which* it is visually presented" (Foster 1991, p. 218). Furthermore, when we are visually aware, we are also aware of being visually aware *from the inside*—aware of *ourselves* being visually aware. So on this account, SE is inseparable from at least a rudimentary kind of self-awareness.

Suppose we reject the act-object model. But then this rejection would imply an even closer connection between SE and experience of self. It is because, on this model, the "so-called appearances or sense-data are...'modifications' of the person who is said to experience them...[Hence] in being aware of ourselves as experiencing, we are, *ipso facto*, aware of the self...as being affected in a certain way" (Chisholm 1976, pp. 17–18). So even during a

Humean search, *what* one apprehends when one apprehends heat or cold, light or shade, love or hatred, is simply oneself. Whether one knows it or not, one apprehends *oneself* as being affected or modified.

## 2. Content of Sensory Perception

This sense of self is not always explicit, but it is difficult to see how we can describe our experience without implicit first-person reference. We do not say, "there is an epistemic seeming that..." but we say, "it seems to me that..." Similarly, we would report *our* moods and actions. It might be thought that a visual experience can be reported without such first-person reference. This is not the case. Christopher Peacocke tries to analyze visual experience in terms of scenarios, but any complete description of the scenario would need a center, and so "the pure propositionalist will have to mention the first-person way of thinking in giving his propositional contents of experience" (Peacocke 1992, p. 114). Furthermore, "Identification of places over time requires that states with scenario content contribute to the construction of a cognitive map of the world around the subject. It is, in turn, highly questionable whether we can make sense of the subject engaging in such a construction unless he employs at least a rudimentary form of first-person thought" (Peacocke 1992, pp. 127–8). Consider a simpler example: how can we report the visual experience of the full moon? Try this: "there appears to be a silver circular plate up there." But what can be meant by "up there" if there is no implicit first-person reference at all? The moon is said to be up there because *I* am down here.

## 3. Justification of Sensory Perception

Not only does the content of SE involve experience of self, but the justification of SE is also related to the experience of self. Now suppose we accept the PCT(SE) as a fundamental principle that cannot be further proved. If this is the case, in view of the former analysis, it is difficult to understand why we should not grant introspection the same epistemic status. If we require further justification of SE, say, a person's experience of a table, then that person can only say something like this: "*I* have been there and seen the table." When we ask him why he is sure about that, he can only reply, "*I* seem to see the table and there is no reason to think I am deluded." But why does he think that is the correct description of his experience? It seems that this description is immediately available to him by an introspective experience of self. In this case, it is hard to separate the questions of the validity of experience of self and the validity of SE. Explanatory foundationalism also needs introspective access to *one's* appearance beliefs.

Justification of SE relies on introspection in another aspect. Spatiotemporal continuity seems to be an essential characteristic of ordinary physical objects. But do we have any reason to believe that physical objects continue to exist, perceived or unperceived? I would say yes: we do observe their continuing existence when we keep on perceiving them. We know they persist because *we continue to observe* them. This is assuming the continuity of one's consciousness, which can only be grasped by introspection. One cannot be certain about this, however. Perhaps my consciousness has gaps of which I am not aware. It is possible that we have been hypnotized for some time and then restored to consciousness as if nothing has happened in between. Slote asks: "how does one know, when one is trying to keep one's eye on a thing at all times, that one is continuously conscious? Could one not lose conscious-ness for a time—in which the object under surveillance was replaced—and then regain consciousness without knowing the difference? Application of the criterion of spatio-temporal identity seems to presuppose the ability to judge reasonably about the continuity of one's own experience" (Slote 1970, p. 45). So we need a basic trust in our introspection that reveals to each of us a *continuous* stream of consciousness. The justification of spatiotemporal continuity of physical bodies is itself contingent upon the reliability of intro-spection, which, in this case, is bound up with the continuing awareness of oneself.

Another interesting argument is suggested by the Indian philosopher Vatsyayana (c. 400), who belonged to the Nyaya school of Hinduism. He criticized anatta (no-self doctrine) by asserting, "I touch the very same thing I see" (cited in Sorabji 2006, p. 292). The point is that the coherence of our perception of an external object seems to depend on our sense of unitary self as well. We have seen that the strength of SE derives from the coherence of different perceptions and the mutual reinforcement of several modalities, but this presupposes that all these experiences fall into the same *world*: "if there are only visual sensations and tactual sensations, without a perceiver who has both, then there is no opportunity to think of the sensations of visual and tactual qualities that belong to the same object" (Sorabji 2006, p. 293). Suppose I have experience of an orange, which is constituted by smelling the orange, seeing its color, and tasting it. However, several persons may each have one qualitatively similar experience (*A* smelling something like orange, *B* seeing an orange color, and *C* tasting something like orange), but these experiences cannot reinforce one another. It is because if one does not think of oneself as a unitary perceiver, one cannot think of those qualities that one perceives as "belonging to one and the same external object or even…as residing in the same location. Thus the idea of bodies as unitary owners of multiple qualities depends upon the idea of perceivers as unitary owners of multiple perceptions" (Sorabji 2006, p. 13).

Sorabji anticipates the objection that we can recognize the coherence of these perceptions because they are tied to same location. He replies that the "recognition of the shared location would still require a single perceiver of both qualities, and the location would need to be judged either by the direc-tion and distance of the qualities from the single perceiver or by their direc-tion and distance of the qualities from other entities perceived by the single perceiver. Still less satisfactory…would be the suggestion that the percep-tions need to follow a single route, rather than belong to a single observer. If you had one perception and I another, there would not yet be any reason to ascribe the qualities perceived to one thing" (Sorabji 2006, p. 293).

### 4. Perception of Change

Moreover, it has been plausibly argued that any experience of change or succession would presuppose self-consciousness. "Suppose I hear Big Ben striking. A moment later I—the same subject—hear it striking again...It is a precondition of my apprehending the second stroke *as* the second stroke that I remember having heard the first. But then I do not 'remember' having heard the first...unless I am aware that it was *I*, the being who now hears the second stroke, who heard the first stroke; unless, in other words, I am not merely the same subject, but also conscious of my self-sameness, in the two experiences" (Campbell 1957, pp. 76–7). So the experience of the selfsame self is, in fact, the foundation of our coherent experience of the temporal world.

### 10.4 Belief in the Self and Science

It is mistaken to pit science against the subjective view. As Baker says, "If there were no people with intentional states, then there would be no scientific experiments, no hypotheses, no tests—no inquiry" (Baker 2003, p. 194). Dismissal of the self cannot be discovered in any textbook on physics or chemistry. Subjectivity is also a fact about this world. If we want to have a complete account of the world, both objective and subjective understandings need to be taken into consideration. Moreover, the scientific spirit behooves us to truly attend to our experiences. If we do so, we have reasons to affirm that the First-Person Perspective (FPP) cannot be reduced to the objective third-person view of science.

Lynne Baker has carefully argued for this position. FPP refers to the ability to conceive of oneself as oneself, from "within" so to speak, without any name or description or demonstrative. This way to think about oneself is different from thinking about someone *who happens to be oneself*. For example, Oedipus could think about the murderer of Laius without realizing that the murderer of Laius was *himself*. In contrast, FPP is thinking about oneself as oneself, thinking about one's thoughts as one's own (let us call this I*-thought). This capacity is basic to the self and does not depend on third-person knowledge that ordinarily helps us to identify oneself. So "I do not need to pick myself out as one object among many. I could still have this thought even if I had total amnesia...'I*-thoughts'...the first-person perspective is...a property that distinguishes persons from everything else" (Baker 2003, p. 168).

It follows that "I am absolutely certain that I* exist when I think that I do" (Baker 2003, p. 171). This also demonstrates the irreducibility of first-person knowledge: "First-person knowledge (i.e., knowledge that a knower would express by a first-person sentence) cannot be replaced by third-person knowledge (i.e., knowledge that does not require or presuppose that a knower have a first-person perspective) without cognitive loss" (Baker 2003, p. 175). It is because "There is no third-person way to express my knowledge that I* exist now. My knowledge that I* exist now is not knowledge that Lynne

Baker exists now…I can assertively think, 'Lynne Baker exists now' without knowing that it is true…I see no other candidates for third-person replacement of my knowledge that I* exist now" (Baker 2003, p. 176).

The conclusion is that there is first-person knowledge that is not accessible to the methods of science. This is not unscientific, but it does show scientism to be false.


## 10.5  Anscombe's Criticisms of "I"


Elizabeth Anscombe has some interesting arguments for the claim that "I" does not refer at all. She argues that for "I" to refer, we need a sense to be specified for this quasi-name "I," but she surveys various proposals and finds them all wanting. She first notes that "I" is not a proper name: when different persons use it, they are referring to different persons. So perhaps "I" is just the word each one uses in speaking of himself? But Anscombe points out that "'He speaks of himself' is compatible with ignorance," that is, he can speak of himself without knowing that it is himself that he is speaking of. In this kind of case, we cannot attribute an "I" thought to him. So the former explication of "I" can't be correct. The explication is correct only if "speaking of himself" is interpreted in a first-person way, but then it would be nonexplanatory. Is "I" a pronoun? But she objects that "the sense of the lie 'I am not E.A.' is hardly retained in 'E.A. is not E.A.' So that suggestion is of little value" (Anscombe 1990, p. 142).

She then argues that "I" cannot be assimilated to the demonstratives: "there is a contrast between 'I' and the ordinary demonstrative. We saw that there may be reference-failure for 'this', in that one may mean 'this parcel of ashes' when there are no ashes. But 'I'—if it makes a reference…is secure against reference-failure. Just thinking 'I…' guarantees not only the existence but the presence of its referent" (Anscombe 1990, p. 143).

She claims that this apparent guaranteed referential success of "I," if genuine, can only be accounted for if "I" stands for a Cartesian Ego. This is her tank argument: "now imagine that I get into a state of 'sensory deprivation'. Sight is cut off, and I am locally anaesthetized everywhere, perhaps floated in a tank of tepid water; I am unable to speak, or to touch any part of my body with any other. Now I tell myself 'I won't let this happen again!' If the object meant by 'I' is this body…then in these circumstances it won't be present to my senses; and how else can it be 'present to' me? But…I have not lost my 'self-consciousness'; nor can what I mean by 'I' be an object no longer present to me…Nothing but a Cartesian Ego will serve" (Anscombe 1990, p. 146). But she thinks Descartes can't be right, and the only possible conclusion is that "I" does not refer.

Anscombe's linguistic arguments have been subjected to various criticisms. As for Anscombe's claim that "I" is not a pronoun, Katz replies: "On a more modern approach, pronominal replacement requires only preserving syntactic well-formedness. Anscombe's argument that "I" is not a pronoun fails because her semantic criterion is neither the only nor the most plausible criterion for pronounhood…some singular pronouns have a generic use as a variable, as in her example. But "I" contrasts with them in a way that shows that "I" is a kind of singular designation" (Katz 1990, pp. 172–3).

But the major problem with her arguments is her claim that "I" cannot be explicated as the word each uses to refer to himself. As Baker points out, "himself" can be used in a third-person way or the *first-person way*. The latter use is denoted by "himself*." Consider these two ways to explicate the sense of "I":

(A) "I" is a word that each speaker uses only to refer to himself*.
(B) "I" is a word that each speaker uses only to refer to himself.

(B) is indeed defective, but Anscombe's objection to (A) is only that it would be nonexplanatory. It does not follow that (A) is false. As Taschek points out, "I find nothing incompatible with holding that (A) is *true*, and consequently that 'I' is a referring expression, even while granting that (A) is inadequate as an explanation of the distinctive semantic role of this pronoun" (Taschek 1985, pp. 640–1). The deeper reason is that explication in terms of something else has to come to an end somewhere. By definition, our *most fundamental* concepts can never be explicated noncircularly. It seems eminently plausible to say that our FPP is a fundamental fact about self-consciousness that cannot be forced into a Procrustean bed.

As for Anscombe's tank argument, I agree that the sense of "I" should not be equated with "this body." I am not sure that it must then refer to the Cartesian ego. Brian Garrett asks, "why assume that if the self were something bodily, and were perceived introspectively, it would have to be perceived *as* something bodily?…Anscombe assumes, more generally, that if 'I' refers, its object must be 'present to' the subject. But the thesis that self-reference requires self-presentation has little to recommend it" (Garrett 1997, p. 29). Even if Anscombe's tank argument were sound, his astounding conclusion only comes about if we can be sure that Cartesianism is wrong. I doubt that. So Anscombe has not given us sufficient reasons to abandon the belief that "I" does refer.

## 10.6 Conclusion

If even part of the above arguments are correct, the dismissal of the experience of self is implausible. Finally, I just want to tell a good story about Avicenna: "an eager student came up to him and said, 'Master, Master, have you heard this one? We have no continuous self.' Avicenna said nothing. 'Master, Master', persisted the student, 'Why are you not answering me? Avicenna replied, 'I only answer the person who asked the question'" (Sorabji 2006, p. 297).

# CHAPTER 11

# EXISTENTIAL EXPERIENCE, CRITICAL TRUST, AND GOD

Existential experience is the experience of the self as the existential subject, who is in search of meaning, identity, and wholeness. In the experience of the self as basic subject, one finds the source of the unity of one's experiences. However, in the existential quest, one may find oneself on the verge of disintegration. These two types of experience may look contradictory, but in fact the experience of self-disintegration presupposes the experience of self as the basic subject. Suppose one is torn between two contradictory desires, D1 and D2. This is a problem only if D1 and D2 belong to the same basic subject, himself. Otherwise D1 in one person and D2 in another person may lead to conflict *between* persons, but certainly would not lead to *self*-disintegration.

## 11.1 Varieties of Existential Experience

### 11.1.1 Freedom, Responsibility, and Transcendence

We may begin with Jean-Paul Sartre's distinction between *en-soi* and *pour-soi* (Sartre 1966). The former, like a stone, *is* what it is. However, a human being seems to be characterized not only by what he is, but also by what he is not, by what he negates, and by what he can become. At each moment, a human being is faced with many possibilities, and he seems to be able to choose among these. The choice, in a sense, determines what kind of person he is, and in the process he seems to be able to (partially) create himself. This phenomenon is most clearly seen in some extreme cases of deprivation and limitation. For example, Viktor Frankl speaks from his experience in the concentration camp:

> Man is not a thing among others…but man is ultimately self-determining…In the living laboratories of the concentration camps we watched comrades behaving like swine while others behaved like saints. Man has both these potentialities within himself. Which one he actualizes depends on decision…Our generation has come to know man as he really is: the being that has invented the gas chambers of Auschwitz, and also the being who entered those gas chambers upright, the Lord's Prayer or the *Shema Yisrael* on his lips. (cited in Heaney 1973, pp. 22–3)

Frankl thinks that even intense suffering cannot destroy the meaning of life, because even under extreme circumstances, human beings are still able to achieve a sort of *attitudinal good* by deciding their attitudes toward it.

The examples he gives, as well as other historical examples, do suggest that even when confronted by an apparently unalterable destiny, a person may still accept the plight with serenity, bear his cross with courage, and suffer with dignity.

Sartre, another writer who places enormous emphasis on freedom, has a similar experience during the period of German occupation of France. Even under this extreme situation, some French people could still choose to rebel by joining the Underground Resistance, risking their own lives. So Sartre wrote in his article, "The Republic of Silence" (originally published in 1944 during the war): "Never have we been freer than under German occupation...This total responsibility in total solitude, wasn't this the revelation of our freedom?" (Sartre 1947, pp. 498-500). However, he seems to overgeneralize from this experience and exaggerates the scope of human freedom. He sometimes talks about human beings as if they can generate themselves from sheer nothingness. However, freedom is not just randomness: "It has direction. It is associated with such aspects of our being as cognition, conscience, purpose.... man does not begin as a sheer nothing. There is a something given. There is an initial directedness" (Macquarrie 1982, p. 14). Obviously, my past choices influence my current choices. By consistently making choices in a determinate direction or under the commitment to the same principle, we can *freely* build up our character. The character development of one's personality can reach such a point of stability where he can no longer be blown off course by some chance desire. In such a situation, we can say, "He could not possibly do that !" This is *not* a denial of freedom. In Macquarrie's terms, we need to note both poles of facticity and freedom in human existence.

In contrast with consumers' "freedom," say, to choose between one brand of beer and another, which is by and large trivial, this kind of freedom can be demanding and terrifying. It can shake our identity to its core, because we are confronted with the choice to become who we are, and we seem to stare at a pit of nothingness. This is a freedom that calls oneself to be responsible for *oneself* . Freedom can also be easily lost by letting your life drift away, letting your life be decided by social pressure, fashions, and so on. So freedom also entails the possibility of bad faith or inauthentic existence. Sometimes freedom will generate a dizziness or a vertigo as we gaze before the abyss of our possibilities. That is why we may try to escape from our freedom, for example, through submitting to authoritarianism or collectivism (cf. Fromm's *Escape from Freedom*). This fact is also well recognized by Dostoevsky's Grand Inquisitor (in his novel *Brothers Karamazov*) who told Jesus, who came the second time, to go back because he thought the people didn't want the freedom he gave. People often prefer the security of conforming to socially established patterns of existence and following the line of least resistance.

Despite these tendencies to "escape from freedom," all is not yet lost: the key is courage. "Without courage, neither freedom, nor honesty, nor community can be pursued...Each man loves certain illusions, has favorite evasions, projects a beloved self-image, which even his friends soon learn to be sensitive to, not to crush, occasionally to flatter, often to lament.... men are not noteworthy for courage sufficient to be entirely honest" (Novak 1971, p. 14). However, sometimes when we experience the courage to face our freedom, it seems that "the courage which moves us does not come from ourselves...in some way, our true identity...lies up ahead, calling to us, drawing us" (Novak 1971, pp. 14–15). In Macquarrie's words, we are beings-on-the-way. We are essentially unfinished creatures, and it seems that we are forever called to transcend ourselves. Yet we are also constantly tempted to *fall* into avoidance, self-deception, and inauthentic existence. Again, the tension in the core of *humanitas* seems patent.

### 11.1.2 *The Plasticity and Transcendence of Human Needs*

The human being is an animal and has some basic physical needs. However, the surprising fact is that he also has a plethora of spiritual needs that have no obvious relation to survival. For example, we need to feel being important: "What we fear most in this life is not personal sorrow or suffering, not confusion about the world's great questions, or even the impending nothingness of death; what we fear above all...is that we do not matter" (Gelven 1990, p. 57).

There are other needs that can be connected with survival, for example, will to pleasure and will to power. However, the inordinateness between the *subjective desire* and the *objective need* is also clearly discernible. In many animals, the strength of the desire is regulated by the degree of need. However, in human beings, their desires can run amuck in such extravagant ways that, in most cases, the degree of need is determined by the strength of the corresponding desires. Just consider the "needs" of drug addicts.

As the psychologist Erik Erikson says, "man can eat, drink, and smoke, work and 'love,' curse, moralize, and sacrifice himself to death. For man's instinctual forces are never completely bound in adaptive or reasonable patterns; some are repressed,...perverted, and often return from repression to arouse strictly human kinds of anxiety and rage...If the nutritional instinct...guides the animal in finding...food, this is very different from the oral-incorporative instinctuality which may make man spend a greater portion of his resources on alcohol and soda pop" (Erikson 1969, pp. 428–9).

Human desire again possesses a sort of dynamism: it is never simply satisfied by satisfaction of the "objective" needs; rather, it seems to be able to escalate indefinitely and generate indefinite needs for oneself. Human beings seem to be the only kind of animal who suffers greatly from addiction, concupiscence, and infinite craving for diminishing pleasure. This tragic fact also partly explains why human beings can be inflicted by all sorts of neuroses to quite a unique degree. The psychologist Abraham Maslow is famous for his theory of the hierarchy of needs. While the lower rung consists of biological needs such as food, shelter, and security, the peak of this hierarchy is the need for self-actualization. Moreover, the person who achieves self-realization will usually have peak experiences that are often religious in nature (see Chapter 16).

Another psychologist, Carl Jung, argues that the human psyche possesses a collective unconscious that has the innate disposition to generate a host of symbols (these tendencies are called archetypes), many of them mythical and religious (e.g. dramas of repentance, sacrifice, and redemption). Deep inside humanity, "there is a thinking in primordial images...It is only possible to live the fullest life when we are in harmony with these symbols; wisdom is a return to them" (Jung 1933, pp. 129–30). This integration of all the disparate components of the personality, both conscious and unconscious, is called individuation, which is the process through which the psyche is oriented toward a state of self-fulfillment. In individuation we are also searching for wholeness, a unified psychic totality.

On the basis of his own therapeutic experience, Jung thinks that religion is very important to individuation: "Among all my patients in the second half of life...there has not been one whose problem in the last resort was not that of finding a religious outlook on life...none of them has been really healed who did not regain his religious outlook" (Jung 1933, p. 239). In fact, Jung explicitly endorses numinous experience as the key to therapy.

Certainly, the details of the theories of Maslow and Jung are disputable. However, it is difficult to deny that they at least point to significant data about humanity. They both emphasize the intimate connection of the human psyche with transcendent experiences. Jung's work convincingly shows the symbolic richness of the human psyche, and also the importance of symbols to man. He believes that due to the domination of technology and scientism, modern man has largely deprived his soul of these symbols, and this is the source of many mental problems. That is why Jung talks about *Modern Man in Search of a Soul*. The process of soul-searching also manifests the inherent human tendency toward wholeness. But the sad fact is that we often find ourselves divided or fragmented. For Jung, an important factor for overcoming fragmentation and achieving wholeness lies in the submission to the archetype of Self, which also has religious overtones.

### 11.1.3 Shock of Non-Being

There are other experiences that are characterized by negative feelings. For example, there is *angst*, the vertigo of freedom, which reveals the incompleteness of the human being, his non-being and contingency. It is a curious fact that negative feelings can be provoked when all seems so well and pleasurable: "If all we do is sleep and feed, if all we want is the fun of rutting in the ditch, if all that matters is our satisfaction or our happiness, then, these fellow-beasts ask: What does it mean? Disgust. But, why does our nature disgust us? . . What else could we possibly want save that which satisfies our wanting? This disgust is the origin of spirit. It begins, then, as a negation. It is the reaching out beyond ourselves" (Gelven 1990, p. 6). The case of Tolstoy is a good illustration. He confessed this feeling when he had everything he wanted: "I felt that something has broken within me on which my life had always rested, that I had nothing left to hold on to...An invincible force impelled me to get rid of my existence...Behold me then, a man happy and in good health, hiding the rope in order not to hang myself."

Tolstoy himself found his experience strange because he "ought to have been completely happy," but he was not: "I had a good wife who loved me and whom I loved; good children and a large property...I was more respected by my kinsfolk." Yet he was tormented by these questions: "What will be the outcome of what I do today? Of what I shall do tomorrow?...Why should I do anything? Is there in life any purpose which the inevitable death which awaits me does not undo and destroy? These questions are the simplest in the world...Without an answer to them, it is impossible, as I experienced, for life to go on.... the very thing which was leading me to despair—the meaningless absurdity of life—is the only incontestable knowledge accessible to man" (Tolstoy 1980, pp. 16–17).

If a cockroach or a pig knew about Tolstoy's questions, would they find a resonance in their minds, or just find him amusing? Suppose you are a naturalist and now have a chance to encounter a highly intelligent alien who comes to visit the earth. Besides expecting much more advanced science and technology, do you expect him to be tormented by Tolstoy's questions? I doubt it. *Homo sapiens* is indeed a curious species.

Suppose we find out that the alien is not only afflicted by abstract and impractical questions such as the meaning of the alien's life, but also often has experiences of despair that drive him to the edge of committing suicide (as Tolstoy was tempted to). Wouldn't it be even more curious? After all, the strongest and most fundamental instinct of a biological species should be the will to survive. According to a survey in Hong Kong, 36 percent of the students in the primary and secondary schools have thought of committing suicide (*Ming Pao*, March 28, 2002). In one shocking case, one teenage girl suffering from the breaking up of a relationship wanted to kill herself. Her two teenage friends, who apparently did not have any intense suffering, showed "solidarity" by killing themselves, too. Their actions were, indeed, more inexplicable than that of the girl who suffered from a broken relationship—but have you seen a cat commit suicide because of a broken relationship with other cats? Humans do have a will to survive, but strangely, their urge to find love or meaning may, at times, trump this will.

Despair often results from alienation from oneself, others, and the cosmos. Kierkeggard's analysis (the *Sickness unto Death*) shows that various ways of missing one's true self (e.g. due to living exclusively on the aesthetic plane) will lead to *despair*. Of course, the biological advantages of finding one's true self are far from obvious. If despair can drive one to eliminate one's being, together with *his whole world*, then this experience is not only about this or that event, but seems to reflect a judgment about the Whole, even an experience of the Whole in absence. So according to Marcel, despair is a "total submission to [the] void, in such a way as to allow oneself to be dissolved interiorly by it. The closed time of despair is a sort of counter-eternity, an eternity forced back on itself, the eternity of hell" (cited in Nichols 1991, p. 158). Despair seems to be unique to the human species, which is constrained by biological necessities, but at the same time plagued by the sense of the Eternal.

When we survey these kinds of negative feelings, we can't help being surprised by the extravagance of the human psyche. Perhaps such experiences can make a poet, a novelist, or a tragic hero. But all these emotions, if not positively "harmful," hardly contribute to our animal survival. It looks more and more as if the "natural" can't fathom the depth of the human spirit.

### 11.1.4 Quest for Meaning, Wholeness, and Identity

The above negative experiences in fact presuppose the spiritual quest and point to the restlessness of human spirit, as if nothing finite can satisfy it. Many of us may not explicitly manifest the quest for meaning. However, in our ceaseless activities, strivings, and perhaps also our moments of boredom, disgust, or despair, the need to affirm a meaningful existence seems to show forth. This is all the more striking if we put the matter into historical perspective. We may think the quest for meaning is only due to the suffering and fragility of lives in ancient and premodern societies. However, in many modern societies, the goals of liberation from material suffering and hardship, sickness and oppression, have been significantly achieved. We have gotten rid of the worst kinds of drudgery and achieved an unprecedented freedom.

So we should expect a great increase in happiness. Yet modern society is characterized by a sense of alienation, futility, and meaninglessness, and not by an increase in contentment. After we are relieved from our more immediate anxieties, we still need to confront our existence as individuals, but it seems to be individuality in a void, with nowhere to go. And *yet we still want to go somewhere*. In the words of Fromm: "the observable data show most clearly that our kind of 'pursuit of happiness' does not produce well-being. We are a society of notoriously unhappy people: lonely, anxious, depressed, destructive, dependent—people who are glad when we have killed the time we are trying so hard to save" (Fromm 1976, pp. 5–6). So the whole historical experiment seems to show that the "pursuit of happiness" can't be the final answer to the question of meaning.

The same conclusion can be drawn from reflection on the opposite extreme: experience of extreme suffering and deprivation. Frankl speaks of the "purgatory" that he himself endured in the concentration camp after the loss of the manuscript of his first book:

> Later, when my own death seemed imminent, I asked myself what my life had been for. Nothing was left which would survive me. No child of my own. Not even a spiritual child such as the manuscript. But after wrestling with my despair for hours, shivering from typhus fever, I finally asked myself what sort of meaning could depend on whether a manuscript of mine was printed. I would not give a damn for it. But if there is a meaning, it is unconditional meaning, and neither suffering nor dying can detract from it. (cited in Dulles 1971, p. 252)

So the removal of suffering alone cannot satisfy the will to meaning; nor can the inflicting of suffering quench the will to meaning. The intimation is that if it is to be satisfied, it can't depend on finite and contingent factors.

We have already talked about the quests for identity and wholeness. The quest for identity itself is a puzzling phenomenon. A psychologist asks: "How did man's need for identity evolve? Before Darwin the answer was clear: because God created Adam in His image, as a counterplayer of His identity...I admit to not having come up with any better explanation" (Erikson 1968, p. 40). The search for identity is closely connected with the search for wholeness.

According to Jung, individuation is achieved through systematic confrontation, step by step, between the ego and the contents of the unconscious. For him, the conscious ego has to be distinguished from the Self, the transcendent center of personality, which organizes all the psychic functions, the unknown yet benevolent power to whom the person must submit himself in order to achieve wholeness. Jung also suggests that "Christ" is actually the symbol of the Self. We don't need to endorse the whole Jungian theory to accept his insight that human beings are endowed with a drive to wholeness and integration, and this is the condition for true human fulfillment. Somehow, to achieve genuine wholeness and fulfillment, the ego has to achieve a proper relation with *something other than the conscious ego*. So the quest for wholeness, together with the quest for meaning, seems to point *beyond* the finite realm by its dynamics.

Carl Vaught has devoted a book to study this problem: *The Quest for Wholeness* (1982). He also agrees that "wholeness is a religious phenomenon and that the quest for wholeness finally brings us face to face with God" (Vaught 1982, p. xi). According to Vaught, the "quest for wholeness moves forward toward a larger, more inclusive unity, but it also leads us back to the origins of our individual existence" (Vaught 1982, p. 4). I call it the double movement of the quest for wholeness: there is a forward and a backward movement.

In the forward movement, we find that "wholeness can never be found apart from the community, for the meaning of human existence is partly constituted by the human bonds that tie us together," and "fragmentation we experience is often caused by separation from others, and it is fragmentation of this kind that drives us toward the community to seek the fulfillment...On the other hand, the individual must not lose himself in the larger world, for to do so would be to lose the center of the fragmented self, and to abandon the hope that wholeness can be found in a fashion uniquely appropriate to oneself" (Vaught 1982, p. 3). In short, we need a balance between individuality and community. The person searching for wholeness needs to place himself in a larger context, but at the same time needs to understand "what it means to be a particular individual, living here and now as *a unique center of power* that can never be reduced to its place within a larger context" (Vaught 1982, p. 7).

In the backward movement, we want "to make contact with the past, and pointing to the possibility of a positive relationship with the sustaining ground of our existence" (Vaught 1982, p. 4). The significance of this quest is reflected in the human urge to understand the origins of our individual existence, as witnessed in the desire of orphans to find their biological parents. The traditional Chinese culture has a high regard for the link of an individual to his ancestors (even very distant ones). In all the villages, there is a special place to honor the ancestors and to ask for their blessings. These traditional practices allow us to know where we come from, induce in us a sense of belonging to a larger whole, or even a feeling of gratitude as we realize our being is indebted to others. As Vaught says, the backward movement is "not primarily to recover our finite origins, but to confront our infinite ground...it is this foundation that can supply us with a source of originative power in terms of which the power of fragmentation can be overcome" (Vaught 1982, p. 7).

So it is plausible to say the inner dynamics of the quest for wholeness are "pointing to the Ground from which we come and to the Whole toward which we develop" (Vaught 1982, p. 7). The quest will not be satisfied by an arbitrary termination in a localized whole that is incongruous with the larger Whole. That is why naturalism ultimately cannot provide a satisfactory answer to this quest. Suppose we find it meaningful to find oneself in communion with others. However, in the context of a naturalistic world, the whole human community (the localized whole) is also a cosmic accident, not anticipated or known by the larger Whole, which is the lifeless Universe. The human community is not sustained by this Whole in any other sense than a causal grounding. However, this causal grounding is contingent and, according to contemporary science, will be withdrawn when our sun explodes in the distant future, or when a meteor hits the earth (which may occur sooner). Concerning the backward movement, the naturalists may find some satisfaction in the view that we belong to this whole drama of evolution and that our ancestors also include fish and amoeba. However, to whom should we be grateful, when nothing is planned and everything is an accident? How can we find our unique form of human existence sustained when our ultimate origins in the random collisions of the physical particles cannot comprehend our passions and spiritual quest? So the naturalistic worldview can give no real answer to our quest for wholeness concerning both movements.

In contrast, God can uniquely fulfill these roles of the Ground and the Whole. So "in the final analysis, the quest also requires that we move beyond the finite order and that we stand face to face with what is ultimate and unconditioned" (Vaught 1982, p. 3).

## 11.2 Fusion of Existential Experience with Theistic Experience

### 11.2.1 Freedom and Transcendence

For Macquarrie, when people are exercising their freedom, "they are themselves experiencing creativity. They are at their most godlike, for in a dimly analogous way they are participating in the divine experience of creating out of nothing" (Macquarrie 1982, p. 14). As discussed above, there is the danger of self-deception, but sometimes we can also face the darkness concerning ourselves that arises from a commitment to unceasing honesty. If this commitment seems to be some kind of urge or calling, then it leads us to suspect that, in being honest, we not only face ourselves, but also hear a calling from some Other.

The experience of Mark T. Clark, a professor of political science at California State University, San Bernardino, is a good example. Clark had some vague encounters with God when he was young, but in the end was not engaged with religion. During his years in the marines, he resumed some kind of spiritual search. One night he was reading some religious literature. Corporal R. asked him, "Are you reading that crap too?" He felt embarrassed and said, "No, just looking at some material." He then turned off the light and slid the book back under his pillow. Then suddenly he had an experience, as if a brick hit him: "It felt as if God...held up a mirror to my soul and *showed me my real self*. I was a coward. Maybe I was tough physically...But I was miserable...I shrank from doing what I really wanted because of peer pressure...I realized in a flash that for me to take charge of my life, I would, in a sense, have to give it over to Jesus Christ. *I had to obey him in order to be really me*. I turned the bunk light back on, grabbed my book, and told R. that I too was reading that 'stuff.'...the struggle I had that evening on my bunk...centered on *moral courage*. I had to decide, and publicly, to obey the truth...As timid as I was when I turned my life over to Christ, I began to feel more alive than ever" (Anderson 1998, p. 124; italics mine). Here the experience of discovering the true self, moral courage, and experience of God were fused together.

### 11.2.2 Meaning and Wholeness

Even in the modern world, many intelligent people are driven to religion by their quest for meaning. An example is the experience of David Raup of the University of Chicago. He says, "By most standards my life would have been considered a success story. I had a wonderful wife and family, a new home and a successful career. I thoroughly enjoyed science and felt fortunate to have a career in that field. Yet I felt an emptiness, a lack of purpose and meaning...Was this all there was to life? The beauty, order and design evident in the world I observed as a scientist only whetted my desire for spiritual understanding" (Anderson 1998, p. 20). Later he had experiences of Jesus Christ, and the New Testament amazed him: "Here was a blueprint for living and a description and explanation of the sense of separation from God that I had been experiencing" (Anderson 1998, p. 21). It is interesting to note that the earlier experience of emptiness is now understood as an implicit experience of "separation from God."

Others experience God at moments of brokenness *and* healing. Listen to Patricia Raybon, a Black professor of journalism and mass communication in the University of Colorado. When she was just 23, she was divorcing her

husband, and was a single mother with a one-year-old child. She was job-
less and broke, and had a broken relationship with her family. The experience of healing was first mediated by the grace of her Christian parents,
who welcomed her back unconditionally. She described her experience as
"a prodigal daughter coming home for atonement and renewal in my good
parents' home." Her parents were just remarkable: "They never once said
'we told you so.' They just put up a crib in my old bedroom...They bought
baby food and diapers. They ordered nursery books and toys. Then my
daddy...spoke in his soft voice the words that would change forever my
mortal life: 'You need to open your Bible'" (Anderson 1998, p. 159).

She did open her Bible at daybreak, and that's when she first met Jesus. She
came across these passages: "*There is therefore now no condemnation to
them which are in Christ Jesus* (Romans 8:1)...Through fresh tears, I dared
now to ask that Savior for forgiveness for myself...Help me, Jesus. I cried at
daybreak" (Anderson 1998, p. 160). As she prayed to Jesus, she experienced
a "peace that passeth all understanding," but this was just the beginning of
healing and the road to wholeness. Eventually she remarried, and her new
husband said years later that Jesus was rounding them out. First, she had to
deal with her hatred for white people: "I hated white people...*that* problem,
said Jesus...was the problem I needed to tackle...So I wrote a book about
making peace with white people...It carried me into crevices in my soul
that only a merciful God could heal" (Anderson 1998, p. 165).

Then she needed to deal with old family hurts, and she was stunned by
this: "The book I was writing became a book about making peace first with
my family and with myself and even with my God. And I cried as I wrote the
book because the damage was big...Jesus cuts clean, healing those wounds
and covering them with a fresh outlook. And the pain ended." She summarized the power of faith to heal and make us whole, individually and
racially, this way: "I am elevated by Jesus. With him I rise above the fickle-
ness of race consciousness" (Anderson 1998, p. 169).

## 11.3 Coherence of Existential Experience with Theistic Experience

### 11.3.1 Freedom and Transcendence

Let us consider the following data:

$e_7$: We have experiences of a subject which strongly suggest that human persons
are finite yet free agents.
$e_8$: Human persons *are* finite yet free agents.

Since $e_7$ is just the description of our *experiences* of freedom, it is hard to
deny. In contrast, $e_8$ is more controversial because it refers to the epistemic
seemings embodied in those experiences of freedom. However, if our existential experiences do have some PFEF, then $e_8$, which just assumes we
have *some* degree of freedom, is one of those well-established presumptive
data because each and every one of us does have an awful lot of epistemic

seemings (or intuitions) about our freedom. To deny $e_8$ is to declare all these experiences of freedom delusory.

$P(e_8/H_n)$ would be pretty low. "It is very difficult to account, on purely naturalistic principles, for man's freedom, his openness to the future, his self-transcendence and creativity...not only are freedom and creativity hard to explain 'from below' by reference to...'bottom-up' causality...they are also positively suggestive of a 'top-down' final causality whereby the creature is drawn out of nature into spirit by and from the world of spirit itself" (Hebblethwaite 1988, pp. 93–4). In fact, many naturalists have long expressed misgivings about the "obscurantist" notion of free will. So their move is to reject $e_8$. I want to point out the intellectual cost of accepting naturalism: it seems arbitrary to reject all our experiences of apparent freedom. Eliezer J. Sternberg is a neuroscientist who recognizes the PFEF of our experience of freedom: "As we act, we feel that we are consciously, freely, controlling our behaviors. If that notion, which some might consider the most basic and essential to understanding our humanity, is to be done away with, we need to be given proof" (Sternberg 2010, p. 153).

The naturalists have tried to provide defeaters for $e_8$. One popular argument is that belief in free will is contradicted by recent neurological research, which seems to show that all our decisions are only features of our brains caused by prior events over which we have no control. Sternberg, however, has assessed this scientific argument against free will, and found it wanting. Sternberg appeals to the case of Jean-Dominique Bauby, which shows the "depths of consciousness." On December 8, 1995, French journalist Jean-Dominique Bauby, editor of the magazine *Elle*, experienced a terrible stroke and fell into a coma. The stroke left him paralyzed, and Bauby could do little more than blink his left eye. However, while his body lay still, his mind was surging with activity, a flood of pain and regret, longing and melancholy, but also of thought and reflection, ideas and creativity. He decided to keep writing. Using only the blinking of his left eye, Bauby dictated to a friend, letter by letter. After over 200,000 blinks, Bauby had completed a book, *The Diving Bell and the Butterfly*. Bauby died of heart failure 2 days after the book was published (Sternberg 2010, pp. 143–4).

Bauby writes, "My heels hurt, my head weighs a ton, and something like a giant invisible diving bell holds my whole body prisoner...[but] my mind takes off like a butterfly...in space or in time" (cited in Sternberg 2010, p. 144). But is the free movement of this butterfly an illusion? Sternberg asks a lot of questions: "Could Bauby's achievement really have been determined by neuronal calculations beyond his control? Something about that conclusion just doesn't sit well with me...could we have written the book for him, word for word, just because we understood the states of his brain?" (Sternberg 2010, pp. 144–5). I agree that the denial of Bauby's freedom is counterintuitive.

In his book, Sternberg has reviewed the research done by Benjamin Libet, Daniel Wegner, Apostolos Georgopoulos, Gazzaniga, and so on. Many people claim that their results prove the truth of determinism. However, Sternberg shows without much difficulty that the inference from scientific results to determinism has a great gap. He uses the analogy of F-16 fighter jet and the pilot. If you were to damage the engine, the plane's flight pattern would, of course, change. However, this does not imply that the pilot does not really control the plane (Sternberg 2010, p. 148).

Sternberg also argues that the above inference is an illegitimate extrapolation that ignores the change of context. He appeals to some concrete examples to argue that "no matter how many rules someone creates—no matter how complex the formulas or algorithms that are used—there is simply no way that a rule-based system can account for the depth of the human moral decision-making process" (Sternberg 2010, p. 159). It is because our reflection, in many cases, is done in the context of boundlessness: there will always be an immeasurable number of details that we miss, and there are far too many concepts to list. There is no standard way to determine which information is relevant. And once relevant concepts are discovered, there are countless ways to interpret them. However, since a deterministic system (like the brain) governed by laws is algorithmic, the brain alone cannot fully account for our self-reflective, conscious deliberation in *the context of boundlessness*.

But in composing his book, Bauby was engaging exactly this kind of self-reflective, conscious deliberation: the scientific "evidence against free will doesn't really address the depth of Bauby's contemplation. The decisions studied were those, like wrist flexions, that require little forethought" (Sternberg 2010, pp. 150–1). So he concludes, "Our ability to go beyond the algorithms—to achieve understanding, to appreciate meaning, to imagine, to consciously deliberate, to reason through boundless problems, and to act as free agents—is what separates us from the lower animals…and all other machines" (Sternberg 2010, p. 179). This again shows the transcendence of the human mind.

I think Sternberg has provided a good case against the scientistic critique of free will. Of course, there are still many challenges. I can only suggest that the PFEF of experience of freedom (as manifested in the conspicuous cases of Frankl and Bauby) is too strong to ignore, and there are plausible replies to other challenges (see Goetz 2008). Anyway, $e_7$ seems undeniable, and it is incumbent upon the naturalist to provide good explanations of the "illusion" of freedom. However, even if those explanations can show the *compatibility* of the experience of freedom with naturalism, it is doubtful that we can *expect* these experiences of freedom on naturalism—do we really expect an animal as paralyzed as Bauby to have the "illusion" of flying like a butterfly? So $P(e_7/H_n)$ may not be high, whereas $P(e_7 \text{ and } e_8/H_t)$ is very high. Theism still provides a neater explanation of $e_7$ and $e_8$.

### 11.3.2 Desire, Meaning, Wholeness

Consider another set of data:

$e_9$: Human beings have a distinct set of spiritual needs.
$e_{10}$: Human desire has a tendency to escalate indefinitely, and this transforms the human being's natural needs.

$e_{11}$: Human beings are characterized by a dynamic quest for meaning, wholeness, or identity.

$e_{12}$: There are human experiences of anxiety, alienation, and despair.

The pattern of spiritual needs and the dynamism can be neatly explained by the spiritual origin of human being: If theism is true, then human subjectivity is, indeed, made for the Eternal and the Infinite. So it is not surprising to find a human tendency to continually surpass our own achieved satisfactions. The above framework can also explain the experience of despair. If there is indeed an implicit drive to achieve a proper relationship with the Infinite, and this is originating from our *imago dei*, then it is to be expected that such a relationship is also the source of our telos, our meaning and wholeness. If we neglect this, for example, by leading an entirely aesthetic existence, we are naturally driven to despair. Indeed, the unconditioned seriousness of these experiences can be interpreted as an "expression of the presence of the divine in the experience of their separation from it" (Schilling 1974, p. 120).

All our existential experiences converge on this observation: the extravagance of the human psyche or spirit *from the naturalistic perspective*. We can't help wonder: why did these particular patterns of archetypes, particular capacities for peak experiences, and our craving for infinite love, and so on emerge? Man did not make up the structure of his own psyche. However, the convergence of human psychological structures and theological framework is striking:

> the psyche is an endlessly convoluted form, full of phenomena which have little obvious relation to survival. The positive function of religion in primitive societies is often pointed to as the reason for its development. Religious beliefs, it is said, comforted man, stabilized society and offered primitive explanations for mysterious phenomena. Since the contrary may also be asserted with equal force (religion frightened man, caused stagnation in society and spread superstitious misinformation), *the argument for the utility of religion fails to explain the extraordinary energy which has poured into the evolution of the human psyche and its various theophanies. Far from having developed along clean, functional lines, the psyche seems a singularly extravagant anomaly.* (Clasby 1988, p. 88; italics mine)

Maybe this is a fluke of the evolutionary process? I am doubtful. First, I deny that such "explanations" have much *positive* explanatory power. Second, I have tried to assemble a large number of "signals of transcendence," which point in the same direction (many others more in later chapters). A "fluke explanation" may be acceptable for several of them, but it becomes increasingly ad hoc and unlikely if such "flukes" accumulate in a determinate fashion. So the more coherent theistic explanation is, indeed, better.

### 11.3.3 The Argument from Meaning

Let us now further explore how theism can throw light on our quest for meaning. I contend that an adequate answer to this question needs to satisfy four kinds of constraint:

1. *Cosmological constraint*: the proposed answer needs to account for the meaningful position of a human being in the whole universe. Human beings are part of the Whole, the universe. It is difficult to make sense of how human existence can have meaning if the whole universe does not. As Urban says, "Denial of all meaning to the whole must…ultimately mean denial of genuine meaning to any of the parts" (Urban 1951, p. 199).
2. *Anthropological constraint*: the proposed answer needs to provide a telos for human existence. This constraint guarantees that there is some coherence to human existence.
3. *Moral constraint*: the proposed answer needs to be compatible with and account for our moral experience: "life has no ultimate meaning except as it is the 'good life'…[Hence the] question whether the world has a meaning resolves itself into the more ultimate question whether values are realized in the world and when realized conserved" (Urban 1951, p. 194).
4. *Subjectivity constraint*: the proposed answer needs to be a feasible way of living that can provide us a subjective sense of lasting satisfaction, blessedness, or the like.

It is important to keep all four constraints together. If we consider the subjectivity constraint alone, there is no way to bar a pathological serial killer, who finds immense satisfaction in wanton killing and torturing of the victims, to claim this is exactly his meaning of existence! Cottingham points out the disturbing feature of the pluralistic account of life's meaning provided by secular humanism: "if there is no overarching structure or theory that confers meaning on life, no normative pattern…then a meaningful life reduces to little more than an engaged life in which the agent is systematically committed to certain projects…irrespective of their moral status" (Cottingham 2003, p. 26). On the other hand, without the subjectivity constraint, we are hard put to explain our sense of revulsion against some religious fanatics who see their meaning of life in the pain caused by their acts of self-mutilation.

With these four constraints in place, it is plausible to argue that only a worldview like theism can provide an adequate answer to the quest for meaning. Block proposes such an answer: "The mystical union of the soul of man with G-d through love is the ultimate meaning of life…because it is the origin of all existence, and the search for this mystical union *is* the basic drive of the human soul" (Block 2007, p. 128). Since this mystical union is part of the whole Creation plan, it satisfies the cosmological constraint. Since the purpose is already built in when human beings are created, this is exactly our telos. Anthropological constraint is satisfied. Since a union with God is also a union with the Standard and Source of all goodness, no doubt it satisfies the moral constraint. Since love is something we naturally crave and find intrinsically satisfying, it also satisfies the subjectivity constraint. This claim is supported by many concrete examples adduced in this book.

If there is no God, it is difficult to conceive anything else that can satisfy all four constraints. So Urban's argument here is plausible: "If the world has a meaning, God, the Supreme Spirit, must be its origin, ground and goal. But the world has a meaning indubitably. Therefore there must be a ground or goal of the nature" (Urban 1951, p. 198).

Now let us consider some common objections to the theistic solution. First, there is the Debasement of Humanity Objection. For example, Kurt Baier considers it an insult to humans to suppose that God has created them for a purpose. Human beings seem to lack intrinsic significance or meaning in themselves. They are reduced "to the level of a gadget, a domestic animal, or perhaps a slave" (Baier 1980, p. 52).

To this objection, Block replies, "This misconstrues…the relationship of love and awe that connects one with G-d. G-d loves every human being as a father loves a child…if one loves G-d in return, one will not consider it a menial task to fulfill His wishes" (Block 2007, p. 120). Suppose two lovers are so deeply in love with another that they both feel that their meaning of existence is to enter into a loving union with the other. I cannot see that by claiming this, one is trying to debase the other.

Second, there is the Diversity of Goals Objection. This points to the fact that human beings are all unique in their background, needs, desires, and values. So it is implausible to say there is only one telos for all human beings. To say so is to curtail the diversity and spontaneity of human existence by imposing a monotonous goal on all. In reply, we need to note that infinite diversity amounts to denial of any objective answer to the quest for meaning. So the important point is to guarantee sufficient diversity, and not to deny all common goals to human beings. If there is indeed an Infinite Loving God who is also the Creator of all, it does seem plausible to claim that a relationship with this God is a great good for all. Any cavalier dismissal of this claim is begging the question against theism.

Perhaps the critic can appeal to our experience that if we narrow our concern to just one good, our life will feel monotonous. Suppose we ask a friend where he will go to spend his leisure time, and his answer is the same every time—"Victoria Park" (in Hong Kong). We can't help feel that his life seems a bit monotonous. However, we have this feeling because there are many other interesting and beautiful places in Hong Kong. So by restricting his choice so narrowly, our friend is missing out on a lot of values. However, if, per impossible, Victoria Park were infinitely large and contained an infinite variety of sites and facilities, then our feeling would be different. In this case, he may not have missed out on anything at all. Similarly, God is the source of all values, and contains all values in His Infinite Life. Participation in His Life also means an appreciation and sharing of all values, in their infinite varieties. So a union with God will not be found monotonous, because there is always something new, something exciting to explore.

### 11.3.4 Naturalistic Alternatives to the Theistic Solution

#### 1. Heroic affirmation of absurdity

Perhaps the critic can flatly deny Urban's assumption that the world does have a meaning. For example, atheist existentialists such as Sartre and Camus forthrightly affirm the absurdity of life: there can't be objective meaning in the world. Life is a useless passion, or is, like Sisyphus's task of forever rolling a stone up the hill—just futile. However, it is arguable whether this denial of meaning is contradicted by our implicit confidence in life: "We must ask...whether we could make any moral choices whatever, unless we could, to some extent at least, put our hearts into them—unless we were, in some slight degree, already confident of their long-term significance, whatever happens" (Ogden 1967, pp. 35–6).

Ogden challenges the "absurdist": "The one thing for which none of us can rationally decide, whether his particular choices, is the eventual nullity of his decisions. Even the suicide who intentionally takes his own life implicitly affirms the ultimate meaning of his tragic choice" (Ogden 1967, p. 36). In fact, the claims of Camus and Sartre that life is absurd seem to be contradicted by their actual life and defiant commitment—both joined the Underground Resistance and later maintained a passion for politics. If all our actions are in principle absurd, then Camus's heroic rebellion against absurdity, as well as the concern for the plight of the French people, must be absurd, too. We can also note that in *The Plague*, Camus seems to affirm the profound significance of the heroic choice of Tarrou to relieve others' suffering at the expense of his own life, though he is at the same time puzzled about the possibility of an atheist saint.

The problem for Camus here is how to make intelligible the profound meaning of moral transcendence in a naturalistic world that is indifferent to morality. Gelven thinks that "to assert that one has autonomous, non-subjective importance forfeits the possibility of explaining this importance in terms of private wants or individual goals. One must assume some kind of world-plan, divine providence, world-significance, or even something as vague as the general scope of ultimate reality" (Gelven 1990, pp. 61–2). This means that the meaning of life and a cosmic meaning are not really separable. The atheist answer seems to fail the cosmological constraint.

In any case, complete nihilism is very difficult to maintain, and the categorical rejection of meaning is perhaps *not consistently livable*. There is every pragmatic reason not to accept this option. Indeed, child psychologists (e.g. Erikson) tell us that there can be no maturation without the presence of this faith at the outset of the socialization process. Hence at the very center of the process of becoming fully human, at the core of *humanitas*, we find an experience of trust in the order of reality. For the sake of argument, let me concede that we cannot theoretically prove that the world has a meaning. But neither can we prove that it has no meaning. In this situation, we can appeal to an argument such as William James's will to believe to show that it is reasonable (or even more reasonable) to accept that the world has a meaning, given the considerations adduced above.

## 2. Meaning Can Be Invented

Usually secular humanists will agree that there is no meaning in the world, but this is not a problem at all, because we can *create* meaning. For example, Paul Kurtz takes this view, and thinks that meaning can be freely invented by human beings (Kurtz 1989, p. 116). Lloyd Geering is a kind of death-of-God theologian in New Zealand. He admits that science cannot provide the answer, but "each of us is now responsible for creating our own personal meaning system" (Geering 1994, p. 201). Geering's own proposal is that we should construct an earth-centered meaning system and acknowledge the sacred character of the earth: "The whole earth *must* become resanctified in our eyes...This imperative to care *must take precedence over lesser loyalties and over all differences* of race, nationality, gender and personal beliefs. It is the kind of love which is ready to sacrifice individual self-interest for the *greater good* of the whole" (Geering 1994, p. 235; italics mine).

However, we know how to invent a machine, but what does it mean to talk about "inventing a meaning?" If I am a naturalist who originally sees the world as devoid of meaning, can I force myself to believe the world will be filled with meaning just because I make a choice or invent a purpose? If we were doing this unconsciously, this might be possible. But how can I create a meaning that has normative implications while all along remaining very conscious of the fact that it is *only my creation*?

Second, Geering's position, in fact, has nihilistic implications. If each of us is now responsible for *creating* our own meaning, then there is no reason a sadist or criminal cannot construct a meaning system that glorifies sexual perversion or crime. Geering seems to be caught in a dilemma. If he really believes that it is "vain to search in general for the meaning of life," then he cannot legislate how other people should create their meaning. He should make it clear that his own preference for an earth-centered meaning system is just his "bias," no better than the man-centered or money-centered systems. Even if he thinks some of these systems will lead to "bad" consequences, for example, the ecological crisis, he should bear in mind that what is deemed good or bad is also a subjective construction. There are, in fact, some people who deem the destruction of humankind a "good" thing, for example, the Unabomber. So to be consistent, Geering should avoid phrases like "the greater good." There is no reason people cannot construct their own imperatives that put higher priorities on their "lesser" loyalties. Why are they not free to invent as they see fit?

So the idea of the "creation of meaning" faces enormous difficulties. In contrast, the traditional Christian answer to the quest for meaning does not have these problems. Even Geering once said, the "greater strength of Christian dualism is that the other-world provided the meaning for this-world" (Geering 1994, p. 115)!

## 11.4 Conclusion

When we survey the whole range of existential experiences considered above, we can't help be surprised by the extravagance and transcendence of the human psyche. Perhaps such experiences are compatible with the naturalistic worldview, but they are hardly to be expected. It is not clear that they contribute to our animal survival—just contemplate the fact that not a single species, other than human beings, seems to have agonized over its existence. The existential experiences seem to complicate our lives unnecessarily. We may be entitled to expect biological organisms that would think more about the concrete ways to improve their chance to survive and propagate their genes. It seems to be a huge waste of time to agonize over the meaning of one's existence (as did, for example, Tolstoy) and languish over the fact that our accomplishments cannot last (as in, for example, Russell's *A Free Man's Worship*). What is the use of all these? Perhaps we need a new cognitive science of existential experiences? But even this cognitive science cannot really *explain* the existential experiences. The more basic problem is that the naturalistic categories, such as natural laws, biological survival, matter, and energy, cannot reveal the positive meaning inherent in these existential experiences.

In contrast, all these existential experiences testify to the same conclusion: human experience originates from the human spirit, and this fact can be well integrated into the theistic scheme. Human persons are characterized by a structure of polarities between the finite and the infinite, which is manifested in human action, intellect, desire, spiritual quests, and so on. This point will be further reinforced when we explore the theistic explanation of moral experience, aesthetic experience, intellectual experience, and so on. We will see that it is remarkable that such polarities are almost all-pervasive in human experience, and it is not unjustified to speak of this as a *structure* of human personhood. Upon reflection, it is also clear that $H_t$ entails this structure. So theism is more coherent with the existential experiences than its naturalistic rival.

For the naturalists, each type of existential experience is not to be expected, and each type is independent of the other. For example, we can have a sense of freedom within a limited scope without the tendency to use symbols and myths. So these data do not have any consilience in naturalism. $P(e_9.e_{10}.e_{11}.e_{12}/H_n)$ would become much smaller than the individual probabilities. However, $P(e_9.e_{10}.e_{11}.e_{12}/H_t)$ would not be reduced to any significant degree. First of all, the individual conditional probabilities are closer to one. Second, they are more intrinsically connected in the theistic explanation. Hence the data seem to exhibit a consilience in relation to $H_t$, but not $H_n$.

# CHAPTER 12

# INTERPERSONAL EXPERIENCE, CRITICAL TRUST, AND GOD

## 12.1 The Nature and Significance of Interpersonal Experience

I have employed the term "interpersonal *experience*" quite often, but no doubt some philosophers will challenge the legitimacy of this. For them, we have a very serious problem of other minds or persons because "we cannot show the existence of other minds *on the basis of experience*, since the data of experience are one and all objective" (Vendler 1984, p. 20; italics mine). On the other hand, Ott claims that "we know the reality of interpersonal relationships...because we continually have *experience* of them" (Ott 1974, p. 43; italics mine). So can we properly speak of interpersonal *experience* (IPE) or perception?

### 12.1.1 Mediated Immediacy

Let us consider Farmer's account of our interpersonal experience:

> As I talk to my neighbour, hear his views,...watch the play of his features, gaze into the eyes...it is totally impossible for me to react to him in the same way that I would react to the dog, and still more impossible to entertain the idea that he might after all be only a mechanical talking doll. There is something intrinsically coercive and self-evident...The whole thing is *sui generis*...it has an intuitive and intrinsic certainty" (Farmer 1935, pp. 14–15).

I find Farmer's account phenomenologically quite convincing. I would interpret Farmer's claim of "direct awareness" as a sort of intentional immediacy. So my claim for IPE is that we often have non-inferential, spontaneous epistemic seemings about other persons and their mental states. For example, when I see that my friend is smiling, no doubt it is mediated by the experience of his facial features, and so on. However, I would be hard put to tell you what those features are that constitute the smile. My epistemic seeming is directly of the smile, though it is mediated by a SE of his face. It fits exactly with the model of mediated immediacy. This kind of epistemic seeming is also imbued with a sense of reality: one that is different from an awareness of physical things, but appropriate to persons.

Some recent neurological studies also show that our knowledge of the mental states of others is akin to direct awareness. According to Stump, "a pre-linguistic infant can know her primary care-giver as a person and can even...read the mind of her care-giver to some limited extent"; this "capacity for social cognition is foundational to the infant's ability to learn a language or to develop normal cognitive abilities in many other areas" (Stump 2009, p. 553).

The scientists discovered that a brain structure, called mirror neurons, is foundational for our recognition of others' intentions and emotions. In fact they "fire both when one does some action oneself *and also* when one sees that same action being performed by someone else" (Stump 2009, p. 555). So the knowledge of people at issue here is direct, intuitive, and hard to translate without remainder into knowledge-*that*, namely, propositional knowledge. These findings seem to support IPE as a basic source.

### 12.1.2 Emotions and Interpersonal Experience

This awareness is also accompanied by different sorts of noetic-qualitative complexes that are appropriate to people, and often they are implicitly embodied in our feelings toward others. Consider the experience of sympathy, which is possible only if the emotions of others are accessible to one. Consider also the experience of shame, in which the others are so obtrusively present. Other states, such as admiration, loyalty, expectation, anxiety, loneliness, or boredom, also seem to have implicit reference to the other.

### 12.1.3 Interpersonal Experience: Basic or Nonbasic Source?

Are we entitled to have a basic prima facie trust in our IPEs, or are we required to justify them by other sources? I'll consider the attempt to justify IPE as the alternative to a basic trust. First of all, there are arguments to the effect that the concept of "other minds" is inescapable. For example, it can be argued that our language actually entails the existence of other minds. However, Vendler replies:

> I agree that the use of P-predicates (person predicates) in the language presupposes *belief* in the existence of other minds. For that matter, so does the existence of language *simpliciter*. But this dependence does not show that the belief is correct.... we can imagine a tribe of robots, exactly like us in all outward manifestations, including 'language' containing P-predicates. (Vendler 1984, p. 13)

I tend to agree with Vendler. Suppose he is wrong, and the existence of *some* other minds can indeed be inferred. I can still ask, "Are they the people I suppose myself to have met?" The issue I am raising is whether *my* whole stream of IPE can be trusted. I cannot see how the affirmation of the existence of *some* other minds somewhere would solve this problem. For example, in the brain-in-a-vat scenario, those other minds that exist refer to the super-scientists who create the brain-in-a-vat and endow it with a linguistic program.

There are also arguments that emphasize that "An original or native solipsism is surely a chimera" (Webb 1966, p. 27). The point is that the development of self-consciousness is parasitic on the consciousness of others, and facts like the following are appealed to: "The child…is apt to speak of himself in the third person before he acquires the habit of using the first" (Webb 1966, p. 31). However, I cannot see how this view about the historical origin of the concept of "self" would help to solve my problem here. The skeptic can still retell the whole story in terms of *apparent* experience of parents and others and so on. As for the Wittgensteinian argument that the inner stands in need of the outer as criterion, let us suppose it succeeds in the much-discussed case of (intense) pain. The argument is still of limited applicability. What are the criteria for a mild itch or a deep grief? Many mental states have no clear criteria for their existence. (For a critique of Wittgenstein's private language argument, see Ayer 1967; Chihara and Fodor 1967.)

The only other plausible possibility seems to be the argument from analogy:

1. I observe the regular concomitance of certain mental states and certain behavior in my own case.
2. I observe similar behavior manifested by other bodies.
3. By way of analogy, those bodies are probably associated with minds that possess the corresponding mental states.

The problems with this argument are legion. The premise (1) above is doubtful for many mental states: unless I constantly look into the mirror, I rarely directly observe the behavior of my body, especially my facial expressions. Inference to (3) is shaky. I know of one case only, and I have no way of knowing whether this way of sampling is fair or not. The conclusion (3) is also too weak to support many pieces of IPE that are well-nigh certain.

Perhaps the defender of other minds can claim that it is the best explanation of others' behavior. It allows us to understand and predict specific aspects of the behavior of other people. There just seems to be no viable alternative—the skeptical hypothesis, like the Cartesian one, is simply too outlandish to be credible. Certainly the denial of other minds will appear outlandish to most of us, but it is not the result of a careful comparison of the merits and demerits of both hypotheses. Instead, it is because they have immediate awareness of other minds.

If we try to remove the "bias" of these epistemic seemings and "objectively" consider the evidence of SEs alone, can we really vindicate the commonsense hypothesis? Hallett asks pointedly "why others' behavior requires an explanation. Explanations must end somewhere; why not with others' behavior?" Even if we insist on the need for an explanation, "why not explain human behavior…by means of physical causes? There is no need to dream up evil geniuses…A neurological explanation stands ready at hand. We believe that others' actions do in fact have neural correlates; why assume anything more?" (Hallett 2000, pp. 110–11). The other minds hypothesis needs to posit distinctive mental states and events behind physical behavior. In contrast, the neurological explanation merely posits certain physiological states, and can still do the same job. The latter hypothesis seems to be more economical. Well, both sides can go on to make claims and counterclaims about which is the better explanation for quite some time. Shall we suppose that the justification of our everyday beliefs about other minds is hanging in the balance, waiting for the conclusion of this debate?

I think the problem of other minds is insoluble if narrow empiricism is assumed. So if we want to avoid skepticism about other minds, we do need to have a basic trust in our IPE, and abandon narrow empiricism. My conclusion is that the Type PCT is applicable to IPE. Of course, IPEs can also be subjected to defeaters and enhancers (e.g. consensus, considerations of analogy, or best explanation). But no doubt, in the framework of CTA, our awareness of other minds in the context of a deep, responsive, and long-term relationship will often be justified.

## 12.2 The Distinctiveness of Interpersonal Experience

### 12.2.1 *General Observations*

The reality of other people is qualitatively different from the reality of physical objects, and hence our ways of knowing in IPE are also different. First, in IPE there is the "awareness of the other's will as standing over against our own...and over which there is no passing save in so far as he invites us so to do" (Farmer 1935, p. 19). In other words, our knowledge of other people depends to a significant extent on their decisions to reveal themselves to us. As a rule, the secret thoughts and motives of one's mind are not open to public inspection. So how can we know them? We need to be told. Naturally, this brings us to the second point: the distinctive and wonderful phenomena of speech and communication, which not only allow us to gain deep knowledge of others, but also help to establish a strong sense of rapport between people. Intimate and extensive conversations between friends and lovers are no doubt the main way to build up their relationship and communion.

Third, in IPEs, we do not just observe one another: we *can* also participate in one another's lives, and a deep IPE seems to "invade" one's inner self and change one's sense of identity. This can be shown by the experience of deprivation "which we suffer in the separation from others through, say, death, or divorce...In such a case we are forced to 'reassemble' ourselves" (Chatterjee 1963, p. 221). There is also the experience of presence, of mutual participation. As Marcel says, "I am unable to treat him as if he were merely placed in front of me;...he is also within me." At the same time, he is *with* me. So presence is neither a relationship of inherence nor exteriority (Marcel 1948, pp. 24–5).

Fourth, other people are experienced as *transcendent and mysterious* in some sense. This is related to the awareness of the independence of the other's will. The sense of reality is heightened when we find that our conceptual framework can't contain them and predict their behavior. They are experienced as agents in their own right, who can produce surprising effects, sometimes, on us. They are also felt to be selves who have an incommunicable depth, who are irreplaceable individuals. "As soon as another person becomes important to us...we are to a certain extent astonished by his individuality. From time to time we pause in his presence, and allow the incomprehensible fact of his being in the world to dawn on us" (Scruton 2009, p. 50).

We have this sense of mystery when confronted with both the beginning and end of life. Concerning the experience of childbirth, Denis Edwards observes: "parents...who certainly know that the child is the product of their own bodies, still find themselves overwhelmed by the mystery of the child they hold. They sense that they are co-creators of this child with something that is beyond them" (Edwards 1984, p. 31). The case of Verna Benner Carson in the School of Nursing of the University of Maryland is a good illustration. She had a childhood faith in God and slipped away from faith during her college years. She says, "My own heart grew cold and I moved away from [God]...He was calling me back. I continued to resist until my first son was born. My pregnancy and the subsequent birth of my son Adam were spiritually rich experiences. I was very much aware of being a cocreator with God" (Anderson 1998, p. 95).

This sense of transcendence in IPE is also present in our encounter with death: "we look with awe on the human body from which the life has fled...The dead body is the object of rituals and acts of purification...in order to overcome the eeriness, the supernatural quality, of the dead human form" (Scruton 2009, p. 177).

In SE, most of the objects we encounter are replaceable. One copy of today's *New York Times* is as good as another, and we do not experience each copy as an incommunicable individual. John Crosby (2001) contends that this awareness is crucial for our ascription of dignity to other persons. He imagines someone denying the dignity of Socrates on the basis that everything about Socrates is, in principle, repeatable. Crosby observes, "Those who knew and loved Socrates...will insist that there was in Socrates something absolutely unrepeatable." We are aware of "something ineffable, something too concrete for the general concepts of human language; something knowable through love but not utterable in concepts" (Crosby 2001, p. 298).

### 12.2.2 I-Thou Relationship

Martin Buber's distinction between the I-Thou relationship and the I-It relationship has been very influential. He emphasizes the prevalence of meeting (or encounter) in our life, a relationship that cannot be reduced to propositional or conceptual knowledge. The social nature seems to be an essential pole of human existence. Every human being has a long period of dependence on his family members, and it is in the context of these I-Thou relationships that the human self begins to be formed. It also seems true that an individual's human growth is inseparable from his dependence on other persons. Everyone seeks the understanding, affirmation, and love of others *for their own sake*, and to understand and love another (perhaps to a smaller extent). Of course, this points to the desire to participate in a community of mutual understanding and love. A mature I-Thou relationship is *creative*: "community brings into human experience the sense of mutual creation. One person's praise, approval, love makes the other break forth in abilities he (she) did not know he (she) had…One person's relentless criticism, honesty, different sense of reality calls another's attention to self-deceptions, fraudulence, inauthenticity he (she) might never have noticed in himself (herself)…. They mutually create each other's humanity" (Novak 1971, pp. 13–14).

Knowledge and affirmation of others seem to be inseparable from self-knowledge and self-affirmation, and their relationships are dialectical. On the one hand, without adequate self-knowledge and self-affirmation, it is difficult to truly understand and love others. When our desire for personal community is coupled with self-deception, all sorts of inadequate and illusory substitutes will arise in our IPE: "we canonise inadequate self-images, putting them in a position that cannot be questioned…. giving inadequate values our unconditional assent. We want so much to be loved for our own sake that we are unable to love others for theirs. Everyone is in the same situation; each person needs to be understood and loved if he is to be able to love and understand others" (Shutte 1987, p. 168).

This seems to be a deadlock, and to break it, we need someone who can love without being loved, a kind of Prime Mover in love. But where can we find the Prime Mover in love, and the source of genuine and life-transforming personal communion? The obvious question is: "if *every* finite human person, for him to grow to maturity, has to experience first the love of a mature person, then how can the whole process start in the beginning?"

### 12.2.3 Love and Sex

As already pointed out, the I-Thou relationship, upon reflection, seems to disclose a sort of mystery. The Thou seems forever transcending our grasp, but also given as a *gift*. This feeling can be more conspicuous in an intense love relationship. "Young couples preparing for marriage, if asked…whether their mutual love is not itself a most amazing and unaccountable gift, will often answer with a strong 'Yes!' with a sense of gratitude that this mystery has been articulated" (Edwards 1984, p. 30). In a mature marital relationship, there are ecstatic moments when loving and being loved is an overwhelming joy. There are times of passionate abandonment and radical trust, but also times of struggle, during which the couple has to cope with doubts and breach of trust. The marriage may end in failure, but there are also occasions when the couple can endure the pain and come to reconciliation, feeling an even deeper and richer relationship. All these are common experiences that show the depth dimension in a loving relationship.

Denis Edwards also notes that a deep experience of love will change one's whole life, and may open the person to the whole of reality. In accordance with the model of transcendental Thomism, he thinks that our experience of love presupposes "a pre-conceptual awareness of being without limit and an opening out of ourselves in trusting love toward the whole of life," and an implicit experience of grace that is immanent in our day-to-day existence. While Edwards's interpretation is not uncontroversial, he does help us to focus the spiritual dimension of our "ordinary" IPE, which is, in fact, suffused with meaning and significance. For example, even in the simpler experiences of friendship, we experience the joy of meeting old friends, the sense of absolute trust in a close friend, and the redeeming power of a friend's trust and encouragement, which help us face our own inadequacy and recover from inner despair. There are also more dramatic IPEs, such as the breaking up of a close relationship followed by the experience of forgiveness and reconciliation. In short, deep relationships open up a depth dimension in IPE. Even atheists can feel this—see the story of Patrick Glynn below.

A sexual relationship in human beings is, again, not just "natural." Macquarrie claims that "in the sexual relation the individual goes out from himself to the other in a unity of being-with-the-other. The sex act is not only ecstatic, it is also total.... 'the mystery of sex is the mystery of total contact between created existents'" (Macquarrie 1973, p. 87). Sexual union can sometimes lead to a mystical experience: "the ecstatic...moments of the heights of sexuality often provoke interruptions of consciousness and are phases from which lovers return to themselves as if stunned or confused by paroxysmal feeling and emotion" (Evola 1983, p. 4). In his study of peak experiences, the psychologist Abraham Maslow also affirms that orgasm can be experienced "as a unifying experience, a holy experience, a symbol, as a miracle" (Maslow 1970, p. 115).

Another way to reflect the personal nature of human sexuality is to explain why the saying "An animal is sad after coitus" can be true of the human animal. For Evola, "the explanation is given by that very saying itself inasmuch as it refers precisely to animals, that is, to a human love more or less *more ferarum* (according to the wild beasts). In particular, these negative or depressed states follow false unions, those occasions when one or both partners seek their own pleasure" (Evola 1983, p. 97). Evola's observation seems to be borne out by our historical experience. Modern society offers plenty of sexual experience for people. However, despite the immense increase in the number of copulations, modern people do not seem to be much happier. Instead, there is a widespread sense of disillusion and alienation, and the teenage suicide rate is generally on the rise.

Fidelity is a crucial component of a love relationship. The human language contains speech-acts of promising, engaging, committing, and vowing faithfulness. It witnesses our capacity to bind oneself with a promise, to commit oneself so unconditionally that the remit of commitment can extend to the sacrifice of life itself. For Marcel, this suggests the "supratemporal identity of the subject," and love leads of its nature to a proclamation of the indestructibility of communion. This and other unconditional features of fidelity seem to suggest a wider context in which these are intelligible. "If fidelity is really to be a total, irrevocable commitment of self, then it has to be grounded in a Presence that cannot fail...In its higher reaches, then, fidelity is a sharing in the infinite faithfulness of an absolute Presence or Thou" (Nichols 1991, p. 160).

### 12.2.4 Community and Solidarity

We also have a basic need for a larger community. This is crucial to foster our sense of belonging. Of course, it can also be the source of the inauthentic existence. The existentialists often speak scornfully of the mass, the "they," the crowd, and so on. It is true that one can lose oneself in the crowd and let one's life drift away. Reinhold Niebuhr also points to the dangers of a collective egoism. The spell of collectivism can be extremely disastrous when it is manipulated by evil charismatic leaders: just think of Hitler's Youth and the Red Guards who were crazy for Chairman Mao. However, the above is far from the whole story. Participation in a community can also be an act of transcendence, especially if the community is struggling for value-realization at great costs. When the whole community is suffering for a righteous cause, for justice, in opposition to tyranny, the individual who participates in such struggles sometimes would have an almost mystical experience of solidarity, and an almost tangible feeling of sharing in the *spirit* of the community.

Consider the Polish experience of Solidarity (the Union Movement led by Walesa) and the Mass for the Motherland, which was initiated by Father Jerzy Popielusko. He was brutally murdered by the Polish secret police, but his death sparked off another burst of Solidarity activities (see Sikorska 1985). A more recent illustration of the experience of solidarity is the Orange Revolution in Ukraine in 2004. The sociologist David Martin observes, "Up to one million people stood for two weeks in the freezing cold in the Maidan, the main square of Kiev, stimulated by television and a continuous concert.... the television coverage (BBC 4, May 15, 2005) suggested a more explicit religious link by cutting from the charismatic outpourings of the assembly to Ukrainians around the common table sharing the bread and wine of the Eucharist, as a kind of analogue of the self-sacrificing provision by support workers of comfort and sustenance to the thousands in the square. The assembly represented a kind of mystic marriage between people as persons, once strangers and aliens, but now as one in the spirit: 'I in you and thou in me'" (Martin 2010, p. 172). So there was an "I-Thou" relationship suffusing the whole assembly. People spoke of being "born again and of having been willing to set their faces to go to the capital and if necessary give their own precious blood for the fraternity of freedom and the rebirth of the nation" (Martin 2010, p. 173). In both the Polish and the Ukrainian movements, it is notable that the experience of solidarity and religious experience are intertwined as manifested by the merging of ecclesiastical and national liturgies.

The Ukrainian experience reminds me of the Chinese experience of solidarity during the student democracy movement in 1989. The peaceful actions of the university students earned the sympathy of the citizens in Beijing, and they came out in support in great numbers. The scenes were often moving. During those few months, the Hong Kong citizens were also greatly concerned about the students. When the situation became dangerous, in May 1989, around one and a half million people joined a peaceful demonstration for the students. When you saw 20 percentof the entire population walking on the street with you, fighting for a worthy cause together, your heart was warmed and your spirit elevated. The sense of solidarity was almost palpable. If it was not an explicitly religious experience, then it was at least spiritual. It was, indeed, a memorable moment in the history of Hong Kong.

How should we understand the intimate relation between social experience and spiritual/religious experience? As a sociologist, David Martin is, of course, familiar with the reductionist view (e.g. Durkheim). However, Martin contends that we do not need to reduce the transcendent to the immanent. Instead, these experiences have manifested "the transcendent in the immanent" (Martin 2010, p. 175). The human urge toward love, communion, and solidarity is a reflection of the shared *imago dei* in human society. Since human beings are made in the image of the Trinitarian God, there is a tendency to find fulfillment in a community—a smaller unit like a family, or a larger social movement. In Martin's words, there exists a "generic human experience of kenotic outgoing of spirit from one to another in love" (as reflected in experience of community, for example). Ultimately, the source of this kind of experience is "the kenotic self-giving of Christ as expressing God's Being realized in relation and going out, from the One to the other, that is love" (Martin 2010, p. 171). Since human beings are made in the image of God, the human acts of love are an imitation of the Divine Act. This kind of understanding is embodied in the Christian liturgy (e.g. Holy Communion). Interestingly, the ecclesiastical and national mobilizations have common liturgical and charismatic features. This can also be explained by the shared *imago dei* thesis.

However, from the Christian perspective, the doctrine of sin reminds us not to identify these experiences of community and solidarity simplistically with the work of the Spirit. These experiences are a great good, but they can also be deformed or abused. The human personhood and God's community are only realizable eschatologically. So in the Ukrainian experience, the "*imago dei* in each and every one present becomes clouded over with the cast of sin, renewed alienation, and despair…corruption and internal conflict rapidly dissipated the spirit of Ukraine's Orange Revolution…the eternal relations of the trinity remain as a transcendent ikon even when the heavenly city, New Jerusalem, hovers tantalizingly for a moment over the city of man" (Martin 2010, p. 173).

I think Martin's emphasis on the eschatological perspective is important. In this book, I argue for the significance of detecting divine immanence in human experience and history. However, we need to remember that in both our moral experience and religious experience, we also have experiences of sin and fallenness. The Chinese experience can provide ample illustration of Martin's thesis. Consider the experience of the red guards gathering in Tiananmen Square before the presence of Mao Tse Tung. It was an experience of ferventness and ecstasy, surely, but also fanaticism, as their violent actions later showed. If we forget this eschatological perspective, we would likely commit the mistake of idolatry. For example, in the 1960s, some contextual theologians hastily identified the Cultural Revolution as the work of the Holy Spirit, and even regarded it as the Chinese Exodus! (Song 1976, pp. 218–19; Samartha 1976, p. 240). As it turned out, the Cultural Revolution was, in fact, 10 years of disaster.

## 12.3 Fusion of Interpersonal Experience with Theistic Experience

### 12.3.1 *Epiphany of the Other*

One important difference between IPE and SE is that in an encounter with other persons, we always feel a sense of demand, which is absent in our encounter with inanimate things. In Emmanuel Levinas's *Totality and Infinity*, he elaborates a phenomenology of the Other that will lead us to God eventually. (The following discussions draw heavily on Fischer 2005, pp. 285–305.) We cannot treat Levinas's phenomenology as a kind of inference. Instead, Levinas is talking about "the relationship with the countenance of the other and the encounter with infinity in an event which can only be experienced" (Fischer 2005, p. 297).

First of all, the other is encountered as external reality, but at the same time "the other breaks through the self-containedness of each one's interiority" (Fischer 2005, p. 290). We have observed above that IPE possesses a strong sense of reality, but in IPE we also sometimes find our boundaries of selves invaded. Levinas is arguing against totality, which tends to eliminate the Other by subsuming all subjects in a single Whole. Instead, he upholds the pluralism of subjects, and this is founded on the "epiphany of the other in the countenance." Of course, the word "epiphany" suggests a kind of moral experience that has religious overtones. The occasions for this epiphany of the other can be an urgent demand for justice, or the misery in the countenance of the stranger, the widow, or the orphan. In this epiphany, the face of the other may become the gateway to the infinite: "human access to God occurs when the dimension of the divine is opened in the encounter with a human face...the face's statement changes into a categorical imperative...[e.g.] its infinite opposition to murder.... The face of the other becomes a gateway to the infinite" (Fischer 2005, p. 291).

This categorical imperative may generate a deep sense of responsibility: "As soon as I am conscious of the responsibility, I become obligated, irreplaceably and unconditionally: I cannot divest myself of the countenance of the anguished other without failure and guilt. That the other has no place of refuge is perceived like cries poured out to God. When the cries are truly understood, brotherhood is met as responsibility for the other, pointing to the father of all. In *the infinity of the challenge*, difference and sameness reveal themselves as the unattainableness of what is commanded and as the unconditionality of the validity" (Fischer 2005, p. 303; italics mine).

What is the force of Levinas's analysis of moral/interpersonal experience? Can it claim to be universal? Perhaps some critics will contend Levinas's analysis is exaggerated—we do feel the call of obligation, but there is no need to say that obligation and responsibility are infinite. Moreover, they can point to many people who are morally lethargic or indifferent. In fact, some philosophers argue that the moral claims are, in the end, erroneous, or real, but limited.

As far as phenomenology is concerned, there are impressive cases that support Levinas (e.g. the case of Liu Xiaobo, the Chinese political dissident who received the Nobel Peace Prize in 2010). As for the morally lethargic, they need not be considered as contradicting evidence if they admit in their hearts the unconditionality of the moral imperative (despite their less than enthusiastic practice of morality—perhaps due to weakness of will). Some may regard intense experiences of moral obligation as odd, or even pathological, as some critics contend that religious experiences are odd. Statistically speaking, this may be partly true. Indeed, naturalists who deny the objective reality of moral obligation should regard those who are "obsessed" with the face of the others, who experience the unconditional call of conscience, as pathological—after all, these people sacrifice their whole lives on the altar of a sheer delusion. But it seems that apart from the psychopath, most people, even if their moral practice is only mediocre, will not regard people such as William Wilberforce, Martin Luther King, Mother Teresa, and Nelson Mandela as pathological. It is more likely that they will be recognized and admired as moral heroes. Some philosophers will be forced to dismiss the force of the epiphany of the other by their prior commitment to naturalism. However, it seems reasonable to say that at least they have some PFEF to overcome, and this shows that we are implicitly invoking the PCT here.

### 12.3.2  Depth Dimension of Personal Encounter

For some, an experience of God is implicit in our experience of a community (e.g. David Martin) or an intimate personal relationship. For example,

Shutte says: "Human goodness wherever it shows itself is a sign of grace.... each human individual...is open to the presence and the power of God. And God's grace exists as an immediate and continuous pressure upon him through his normal relationships with other persons" (Shutte 1987, p. 177). Not that we can recognize this presence all the time; but it is there, and in rare moments of clarity we do sense it.

Probably Buber would agree to this. For him, "Extended, the lines of relationships intersect in the eternal You. Every single You is a glimpse of that. Through every single You the basic word addresses the eternal You" (Buber 1970, p. 123). One illustration is the story of Patrick Glynn. He is a philosopher who had been an atheist for many years. However, through the combined force of his moral and interpersonal experience, and arguments of natural theology, he has become a theist. The first sign of his awakening was his self-reflection, which led to his realization that nihilism couldn't be a basis for moral decision making. This was the process of "finding through experience [of being an atheist for many years], that a nihilistic outlook was existentially unsustainable" (Glynn 1996, p. 12). Of course, he maintained some "skin-deep" morality, but "at some level one had the secret atheist insight: If God is dead, then everything is permitted...if you come to imagine that there is no moral order to the universe, the incentives to good conduct, particularly in private life, are, unfortunately, much weakened. There is little to justify great self-sacrifice or deep personal commitment. Indeed, it is hard...to feel or express love to the fullest extent...What is there in the nihilist's universe to call forth sacrifice?...Such was my state in the early 1990s, when rather than work on a marriage much in need of repair—... I sought a divorce" (Glynn 1996, pp. 13–14).

However, reading Buber made a deep impression on him, in particular this saying of Buber's: "The You, when truly encountered, is *immeasurable* and directs us back to the *Immeasurable*." Glynn came to an honest self-evaluation: "In embracing reason as my idol, I had turned my back on everything *immeasurable* and with it on the entire realm of I-You. I had submersed myself in a world where, in the final analysis, there was only I-It" (Glynn 1996, p. 15; italics mine). A moral decision came after this moment of truth: one afternoon in the early 1990s, he decided to live honorably thereafter. Another important event was his subsequent wonderful romance with Gabriele. For Glynn, this was "an encounter with love sufficiently deep to bring *an intimation of the divine*...these romantic feelings pointed me toward something deeper...For reasons that I hardly understood, I began to utter from time to time a little *prayer of thanksgiving*" (Glynn 1996, pp. 16–17; italics mine). Notice that this process of transformation was gradual and mostly implicit, guided by the heart and not the mind. Glynn's experience is a perfect illustration of the thesis that a powerful experience of love would induce a strong sense of gratitude, and an implicit experience of grace. Indeed, every particular "Thou" is a glimpse through to the eternal "Thou."

### 12.4  Coherence of Interpersonal Experience with Theistic Experience

#### 12.4.1  *Analogy of Interpersonal Experience with Theistic Experience*

The above discussions of IPE seem to show the convergence of epistemology in the areas of TE and IPE. First, propositional knowledge (knowledge *that*) does not exhaust all there is to know. Our IPEs are often hard to express by propositions and, to some extent, ineffable. The best way to express them is often to tell a story, using metaphors. IPEs also have an important intuitive dimension. Our knowledge of others depends on in-depth interaction with them in an I-Thou relationship. These conclusions further demonstrate the inadequacy and superficiality of scientism and narrow empiricism. Recognition of the limitations of knowledge-*that* also supports the movement toward a post-foundationalist epistemology and opens the way for an integrated empiricism. We have also talked about the positive role of love in our knowing in IPE. So N. H. G. Robinson argues that just as "on the human level,...sympathy and obligation are the organ of personal knowledge,...obedience is the organ of spiritual knowledge" (Robinson 1969, p. 18). I think that the combined weight of IPE, together with many inseparable moral experiences, is already a sufficient reason for abandoning the straitjacket of narrow empiricism.

IPEs are, in many aspects, analogical to TEs, and this coherence enhances the epistemic status of both. As Hallett says, "on the one side, that the premise of God's existence strengthens the case for other minds ('It would be puzzling to suppose that an all-good God constructs creatures with cognitive faculties designed only to mislead and generate systematically mistaken views'). On the other side, it is evident that the premise of other minds strengthens both the teleological evidence for God and the evidence based on others' testimony" (Hallett 2000, p. 118). It also helps remove many objections to TE. "If the major monotheisms are right, then even to understand what is ultimately real, we will need to have not just physics and cosmology but also the non-propositional knowledge of persons; which cannot be mediated to us by the sciences" (Stump 2009, p. 565). If this is true of our mundane IPEs, it seems difficult to deny that it is at least possible for us to have a personal encounter (I-Thou relationship) with God, and our knowledge of God may be largely intuitive and non-propositional, building on our lifelong interaction with the Eternal Thou. Some philosophers have queried whether it makes sense to talk about the experience of God's love, since love is a dispositional property, and not a phenomenal property. Only the latter, and not the former, it is alleged, is experientially accessible. However, this model is falsified by both the phenomenology of our IPE and recent neurological studies of, say, the mirror neurons. They both show that we can have a direct awareness of others' joy, grief, or love, often mediated by profound emotions. It is likewise coherent to suppose we can directly experience God's love. In fact, this is what many people have actually experienced.

## 12.4.2 I-Thou Relationship and Community

$e_{13}$: Human beings have an innate desire for an I-Thou relationship and community.

$e_{14}$: Human beings' fulfillment depends partly on a participation in an I-Thou relationship and community.

$e_{15}$: Formation and growth of an individual depends partly on a mature community.

Now, it seems that theism provides good and illuminating explanations for the above data. The basic structure of personhood is not freely chosen by us, and it is, in a sense, given, part of the reality. Now, if the above data are correct, then it is part of reality that human persons are structured in such a way that they need one another for fulfillment. In this way it provides a telos and drive for human activities. This telos is, at the same time, perceived as objectively valuable. Any explanation has to do justice to both facts. Now, there is no special reason evolution has to build us in such ways. To "design" us as more pragmatic and prudential beings would seem to be more conducive to individual and corporate survival. Love and human relationships typically generate non-prudential behavior, not to mention the sacrifices needed to build up such relationships.

In the framework of evolutionary naturalism, we should expect sexuality to be the easiest thing to explain, and yet my earlier discussions suggest that human sexuality is not merely a biological phenomenon; it has integral spiritual elements as well. The strength of our sexual desire certainly has some biological and sensual roots, but when we look at its phenomenology more carefully, we find that the deeper driving force is the search for intimacy, union, the overcoming of loneliness, and so on. All these features are not substantially related to the propagation of one's genes, and in modern society people typically take deliberate measures to prevent the propagation of their genes during their sexual experiences. How should we explain these strange sexual phenomena? It is arguable that a religious worldview is even more adequate to such data—which appear at first insight to be the most naturalistic facts.

If a plausible naturalistic explanation is forthcoming as to why such a structure of personhood has evolved, it would also explain away its "halo," its unconditional and binding character. Such explanations would appeal to historical contingencies and expediencies, and our "commitment" to people would then also be contingent. If fidelity is just a useful tendency in the past, there is no obvious reason I have to stick to it if I no longer find it useful. Marcel's analysis of the experience of fidelity would then just be nonsense. Of course, those who are skeptical of *all* such experiences of value would not be convinced, but the adoption of global moral skepticism is a very costly option.

In contrast, theism gives a natural interpretation of this structure. In the Genesis narrative, the incompleteness of Adam is highlighted, and the implication is that people are made for one another, as well as for communion with God. It also explains the paradox between the individual and the community. Their mutual dependence seems to generate either a circle or infinite regress. Perhaps a plausible explanation is that the whole structure of the interdependence of individuals and community is based on the Infinite Person, who provides the creative ground of persons-in-community. If this is true, it would also explain the sense of gift we have in deep relationships. So $P(e_{13}.e_{14}.\ e_{15}/H_t)$ seems greater than $P(e_{13}.e_{14}.\ e_{15}/H_n)$.

### 12.4.3 The Argument from Fidelity

Earlier we discussed the experience of fidelity and Marcel's claim that this experience reveals the Presence of a larger Being. Brendan Sweetman (2008) defends a similar claim, in the form of an inference to the best explanation. The basic point to note is that fidelity appears to have an unconditional element to it. Fidelity is essential to simple promise making, to friendships, to marriage vows, and to a commitment to general welfare, and "this experience evokes in us a sense of an eternal, timeless, unchangeable value, to which the individual is faithful. Its value is so high that it demands of us an unconditional...commitment" (Sweetman 2008, p. 63). He gives the example of making a promise to make a return visit to a sick friend who is lonely in the hospital.

However, questions arise: "To whom do I make the commitment?...it cannot be to myself because this would not capture the experience of giving that seems essential to making a promise...[there are] cases in which the other person does not know they have a claim on me...where I have made a promise to a person without even telling them that I have made it. I can also make a promise to a person...who tries to release me from it; or perhaps to a person who later dies...Marcel holds, the person who has made the promise still experiences that the pledge is a commitment." It is "best explained if they are understood as being pledged to an absolute, transcendent reality...'Unconditionality is the true sign of God's presence'...the love between a man and a woman is unconditional, and as unconditional is ultimately grounded in an 'Absolute Thou'" (Sweetman 2008, p. 73).

### 12.4.4 Interpersonal Experience, Individuality, and Pantheism

When we reflect on the content of our IPE, there seems to be a tension between two forces that pull us in opposite directions. On the one hand, when we meet with the Other, we are impressed by the transcendence of the Other, which suggests he is an independent individual. On the other hand, in our experiences of intense love, solidarity, and community, there is an opposite tendency to lose oneself in a larger Whole. This issue is relevant to the resolution of the tension between theism and pantheism or monism.

For those who are attracted to monism, they usually feel that individuality is a curse that has to be lifted, and hence the goal of transcending the subject-object distinction by being absorbed into the All is desirable. Goethe's poem *One and All* is a good illustration of this urge:

*To find oneself unlimited, say,*
*Gladly the individual fades away,*
*There, all satiety given flight;*
*No more hot wishing, wild wanting,*
*No irksome demanding, strict 'shalt not'ing;*
*Relinquishing oneself is delight"* (cited in Fischer 2005, p. 297).

However, Levinas's account of IPE draws us in an opposite direction. Because of the epiphany of the Other, he strongly emphasizes a pluralism of persons. He thinks that seriously taking into account the personal "I" is incompatible with pantheism. Even in deep IPEs like sexuality, "the subject enters into relationship with what is absolutely other…Fusion of persons does not take place in the erotic event" (Fischer 2005, p. 293). He explicitly argues against pantheism and mysticism, which "lead the subject into ecstasy and dissolution of the selfhood into oneness and wholeness and interpret the downfall of the individual as individual a good thing" (Fischer 2005, p. 296).

Levinas's key concepts "totality" and "infinity" can be used to distinguish monism and theism. They seem to be incompatible, but both poles seem to have some roots in our deep IPE. Which way should we go, the way of totality or the way of infinity? It seems to me these two dimensions are both needed and are not, in fact, incompatible in a genuine I-Thou relationship. Levinas has not paid sufficient attention to the dimension of solidarity in which our individuality, though not denied, is also to some extent transcended. For example, in our experience of sexuality, although fusion of persons does not *literally* take place, the erotic event is not a "relationship with what is *absolutely* other," either. There is no metaphysical fusion, but, on some occasions, there is a personal union in which the other, while remaining the other, is experienced to be intimately connected to oneself.

As John Macquarrie says, "Both sociality and individuality belong ineluctably to humanity…No doubt there is a tragic potential in this separateness of human beings, yet it is also the necessary condition for the joy and richness of personal relations, which could not arise if there were no subjectivity. Up to a point, each one's subjectivity can be opened up to another in intimacy, yet there will always be that which is inaccessible and inexpressible and which on this very account adds to the depth of the relation. There is an inwardness in every human being constituting the core of his or her individuality" (Macquarrie 1982, p. 84). The irreplaceability of unique individuals is not a contradiction of personal union; it is its presupposition. The personal union does not abolish individuality; it revitalizes it. "One mind has joy in another by empathy, and seems to 'fit into' the other mind and be submerged in it. Nevertheless, so far from there being a fusion or disintegration of consciousness by this submersion, the mind enjoying the empathetic experience finds itself more fully integrated than before" (MacGregor 1947, p. 195).

So both the social and the individual poles seem equally original in the being of man. Moreover, we long for a personal union with the other, in which alone we can find personal fulfillment. So totality and separation are not the only choices. The third possibility is Buber's realm of the "between," in which the poles of "distance" and "relation" need to be kept in balance. This is also the fundamental structure revealed in our IPE. The best account of our experience needs to take both of these into consideration: the urge to be oneself and the urge to lose oneself. It seems that the model of personal encounter (loving union) can integrate the two. Theism is largely consonant with this model. God does not absorb the finite person, but rather confirms its being. He is also the enabler of genuine interhuman relationships, the author and the sustainer of the "between," the guarantor that the personal and the interpersonal have ultimate worth and significance.

We can recognize that the urge toward monism has deep roots in humanity without affirming the literal dissolution of individuality. What needs to be transcended is the false sense of individuality that refuses genuine communion with and openness toward the other. If the above account of IPE is correct, then it is arguable that TEs that presuppose a personal encounter model are more coherent with our IPE than monism. This point is important when we come to the conflict between theism and monism. In fact, this point was felt in the experience of Basil Mitchell, and this was the major reason for his conversion from Sufism to Christianity (in the following account, I basically follow Overman 2009, pp. 137–40). Mitchell was born in Bath, Somerset, in 1917. In his early years, he was greatly influenced by the Sufis, and was repelled by the Christian emphasis on the particular, as shown by the doctrine of incarnation.

During the Second World War, he had a personal struggle over whether to fight or remain a pacifist. His Sufi advisers pointed to the Bhagavad Gita for the answer, and Mitchell read this work. However, to his dismay, he did not find it helpful: "The Gita's answer was that as warrior Ksatriya had a duty to fight, not because of right or wrong, but simply as a duty... Not only was the concept of duty deriving from one's social status totally irrelevant to my situation,... I felt profoundly that what was at stake in Europe was... a fight of good against evil and that the outcome was of momentous importance" (cited in Overman 2009, p. 138).

After that time, the Sufi influence began to lose its hold on him. Mitchell later also had some romantic experiences, which made a deep impression on him. In short, Mitchell finally rejected monism because it seemed to be in conflict with his deeper experience of love, which intimated the importance of individuals, and also his historical experience of the distinction between good and evil.

## 12.5 Conclusion

When we are open to the richness and depth of human existence as we examine the rainbow of experiences one by one, I believe it will become clearer and clearer that no "scientific" or naturalistic account of human life *in its fullness* is adequate. Our IPEs already reveal the mystery of person, and also the inseparability of existence and value. Let us now turn to another component of the rainbow of experiences: moral experience.

CHAPTER 13

# MORAL EXPERIENCE, CRITICAL TRUST, AND GOD

## 13.1 The Nature and Objectivity of Moral Experience

### 13.1.1 The Idea of Moral Perception

Despite the protest of the purists about experience, there is such a thing as "moral experience" or "moral perception." Actually, some even talk about "moral observation":

> if one takes an observation to be any belief reached noninferentially as a direct result of perceptual experience, there is no reason to deny that there are moral observations. After all, just as we learn to report noninferentially the presence of chairs in response to sensory stimulation, we also learn to report noninferentially the presence of moral properties in response to sensory stimulation. (Sayre-McCord 1988, pp. 258–9)

Even a moral antirealist like Harman would grant this: "If you go round a corner and see a group of young hoodlums pour gasoline on a cat and ignite it, you do not need to *conclude* that what they are doing is wrong; you can *see* that it is wrong" (quoted by Lycan 1988, p. 169). Lycan also agrees:

> Spontaneous moral judgments are almost impossible to ignore or to write off.... Moral intuitions can seem as hard to disdain as are perceptual appearances, and in the perceptual case this difficulty is felt to indicate the presence and activity of delivery mechanisms. (Lycan 1988, p. 170)

So we do have moral epistemic seemings that are spontaneous, noninferential, and imbued with a sense of reality. An important part of our moral life consists of moral perception: when the moral qualities of some people, actions, or situations "stare us in the face."

If we pay attention to the phenomenology of moral experience, I think a cognitivist interpretation of our moral locutions is more plausible, that is, they are *meant* to describe objective states of affairs, rather than one's subjective states or preferences. I cannot fully argue for it here, but even moral antirealists, for example, Mackie, would tend to grant it. I think this capacity for moral perception is nearly universal, and it shows forth unmistakably in cases of horrendous evils (see below). That this capacity is indeed very deep-rooted can be shown by this confession of Putnam:

> Anyway, in the middle of this [moral antirealist] period I found myself with a severe moral problem in my own life…I found myself agonizing over whether what I was doing…was *right*—*really* right…it never occurred to me that there was any inconsistency between my meta-ethical view that it was all just a choice of a "way of life" and my agonized belief that what I was doing had to be either *right* or *wrong*.… I would not want to give the impression that this inconsistency was peculiar to me, however. My emotivist teachers…Reichenbach and Carnap—were fine and principled human beings.… both had deep convictions about right and wrong. (Putnam 1990, p. 145)

I suspect many convinced moral antirealists would also be haunted by this spontaneous (implicit) belief in the objectivity of values. If this is true, then moral experience is not entirely dependent on prior metaethical beliefs. This also demonstrates the fact that spiritual experience can occur against one's belief.

Third, I would like to point out that in our actual experience, SE and moral experience are closely connected and fused. In other words, the experience of "fact" and the experience of "value" are not separate domains of our *Lebenswelt*.

> In life as we all…live it, all is given, facts and valuations together, in an undivided whole.… Our respect for parents, our love for our friends, our loyalty to our country, our adoration of the divine, all are specific responses to specific features in an actual whole which is, in the first instance, given and not made. (Taylor 1930, pp. 55–6)

### 13.1.2 Emotion and Moral Perception

The ethologist Konrad Lorenz also defends the "realness, and the life-sustaining importance, of the perceptions by humans of values" (Lorenz 1988, p. 70). This perception of value is different from biological instincts. For example, "mother love is regarded as something noble; the nagging fear of never getting one's proper share is thought to be despicable—although both…are reckoned among the instinctive aspects of man's 'ethogram'" (Lorenz 1988, p. 96). He regards moral experience as "inborn forms of experience. They correspond to the phylogenetically programmed behavior norms of humans…they belong…to a species-preserving, meaningful system of human social life and are, thus,…teleonomic" (Lorenz 1988, p. 96).

One interesting aspect of his theory is his emphasis on the mediation of moral perception by emotions. "The murderer or the ruthless terrorist elicits feelings of horror and deep indignation; we regard them as nonhumans, as monsters or fiends" (Lorenz 1988, pp. 103–4). This is supported by the fact that "in emotions, and especially in the realm of perceived value, there is shared commonality...[e.g.] indignation we feel when the rights of fellow humans are seriously violated" (Lorenz 1988, p. 84). This again shows that emotions need not be cognitively superfluous and harmful.

### 13.1.3 Moral Experience: Basic or Nonbasic Source?

If the above account is correct, isn't it clear that we should at least grant prima facie force to our moral experience? Brink expresses this intuition in this way:

> [realism alone] provides a *natural* explanation or justification of the way in which we do and can conduct ourselves in moral thought and inquiry.... if this claim about the realist nature of moral inquiry is right, we have reason to accept moral realism that can be overturned only if there are powerful objections to moral realism. (Brink 1989, p. 24)

There is a complicated debate about moral realism and antirealism that I cannot go into here. I trust that the intrinsic force of moral experience will be obvious to many.

## 13.2  The Distinctiveness of Moral Experience

### 13.2.1  Experience of Value

Human freedom does not entail arbitrariness. We find that our actions and our choices are constrained, in some way, by what we perceive as values. The human *Lebenswelt* is, through and through, value-laden. Values "come to us with the character of 'oughtness', and that character is intrinsic to their very nature.... The good is...different from other essences in that in the 'ought-to-be' which is part of its essence as such, is the drive to realization" (Urban 1951, pp. 195–6). Baron von Hugel writes, "Everyone who believes fully in anything at all, be it the obligation to truthfulness, in the more than utilitarian worth of his wife's or daughter's chastity, even in the more than empirical worth of natural science, believes that these things are part of a moral order and...'in the more than human character of this order moral'" (cited in Urban 1951, p. 196).[1]

### 13.2.2  Experience of Evil

In human experience, we are also confronted by evil. A writer claims, "Evil is directly experienced and directly intuited. A young woman is beaten; an old man is mugged; a child is raped; a terrorist rips a plane apart in midair...Those whose minds are not bent by personal or societal madness immediately respond to such actions with justifiable anger...evil is real and tangible" (Jeffrey Russell 1988, p. 1).

Consider the case of the Moors Murderers, Ian Brady and Myra Hindley, who lived near Manchester. They tortured and murdered a number of children and then buried them in the Saddleworth Moors. Robert Wilson, a journalist, wrote of the trial of this couple, "I'd expected to see a couple of monsters, and here was a perfectly normal looking young couple, just looking around the court as if they'd been accused of nothing more serious than riding a bicycle without lights...Ian Brady...sat throughout the proceedings without seeming to give a damn as to what was going on around him—that, I think, was possibly the most frightening evil aspect of it all.... tape recordings of Lesley Anne Downey's last screams for mercy...Myra Hindley was heard saying, in a very matter-of-fact way, 'Shut up, or I'll hit you.' The little girl was appealing to the maternal instincts of the couple, even referring to them as 'mummy and daddy', but it fell on deaf ears. I don't think the sound of those tapes will ever leave me. Again, even while the tapes were being played, Brady and Hindley kept up the same poker-faced facade, as if it was nothing. They had no sort of remorse" (Babuta and Bragard 1988, p. 20).

"Almost everyone connected, even distantly, with the case feels *compelled* to use 'evil'...they would often search for an alternative word, but would invariably return to 'evil', sometimes in exasperation, *as if forced to use it*" (Babuta and Bragard 1988, p. 20; italics mine). Another journalist wrote, "There was a general presence of evil around Brady and Hindley that transferred itself to everyone in the court-room...this aura was almost demonic" (quoted by Babuta and Bragard 1988, p. 22).

There are also the horrors of group evil, for example, the Holocaust and the My Lai Massacre. Consider this: "A French woman was interviewed in a television programme called *The World at War*. She had witnessed, over a long period, a young Nazi officer sending trainloads of (mainly) children to the death camps. She said that every day since then she had asked herself how it were possible for him to do it...It expresses a sense of mystery at that kind of contact with evil...a sense of the reality of evil as something *sui generis*" (Gaita 1991, p. 33).

Babuta and Bragard even claim that "the hypnotic hold that evil seems to exercise over the observer can be seen as partly a numinous experience, instigated by an external *mysterium tremendum*, separate and independent of the individual" (Babuta and Bragard 1988, p. 52). We can see that profound moral experiences often provoke the spontaneous use of religious categories like the demonic, the numinous, or so on. Some of the above experiences may be regarded as proto-REs.

Numinous experience is to do with the sacred, while absolute evil is sacrilege. However, even sacrilege in a strange way bears witness to the sacred: "sacrilege cannot exist except where there is a persistent awareness of the sacred; this awareness must persist just sufficiently for the infraction committed to retain its value *qua* infraction and, so to say, its savour; but it must not persist more strongly than that, for if it did a reverential fear might in the end prevent the sacrilegious person from carrying out his purpose"

(Marcel 1952, pp. 34–5). Marcel supports this claim by these reflections on the concentration camps: "it was a matter of degrading these victims morally by encouraging them to spy upon (one another)...We are here in the presence of the *most monstrous collective crime in history*; only poisoned and poisonous imaginations could have conceived it in the first place" (Marcel 1952, p. 32).

Why do the torturers in the concentration camp do all the above actions? The motivation seems to go beyond mere utilitarian considerations, because there is a "wish to humiliate...to destroy in another human being that being's awareness...of having a value.... the persecutor strengthens in himself the sense of rightful superiority.... the man who has perfected a technique of degradation, and is a past master in it, feels a delight and exaltation in applying it, comparable to the delight and exaltation of sacrilege" (Marcel 1952, p. 34).

To be confronted with such evil can be a very unsettling experience. It naturally drives us to ask, Why? There is something deep down in us that demands an explanation, not one in terms of causes and general laws, but one in *meaning*. Another deep-rooted reaction would be outrage, or even *damnation*. In face of such monstrosities, "condemnation can be posited as an absolute and compelling necessity...Indeed, a refusal to condemn in absolute terms would appear to offer prima facie evidence not only of a profound failure in the understanding of justice, but more profoundly of a fatal impairment of *humanitas*.... these deeds...seem to violate a fundamental awareness of the constitution of our humanity" (Berger 1970, p. 86). This absolute and certain condemnation seems to look beyond the realm of our "natural" experience for a validation. In this context, we might even be tempted to talk about hell: "These are deeds that demand not only condemnation, but *damnation* in the full religious meaning of the word—that is, the doer not only puts himself outside the community of men; he also separates himself in a final way from a moral order that transcends the human community, and thus invokes a retribution that is more than human" (Berger 1970, p. 87).

### 13.2.3 Conscience and the Unconditional Imperative

The positive expression of conscience can be described as the summoning of the Unconditional Imperative. It could be interpreted as Kant's categorical imperative to perform duty for duty's sake alone. Or it can be interpreted as the unconditional call to be the authentic self, to be completely honest and to renounce the bad faith and so on. Either way, the summons seems to be characterized by a sense of otherness, and yet also by the sense that it most intimately belongs to oneself. In the words of Ebeling, "It is the mystery of human personal being that it is summoned from elsewhere, that it exists in response and as response, and that man is therefore wholly himself when he is not caught up in himself, but has the real ground of his life outside himself" (cited in Schilling 1974, p. 130).

### *13.2.4 Guilt and Remorse*

However, conscience seems to be better discerned by its negative expression: guilt or remorse. This state can be characterized by such seriousness that Gaita is tempted to say that guilt is "like a leak from another realm or world into this world—we stand within and without nature" (Gaita 1991, p. 50). It has a strange character that it can't be relieved by being shared: "suffering…may be consoled by being seen in the light of the suffering of others…That is not true of the sufferings of the guilty…. there can be only corrupt consolation in the knowledge that others are guilty as we are" (Gaita 1991, p. 47).

Proper remorse is not self-absorption, but a form of the recognition of the reality of others—those we have wronged. It is the acknowledgment of the sacredness of others. That is why lack of remorse in the Moors murderers is so horrible—this is tantamount to the denial of the sacredness of others. As Gaita also points out, time is often the best way to heal our suffering (physical or psychological). However, this does not work in the case of guilt: "time, working alone, is denied the right to heal guilty suffering…What may heal it is as strange as the suffering: repentance, atonement, forgiveness, punishment. We are so familiar with this that we have lost a sense of its mystery" (Gaita 1991, p. 51). For John Baillie, these experiences are indeed religious: "It is just such a sense of union—of oneness, of communion and, after estrangement, of reconciliation—that we have in mind when we speak of religion; and the perfect achievement of this union is what we mean by Eternal Life" (Baillie 1928, p. 326).

## 13.3 Fusion of Moral Experience with Theistic Experience

### *13.3.1 Experience of Conscience as the Voice of God*

Newman's argument from conscience is well known, and he is worth quoting in full:

> If…we feel responsibility, are ashamed, are frightened, at transgressing the voice of conscience, this implies that there is One to whom we are responsible, before whom we are ashamed, whose claims upon us we fear. If, on doing wrong, we feel the same tearful, brokenhearted sorrow which overwhelms us on hurting a mother; if, on doing right, we enjoy the same sunny serenity of mind, the same soothing, satisfactory delight which follows on our receiving praise from a father, we certainly have within us the image of some person, to whom our love and veneration looks, in whose smile we find happiness, for whom we yearn, toward whom we direct our pleadings, in whose anger we are troubled and waste away…we have no remorse or compunction on breaking mere human law…yet…conscience…[also] sheds upon us a deep peace, a sense of security, a resignation, and a hope, which there is no sensible, no earthly object to elicit…If the cause of these emotions does not belong to this visible world, the

Object to which his perception is directed must be Supernatural and Divine."
(Newman 1973, pp. 109–10)

This idea is supported by the phenomenology of moral experience: the element of otherness that seems to be inherent in the moral imperative. The sense of otherness is supported by the intuition that there is no obligation that is not an obligation *to* some living self, other than myself. This intuition is attractive, but here I do not contend that it is a necessary truth. It might be possible that we are just obliged by some Platonic moral reality that is impersonal. However, the personal God seems to provide a better interpretation of the personal features highlighted above: a conscience that threatens and promises, rewards and chastises.

Louis Dupre agrees that we can have a TE mediated by conscience, but if it is put forward as an argument, he has two objections. First, perhaps our conscience has this kind of phenomenology only because it is already conditioned by religious education. So this cannot be used as independent evidence for the existence of God. Second, there are some secular heroes, and "for them at least the moral imperative is not the voice of a transcendent Being" (Dupre 1977, p. 167). I do not think these objections are very strong.[2] The first objection concerns the role of conceptual framework in our experience. I have already pointed out that this itself cannot be regarded as a defeater. Similarly, we cannot experience an oscilloscope *as* an oscilloscope apart from some scientific training, and we will not watch a football match *as* a football match without some social training. Moreover, religious belief is not a sufficient condition for a deep experience of conscience (many religious believers do not have it); nor is it a necessary condition (see the experience of Glenn Tinder below). We have also discussed the interesting case of Wittgenstein, who feels the conscience as the voice of God despite his ambivalence about religious belief.

As for secular heroes, our model does not maintain that we will always *explicitly* experience conscience as the voice of God. A strong experience of conscience as objective (and even unconditional) is already some evidence for God (see the discussions below). Nevertheless, there are cases that show that the theistic phenomenology is even acceptable to atheists. One Chinese intellectual in exile after June 4, 1989, Yan Jiaqi, interestingly talked of his decision to follow his conscience as hearing God's voice despite his years of atheist education. Talking about his open rebellion against the Chinese communist government, he says, "Human beings have reason and conscience. When one's conscience and reason are no longer suppressed, and he makes a decision according to his conscience and reason, he will feel close to the decision of 'God'" (Yan 1992, p. 208). Once he visited Portsmouth in America, and felt impressed by the early immigrants to America from Europe, who were inspired by their religious faith. He says, "The most precious riches from God are exactly conscience and reason...When I left Portsmouth, I felt that I had discovered God, and my body was suffused with Infinite Power" (Yan 1992, p. 209).

He deeply believes that "in the innermost depth of our hearts, our judgments made on the basis of conscience would be largely the same...By September 1989, I have already understood the difference between 'the decision of God' and 'the decision of man'... Man can get closer to 'God' through his conscience and reason. The voice of conscience is the voice of God. Although I understand 'God' in this way, I still do not believe in a supernatural 'God' in the universe because of my deep-rooted convictions about physics and natural science" (Yan 1992, pp. 213–4). I find this interesting. Despite his disavowal of any belief in God, the sense of the transcendence of conscience comes through strongly in the above passages. This again confirms my thesis that spiritual experiences can happen against one's settled beliefs. In fact, Yan's experience of conscience cannot be derived from his existing belief system, which is atheism. Nonetheless, some powerful experiences obviously occur to him spontaneously and involuntarily. Shall we say that despite his lack of an explicit belief in God, he does have some implicit contact with the Divine Reality through his irrevocable commitment to the moral reality?

However, as our epistemology needs critical elements, it is important to point out that conscience cannot be equated to the voice of God in a simplistic fashion. Conscience may remain undeveloped or rendered dysfunctional through habitual violation. Sometimes an erring conscience, say, plagued by self-deception, may even bring disastrous results. These phenomena are, in fact, anticipated in our model. So the voice of God in our conscience can be more reliably heard in the general summons to be a kind of morally honorable person (see the experience of Glynn in Chapter 12), than in the call to a *particular* moral decision. The former summons is the foundation of all the particular decisions we make, but it can never be wholly objectified as a universal standard of conduct.

The decision to be an honorable person needs to be renewed in every moment of existence, and to be actualized in various concrete situations. In this process, we inevitably make mistakes. In order to test whether an experience of conscience as the voice of God is veridical, it is more important to look at the person's general quality of life than to focus on a few particular decisions. If the experience of God's presence in conscience is not a sporadic, but a constant, feature of some person's experience, and this is manifested in an impressive moral practice in general (which also sometimes includes some noble acts of self-sacrifice), the case is harder to deny. Shall we say it is again just a deep-rooted and persistent illusion in his life, and this illusion completely explains his moral integrity and occasional nobility? Wouldn't it be more reasonable to trust that his experience at least indicates some truth about reality?

### 13.3.2 *The Case of Glenn Tinder*

The interesting conversion experience of the political scientist Glenn Tinder vividly illustrates the fusion of moral experience and TE (Anderson 1998, chapter 15). Tinder was baptized only in his early forties. He regards his own conversion as a miracle, because "there was nothing in my childhood and youth, and nothing in the spiritual setting I inhabited as an adult, to explain it...nowhere in my background or environment were there Christians (the quiet sort aside)" (Anderson 1998, p. 146).

The important experiences that set him on the spiritual path happened during the three years he served in the Navy. In March 1945, his ship sailed into Manila Harbor. While carrying out his duties, he killed two unarmed Japanese soldiers. Initially, he was entirely untroubled. However, a few days after the second expedition, he suddenly had this experience: "I was nearly felled with the realization that I was responsible for the needless loss of two human lives. I had been officer in charge of the two exploratory expeditions, and I had fired my gun into the bodies...The terrible word *murder* invaded my mind...I realized that I had committed an offense against something holy...I had never had anything like 'a religious experience.'...Now, unexpectedly, an angry God...towered over me" (Anderson 1998, p. 150). This moment of "metaphysical panic" changed his life forever.

He was tormented by moral agony for several weeks, only to be relieved by another TE: "I was leafing through the Bible in a mood of desperation,...[I came across] Psalm 118:24: 'This is the day which the LORD hath made,...we will rejoice and be glad in it.' I knew in an instant that in spite of what I had done God's universe remained intact, that I inhabited a day that God had made, and that I could live. The inward experience immediately found an outward symbol. The sunlight on the waves of the blue Pacific Ocean took on a splendor and significance they had never before had but never lost during my time at sea. In the sunlit waves that were all about me every day I saw a sign of the divine power that could, in a way still utterly beyond my understanding, deliver me from guilt and give me life" (Anderson 1998, pp. 150–1).

Tinder's case confirms the claim that RE can happen unexpectedly to someone *despite* his background. Moreover, he may find it hard to understand the experience. Second, several types of TE can merge together. In Tinder's case, it is the fusion of moral experience (guilt), sudden enlightenment through reading Scripture, experience of grace mediated by aesthetic experience (natural beauty), and the long process of intellectual integration.

### 13.3.3 *Experience of God through the Struggle for Justice*

People also claim to experience God through a struggle for justice. Schilling talks of God's presence in some contemporary social movements, for example, the anti-war movement: "In movements like these in behalf of social, economic, and political justice many religious persons have experienced in dedicated action an awareness of the living reality of God which far surpasses in vividness and power anything which they have known as participants in corporate worship in church or temple.... Thus the distinguished Jewish theologian Abraham Heschel remarked, 'When I marched with Martin Luther King in Selma, Alabama, I felt my legs were praying'" (Schilling 1974, p. 145).

Of course, King himself was a Baptist minister, and his commitment to the civil rights movement was inspired by his Christian faith. The noble vision reflected in his 'I Have a Dream' speech at the 1963 Washington rally was also indebted to his understanding of the Biblical drama, for example, the Exodus event. Moreover, his persistence in the movement despite setbacks and challenges was sustained by his experience of God: "During the Montgomery bus boycott he was terrified one night by threats against his life. He tells of sitting alone in the kitchen and of experiencing the presence of God, which reassured him to persevere" (Bianchi 1972, p. 117).

Mohandas K. Gandhi is another impressive example illustrating how we can experience God in moral struggles. Gandhi used to say, "God never occurs to you in person but always in action" (cited in Erikson 1969, p. 93). This is what we call participatory knowing. Gandhi's political actions and his RE are inseparable. Gandhi wrote to C. F. Andrews: "I have taken up things as they have come to me and always in trembling and fear...I fancy that I followed His will and no other and He will lead me amid the encircling gloom" (cited in Erikson 1969, p. 411). In fact, prayer meetings were often held before his social actions. "In his ashrams the day began and ended with prayer, readings (mainly from the Gita), hymns (including some Christian hymns)" (Hick 1999, p. 150).

Gandhi is often guided by his "inner voice," which clearly has a mystical and religious meaning. Listening to this inner voice is important for the discernment of "the truth," and of course Gandhi's famous strategy of Satyagraha depends on the unmistakable experience of this "evasive" truth. This is not abstract propositional truth that can be calculated by an algorithm. "The sudden conviction that the moment of truth *had* arrived always came upon him as if from a voice which had spoken before he had quite listened. Gandhi often spoke of his inner voice, which would speak unexpectedly in the preparedness of silence—but then with irreversible firmness and an irresistible demand for commitment" (Erikson 1969, p. 411).

It is the truth in being and the truth in action. Each individual needs to face an absolute Being who alone is truth. He needs to be true to himself, to refuse *bad conscience*, *negative identity*, and *hypocritical moralism*, which characterize the division of men into pseudo-species. By learning to love the opponent, he needs to make sure that his actions are not motivated by his egotistic hate. The supreme test of the truth is the readiness to suffer, to get hurt and yet not to hurt (*ahimsa*). The religious origins of these ideas are obvious. So Gandhi's experiment with Truth has an implicit reference to the quest for God. "The satyagrahi, who has been presented for the most part as a political activist of a particular kind, is actually...a religious type...Gandhi as a satyagrahi himself was no doubt one who 'relies upon God as his sole refuge'. His inner life was nourished by a very deep faith" (Chatterjee 1983, p. 92).

Gandhi's experience of social actions is, at the same time, his experience of God. The language and practice he uses is basically theistic. As Hick points out, "For Gandhi there was in practice no division between religion and politics...the great aim of his life was, in his own words, to 'see God face to face'...man's ultimate aim is the realization of God, and all his activities...have to be guided by the ultimate aim of the vision of God" (Hick 1999, p. 150). True, sometimes Gandhi's language about God may look monistic. For example, he emphasizes that God is beyond the scope of all human ideas, and talks about the "worship of the Formless" (Hick 1999, p. 151). Gandhi also said, "I believe in advaita, I believe in the essential unity of man and for that matter of all that lives" (cited in Hick 1999, p. 152). However, his focus was not upon the Advaita Vedanta philosophy as such, but on its practical significance. Gandhi is talking about the union of all life or souls, and not about the union of souls with Brahman. This is not incompatible with theism, and Gandhi sometimes expressed the truth in a theistic way—"we are all children of the same God" (cited in Hick 1999, p. 161). In fact, after talking about the unity of all, Gandhi goes on to say, "The rays of the sun are many, through refraction." The Indian philosopher Margaret Chatterjee points out that this image "is pluralistic. To speak of a common source is not to speak of identity" (Chatterjee 1983, p. 105). She unambiguously affirms that Gandhi "does not belong to the tradition of those who see liberation in terms of the attaining of a superior state of consciousness beyond good and evil...the vision of God, and listening to God, presuppose a discreteness, distance which is to be bridged both by devotion and grace, but which does not terminate in a state of identity. Gandhi is not a mystic, nor is he a philosophical monist" (Chatterjee 1983, p. 107).

I am not trying to make Gandhi into a Christian, though nobody doubts that he has been significantly influenced by Christianity, the Sermon on the Mount in particular. Gandhi was clearly shaped by the theistic tradition in Hinduism, for example, the Bhagavad Gita, which was his favorite devotional literature, and the way of Bhakti (loving) devotion. So the world-shaking actions initiated by Gandhi were, indeed, sustained by his experiences of God: "If I did not feel the presence of that living God, at the painful sights I see in the world, I would be a raving maniac and my destination would be the Hooghli (river). As, however, that Indweller shines in the heart, I have not been a pessimist now or ever before" (cited in Chatterjee 1983, p. 53).

### 13.3.4 *Experience of God through Conspicuous Sanctity*

We can experience God through an encounter with conspicuous sanctity or moral heroism. Eleonore Stump (1997) has provided the impressive example of Philip Hallie's study of Le Chambon, the French village that gave unstintingly in its attempts to rescue Jews during the German occupation of France. (The following basically follows Stump's account.)

This heroic act was inspired by their religious faith. In the beginning of the study, Hallie was not a religious believer. He tried to study the events objectively. However, he was so deeply moved that he says, "For me [the] awareness [of goodness] is my awareness of God. I live with the same sentence in my mind that many of the victims of the concentration camps uttered as they walked to their deaths: *Shema Israel, Adonoi Elohenu, Adonoi Echod*" (cited in Stump 1997, p. 283). Hallie was overwhelmed by the greatness and goodness of what the villagers had done. This led him to a commitment to God.

Another experience of conspicuous sanctity is told by a writer in Taiwan, Sima Zhongyuan. Father Zhang Zhihong was a Catholic priest who went from San Francisco to Shanghai in 1949. Soon after China was taken over by the Communists. Zhang was imprisoned for a long time, and cruelly tortured in the prison. This has permanently damaged his health. For example, both his hearing and eyesight were severely impaired. However, as the author says, "He is completely devoted to China. From the religious perspective, the human heart is the temple of God. Although violence can enslave the human body, it cannot occupy the temple of God. So after a brief period of recovery, he has returned to his original calling...to serve China" (Sima 1981, p. 16). After Zhang was exiled from China, he went to Taiwan. There he has for many years faithfully served the Chinese by promoting arts and literature, organizing social services, and helping a lot of young people. Sima has been the friend of Father Zhang for several years, but Zhang has never tried to proselytize him. Nevertheless, Sima comments, "The light shining forth from his humanity is his Word, which radiates toward you directly. This helps you learn to be tolerant and loving. From his life, suddenly we come to realize some spiritual insight. I can't help believe that the genuine Word does not need to be preached by the mouth. Father Zhang is not so much a preacher as an embodiment of his spiritual faith in his life!" (Sima 1981, p. 18).

After many years of tireless service, Zhang had grown old and became half-deaf and half-blind. People advised Zhang to retire and go back to America. Zhang pointed to the ground and said, "My home is here—China. I love this place, and the people." Yet he still led a team of young people in a trip to the heart of the mountains. One day, a truck knocked him over the cliff. When the people finally found him unconscious in the valley below, they tried to resuscitate him. When he became conscious again, he just said, "Sorry, I cannot lead your way back!" Not long after, he died in the ambulance. Sima later attended the Memorial Mass for Zhang. He reported this experience, "Death is only a door that looks dark. Inside the door is the Light of eternal life...That night, I saw that Light...Every young face is lovingly caressed and illumined by that Light" (Sima 1981, p. 22). Zhang's story may not be as impressive as that of the villagers of Le Chambon, but perhaps it is more common. They both illustrate the point that sometimes we can strongly feel the Presence in a life beautifully lived.

### 13.4  Coherence of Moral Experience with Theistic Experience

#### *13.4.1  Value, Evil, and Duty*

Consider, now, these data:

$e_{16}$: We have experiences of value, evil, and duty, which strongly suggest
that these are objective realities.
$e_{17}$: There *are* some objective values.
$e_{18}$: There *are* absolute evils.
$e_{19}$: There *are* absolute evils that demand a vindication of justice.
$e_{20}$: There *are* some objectively binding duties.

It seems to me that a naturalist who accepts any of these has a job on his
hands. So, again, the characteristic move is to reject all of these claims. Of
course, he still has to explain $e_{16}$, and various accounts, such as projectivism,
have been offered. If neither the rejection of values nor the non-cognitivist
account of moral and value experience is plausible, then the probability of
naturalism, given such data, is quite low.

On the contrary, theism seems to provide plausible explanations of these
data and also to weave them into a coherent whole. The objectivity of values
can be grounded in the divine being *in some way*, though this account is
by no means without subtleties. However, if some plausible account of the
divine grounding of values can be provided (e.g. Adams 1999; Evans 2010),
then $e_{17}$ would then be intelligible. The other two pieces of evidence, $e_{18}$ and
$e_{19}$, point even more clearly to the divine. I have argued that the perception
of absolute evil is akin to a perception of the violation of something sacred,
a sacrilege. It is only fully intelligible if the value violated is grounded in the
divine being and the *holy* moral law at the heart of reality. The demand for
vindication is not necessarily equal to a demand for vengeful retribution. It
just insists that the perpetrators of such hideous crimes *will not get away*.
This is only possible if there is an omniscient, omnipotent, and holy Judge.

The *unconditional* character of conscience again becomes intelligible in a
theistic world. It is hard to see how the world could bring forth moral experience carrying the note of obligatoriness, pressing upon us in a way that we
would describe in metaphors drawn from external objects, and calling upon
us for our dutiful response—unless it were itself originated and so always
sent us back to God as its final and absolute foundation. In fact, even the
staunch atheist John Mackie agrees with this logic: "objective intrinsically
prescriptive features, supervening upon natural ones, constitute so odd a
cluster of qualities and relations that they are most unlikely to have arisen
in the ordinary course of events, without an all-powerful god to create
them. If, then, there are such intrinsically prescriptive objective values, they
make the existence of a god more probable than it would have been without
them" (Mackie 1982, pp. 115–16). His way out is to deny the objectivity of
moral values. As I have explained, this is a costly "solution." In fact, Mackie

implicitly admits that moral experience is more coherent with theism than with naturalism.

Similarly, guilt points in the same direction. We have seen that a sudden realization of the gap between what we are and what we ought to be can be terrifying, shaking us to the core. Most people have similar experiences to a lesser degree. This consciousness of "the gap" can be explained by an implicit awareness of God: "It is the underlying relation to God which reveals to man the disparity between himself and his world, sets him at odds with that from which he came, brings him to that pass to which the animal cannot come—an unwillingness to take his world as he finds it, a consciousness of the everlasting No, and a defiance of it...it is his original knowledge of God that has made this alienation possible" (Schilling 1974, p. 153). The above arguments are further defended below.

### 13.4.2 *Naturalistic Explanation of Moral Obligation*

It is difficult to understand the objectivity of moral obligation in a naturalistic worldview. The reasons have been indicated by Mackie's argument from queerness. If naturalism is assumed, in fact, I agree with Mackie's judgment. My contention is that this cannot be assumed. The problem is further aggravated by trying to figure out how the evolutionary process would produce morality. Many evolutionary naturalists make it clear that the evolutionary account of morality in the context of naturalism is detrimental to the belief in the objectivity of morality. For example, Michael Ruse honestly struggles with the problems of the evolutionary explanation of morality. Ruse recognizes the intrinsic force of moral experience, but unfortunately he finds himself driven by his belief in evolution to moral non-realism: "for such claims as that one ought to be kind to children...ultimately there is no justification which can be given!...the Darwinian approach to ethics leads one to a kind of moral non-realism...substantive morality is a kind of illusion, put in place by our genes, in order to make us good social cooperators...the reason why the illusion is such a successful adaptation is that...we...believe that substantive morality does have an objective foundation...the phenomenological experience of substantive ethics is...that we feel that we ought to do the right and proper thing because it truly is the right and proper thing...an important part of the moral experience is that we objectify our substantive ethics" (Ruse 2003, pp. 152–3). But moral objectivity is only an illusion!

Indeed, Ruse further develops an argument from evolution against moral objectivity. The basic idea is that since evolutionary explanations are always contingent, it is a real possibility that an entirely different morality would have evolved. Evolutionary naturalism simply does not have the resources to say one kind of morality is more objective than another. Ruse explains, "evolution is a directionless process...there is really no reason why humans might not have evolved in a very different sort of way...From the Darwinian perspective, there is no ontological compulsion about moral thinking...we might well have evolved as beings...where the highest ethical calling would not be 'Love your neighbour', but 'Hate your neighbour'. But remember that your neighbor hates you and so you had better not harm them because they are going to come straight back at you" (Ruse 2003, pp. 154–5). This system of "morality" may also work. He asks, "if there is an objective foundation to substantive morality, which of the two is right?...What most people mean by objective morality incorporates the fact that it is going to be self-revealing to human beings...So, given Darwinism, we have a refutation of the existence of such a morality...We might be completely deceived, and since objective morality could never allow this, it cannot exist" (Ruse 2003, p. 155).

On the other hand, Ruse goes on to say, "we can dismiss National Socialism as evil" (Ruse 2003, p. 156). I am puzzled. Ruse has just argued for moral non-realism. So on what foundation can he dismiss Nazism as evil? Ruse himself acknowledges the limits of evolutionary explanations of morality: "why do things work as well as they do?...if you look at today's large societies, especially those that do function reasonably well...it is surely remarkable that they are simply based on rules of conduct forged in times and places very different from our own...Darwinism—can say little or nothing more" (Ruse 2003, pp. 156–7). He is open to the possibility that we might claim that moral realism is embedded in the will of God. I, indeed, think this is a better option, given the intrinsic force of moral experience that Ruse recognizes.

### 13.4.3 Naturalistic Explanation of Radical Evil

The problem of evil is the greatest intellectual obstacle to belief in God, especially in the form of the argument from horrendous evil. However, I also believe horrendous evil or radical evil is hard to make sense of in a naturalistic world. The comments of an agnostic, J. C. A. Gaskin, are revealing. He admits the atheist is "conscious of the potential damage he has done to the standing of the sort of morality to which he still (largely) wants to subscribe," and he may try to find some substitutes. However, in the end it is "very difficult for the atheist to do entirely without something like the authority...of God" (Gaskin 1984, p. 163).

One "glaring intellectual defect" of atheism is that its account of radical evil does not seem to capture the full force of our experience: "on the one hand we have indulged and planned destruction and evil on an organized scale never before experienced or contemplated by man; on the other hand our concepts of good and evil have shrivelled to social minutiae and utilitarian niceties of a purely local and restricted character" (Gaskin 1984, p. 163). The following is an important admission by an agnostic: "the effect of atheism in secularizing morality has been and is to trivialize the language of morality by confining its concepts to social and humanistic needs which leave us bereft of the moral eternities of good and evil which alone seem able to measure the scale of the actual good and evil, creation and destruction, which we now contemplate as real possibilities" (Gaskin 1984, p. 164).

It even appears to Gaskin that "only when set against the powers of an eternal or divine good or of a Satanic evil can the things we are now capable of be *adequately experienced in moral terms*" (Gaskin 1984, p. 164; italics mine). The above seems to support my contention that there is an awareness of something absolute and transcendent in our moral experience of obligation and evil.[3] If we take seriously our moral experience, as we should, then at least we can say that the inadequacy of the naturalistic explanation of our most profound moral experiences counts against naturalism. Perhaps our outrage at radical evil is the implicit participation in God's holy anger.

### 13.4.4 The Argument from Moral Obligation

Some naturalists who appreciate the force of moral experience have tried many ways to reconcile the apparent conflict between moral experience and naturalism. Some try to argue that even if morality is subjective, it can still be useful and serve as a guide to our life (quasi-realism). Many years ago, Baillie convincingly argues against these attempts. He believes that morality needs the support of Reality (this capitalized word is used by Baillie to indicate *ultimate* reality): "Our values refuse to hang in a permanent state of suspension in the thin air of the ideal; rather do they, as soon as apprehended, demand a cosmic setting for themselves" (Baillie 1928, p. 346). It is first of all supported by our experience of conscience: "No obligation can be absolute which does not derive from the Absolute" (Baillie 1928, p. 350). But something can hardly be called absolute if it does not even have a cosmic significance. So Baillie queries:

> Can any possible meaning be attached to absolute obligation, or to ultimate value, if these are conceived as having no sanction in the all-enclosing system…can this mean less than that reality demands these things of me? And if reality demands these things of me, then reality must be interested in moral value…it must be on the side of the good and against the unworthy and the evil. But that is to say that it is a moral Being itself, not indifferent to moral distinctions…the ultimate reality must thus be One Who loves the Good." (Baillie 1928, p. 352)

Having exhibited the inadequacy of naturalism, we can consider how the theistic grounding of moral obligation not only preserves its intrinsic force, but also leads to the fulfillment of the deeper drives of morality. Baillie's explication of religion as moral trust in reality is helpful here. In the religious perspective, the inner core of reality must be continuous with the moral consciousness, and we have the conviction that no value perishes out of the world. It follows that "conscience must be no more sojourner and resident alien in the universe, existing only on sufferance, but must rather be its own native burgess, exercising all the functions and enjoying all the privileges of citizenship" (Baillie 1928, p. 325).

Baillie writes beautifully about this moral trust: "It gives me the assurance that in following the gleam of righteousness and love and honor I am not entering into an unsubstantial region of my own fancying, but am rather identifying myself with the inmost nature of things, and bringing my finite will into line with the Infinite Will that made and moves the stars...I am now at home in the universe...I am not fighting alone, against impossible odds, for a fantastically hopeless cause, and with the paralyzing suspicion in my heart that it cannot really matter whether I win or lose...rather it is Reality's own battle that I am fighting, and the stars in their courses are fighting with me...[Reality] is nothing else than Love, the very Love whose feeblest earthly counterpart burns in my own heart and moves my hands to fight" (Baillie 1928, p. 326).

### 13.4.5 Morality, Theism, and Monism

Even if we agree that morality needs a grounding in Reality, critics may argue that this Reality need not be personal. Here Baillie correctly points out the intrinsic relationship between value and spirit, or morality and personality. It is difficult to understand a purely impersonal moral order, especially when we remember that morality is primarily about practice, and not just the existence of some abstract standard of rightness and wrongness. If the objectivity of morality means that the universe is not entirely indifferent to the conservation of values, then a precondition is that the universe can understand and discern values. If the universe cannot even understand values, in what sense can we say that morality really has an important role in Reality? Baillie says, "we are ascribing to it [moral order] the ability to conserve what is valuable. But plainly it cannot conserve what is valuable unless it be alive to the value of it...the balances in which all things are finally weighed should be sensitive to the subtlest moral distinctions, that they should record with infallible discrimination the finest and most inward fruits of spiritual development...can anything less than mind, soul, spirit be thus alive and thus sensitive?" (Baillie 1928, p. 390).

Moreover, the fullness of morality (e.g. moral beauty, a character with moral integrity, love, and communion) cannot be divorced from personal categories: "It is only to spirit that the beauty of goodness can in any wise be apparent. It is only personality that can appreciate character" (Baillie 1928, p. 391). In fact, the "personal communion with the Divine" can be said to be the fulfillment of morality in which "uprightness and honor and self-denying love, and all the things which really count, can live and grow and find their full fruition and be realized in their deepest meaning" (Baillie 1928, p. 392). So "whatever more God may be than a moral personality, He cannot, if our finite personalities are not to be spiritually homeless, be any less...[Theories which postulate] God as a mere 'immanent purposiveness'...come to grief on the fact that they would make personal religion, in any high form of it, impossible" (Baillie 1928, p. 391).

He explicitly criticizes the monistic interpretation of morality (e.g. that of Spinoza, Hegel, Bradley): "in trying to transcend morality they fall below it and present us with an Absolute conceived, if not in entirely unspiritual terms, at least in terms of lower potencies of our spirits than moral personality and the knowledge of good and evil…we cannot…agree…that in religion we are ever carried 'beyond good and evil,' or beyond the leadings of our highest values" (Baillie 1928, p. 328).

### 13.4.6 *Non-Naturalistic Non-Theistic Moral Realism*

The critic may claim that I have overlooked an important alternative to theism: non-naturalistic non-theistic moral realism as defended by Erik Wielenberg. He acknowledges the force of moral experience and agrees that naturalism does not give any enlightening explanation. However, he thinks that we do not need to appeal to God, because there can be basic ethical facts in the universe that are brute facts—fundamental truth that does not admit of further explanations. These ethical facts take the form of metaphysically necessary truths such as "in all metaphysically possible worlds…causing pain just for fun is wrong" (Wielenberg 2009, p. 27). I think this is an interesting option, which deserves attention. Here I can only briefly indicate why this alternative would not endanger my ARE.

Wielenberg only argues that theism cannot perform better than his theory (which is not a form of naturalism). He does not argue against theism, just that it is not absolutely required for the belief in moral objectivity. So the case for the claim that moral experience is more coherent with theism than with naturalism still stands. Moreover, my Rainbow Argument covers many types of experience other than moral experience. So unless Wielenberg's position can extend to the entire rainbow of experiences, there is no reason to think that there is a better alternative, which can better explain all our experiences.

Moreover, his theory has quite a few drawbacks. First, perhaps the alleged metaphysically necessary ethical fact about the wrongness of causing pain just for fun is plausible. But can we extend the same reasoning to moral duties such as helping strangers or sacrificing one's life to save others? I think many people will be surprised to hear that "in all metaphysically possible worlds, it is wrong not to help strangers or not to sacrifice one's life to save others." They will naturally ask, why is that? Second, in Wielenberg's scheme, the universe consists of two parallel realms, one of nature and the other of necessary moral facts. It introduces complexity in the worldview. Certainly this would not be a favorable option for tough-minded metaphysical naturalists. This theoretical demerit shows that theism is the better alternative, because it can give a unifying, coherent explanation of both realms.

Third, there is the further question of how these two realms interact. The moral facts themselves are presumably causally inert. Nature in itself does not know about the moral facts. Then the problem of moral knowledge becomes very acute (see Linville 2009). Similar problems occur for our knowledge of logical truths (see Chapter 15). Fourth, there is no further explanation as to why some moral facts, rather than others, obtain. Why isn't it the case that in all metaphysically possible worlds, causing pain just for fun is right or permissible? Is there any logic behind this? For Baillie, the data of moral experience show that value and existence are identical. In Wielenberg's scheme, value and existence are bifurcated. It is open to the worry of a radical error theory. Because moral facts in themselves are objective, perhaps all our moral convictions are radically mistaken. For example, the following may be necessary ethical facts for all we know: rocks and other inanimate things have immensely superior value than life and mind. So it is necessarily wrong to break the door of a car in order to save a human being trapped inside! Why? This is just a fundamental moral fact. What can Wielenberg say to this claim? However, for theism, because man is made in the image of God, radical moral error is very unlikely.

Fifth, what about the problem of cosmic justice? The moral facts are helpless, because they can do absolutely nothing to rectify the situation. In fact, they do not know about these problems at all; nor can they feel for those victims. This position can only lead to a rather truncated picture of morality as a whole. A sufficient explanation of morality should not only explain the basis for moral objectivity, but also the exigence of moral obligations, the integration of value and existence (for example, personal beings), and the possibility of cosmic justice. Sixth, there is also the question of phenomenology of moral experience. I have argued that this phenomenology is readily understood in terms of personal theism. However, it is difficult to understand how the nonnatural moral fact can cause one type of moral experience to occur, rather than another. Even if morality is objective, so what? Why should we feel shame or remorse?[4]

## 13.5 Conclusion

The naturalistic worldview seems to be out of touch with the height and depth of our moral experience, which can be made intelligible by theism. First, we have a TE mediated by various kinds of moral experience, but in such a way that our moral consciousness not only finds a ground, but also finds a transforming goal. So experience of God quickens and enriches our moral consciousness. Second, theism reveals itself as the only means whereby moral desire may be fulfilled. This fulfillment is not only relevant to the moral quest, but also gives an answer to our existential quest. Religion not only guarantees the conservation of values, but also provides a spiritual home, saving us from spiritual homelessness and isolation. Ethics is also transformed in the process—a personal faith transcends legalistic moral codes and places the moral quest within a free and loving relationship with God—we are no longer slaves, but sons.

# Chapter 14

# Aesthetic Experience, Critical Trust, and God

## 14.1 The Nature and Significance of Aesthetic Experience

For many people, an aesthetic experience is simply one that can give you pleasure and art is just the expression of feelings. Although aesthetic experience certainly has something to do with pleasure or the expression of feeling, the former cannot be reduced to the latter two. Eating a delicious steak will give one pleasure, and tearing a book to pieces can express one's anger, but these two experiences are not aesthetic. Eliseo Vivas offers the following definition: "the aesthetic experience is an experience of rapt attention which involves the intransitive apprehension of an object's immanent meanings in their full presentational immediacy" (Vivas 1944, p. 99). In science, an object is apprehended as an instantiation of a general law in the context of causal interaction with other objects. In short, these modes of experience have a transitive character. In contrast, an aesthetic experience is a kind of intransitive apprehension, because during aesthetic appreciation, of, say, a painting, my focus is on the painting itself, and I am not concerned with its causal history or moral impact.

The word "aesthetics" is derived from the Greek *aesthesis*, which means sensation. Obviously, most aesthetic experiences are mediated by our sensations, and this is why we can judge a face, a flower, a melody, and a color beautiful. However, we can also talk about the beauty of a novel, a speech, and a theory in physics, or the elegance of a mathematical proof. So the object of aesthetic experience can be an intelligible object instead of a sensible object. There is such a thing as nonsensuous beauty. As Vivas says, aesthetic experience is about an "object's immanent meanings in their full presentational immediacy." Scruton also agrees that "we call something beautiful when we gain pleasure from contemplating it as an individual object, for its own sake, and in its *presented form*" (Scruton 2009, p. 26). Since the recognition of form inevitably has an intellectual dimension, "the experience of beauty...is the prerogative of rational beings. Only creatures like us—with language, self-consciousness, practical reason, and moral judgement—can look on the world in this alert and disinterested way" (Scruton 2009, p. 33).

To highlight the intellectual character of aesthetic experience, Anthony O'Hear points out that aesthetic appreciation or judgment does not necessarily involve a sense of pleasure or attraction: "I was well aware of the aesthetic fineness of Raphael's work, of its beauty, without ever being par-ticularly attracted to it" (O'Hear 1997, pp. 184–5). Instead, a proper appre-ciation of aesthetic experience seems to suggest a kind of aesthetic realism. Iris Murdoch says: "Good art, thought of as symbolic force rather than statement provides a stirring image of a pure, transcendent value, a steadily visible enduring higher good…what is within us is itself attracted by and pulled to something beyond us, the Beautiful" (Murdoch 1977, pp. 76–7).

To illustrate this world of the Beautiful, let us look at Roger Scruton's discussions of music. The basic idea is that the world of music seems to pos-sess features that are entirely different from and irreducible to the physical world, but at the same time this world seems to be real on its own, and hence it seems to be a pointer to an alternative world, something like the eternal or timeless realm.

Scruton insists on the reality of the experience of music, and "the inten-tional object of a musical perception" (Scruton 1996, p. 149). He goes on to discuss the phenomenology of the musical experience: "In the useless space of music we hear those musical unities—the palpitating stones of melody and harmony—built into living temples in which we wander freely, released from earthly constraints…Music…does not describe the transcendental subject: but it shows it" (Scruton 1996, pp. 148–9). It seems that the mas-terpieces of music can lift us from our time and space into an ideal time and space, ordered by an ideal causality, which is the causality of freedom. From the ideal time of music it is, so to speak, a small step to eternity.

## 14.2  The Objectivity of Aesthetic Experience

We should note the element of "presentational immediacy" in Vivas's defini-tion. While sophisticated aesthetic judgments about a complicated artistic work like a tragedy certainly involve inferences (they are like the scientific inferences in the realm of sense experience), it is obvious that most of our aesthetic judgments are immediate. They are not the second stage of infer-ences after the first stage of perception is complete. This two-stage story "just does not accurately describe what it is like to see, say, a beautiful sunset. I do not see an expanse of coloured cloud, which is not itself seen as beautiful, and then experience a thrill of pleasure to which I give the name of beauty. The beauty of the sunset is woven into the fabric of my experience of it. I see the sunset *as* beautiful" (McNaughton 1988, p. 56).

While aesthetic experience is shaped by the variability of human cultures, this type of experience seems universal to all cultures and, potentially, to all human beings (at least in a rudimentary form). For a type of experience to possess PFEF, we do not need to require most of its token experiences to be ultima facie justified. A core of reliable experiences is enough to avoid outright skepticism about that type of experience. As O'Hear points out, even Hume agrees on the universality of (at least some) aesthetic judgments: "the same

Homer, who pleased at Athens and Rome two thousand years ago, is still admired at Paris and at London. All the changes of climate, government, religion, and language have not been able to obscure his glory.... a real genius, the longer his works endure, and the more widely they are spread, the more sincere is the admiration which they meet with" (cited in O'Hear 2008, p. 17). However, O'Hear disagrees with Hume's view that "the cross-cultural and trans-temporal critical-creative dialogue which elicits the cool, reflective, and disinterested judgment, say, that Homer is a poet of great stature, is ultimately a dialogue about what our feelings ought to be, not about anything objectively or really there." He asks, "why 'ought to be'...*if* these judgments aren't based in something actually there, and actually there apart from any feelings I or anyone else happen to have at a given time? And what is our dialogue about if it is not a dialogue *about* the *Iliad* itself?" (O'Hear 1997, pp. 185–6).

I think O'Hear is right here. There are immense differences between the Chinese and Western cultures, and it is true that some of our aesthetic tastes diverge sharply. For example, many popular forms of music in the West (like rock and heavy metal) are much less appreciated by Chinese, but at the same time many popular English songs are recognized to be beautiful by most Chinese. Moreover, the Chinese by and large will not dispute the status of the works of Shakespeare, Beethoven, Da Vinci, and Van Gogh as artistic masterpieces. Of course, the Chinese are also admirers of natural beauty, such as a beautiful sunset or mountain. In fact, this is one of the major themes of Chinese poetry and paintings.

As for the objections to the objectivity of aesthetic experiences, we find many stock objections that have been discussed over and over. So we can be concise here. One important factor that seems to favor aesthetic skepticism is the irreducibility of aesthetic judgment to formal rules or algorithms. However, we have argued that even the judgment of scientific theories cannot be reduced to algorithmic reasoning. In fact, one of the factors for choosing a scientific theory is exactly its elegance and beauty! O'Hear appeals to "judgments about the guilt or innocence...in court" as counterexample (O'Hear 2008, 16). Second, some skeptics highlight the fact that aesthetic judgment requires a specifically human sensibility to discern. Of course, "just because certain features of the world became apparent only to a particular type of sensibility, it does not follow that what is perceived is not real" (O'Hear 1997, p. 186). All our experiences, including sense experience, depend on human sensibilities conditioned by a human brain. So the above arguments do not provide strong reasons to regard aesthetic judgments as fundamentally subjective.

So if there are no good reasons for a blanket denial of the objectivity of aesthetic experience, in view of the intrinsic force of at least some aesthetic experiences and the surprising convergence of judgment over these cases across cultures and traditions, isn't it reasonable to accord aesthetic experiences PFEF at least? O'Hear again expresses this argument forcefully:

"it is only through their conformity to, and explanatory power over the experiences we have that we grant the statements of natural science the accolade objective...in its own realm, an objectivist account of our aesthetic judgments explains our experience of beauty, ugliness, and other aesthetic properties...that a Mediterranean island sunset, Van Gogh's *Sunflowers*, and Strauss's *Im Abendrot* are all beautiful is certainly something experienced by most of us as true, as demanded by the objects so described, and as authoritative and compelling as anything in science...[In aesthetic experience, they are] speaking about qualities of the things, not about feelings in their own breasts...what is beautiful actually directs, shapes, and explains our sense (experience) of its being beautiful" (O'Hear 1997, p. 187).

My conclusion is that the application of PCT in aesthetics is reasonable. Of course, in so far as the subjective character of a lot of aesthetic judgments is also pretty obvious, the actual application of PCT in aesthetics needs to be careful, cautious, and mindful of whatever second-order critical principles may be justified on the basis of past experiences. Nevertheless, all these still do not entail the fundamental unreliability of aesthetic experience.

### 14.3 Fusion of Aesthetic Experience with Theistic Experience

#### 14.3.1 Natural Beauty

Aesthetic experience can be fused with RE. Hawker's mountain experiences have been described in Chapter 9, which has some discussions of natural beauty. The beauty of nature is ubiquitous. William Wordsworth's poem conveys a sense of presence in his experience of nature:

> And I have felt
> A presence that disturbs me with the joy
> Of elevated thoughts; a sense sublime
> Of something far more deeply interfused
> Whose dwelling is the light of setting suns,
> And the round ocean, and the living air
> And the blue sky, and in the mind of man.
> A motion and a spirit, that impels
> All thinking things, all objects of thought,
> And rolls through all things. (cited in Overman 2009, p. 149)

The beauty of the world seems to have unfathomable depth—when we look deeper and deeper into the underlying structure of the natural world, we seem to encounter limitless riches, but simultaneously the balance of unity and diversity is not broken. The beauty of nature also seems extravagant—the degree of ingenuity or the intensity of beauty seems to transcend the ordinary needs for survival. When a presence is almost tangible through our experiences of the beauty, such experiences also seem to suggest an ultimate harmony between us and the world. "The beautiful scene in nature is not only captivating to our senses, but also uplifting: It resonates with spiritual overtones that awaken our moral sentiment" (Barrett 1987, p. 97). In the bleak picture described by scientistic empiricists such as Bertrand Russell, the world is entirely indifferent to human aspirations, and there is an unbridgeable gap between the objective universe of physics and the subjective world of human values. However, as we are blessed by the natural beauty, and even feel immersed in it, we seem able to transcend this grim separation. We feel that we are in tune with a world beyond ourselves. As O'Hear says,

> Where...do we get a sense that, despite the problems of alienation thrown up by science and morality, we are nevertheless at home in the world? Where else, except from a sense, at times strong, at times fleeting, that despite all the horrors and dilemmas and problems, the world and human life are beautiful, and that this sense is not mere projection on our part?...it is above all in aesthetic experience that we gain the fullest and most vividly lived sense that though we are creatures of Darwinian origin, our nature transcends our origin in tantalizing ways. (O'Hear 1997, p. 202)

In these moments, we may feel grateful for the wonderful gift of nature, and there may even be an implicit awareness of God: "There is the perfection of a single flower that can captivate us, the depths of space at night, lit by stars which entrance us with their loveliness and whose number and size dazzle our minds...These kinds of experiences can be truly moments of grace. They touch us deeply and the human heart spontaneously lifts in thanksgiving...[and] praise" (Edwards 1984, p. 33).

This kind of experience may even happen to atheists who do not believe in any ultimate harmony. Barrett talks about some beautiful scenery that "may shake even the skeptical and positivistic disposition" of some of his friends: "The long line of the mountain folds into the curve of the river, and there just above it, clearing the horizon, the evening star appears...we stand rapt and exalted...feeling that we and this universe may be part of some great meaning which we cannot grasp or articulate but which is almost sensibly present...Under pressure, even some of the more positivistic of my friends will confess to such a feeling—though they may insist that it is, after all, 'only a feeling'" (Barrett 1987, p. 97). Maybe it is, but our CTA advises us to be open to the possibility that it is not *only* a feeling.

The admission of Barrett's agnostic friends show that aesthetic experiences do have some PFEF independent of prior belief, which at least points in a religious direction. Indeed, in some cases aesthetic experiences can be instrumental in someone's conversion or returning to faith. For example, Anne Rice, a successful writer who has written 28 books about vampires, tells of her experience of joy in her book *Called out of Darkness: A Spiritual Confession*. She had a Catholic upbringing, but later became disillusioned with God. Along her gradual way back, experiences of natural beauty were important pointers. One particularly moving scene finds her awestruck, looking at a huge tree lit with golden light, which was moving as if in a great dance. She says, "I knew perfect joy then as I looked at that tree. I knew a joy that was beyond description. All was right with the world...It was a glorious moment, and I think of it all the time." Looking back, she sees the mystical experience of the tree as a comforting whisper from God when her daughter died. She gradually became convinced that she was being pursued by *something*: creation, music, painting spoke to her of God (cf. Crosby 2009, pp. 6–7).

### 14.3.2 Music

TEs can be mediated by different kinds of aesthetic experiences, and music is also instrumental in many conversion experiences. Several years ago, I met a young Shanghai woman. She told me that she had never been to a church, but finally decided to try it one Christmas Eve. However, to her surprise, when she heard the carols, tears just flowed down her cheeks. Deeply moved, she later became a Christian. She probably had an implicit TE at that moment, the content of which was not verbalized, but mediated by her emotions.

Another case of fusion of aesthetic experience with religious experience happened to Plantinga when he was a freshman at Harvard in early 1950s. He says in an interview: "I was coming back from the university dining hall one miserable November evening, and suddenly felt as if the heavens had lit up and opened. I heard music of the most incredible beauty and sweetness… There weren't any voices or anything like that: it just felt like a kind of confirmation of what I'd thought all along. It wasn't as if I could literally see into heaven, but it felt somewhat as though I could… There weren't any actual orchestras around" (cited in Shortt 2005, p. 44).

### 14.3.3 Art

We can also consider the fact of artistic creativity. It is not unusual for an artist to talk of inspiration as if it comes from outside and takes hold of him or her. Both aesthetic appreciation and creativity sometimes lead to experiences of rapture. Experience of creativity can also be, at the same time, a RE. George Frideric Handel, also a Lutheran, was 56 years old when, at a time of crisis in his life, he closeted himself in his room to compose his famous Messiah. "The created object derives its force both from the emotion and from the meaning that it is able to communicate. Handel, for example, having worked at writing the Hallelujah Chorus, reports, 'I think I did see all Heaven before me, the great God himself.' This is something like a mystical experience… Handel had a hold on it; he was able to convey it, or something much like it, to others. The wonder he felt is directly exhibited and so skillfully and powerfully expressed as to startle and move audiences to hum or to rise and sing themselves, expressing the emotion by which they have been overtaken" (Parsons 1969, p. 98).

Aesthetic experiences can be the medium for us to feel the reality of the transcendent realm. In the case of the novelist Susan Howatch, her aesthetic appreciation of the cathedral triggers and mediates her experiences of God.[1]

Howatch's London flat was right in the cathedral close at Salisbury. Once, she caught sight of the cathedral and saw it as if for the first time. It was floodlit, radiant, and astonishingly beautiful. "I felt," she said, "as if I'd been presented with some extraordinary gift." Always, the cathedral, with its slim, tapering spire, seemed to be pointing in every sense to heaven. The cathedral became a presence in her life, and drew her, compelled her, on the road to a spiritual quest.

The above story also illustrates O'Hear's saying, "Art can seem revelatory…It can seem to take us to the essence of reality, as if certain sensitivities in us, and based on our physical constitution and its predilections, beat in tune with reality" (O'Hear 1997, p. 199).

## 14.4 Coherence of Aesthetic Experience with Theistic Experience

### 14.4.1 Aesthetic Experience and Spiritual Existence

Aesthetic experiences obviously transcend our animal instincts and materialistic urges. Aesthetic judgments are fallible, and they require a critical rational conversation directing attention to real features of the world and its objects. O'Hear asks, "Can we imagine the aesthetic responses of a peahen being refined and developed in this sort of way? No…There is only a genetically based response which fires or fails to fire" (O'Hear 1997, p. 197). In an essay on the spirit of tragedy, the Chinese philosopher Liu Xiaofeng argues that the tragic personality has an aesthetic dimension, because in some sense he not only transcends utilitarian needs, but also transcends life and death (Liu 1997, p. 26). One with a tragic personality has an unyielding spirit, and dares to challenge fate and to shoulder the suffering inherent in human history. Through undergoing those tragic ordeals, he realizes his infinite potential and passion. The human struggles and passions revealed in tragedy cannot be explained with reference to animal impulses. They are the manifestation of the human quest for ultimate values and a higher realm of existence. The spiritual quest is the urge to "commit the finite self to something which transcends the self" (Liu 1997, p. 29).

The Chinese political dissident Liu Xiaobo, who was awarded the Nobel Peace Prize on October 8, 2010, is also a philosopher. In his discussions of Shakespeare's tragedies, he argues that the crises of humanism and rationalism in modernity were already foreseen. On the one hand, there is an unconditional affirmation of the secular world and the liberation of human desires. On the other hand, there is a deep tragic appreciation of the selfish nature of human beings and the cruelty of competition among humans. In the end, a big question mark is placed over the Enlightenment hope that by shaking off the shackles of religion, human beings can forever transcend the hell of suffering (Liu 1989, p. 225). Liu Xiaobo has a keen understanding of the evil impulses of humanity, and he emphasizes, like Pascal, the inherent tension within human nature: while our feet are solidly planted on the earth, our souls desire to transcend the mundane reality and find a Paradise. This intrinsic paradox within human nature is tragic (Liu 1989, p. 276). Although Liu is not a Christian, he has a deep appreciation of the spirit of transcendence in Christianity. He even says, "The arrogant people will never honestly face themselves...and they will tread the wrong path. In this sense, the tragedy of the Chinese is the tragedy of the absence of God. Exactly because the Light at the other shore disappears, the darkness at this shore is mistaken to be 'light.' I believe that people in penitence and confession are the most pious, the most transparent, most full of vitality and passion" (Liu 1989, p. 74).

What makes people admire Liu is his persistence in his struggle for democracy despite the certainty of suffering under the Communist government. He has been imprisoned several times, and now is still serving a sentence of 11 years that began on the Christmas day of 2009. Liu already says that human existence on the whole is tragic, but nonetheless he still chooses to struggle and rebel. He knows that China's road to freedom "may be the longest and most arduous process in human history...During this long process, the suffering is unbearable, but bear it we must. The contemporary Chinese simply have no other choice" (Liu 1989, pp. 44–5).

Liu Xiaobo's personal example seems to be a perfect illustration of Liu Xiaofeng's account of the tragic personality, and also demonstrates the nobility of the human spirit of transcendence. So various kinds of aesthetic experiences confirm our spiritual nature, and this fact itself seems more consonant with theism than with naturalism (I will evaluate the naturalistic explanations of aesthetic experience below). It is surprising that Liu Xiaobo as a nonbeliever has such a keen sense of the absence of God, which reflects his longing for transcendence, or even longing for a God whom he does not yet believe in. His commitment to the struggles for freedom in fact presupposes his strong perception of transcendent values, and manifests his experience of the call of conscience. When he says the Chinese have no choice but to bear the birth pangs of democratization, it is only intelligible from the moral perspective—because, in fact, many Chinese try to avoid the problem altogether. Taken together, Liu's experiences seem to be intelligible in a theistic world as a manifestation of the transcendence of *imago dei* in his humanity. It may even be plausible to say that Liu has an implicit experience of the God Incognito through his conscience and longing for transcendence. As Marcel says, "I aspire to participate in this being, in this reality—and perhaps this aspiration is already a degree of participation, however rudimentary" (Marcel 1948, pp. 4–5).

### 14.4.2 The Prima Facie Conflict Between Aesthetic Experience and Naturalism

We should distinguish between two different tasks of a naturalistic explanation. The first task is to explain the epistemic seemings contained in our most-established aesthetic experiences. The second task is to explain why those aesthetic experiences occur, regardless of the truth or falsity of their intentional content. Concerning the first task, naturalists will hardly admit that the transcendent realm suggested by powerful aesthetic experiences really exists. So aesthetic experience, by its very nature, is either a falsification of reality or the intimation of entirely ungrounded beliefs. No matter how deeply we are impressed by the sunset in all its glorious hues, or the striking beauty of the rainbow, they are "really" nothing but phenomena caused by the refraction of white light through particles or raindrops in the atmosphere. If some aesthetic experiences suggest an ultimate harmony between us and the world, then again this must be regarded as wishful thinking, because it is difficult to understand how our sense perception of a limited part of the physical world can reliably arrive at such a wide-ranging and deep truth! Well, does this mean that naturalism will be falsified by our aesthetic experiences? Not necessarily, but the naturalist has something to overcome. In fact, if the aesthetic experiences are strong enough, they alone can create an epistemic dilemma for the naturalist. This seems to be the case in O'Hear.

O'Hear is a staunch defender of the objectivity of aesthetic experience, and his analysis of the content of aesthetic experience also shows that it points to a transcendent realm. However, since he is an agnostic or atheist, he backs off at this point: "how could we think of an aesthetic justification of experience, that really was a justification and not just a momentary narcotic, unless our aesthetic experience was sustained by a divine will revealed in the universe, and particularly in our experience of it as beautiful?... Aesthetic experience *seems* to produce the harmony between us and the world that would have to point to a religious resolution were it not to be an illusion. But such a resolution is intellectually unsustainable, so aesthetic experience, however powerful, remains subjective and, in its full articulation, illusory... This is a dilemma I cannot solve" (O'Hear 1997, p. 201). Obviously, an unsolvable dilemma at the center of a worldview certainly is a demerit. Moreover, if the weight of aesthetic experiences alone is not enough to overturn a prior belief in naturalism, I think the combined weight of the rainbow of experiences should be sufficient, especially in view of the fact that the arguments for naturalism are less than conclusive. John Schellenberg has strongly argued for this point (Schellenberg 2007, chapter 7), although he himself is a religious skeptic.

It is interesting to note that in later works, O'Hear becomes more open to religious truth. He is now openly critical of scientism as dogmatic and shallow (O'Hear 2008, pp. 18, 153), and even explores the convergence of science and religion (O'Hear 2008, pp. 147–9). While he continues to reject natural theology,[2] he now admits "there is within our human world a need to push out into both those other worlds [of science and religion]" (O'Hear 2008, p. 157). The major reason seems to be that "any purely secular account of morality and aesthetics... will struggle to make sense of moral obligation and of the apparently timeless and transcendent sense of rightness one sometimes has in the experience of something beautiful" (O'Hear 2008, p. 154).

He updates his criticisms of evolutionary explanations of aesthetics and identifies the tension between aesthetic experience and naturalism again. He still says the intimation of transcendence in aesthetic experience may be an illusion, but now he is concerned that the obliteration of the sense of transcendence will likely cause art to degenerate into what Ruskin called "'mere amusement, ministers to morbid sensibilities, ticklers and fanners of the soul's sleep'—much like what you can see in today's most admired galleries of contemporary art, in fact" (O'Hear 2008, p. 27). He believes that in the past, great works of art have been sustained by "the shared symbolic order of Christianity. It is partly the waning of that capital in the world as a whole that makes the predicament of artists today more difficult: for how can mere artists exalt the human spirit if there is no spirit to exalt and no cosmic power to do the exalting? They cannot, so in all artistic media at the end of the millennium, they revel in our baser nature " (O'Hear 1999, p. 189).

Although he admits that the naturalistic story about aesthetic experience may be true, he comments, "in which case aesthetic experience has no more ultimate significance than a warm bath or Prozac or some other way of affecting the chemistry of the brain. All I can say about that is that this is not how the experience of say, *King Lear*, or Beethoven's *Op.132* actually *feels*" (O'Hear 2008, p. 64). It is clear that his personal inclination is to take the intentional content of those aesthetic experiences seriously. In the end, while still rejecting dogmatic religion or traditional theism, he seems to be tempted by a kind of piecemeal supernaturalism—a vague belief in some kind of good superpower (O'Hear 2008, p. 65). O'Hear's intellectual odyssey is guided by his sensitivity to the intimation of transcendence embodied in the rainbow of experiences. This shows that aesthetic experience and moral experience do have a kind of PFEF, independent of one's prior framework. In Chapter 9, we explored another way to exhibit the coherence between aesthetic experience and theism without assuming the PFEF of aesthetic experience: the argument from natural beauty. The following discussions will further strengthen this argument.

### 14.4.3  Naturalistic Explanation of Aesthetic Experience

To undermine the argument from natural beauty, one major strategy of the naturalists is to offer alternative naturalistic explanations for the capacity for aesthetic experience as a product of the evolutionary history of human beings. I have argued that even assuming the success of this project, it still cannot rebut the argument from natural beauty. Now I intend to further critically examine those naturalistic explanations to see whether they are really adequate (the hypothesis of biophilia has been criticized in Chapter 9).

#### 1. The Beauty of Biological Organisms

Concerning the beauty of biological organisms, a general naturalistic strategy is the appeal to sex selection. It is an initially surprising fact for the Darwinists that elaborate displays are found among animals and birds. For example, the tails of male peacocks and the songs of many male birds are elaborate, graceful, and beautiful, but also highly clumsy. Since this seems to be harmful for survival, it is a puzzle why natural selection has allowed these organisms to evolve. The Darwinists suggest that everything can be explained on the assumption that birds and animals are capable of appreciating beauty. Suppose the female peacocks find the clumsy tails of male peacocks beautiful and are attracted to them. So the most splendid males are chosen by the females, who in turn produce splendid males, and so on. So the beautiful but clumsy type of peacock ultimately becomes embedded in the population.

For me, the issue of sex selection is not directly relevant to the explanation of human aesthetic experience. Even if the peahens' aesthetic appreciation of the tail of the peacock solves the puzzle of the evolution of the peackcock's tail, why should human beings also find the tail beautiful? Certainly our response has nothing to do with their evolution. It is eminently possible that what the peahens find beautiful will look ugly to us. Perhaps the suggestion is that the aesthetic sensibility of the peahens has been transmitted to us in some way. In any case, it is still very unclear how human aesthetic experiences are conducive to human survival in the early evolutionary context of a forest or the savannah.

Lorenz provides some impressive examples of the extravagance of beauty in the biological world, which are difficult to explain on evolutionary grounds. He believes that "there is the beautiful, the genesis of which in a similar manner [selectionist explanation] must be doubted, for which, in fact, an explication of origin by means of selection seems conspicuously contrived" (Lorenz 1988, p. 108). He points out that "at the lower levels of plant and animal life, there is so much for us that is beautiful, that seems to have no apparent species-preserving value. Many butterflies have exceedingly beautiful color designs with innumerable details that are most certainly not seen by conspecifics and cannot frighten enemies away. The markings on the feathers of pheasant hens and on other birds with protective coloring have, when examined closely, very rich colors in well-regulated patterns although the selection pressure that brought these into being was pointed toward making them as similar as possible to the irregular chaotic coloring of the background...There the selection pressure favors bright colors and variegated forms that are made even more conspicuous through their strict regularity" (Lorenz 1988, p. 109). Then Lorenz makes an astounding observation, which seems to me a profound truth about our world: "it would seem as if the organisms were 'living their lives to the full' as *extravagant works of art*" (Lorenz 1988, p. 109; italics mine).

Lorenz does not offer any enlightening solution to these puzzles. He believes we have a capacity of Gestalt perception rooted in sense organs and brain structures, which can be used to "discover relationships that exist among sensory supplied data or, also, between higher units of perception" (Lorenz 1988, p. 112). This Gestalt perception enables us to perceive "highly complicated polyphonic interactions as harmonies and of reacting to minimal disturbances" (Lorenz 1988, p. 115). Moreover, he believes that "there are value awarenesses which are, in the strictest sense, a priori...they have evolved during the course of evolution and through interaction with extrasubjective givens" (Lorenz 1988, p. 117).

It is not clear how these suggestions help to account for the beautiful design of the butterflies. Our Gestalt perception appears later than those "lower" species, and hence cannot be any causal factor related to their survival. Perhaps the suggestion is that for some yet unknown reasons, or just by chance, the butterflies evolve into *extravagant works of art* (Lorenz's own terms), and then our Gestalt perception somehow constrains us to view them as beautiful. I find this rather implausible. It is perhaps survival-conducive to be able to discover the structure of our sensory data, but the further perceiving of these "units of perception" as beautiful does not seem to do any work. This seems to be entirely epiphenomenal. As for Lorenz's a priori awareness of values (which presumably includes beauty), I find it thoroughly obscure and cannot understand how something in the strictest sense a priori can interact with extrasubjective givens. On general grounds, it is doubtful whether any evolutionary explanation can account for the emergence of noncontingent a priori awareness.

I entirely agree with Lorenz that many biological organisms strike us as extravagant works of art, and this still seems to be a complete mystery in a naturalistic world.

## 2. Neurological Explanation

Neurological explanation is another major tool of naturalists. For example, E. O. Wilson says that aesthetic contrivances "play upon the circuitry of the brain's limbic system in a way that ultimately promotes survival and reproduction...usefulness of curiosity and the search for connections and similarities" (Wilson 1984, p. 61). However, it is plausible to think that "curiosity and the search for connections and similarities" are useful for organisms, but these tendencies are in fact quite different from aesthetic experience, which has been earlier defined as an experience of rapt attention that involves the intransitive apprehension of an object's immanent meanings in their full presentational immediacy. Just as curiosity is quite different from rapt attention, the search for connections and similarities is also poles apart from the mode of intransitive apprehension that focuses on the object itself. Even if the capacity for aesthetic experience were related to curiosity and the search for connections and similarities, it would still be a mystery why evolution did not throw up the latter tendencies alone. On top of these, the capacity for aesthetic experience seems like unnecessary baggage, which should be eliminated by natural selection.

## 14.5 Conclusion

"God reveals Himself...in many ways; and some men enter His Temple by the Gate Beautiful" (Tennant 1956, 93). There are several other gates: Gate

Meaning, Gate Goodness, Gate Truth, and Gate Love, Gate Rainbow, in addition to the Gate Religion. The intimate relationship between aesthetic experience and religious experience is suggested by the fusion of aesthetic experience and religious experience, and then confirmed by the considerations of theoretical coherence. Aesthetic experience is also closely linked to other kinds of experience. As Tennant points out, "Nature's beauty is of a piece with the world's intelligibility and with its being a theatre for moral life; and thus far the case for theism is strengthened by aesthetic considerations" (Tennant 1956, p. 93).

Besides the convergence of aesthetic experience and intellectual experience, there is also the mutual penetration of aesthetic experience, moral experience, and IPE. As many experiences of social movement show, the use of music is very important to sustain or express the sense of solidarity. For example, David Martin points out that in the Orange Revolution, the "spirit of the demonstrators in Kiev was in part maintained by music…, music…has strong historical links with both [politics and religion] in terms of parades and processions…[e.g.] music provides a deeper resonance to the Remembrance Day ceremony in Whitehall" (Martin 2010, p. 177). When the people sing together in the face of sacrifice and death, the complete equality and unity of everyone is beautifully and movingly expressed.

In short, the coherence of the rainbow of experiences is itself a datum expected by theism. If these types of experience are all accidents in the evolutionary history of human beings, then there is no particular reason to expect their convergence or coherence in an overall intelligible picture.

# CHAPTER 15

# INTELLECTUAL EXPERIENCE, CRITICAL TRUST, AND GOD

## 15.1 Varieties of Intellectual Experience

### 15.1.1 Reason and Intellectual Dynamism

Reason has been regarded by some as *the* distinctive mark of humanity. Though I think this is mistaken, it is still true that the human exercise of the rational capacity is one clear mark of human transcendence. First of all, we can draw attention to the intellectual dynamism that is emphasized by the transcendental Thomists such as Rahner, Lonergan, and Joseph Donceel. According to them, the intellect is always striving for infinity. This can be shown by our everyday knowledge of a finite reality *as finite*. "Whatever reality we know in everyday experience we know as finite.... Now I can know them as finite, as limited, only because something in me is always already beyond them and strives beyond all limits, toward the unlimited...It is not just this or that or the next limit which I thus transcend; it is every conceivable limit, it is the limit as such" (Donceel 1979, pp. 55–6).

Alternatively, we can illustrate this intellectual dynamism by noting the unrestricted capacity of reason to question. Even parents know well that the drive to question, once given its rein, cannot arbitrarily be brought to a halt. It is, in principle, unrestricted. It seems that only the ultimate and the unconditioned can satisfy the unrestricted drive to question. The transcendental Thomists want to claim that "by knowing all the finite as finite, I always co-know the Infinite" (Donceel 1979, p. 56). Even if this more controversial conclusion is uncertain, the experience of intellectual dynamism still seems to be real and significant.

The above portrayal of human reason seems one-sided: reason is alleged to be able to soar effortlessly above every conceivable horizon. In fact, it seems that human reason is heavily fettered in actuality, and it possesses an inertia that is difficult to overcome. This more dialectical portrayal of reason is brought out by Anthony O'Hear (1991). Of course, practically speaking, human beings have no option but to accept the validity of some practices, and to trust their deliverances and standards as the criterion for the reasonable. I have stressed this point so far, but at the same time our reasoning ability itself cannot be constrained by the practical alone. This is shown by the activity of reason in philosophy, which insists on critical questioning of what is taken for granted ad infinitum. Indeed, philosophy is not regarded by many as "practical."

The possibility of skeptical reasoning exactly demonstrates the fact that reason can question everything. It can step outside our cognitive and practical frameworks, and raise fundamental question about their validity. Reason seems to take the role of a transcendent judge: whatever we might put in place of what our questioning undermined will be vulnerable in its turn to further rational criticism. Hence the resulting picture of reason is a dialectical one: "the infirmity of reason and its transcendence, its infirmity or limitation regarding content and its transcendence as process, its need to find truths and standards which stand absolutely justified and its inability to discover any" (O'Hear 1991, p. 119). O'Hear recognizes that this picture seems to call for a natural fulfillment of reason in religion, but he resists this move. The point I want to raise here is that the above dialectical picture of reason is also a tragic one. If reason is at the center of humanity, then humanity would also be infected by the above tragic contradiction. It seems to generate a burning question: why does human reason have such a character? How can this kind of rational capacity arise in the universe and become a defining feature of an animal that accidentally evolved in the struggle for survival?

### 15.1.2 A Priori Intuitions

George Bealer's understanding of intuition is similar to mine: "For you to have an intuition that A is just for it to seem to you that A. Here 'seems' is understood as...a term for a genuine kind of conscious episode...this kind of seeming is intellectual" (Bealer 2000, p. 3). Intuitions are necessary for our assessment of the validity of deductive reasoning: "the relevant logical insight must be construed as non-propositional in character, as a direct grasping of the way in which the conclusion is related to the premises and validly flows from them" (Bonjour 2005, p. 100). Suppose we think $A$ entails $C$. If this connection cannot be directly grasped, perhaps we can find a $B$, such that we can see that $A$ entails $B$, and $B$ entails $C$. Since we cannot go on interpolating terms ad infinitum, sooner or later we come to a point where we have to credit ourselves with the ability (at least in some cases) to *see* that "$p$ entails $q$" is a necessary truth.[1]

Katherin Rogers emphasizes the character of strong intuition as a strongly certain belief, which has a luminous quality: "If I am strongly certain that x, then I know that I know that x ... [It is] ... direct recognition ... There are no intermediaries between the intellectual 'seeing' and the content seen ... In addition to my 'grasp' of the bare proposition, like '2+2=4,' there is recognition of the necessity of the proposition" (Rogers 2008, p. 32).

### 15.2 Application of the PCT to A Priori Intuitions

Bealer points out that intuitions are regularly used as evidence (or reasons) in our standard justificatory practices such as elementary logic, number theory, set theory, and philosophy. For example, the appeal to Gettier examples and the twin-earth example involves intuitions about whether certain situations are possible and whether relevant concepts would apply. So philosophers are at least implicitly applying some form of PCT to logical intuitions in the realm of necessary truths.

One kind of necessary truth concerns whether some states of affairs are logically possible. I argue below that, ultimately, there is no other way to determine logical possibility apart from a prima facie trust in our epistemic seemings in this area, especially when we find those states of affairs imaginable. However, we need to consider the distinction between metaphysical possibility and epistemic possibility, which is frequently used in the philosophy of mind, especially to refute Cartesian dualism. Consider Peter Carruthers's discussion. "if I imagine a pig flying, what I really do is represent to myself how it would look to me if a pig flew: I imagine a sequence of experiences which I should naturally describe as being 'of a pig flying'. But this does not by itself show that it is logically possible for a pig to fly...The most that it shows is that it is possible to hallucinate a pig flying" (Carruthers 1986, pp. 95–6).

Here Carruthers exposes the gap between the *psychological* state of judging a proposition to be possible and the proposition's *logical* status. In some cases, the former psychological state consists of imagined images, but in most cases don't. The problem here is how Carruthers is going to close the gap. He points out that real possibility does not follow *deductively* from psychological imaginability. Certainly that is true, because nothing can fulfill Carruthers's stringent requirement but another logical truth! *Nothing* entails a logical truth except another logical truth, but we can have cognitive access to logical truths only through *our judgments*, which are necessarily psychological states. So skepticism follows immediately if Carruthers's demand is legitimate. I am not sure how he is going to justify his conviction that pigs' flying is logically possible. He does not seem to allow imagination to do the job. The alternative route may be via scientific inquiry. However it is not likely that any scientific discovery can entail the proposition $q$ that "it is logically possible for pigs to fly." The only way to deny this is to posit a posteriori necessary truth about pigs discoverable by science. For example, it may be claimed that $p$: "a pig has a certain set of chromosomes" is a necessary truth. But it is not obvious how this can entail $q$. Suppose you think it does. The natural retort is that it only shows that it is possible to *hallucinate* that $p$ entails $q$, but not *that $p$ entails $q$*.

Furthermore, the same move can be brought against the simplest logical intuitions. For example, I hold that I can see that $A$ and $B$ entails $A$. If you ask me why, I can only say that I can't imagine any world in which the antecedent holds, but not the consequent. You can challenge me that what it shows is the "epistemic impossibility" of the negation of the above proposition. It doesn't follow that it's really a logical impossibility. I would then be hard-pressed to find another reply.

### 15.3  Is A Priori Intuition Dispensable?

Despite the prima facie case for intuitions, empiricists and naturalists always have a strong tendency to doubt intuitions and try to dispense with them. For example, Ernest Nagel points out that since the naturalist "professes to accept the methods employed by the various empirical sciences for obtaining knowledge about the world, it cannot with consistency claim to have a priori insight into the most pervasive structure of things" because it is "not subject to experimental refutation" (Nagel 1944, p. 211). More recently, Michael Devitt claims that the thesis of naturalism is that *all* knowledge is [empirical]; there is only one way of knowing" (Devitt 2005, p. 105). So he rejects the whole idea of the a priori.

Both Nagel and Devitt make it clear that their rejection of logical intuitions is motivated by their prior commitment to naturalism. But when two things conflict, the direction of disconfirmation can go either way. The fundamental contention of holistic empiricism is that we should determine the nature of the world on the basis of what we can know (as revealed in the rainbow of experiences), and not vice versa. Perhaps we should take seriously the deliverances of our reason, and this shows the mind's transcendent capacity. Then we can argue that in theism, it can be explained. Here we are anticipating an argument for God from logical intuitions recently advocated by Katherin Rogers (see discussions below).

We have briefly indicated the apparent indispensability of intuitions for our rational activity. For those who insist empirical knowledge is all that there is, the thorny question is: how should we account for the rationality of forming beliefs on the basis of empirical evidence? If our "knowledge" is entirely an instinctive matter, that is, the constitution of our being causing us to have every belief we have in a fully deterministic way, then no such questions arise. However, we are reflective beings, and our empirical evidence always needs to be interpreted and does not fully determine our higher level beliefs. So the former question is inescapable. Either there are some rational criteria on top of the empirical evidence, or we depend on empirical evidence alone to decide how to adjudicate our empirical evidence. The latter option seems to be arguing in a circle. If we infer from some empirical evidence to a conclusion, we typically claim that our evidence provides us with *reasons* for believing in the conclusion, either in a deductive, inductive, or abductive fashion. It seems difficult to understand this rational activity without relying on some fundamental rational criteria legitimated by a priori intuitions. The radical empiricist picture seems to be facing fundamental difficulties. So for those who want to go without them, there are two important questions:

1. How do we account for the intrinsic force of a priori intuitions?
2. What are the substitutes that can replace intuitions, but can still perform their roles?

Let us examine more closely whether the radical empiricists have adequate answers to these questions. Nagel's basic idea is that logic is only necessary because we have adopted some regulative principles about the use of language in order to fulfill some functions. For Nagel, "since logical laws are implicit laws for specifying the structure of a language, and since their explicit function is to link systematically statements to which data of observation are relevant, logical laws may be evaluated on the basis of their effectiveness in yielding systems of a desired kind" (Nagel 1944, p. 232).

Of course, the obvious objection to Nagel's theory is that logic becomes arbitrary in his theory. We can alter logic simply by deciding to use different rules of language. The criteria for logical truths suggested by Nagel are the effectiveness to fulfill certain functions, but obviously the choice of functions here is relative to contingent human desires or historical development. For example, the function to link statements to data of observation systematically has not been regarded as an important function in many cultures. So Nagel's substitutes for logic or intuitions cannot really replace logic. Nor has he really accounted for the intrinsic force of logical intuitions.

A more influential attempt to naturalize knowledge and logic is Quine's naturalized epistemology. Quine is famous for his attack on the analytic/synthetic distinction, and basically he denies that there is such a thing as necessary truth. For Quine, "The proverbial necessity of mathematical truth resides merely in our exempting the mathematical sentences when choosing which one of a refuted block of sentences to revoke. We exempt them because changing them would reverberate excessively through science" (cited in Rogers 2008, p. 32).

Rogers replies: "Either the fallibilist offers an argument for his position or he does not. If he does not, then we have no reason to accept his counterintuitive conclusion…But if he does give an argument, then it will have premises, and the premises will inevitably be more dubious than the claim that 2+2=4 is a necessary truth. Quine's story…involves many claims about conditioning, animal expectations, the molding influence of evolution, language acquisition, and so on. But any of these claims is far, far more dubious than '2+2=4' cannot possibly be false" (Rogers 2008, pp. 32–3).

Bealer also argues against the radical empiricists, and his strategy is to show that those who reject intuitions as evidence will end up with a self-defeating epistemology. He mainly targets the Quinean philosophy which consists of three theses:

(i)   the principle of empiricism: A person's phenomenal experiences and/or observations comprise the person's evidence.
(ii)  the principle of holism: A theory is justified for a person if and only if it is, or belongs to, the simplest comprehensive theory that explains all, or most, of the person's evidence.
(iii) the principle of naturalism: The natural sciences (plus the logic and mathematics needed for them) constitute the simplest comprehensive

theory that explains all, or most, of a person's phenomenal experiences and/or observations. (Bealer 2000, p. 5)

However, the problem is that the principles contain the familiar terms "justified," "simplest," "theory," "explain," and "evidence." These terms do not belong to the primitive vocabulary of the simplest formulation of the natural sciences. In particular, "this formulation of the natural sciences does not contain an apparatus for indicating definitional relationships (or relationships of translation, synonymy, abbreviation, property identity, property reduction, or anything relevantly like them)…[So] principles (i)–(ii) do not count as justified according to principles (i)–(iii)…[The Quinean philosophy] is epistemically self-defeating" (Bealer 2000, p. 6).

Bealer's argument above is a particular illustration of the general point I make above. When we engage in reflective epistemic appraisal of our empirical evidence, and then claim that naturalism is supported by the evidence, we already rely on rational principles grounded on our intuitions. If the resulting worldview categorically rejects the force of intuitions, then it will end up in an epistemically self-defeating position. Alternatively, the naturalists may claim that the justifiability and superiority of the naturalistic worldview is just obvious, and it does not need any grounds, because any grounds offered will be less impressive than the naturalistic worldview itself. So circular reasoning is not necessarily a bad thing, as long as it circles around empirical data. We should note that this argument also relies on something that is "just obvious." This looks like another kind of intuition. Second, naturalists are always proud of their rationality when they attack religions as dogmatic, relying on unproven revelations and always arguing in a circle. It is ironic that now their own worldview seems equally dogmatic. In fact, circling around empirical data may not be necessarily bad, if we really attend to all our experiences. The major problem with the above strategy of naturalism is that it is not empirical enough. It has arbitrarily excluded most of the rainbow of experiences in an a priori fashion.

## 15.4 Fusion and Coherence of Intellectual Experience with Theistic Experience

### 15.4.1 Reason and Intellectual Dynamism

The transcendental Thomists claim that the analysis of intellectual dynamism can vindicate the existence of God, the Infinite, the Unlimited, or the Ultimate Ground of Intelligibility. To this conclusion, Peter Baelz dissents: "Granted that man possesses, or is possessed by, an unrestricted drive to question; granted also that the act of questioning itself presupposes a faith in intelligibility, an affirmation, a demand that what is can in principle be rationally understood; it does not seem to follow necessarily that this demand will in fact be met" (Baelz 1975, p. 30). So intelligent inquiry may point us beyond the finite and conditioned toward the *possibility* of the infinite and unconditioned. But we cannot yet say whether this *possibility* is realized or not.

Perhaps a tight demonstration of the existence of God from intellectual dynamism is not obviously successful. However, neither is the argument completely without force. We need to bear in mind, especially, that such arguments are not meant to be ordinary deductive arguments. They are called by the transcendental Thomists "retortions"—arguments from self-referential inconsistency. They aim to show that the existence of God is *undeniable* because in the very act of denial his existence is also implicitly affirmed. If we concede that in every act of knowing or questioning we implicitly affirm the Unconditioned, then the transcendental Thomists can be contented.

Now let us turn to O'Hear's account of reason, which seems to call for a religious explanation. It is true that "our beliefs about the natural world and our science may appear constrained by the limits of our minds and perceptual faculties. But in religion we gain an assurance that our knowledge does stem from God, who is the source of all truth, and that we are not completely limited by the finiteness of our minds.... religion in its intimations of human limits and their overcoming mirrors very precisely our nature as thinkers and reflective agents who are nevertheless constrained in practice by the finitude of our powers.... Religious belief...also sees our drive to something transcending human powers as reflected in the fabric of the universe, our yearning as for something which actually exists" (O'Hear 1991, p. 120).

O'Hear thinks that the search for the Truth is inevitably linked with the emergence of *self*-consciousness. Even as an atheist,[2] he still appreciates that the emergence of self-consciousness is a mystery and it is "natural for the religious to interpret this emergence...as revelatory of something deep in the universe, something inexplicable by physics, something behind the material face of the world" (O'Hear 1991, p. 121). He also seems sympathetic to the view that self-consciousness itself intimates a world other than the material, physical world, a world where...absolute truth and absolute goodness exist. Hence, "in our self-conscious search for what is true and good, absolutely speaking, we attempt to attain a perspective which is gestured at by religious conceptions of the divine." Nevertheless, "such reflection does not by itself make religion any more believable" (O'Hear 1991, p. 121).

O'Hear has done a very nice job in exhibiting the coherence of a religious worldview with the transcendent dimensions of reason. However, he is wrong in asserting that such reflection would not make religion any more believable. The coherence itself is *some* reason to make religion *more* believable, a kind of enhancer. As before, let $H_t$ denote the theistic hypothesis and $H_n$ the naturalistic hypothesis. Let $e_{21}$ be the fact of intellectual dynamism and the transcendent dimensions of reason. It seems that the prior probability of $e_{21}$, symbolized here by $P(e_{21})$, is quite small. However, if $H_t$ is true, then the humble origin of man would entail his finitude, while the *imago dei* would entail some drive toward the Infinite. So something like the "contradictory" nature of human reason is to be expected, that is, $P(e_{21}/H_t)$ is close to one. Therefore the theistic hypothesis is significantly confirmed.

Now consider the probability of the purely naturalistic emergence of a rational human being whose reason has transcendent dimensions, that is, $P(e_{21}/H_n)$. Let us first shirk the question whether reason can be reduced naturalistically. For a human phenomenon to be *positively explainable* by $H_n$, it is a necessary condition that this phenomena should have survival value *in the evolutionary context*. It is not enough to say that it is a fluke or an accidental outgrowth, because these are very weak explanations. To say these things is to admit that evolution gives no positive reason to *expect* such phenomenon, that is, $P(e/H_n)$ is not higher than $P(e)$. It is also illegitimate to appeal to the *future* survival value of a certain phenomenon, because no selection process can operate on a purely future, as yet nonexistent, survival value. If these comments are roughly correct, then $P(e_{21}/H_n)$ seems to be not higher than $P(e_{21})$, because the transcendent dimensions of reason do not have any *survival value in the evolutionary context*. Would skepticism or the contemplation of the Infinite be biologically useful in a primitive jungle? If anything, this capacity is positively harmful, for it would distract from the severe struggle for survival. Hence probably $P(e_{21}/H_n) < P(e_{21})$. If it is the case, then $e_{21}$ actually disconfirms $H_n$. Hence, it seems fair to say that at least $e_{21}$ confirms $H_t$ relative to $H_n$.

### 15.4.2 The Argument from A Priori Intuitions

Rogers believes that the phenomenon of strongly certain belief is most plausibly explained by God. "The evident fact of our knowledge of mathematical truth, which knowledge could not have its source in the contingent physical universe, shows that there is an eternal, immutable, and transcendent realm of such truth which must be identified with God" (Rogers 2008, p. 34). First of all, let us explore the plausibility of the theistic explanation. We need to distinguish two scenarios:

> First Scenario: There is a Platonic realm of necessary truths independent from God.
>   Second Scenario: Necessary truths do not exist independently from God; they are in fact ideas in the Infinite Divine Mind.

Consider the first scenario. Since God is necessarily omniscient, He knows all necessary truths. Since we are made in the image of God, it is likely that we can have some limited capacity for knowing necessary truths. Since God can implant the a priori intuitions directly in our minds, this "may accord best with the phenomenological quality of immediacy." So the first scenario is one possible explanation. However, Rogers is not entirely satisfied with this explanation because "it reduces Him to the role of a sort of platonic demiurge...Rather, He is Perfect Being, and necessary truth—the laws of logic and mathematics—are the way all being has to be. They reflect the nature of God...there is no explanation at all for God's knowledge of necessary truths beyond the simple fact of His necessary existence...it does not hypothesize a world of ontologically dubious platonic abstracta just 'there' in the universe" (Rogers 2008, p. 43). So Rogers prefers the second scenario.

Hugh Rice also has a criticism of the first scenario, what he calls the preestablished harmony by God. He points out that the major difficulty concerning the explanations about a priori knowledge is the implausibility of the thesis that necessary facts could affect what we contingently believe. However, in the first scenario, a similar problem occurs regarding how knowledge of necessary facts arises in the Mind of God. Even if we explain it with reference to God's omniscience, it still acknowledges that necessary facts can affect what we believe, after all. His final conclusion is that necessary facts can have causal powers in fact, and some kind of a priori perception is possible (cf. Rice 2000, pp. 45–7). Rice's solution is not antithetical to theism. He allows that the explanation by God is one choice. His second choice is the postulation of a human faculty of a priori perception that accounts for our intuitions: "a priori perception provides for the possibility of the shaping of our beliefs by necessary facts...Perhaps it is just a causal process; or perhaps it is not itself a causal process, but provides for a causal relation between our beliefs and the necessary facts" (Rice 2000, p. 47). I think that his second choice would also naturally lead to theism, because a faculty of a priori perception is hardly acceptable to naturalists. If there is no God, evolution of this kind of creature would be rather unintelligible (more on this below). Moreover, his critique of the God theory seems to ignore various accounts by theistic philosophers about divine knowledge of necessary truths. For example, in Rogers's view, the necessary truths do not exist apart from the Divine Mind, and God's knowledge of necessary truths can be assimilated to His intuitive understanding of His own mind. There is no need to posit a kind of a priori perception for God in this case.

### 15.4.3 *Naturalistic Explanations of Necessary Truths*

So there is a coherent theistic explanation of intuitions; what about naturalistic explanations then? Here the major strategy of naturalism, the appeal to evolution, seems to encounter greater, if not insurmountable, difficulties. Even a naturalist like Nagel has some misgivings about the evolutionary accounts of logic: "It is sometimes said that a theory of logic is 'naturalistic' only if it holds that rational operations 'grow out of' the more pervasive biological and physical ones...And it is even less evident how, even if this were the case, the causal account would enable us to evaluate inferential principles, since the cogency of such an account is established only with the help of those principles…a genetic account of logical operations is at best a highly speculative and dubious one;…even if a well-supported genetic account were available, it would contribute little or nothing to an understanding of the present functioning of logical principles or to the explanation of the grounds of their authority. In the absence of a detailed knowledge of the past, the reaffirmation of the historical and structural continuity of our rational behavior with the activities of other organisms is an act of piety; it does not increase the clarifying force of an experimentally orientated naturalism" (Nagel 1944, p. 229). Nagel's attitude is rather different from the contemporary evolutionary psychologists' unlimited confidence in evolutionary naturalism. Anyway, I think Nagel pinpoints the fundamental problems with this whole enterprise.

What are the major options for the project of naturalistic explanation of intuitions here? (There is another option to deny necessary facts, but this has been criticized earlier.)[3]

> Option 1: The causal explanation of our strongly certain beliefs has something to do with the contents of those beliefs, for example, beliefs about numbers, and it is because numbers are in fact part of the physical universe that can interact causally with other physical things.
> Option 2: The causal explanation of our strongly certain beliefs has something to do with the contents of those beliefs, but there is an independent existence of some realm of Platonic abstracta (which consists of abstract objects like numbers and necessary truths).
> Option 3: The causal explanation of our strongly certain beliefs has nothing to do with the contents of those beliefs. For example, a cognitive capacity just accidentally arose in the history of evolution, and it just happened that the deliverances of that capacity largely correspond to the necessary truths.

Consider Option 1. First we need to clarify the nature of entities like numbers as *physical*. Presumably, they should be different from the numbers in the Platonic realm, which are eternal and unchanging. Suppose these physical numbers "might come into or go out of being with the birth and death of the universe…It would not have been the case that 2 + 2 = 4 if some radically different physical universe, or none at all, had existed" (Rogers 2008, p. 35). So this account can hardly preserve the necessity of logical intuitions.

Second, the idea of physical numbers, which can interact causally with other physical objects, have intrinsic difficulties. For example, it is difficult to understand what the constitution of these numbers is, where they come from, and how they are governed by natural laws. There is simply no motivation for this conception in our current scientific worldview, and it is well-nigh impossible to reconcile this conception with that worldview.

Third, there are an infinite number of numbers and necessary truths that are causally active. As Rogers observes, such "a theory depending on a possibly infinite number of agent abstracta at work in the world seems to depart from the empiricist and parsimonious motivations behind naturalism" (Rogers 2008, p. 45). Due to all these problems, Option 1 is untenable, and, as a matter of fact, hardly any naturalist has seriously advocated this option.

What about Option 2, which admits an independent existence of Platonic abstracta? Though naturalists are typically hostile to Platonism, there are a few who accept an existing Platonic realm side by side with the physical world. Nonetheless, "the universe of the naturalist who allows this platonic realm seems a strange, unparsimonious, and indeed schizophrenic place...What sort of 'things' are these platonic abstracta? As Robert Adams notes, they *seem* like ideas. Classical theism solves the problem by placing necessary truth in the mind of God and identifying it with the nature of God" (Rogers 2008, p. 43). So Option 2 seems inferior to the theistic explanation. Moreover, there are reasons to suspect that this option cannot really be a good explanation of logical intuitions. The difficulties are twofold. First, it is plausible to think that the Platonic abstracta are causally inert and cannot interact causally with the physical world. Second, the contents of logical intuitions are mainly about necessary truths, but the *necessity* of any belief is simply irrelevant to biological survival.

Consider these four beliefs:

 B1. If anything is sweet and poisonous, it *must* be poisonous.
 B2. If anything is sweet and poisonous, it is always poisonous.
 B3. If anything is sweet and poisonous, it is always poisonous before the year 2050.
 B4. If anything is sweet and poisonous, it is poisonous before the year 2050, but not poisonous after 2050.

B1 to B3 are true, but only B1 contains a content about necessary truth. B4 is necessarily false. What makes it likely that natural selection will produce a belief like B1, but not the others? As far as the consequences for our survival are concerned, all four of them are equivalent. So Rice concludes, "the *truth* of our beliefs about necessary facts is, in itself, simply *irrelevant* to survival...[a belief's] usefulness does not in any way depend on the *truth* of the metaphysical belief about necessity...So the Darwinian solution will not work for truths to the effect that something *must* be the case... evolutionary considerations provide no more reasons for supposing that our beliefs in necessary truths are well adapted to all possible circumstances, than for supposing that our lungs are well adapted to all possible circumstances" (Rice 2000, p. 44). Not only does the recognition of necessity in itself not enhance our success as reproducers; belief in a necessary falsehood (as in B4) may not even be detrimental to our survival at all. As our previous discussions show, natural selection is a very porous filter, but to catch the necessary truths, we need a very fine-grained filter indeed.

Rogers points out that a successful naturalistic theory needs to explain the reliability of our strongly certain beliefs, their inherently veridical nature, and the unique phenomenology of strong certainty. However, a naturalistic account of knowledge typically has a tracking requirement, that is, our beliefs can reliably track the features of the environment. For example, Devitt is attracted to radical empiricism because empirical knowledge seems to satisfy his idea that "justified beliefs are appropriately sensitive, via experience, to the way the world is" (Devitt 2005, p. 114). In Rogers's words, "An adequate theory of the causes of knowledge must presumably allow for the content of the knowledge, the thing known, to play *some* role in the causal explanation" (Rogers 2008, p. 35). But in the case of knowledge of necessary truths, it is hard to see how this requirement can be satisfied. Platonic necessary truths are supposed to be causally inert. How can they cause the brain states that cause the true beliefs?

A more general problem is this: we have seen that evolutionary explanation of belief is very flexible. The appeal to survival conduciveness is simply too coarse-grained to ensure *truth*. In Chapter 9, we argued that evolution in itself does not lead us to expect the reliability of our experiences. This argument will be even stronger when applied to beliefs in general, and beliefs about necessary truth in particular. So if the evolutionary causal story is indeed the correct account of how we come by *all* our beliefs, then there is at least the *logical possibility* that none of them are true. "But given that I am strongly certain that 2+2=4 I know it is not possible that all my beliefs are false...But this [evolutionary] causal explanation fails for our strongly certain beliefs because there is nothing in the story to account for the inherently veridical nature of these beliefs" (Rogers 2008, p. 36).

So the reasonable conclusion is that the evolutionary account offers no explanation for our modal knowledge. A platonic abstractum cannot "activate" a spatiotemporal causal chain. That being the case, there will be no naturalist causal explanation for the veridical nature, the luminosity, and the immediacy of the strongly certain belief in a necessary truth like 2+2=4.

Option 3 does not fare any better. The suggestion is that our strongly certain beliefs just happen to be true without any *causal connection* between the belief and the true proposition. The basic problem is that this account violates the tracking requirement, and will throw our intuitions into doubt. For example, the fact that 2+2=4 plays no role in the causal history of the strongly certain belief that 2+2=4. The naturalists simply would not use this kind of theory to explain our SE. Suppose our visual apparatus and brain mechanisms are causally disconnected from the outside world entirely, but somehow our brain can still generate veridical perceptions of the external world *all the time*. This theory relies on a colossal accident that is, to put it mildly, immensely unlikely. It is simply unbelievable.

### 15.5 Conclusion

It seems that only a godlike being can provide a sufficient explanation for our strongly certain beliefs concerning platonic abstracta (and necessary truth in general), and so the existence of such beliefs provides some evidence for the existence of God. The argument from necessary truths seems plausible. Even if it is not conclusive, it at least shows the coherence of our intellectual experience with theism, and this is enough for our purpose here.

CHAPTER 16

# RELIGIOUS EXPERIENCE, CRITICAL TRUST, AND GOD

In this chapter I will discuss the nature of various types of RE, especially in relation to theistic experience. I argue that theistic mysticism can be distinguished from non-theistic types of mysticism, and from pure consciousness events. I discuss the nature of the major forms of RE and argue that most of them are compatible with, or even supportive of, theistic experience. I finally defend the ARE from the radical constructivism objection and the conflicting claims objection. I argue that the entire corpus of RE can provide *some* PFJ for the existence of *some* supernatural realm.

## 16.1 Varieties of Religious Experience

### 16.1.1 The Typology of Religious Experience

REs can be further divided into the following types:

1. Theistic experience (TE): a noetic experience whose intentional object is God, the personal and supremely perfect creator of the world. Theistic mysticism will be included in the category of TE. The typology of TE will be discussed in the next chapter.
2. Ecstasy and peak experience (Abraham Maslow).
3. Encounter of the Light Being in a near-death experience (Moody).
4. Experience of evil spirit, angels, or departed saints.
5. Experience of contingency: a spontaneous feeling that the world is not ultimate and is somehow dependent on something beyond.
6. Experience of design: experience of being struck by the beauty and intricacy of the natural order and the feeling that this order is ultimately due to Intelligence or Mind.
7. Nature mysticism, extrovertive mysticism, or cosmic consciousness: a spontaneous feeling that the universe and oneself are one. It is usually induced by contemplation of nature, but a similar experience can also be induced by drugs, for example, mescalin.
8. Pure consciousness event (PCE): a pure state of consciousness without *any* intentional object and uncontaminated by any concept. This event should be distinguished from the monistic mystical experience, which may include a PCE as a part.

9. Experience of minor deities, for example, visions of Kali or Buddha or Apollo.
10. Monistic mysticism, for example, the intuitive apprehension that Atman is Brahman and that All is One.
11. Experience of Nirvana: experience of Nothingness or No-self as the Ultimate.

### 16.1.2 Theistic Mysticism and Non-Theistic Mysticism

How we should classify different types of mysticism continues to be controversial. One possible objection to my typology is that it is illegitimate to classify theistic mystical experience as a separate type. Stace argues that all mystical experiences are basically the same in terms of (phenomenological) content. Theistic mysticism is just the imposition of theistic *interpretation* on this core mystical experience. What is this core experience? "It is the pure unitary consciousness wherein awareness of the world and of multiplicity is completely obliterated. It is ineffable peace. It is the Supreme Good. It is One without a second. It is the Self" (Stace 1960, p. 88). The experience is described by Christian mystics as the experience of "union with God" only because they come to it antecedently committed to a theistic world picture or because they are subject to ecclesiastical pressures. Such a move is in part justified by the claim that a theistic experience, if genuine, would incorporate too high a level of interpretation—an assumption about the origin of the world and a belief in the existence of a personal God.

How does this theory fare with the phenomenological data of the Christian mystics' experiences? Not very well, according to Pike. He urges us to recall "that in the Prayer of Quiet, God and the soul of the mystic are said to be *close*, while in the Full Union and in the culmination stage of Rapture these same two objects are pictured as being in *mutual embrace*...the language is radically dualistic" (Pike 1992, p. 108). Furthermore, "the very same mystic sometimes offers one of these (alleged) elaborative expansions and sometimes another...it is *not* an item of orthodox faith that God is sometimes close to the soul...and at other times enwraps and penetrates the soul...There is also the phenomenon of 'spiritual sensations': "Where in the catechism does it say that God is sometimes felt as a burn or is heard as the whisper of a gentle breeze?...how about the *smell!*" (Pike 1992, pp. 110–11). Pike concludes that a far more likely hypothesis is that these descriptions have their source in experience. I think Pike has built up a convincing case against Stace.

Stace also seems to adopt a bottom-up approach to the distinction between experience and interpretation. I have argued against this in Chapter 3. In any case, my analysis below shows that monism is not identical to the PCE and is also an interpretation *of* the PCE. There is no particular reason to favor the monistic interpretation over the theistic interpretation.

### 16.1.3 *Monism and Pure Consciousness Event*

Concerning the description of the alleged core mystical experience, PCE, we have to distinguish these two experiences:

1. Awareness *of* undifferentiated unity, the One, the Self, and so on.
2. A pure state of awareness that *is* undifferentiated unity.

The first experience is more like an intuition, an insight into reality, but the intentional structure of experience is intact. But there is a tension here: the content of the experience is alleged to be an undifferentiated unity without distinctions; yet the experience itself can still be divided into the subject of awareness and the intentional object of the awareness. This is certainly paradoxical. The second experience is akin to the pure consciousness event (PCE), and it does not have an intentional structure at all.

It is not always clear, when a "monistic mystical experience" is mentioned, which sense is intended. I propose that the phrase should be used to refer to the first intuitive experience, rather than the PCE, because the PCE in itself is not specifically monistic. Indeed it *cannot* yield support to monism by virtue of its epistemic seeming, because there is no conceptual element in the PCE. In fact, the two experiences are logically incompatible: no person can have both experiences at the same time. Consider this report:

> I would settle down, it would be very quiet...and there would just be a sort of complete silence void of content...there would be no thought, no activity, and no perception, yet it was somehow comforting...But I did not yet identify myself with this silent, content-free inner space.... Then...I began to recognize in it the essence of my own self as pure consciousness. Eventually,...'I' as a separate entity just started to have no meaning.... There is no thought, there is no activity, there is no experiencer" (cited in Forman 1990, pp. 27–8).

The description is littered with paradoxes. Certainly, there was a PCE, but it was also "somehow comforting." Did this sense of comfort feature within the experience or not? If yes, the experience is no longer pure. I also wonder how the person can report a PCE afterwards. In the PCE, there is no thought and feeling, and no awareness of any sort. How, then, can the subject later ascribe this experience to *himself*? This must be explained by the continuous operation of the memory, which is somehow hidden during the PCE. But whose memory and whose PCE? To give an intelligible answer to this question, it is difficult to avoid positing a self who possesses this PCE, even though the sense of self is not present *in* the PCE. Indeed, it is the interpretation adopted by the subject originally. But later the subject comes to another interpretation: "there is no...experiencer." Now, if this is the correct description of the experience, then this description cannot be *given* in that experience. So this must be an *interpretation* imposed on the PCE due to subsequent reflection or experience. So the question as to why this interpretation is justified has to be raised.

So why should we think that the PCE can support the monistic experience? Perhaps we can conceive of the experiences as a unity. First, the subject has a PCE without monistic mystical experiences. Surely he can't have both types of experience at the same time. However, when he comes back from this contentless state, *he* immediately has some mystical illuminations that are monistic in content. The two experiences seem to go together, and the PCE *in this context* can then be legitimately interpreted as an experience *of* the Self. I doubt very much that this move is successful in avoiding the conceptual difficulties. Let us waive these. Here I just want to point out that the same move is available to the theists. Pike grants that, in the Rapture, the theistic mystic may experience a "monistic interval lacking subject-object structure as well as sensory and sensory-like content" (Pike 1992, p. 160). However, the phenomenological description of this interval should be determined with respect to the context.

Pike gives an analogy of being knocked into unconsciousness by a baseball. I propose an alternative analogy of "sleeping in the arms of the beloved." Suppose a wife and a husband embrace one another and continue to talk late into the night. The wife slowly falls asleep. Upon awakening, she describes her experience as one of sleeping in the arms of the beloved. No one will dispute this description, but, strictly speaking, during her sleep she cannot be aware of staying in the arms of her husband! But her experience can phenomenologically make sense in the experiential context. Similarly, when the Christian mystics experience a "monistic" interval within the context of dualistic mystical experiences of God, it is legitimate to think that this "moment of experience in which the soul detects no distinction between itself and God is a kind of experiential fiction—appearance only—and is not to be thought of as indicative of reality" (Pike 1992, p. 156). The spirit is simply deluded by love into not noticing the difference between itself and God. There is all the world of difference between an experience of not noticing the distinction between the soul and God, and an experience of noticing that there is no distinction between the soul and God. Even if a PCE occurs amid the theistic mystical experiences, it is normally the former and not the latter. The upshot is that even if PCEs can lend support to monism in certain contexts, they lend support to theism in others.

I conclude that it is legitimate to classify PCEs, theistic mysticism, and monistic mysticism as distinguishable types of RE, though they are also intricately related.[1] Since the intentional object of theistic mysticism is similar to other TEs, it should also be included under the same umbrella.

### 16.1.4 Rapture, Ecstasy, and Peak Experience

Mysticism is only part of the phenomena of RE. Ordinary people who do not consider themselves mystics nonetheless can experience trancelike states of mind in rapture, ecstasy, and peak experience. Moreover, these "extraordinary" states can be induced by a variety of situations *in ordinary life*, for example, art appreciation, sexual love, philosophical insight, athletic success, watching a dance performance, or bearing a child. That is why Abraham Maslow says, "the sacred is *in* the ordinary" (Maslow 1970, p. x), and "the eternal becomes visible *in* and *through* the particular, the symbolic and platonic can be experienced *in* and *through* the concrete instance,...and one can transcend the universe of time and space while being of it" (Maslow 1970, p. 116). This view is consonant with my model of immanent transcendence (Chapter 5).

These experiences do not always have *explicitly* supernatural content, for example, a sudden sense of peace in the face of adversity or before the threat of death. Yet many peak experiences are explicit REs and often theistic. It is also arguable that even for those peak experiences with no explicit religious content, they *implicitly* embody a kind of *Being-cognition*. (This is Maslow's term, and it is sometimes abbreviated as B-cognition. The values embodied in B-cognition are called B-values.) For example, a peace that surpasses rational understanding suggests a kind of Being that is fundamentally harmonious with the nature of humanity. So on the whole, peak experiences can be considered as some kind of proto-REs or implicit REs, which point beyond the persons who have them. When they occur to us, we seem to feel the Presence of something great, and we stand in wonder, awe, reverence, and humility. As Maslow says, "the B-values *are* absolutes of a kind, a humanly satisfying kind, which, furthermore, are 'cosmocentric'...and not personally relative or selfishly ego-centered" (Maslow 1970, p. 96).

I agree that peak experiences can be interpreted in both theistic and monistic frameworks. For example, the core affirmation of B-cognition is the meaningfulness and unity of the universe, but this meaningfulness can be grounded in "the fact that it was all created by God or ruled by God or *is* God" (Maslow 1970, p. 60). However, if we look carefully at the more detailed description of various peak experiences, there is little direct evidence for monism, but quite a few pointers in the direction of personal theism.

For example, peak-perception "is the experience of gratitude,...of grace" (Maslow 1970, p. 79). There are emotions like awe and worship (Maslow 1970, p. 65). I think attitudes of gratitude, awe, and worship are more appropriate for a personal God than for an impersonal Absolute, not to mention the experience of grace. Moreover, peak experiences make a person feel more responsible and are related to the discovery of one's real identity or real self (Maslow 1970, pp. 67, 75). So although there may be a temporary loss of self-consciousness, peak experience cannot be identified as a no-self experience.

Maslow's psychological study of peak experiences shows that Being-cognition is helpful for the process of self-actualization. As the individual finds himself perceiving something of the essential Being, he feels closer to the core of his own Being; he becomes more truly himself, more integrated, and more fully human. Peak experiences are also therapeutically effective. Maslow has two subjects who have peak experiences in which "the whole universe is perceived as an integrated and unified whole," and they feel that they belong in it. Because of such an experience, they "were totally, immediately, and permanently cured of...chronic anxiety neurosis and...of strong obsessional thoughts of suicide" (Maslow 1970, p. 59). Maslow himself concludes, "man has a higher and transcendent nature, and this is part of his essence," and his project is "to become a man...to combine the humanistic, the transpersonal, and the transhuman" (Maslow 1970, pp. xvi–xvii).

The above data about peak experiences lend support to the ARE. They once again show that REs are not odd at all. REs seem to resonate deeply with the human psyche (its needs and its telos), and play an integral role in the process of self-actualization. This is readily explicable on the theistic hypothesis, but not to be *expected* in a naturalistic world. I have already argued for similar points elsewhere in Part B.

### 16.1.5 Extrovertive Mystical Experience

In an extrovertive mystical experience (EME), people have a feeling of unity with surroundings or with other people, a sense of harmony, and an awareness of a sacred presence in nature. These experiences occur during our encounter with the world, and not in the context of intense meditation. It is called extrovertive as a contrast with the introvertive mystical experience, which looks inside. (In fact, EMEs and peak experiences have significant overlap.) Marshall has a thorough study of these mystical experiences, which take place in the modern world—in a surprising variety of circumstances. Again we need to distinguish the EME from the PCE: "As a contentless state of consciousness, pure consciousness does not seem to have much to do with extrovertive experiences, which are often very rich in contents" (Marshall 2005, p. 8).

Marshall has summarized the most common contents of an extrovertive mystical experience: feeling part of the whole; relaxation of individual identity and discovery of deeper self; all-embracing love and sense of being deeply loved; extraordinary beauty; bliss, elation, peace, gratitude, wonder, everything animated with "life," "consciousness," and "energy"; unique sense of reality; a "presence" or "power" in nature (Marshall 2005, p. 27). Looking at these contents, we can see that EME cannot be equated to a monistic experience. Basically, all the contents are compatible with theism, and some of them (e.g. sense of love) even positively suggest a form of personal theism.

Marshall has surveyed many interpretations of EME and takes the theistic interpretation seriously. I find William Inge's theory quite plausible. Inge believes that EME is the realization of the presence of the living God in the soul and in nature. The intelligible world, or the spiritual world, is the world of values—Goodness, Truth, and Beauty—which is grounded in the unity of the Divine Mind. Why, then, should an encounter with the natural world bring blissful feelings, an altered experience of time, a sense of unity, and luminous phenomena? It is because in an EME, the divine presence in the intelligible universe is accessible to the soul, and the nature mystic's experience becomes infused by the characteristics inherent in the Divine Mind (Marshall 2005, pp. 134–6).

So the phenomena of EMEs are congenial to the theistic worldview. In fact, what happens in the EME seems analogous to many implicit TEs in the rainbow of experiences. At times, an EME can be explicitly theistic. For example, an experience occurred to John Franklin, a schoolboy aged 14, in June 1949, when he was lying under a lime tree: "I suddenly found myself surrounded, embraced, by a white light, which seemed both to come from within me and from without...an overwhelming sense of Love, of warmth, peace and joy." In the end there is the "realisation...that the love of God is an ever-present reality...that enfolds us always" (cited in Marshall 2005, pp. 24–5).

## 16.2  The Challenge of Radical Constructivism

In Chapter 5, we evaluated the Theory-Ladenness Objection, which argues that since religious experiences are heavily (or entirely) shaped by the conceptual framework of the experients, they are not useful as evidence for ontological claims. I find this objection still surprisingly common, despite its implausibility in a post-foundationalist context. Perhaps this is founded on the feeling that although all experiences are theory-laden, the problem is especially serious in religious experiences. This is reflected in the popularity of Steven Katz's constructivism in the study of mysticism. I will examine this challenge of constructivism more carefully below.

### 16.2.1  Katz's Constructivism

Katz is not uncommonly classified as a radical constructivist who claims that mystical experience is *entirely* constructed out of the mystic's religious training or framework. However, this may not be entirely fair to Katz, because Katz acknowledges the existence of mystic heretics who challenge their religious traditions. He even explicitly says, "it is not my intention to argue that mysticism...is *only* a conservative phenomenon...mysticism...is a dialectic that oscillates between the innovative and traditional poles of the religious life" (Katz 1983, pp. 3–4). So on paper he is not a radical constructivist. However, in general his work leans toward the constructivist side. He claims that his studies "throw suspicion on those approaches to mystical experience which treat these experiences in non-contextual ways...The thesis that mysticism has strong, if not dominant, conservative characteristics has at least begun to be demonstrated" (Katz 1983, p. 51).

It is understandable that claims like these can easily lend support to radical constructivism. Anyway, my criticisms below are targeted at such an extension of his position. My intention is not to deny the significance of contextual studies of RE. REs are, of course, theory-laden, and in many cases constrained by the experient's prior framework *to some extent*.

However, theory-ladenness is not automatically a cognitively debilitating factor, and *many* REs are also surprisingly independent of the experient's prior framework.

Radical constructivism cannot be the truth, simply because it is contradicted by many empirical data. Two things, *P* and *Q*, have no necessary connection if in reality all these scenarios obtain: *P* and *Q*, *P* and ~*Q*, ~*P* and *Q*. (~*P* and ~*Q* may not be relevant, as the raven paradox shows.) In general, prior belief in *X* and experience of *X* have no necessary connection. Similarly, all these combinations happen in the case of RE.

### 16.2.2 *Religious Experiences Happening to People with No Prior Belief*

Even John Baillie insists that "we can have no religious experience prior to and independently of religious faith" (Baillie 1928, p. 231). So he claims that we cannot experience divine forgiveness apart from faith in a forgiving God. His analysis is mistaken. The primary problem is his misunderstanding of experience. As my arguments in Part A show, a noetic experience that *p* is only an epistemic seeming that *p*. This is a spontaneous inclination to believe in *p*, which is compatible with an absence of belief in *p*, or even with a belief in **not-*p***. This can be easily demonstrated in the case of the Lyer-Muller illusion. So there certainly can be REs apart from religious faith. They can even occur to atheists! In cases of conversion experience, strong REs *result in* faith, but they cannot be determined by *prior* belief, which simply did not exist. So it is indeed possible for a person to come to believe in a forgiving God on the basis of an unexpected experience of God's forgiveness (see Tinder's experience in Chapter 13). Let us look at some more real cases.

Simone Weil (1909–1943) had an unexpected mystical encounter with the divine that transformed her life (in the following account, I basically follow Overman 2009, pp. 133–7). Weil was born into a Jewish family in Paris, but her family was completely agnostic. She participated in the anarchist movement of the Spanish Civil War. After being wounded, she went to Portugal, where she had surprising religious experiences. However, besides not having any religious training, she was not even in search of God at that time. In 1938, when she was at the abbey of Solesmes, she had an unexpected mystical encounter: "Christ himself came down and took possession of me...I had never foreseen the possibility of that, of a real contact, person, here below, between a human being and God.... in this sudden possession of me by Christ...I only felt in the midst of my suffering the presence of a love... God in his mercy had prevented me from reading the mystics, so that it should be evident to me that I had not invented this absolutely unexpected contact" (cited in Overman 2009, p. 135).

Weil should be taken as a serious witness. No doubt she was an intelligent person with moral integrity. She died in Kent on August 29, 1943, at the age of 34. Although dying young, her philosophical works have been highly regarded. Moreover, the reason for her premature death was her decision to show solidarity with those suffering the Nazi occupation in France. Though she was already in a state of poor health, she still declined supplemental food, consuming the same rations that were allowed to her fellow French people.

In his study of extrovertive mystical experience, Marshall also points out that "many cases are situated outside traditions of doctrine and practice, occurring under a variety of non-religious circumstances" (Marshall 2005, p. 190). In many cases, the subjects had no background knowledge of mysticism at all. For example, a schoolboy experienced the world as the "mine" of an "I" that was no longer the "familiar ego," and he later recalled: "The event made a very deep impression on me at the time; but, because it did not fit into any of the thought patterns—religious, philosophical, scientific—with which, as a boy of fifteen, I was familiar, it came to seem more and more anomalous, more and more irrelevant to 'real life', and was finally almost forgotten" (cited in Marshall 2005, p. 191). These childhood experiences of extrovertive mysticism are particularly striking because they are not commonly included in the religious education of children, or the larger culture of society.

The above are not isolated cases. In a UK national poll, "23–24% of those who'd had an experience of a presence or power identified themselves as being either 'agnostic,' 'atheist,' or 'don't knows.'" (Hawker 2000, p. 84)!

### 16.2.3 Religious Experiences Contradictory to People's Prior Belief

Another contemporary counterexample to the constructivist thesis is Rachel Noam's case (see Block 2007, pp. 167–80). Noam was an Israeli woman who was born on a *kibbutz* of Hashomer Hatzair, indoctrinated into the philosophy of dialectical materialism. Naturally she assumed that after death there was absolute nothingness. When she was a young lady, as she was walking in Tel Aviv just after the Yom Kippur war in 1973, she was struck on the head by an eighteen-foot-long wooden beam that fell five stories from a construction site. She then had an out-of-body experience, which surprised her. As she explained, "I always thought that 'I' and my body were identical. I did not know that I was a being that was more than just a physical body.... I did not need any physical organs to see, to hear or to think" (cited in Block 2007, p. 168).

Then she had a mystical NDE of the Light Being: "The magnificent stream of light was accompanied by a flow of sublime love...Faced with this overpowering love,...I simply melted away...No words can describe the enchantment, the wonder, the incomparable, infinite goodness...Any sense of independence, pride, anger and desire vanished...I felt a powerful bond with this marvellous presence. This was the will of a higher Power, a Being of infinite might" (cited in Block 2007, pp. 169–70). The force of compassion finally brought her back into her body.

Despite her experience, she did not develop a religious worldview, nor was she engaged in religious activities. Some years later, she noticed a book on the dining room table, a prayer book called in Hebrew a *siddur*. Then she read this in the prayer book: "Lord of all souls, Who restores souls to dead bodies." This saying greatly struck her: "The thing I dared not speak about for so many years was written here plainly...I was weeping irrepressibly, although...for many years I hardly cried at all.... How is it possible that for thirty years I had not even once read the siddur?" She reflected on the whole process: "For six long years, I had been searching, and now, in the seventh year I had finally found the answer...How many times had I passed a synagogue, yet it never occurred to me to enter!" (cited in Block 2007, pp. 177, 179). This was the beginning of her involvement in Judaism.

This case is quite interesting, and shows again that even persons with secular or even atheist bckgrounds can have strong REs. In this case, her NDE is basically a kind of theistic mysticism, because the experience combines affirmation of a personal Being with a sense of unity (the temporary loss of individuality was the result of being overwhelmed by Infinite Love). However, far from constructing these experiences from her prior religious belief, Noam cannot really interpret the experiences. Only after later reading a prayer book, did she have a sudden realization of the meaning of her REs. This case also illustrates the thesis that the meaning of a RE may already be implicit there, but it can take a long search (6 years for Noam) to fully unravel the meaning. These features all contradict the constructivist thesis. In fact, Noam's experience is not an isolated case. According to P. M. H. Atwater, who has studied NDEs, "it takes the average near-death survivor *seven years* to even begin to integrate the experience" (Atwater 1994, p. 218).

The case of the theologian Sarah Coakley shows that RE can occur in contradiction to prior theological paradigm. Her earlier study of Troeltsch's liberal theology has "utterly dismantled" her belief in traditional doctrines such as Christology and Trinity. However, several years of the practice of prayer of silence has led her back. She says the experience was frightening, but "also uniquely alluring and magnetizing, as if all the fragmented pieces of my life were being lined up and drawn inexorably in one direction...What I discovered as a result of time on my knees was that my earlier dismantling of doctrines such as the incarnation and Trinity was itself being challenged and recast...what has to be abandoned here first...is any sense of mastery...You are being led by the Spirit beyond conventional modes of rationality...[I] rediscover a vibrant and distinct sense of the Spirit, starting on my knees, before I could return to those last strands of Christology and Trinity" (cited in Shortt 2005, pp. 70–1).

### 16.2.4 Religious Experiences Not Happening to People with Prior Belief

The constructivists seem to assume that it is easy for people with religious belief to conjure up a RE at will. However, the case of Mortimer Adler, a professor at Columbia University and at the University of Chicago, is an impressive example showing that a religious belief in God is by no means a sufficient condition for a living TE (in the following account, I basically follow Overman 2009, pp. 141–8). Adler was fascinated with Aquinas's writings, and was convinced that he could construct a rational argument for God's existence. Interestingly, despite his belief in God for many years, he did not have any experience of God until 1984.

In March 1984, after a trip to Mexico in February, he fell into protracted illness. While suffering from a mild depression, this experience happened to him unexpectedly: "I found myself repeating the Lord's Prayer, again and again, and meaning every word of it. Quite suddenly, when I was awake one night, a light dawned on me, and I realized what had happened without my recognizing it clearly when it first happened…Here after many years affirming God's existence and trying to give adequate reasons for that affirmation, I found myself believing in God and praying to him" (cited in Overman 2009, pp. 143–4). On April 21, 1984, he was baptized a Christian at last.

The story of Michael Goulder is an even more conspicuous counterexample. He was a theologian and an ordained minister in the Anglican Church. Certainly he "was a committed Christian, committed to a lifetime's quest of God." He also received intense religious training. However, he confessed, "the reality of God's coming to me was very dim. Neither at this period of early devotion, nor in the bright time of my conversion, nor in the halcyon days of my vocation to the ministry, nor (I now recognize) ever, did I have an awareness of God in prayer" (Goulder and Hick 1983, p. 3)! Of course, this kind of phenomenon is the premise for the argument from divine hiddenness, and poses some difficulties for theism. If it were that easy to construct a vivid RE from one's religious training, then this problem of divine hiddenness would hardly arise.

### 16.2.5 Similar Experiences in Different Frameworks

If REs are entirely constructed out of prior frameworks, then we should expect different frameworks to produce different REs, but this is not always the case. So substantial similarities in mystical traditions in divergent socioreligious contexts is not something to be expected on the constructivist thesis. This is some counterevidence, unless the constructivist "can satisfactorily show in relevant cases that mystics of different traditions read the same books, performed the same practices, expected the same encounters" (Stoeber 1992, p. 112).

Some examples are given by Marshall: "notable similarities between Derek Gibson's spontaneous extrovertive experience (late 1960s, England)…and the clairvoyant-mystical experiences reported by Yogananda (early twentieth century, India)…For Iglulik shamans, an inner luminosity could bring a feeling of ascension, clairvoyance, and precognition…a combination also experienced by the medieval Christian mystic Hildegard of Bingen" (Marshall 2005, pp. 190–1).

The above empirical data about REs show that radical constructivism is not an adequate model. Barring skeptical considerations and a double standard, it seems that the model of critical realism is applicable here as in other types of experience. There seems to be a dynamic interaction between the Real and the mystic as reflected in the mystic's continuous development of his understanding of the Real. In fact, there are similar phenomena in the rainbow of experiences. People have spiritual experiences that do not come from their prior framework and sometimes *despite* their framework, for example, Wittgenstein's spiritual experiences (Chapter 2), Smart's sense of wonder (Chapter 9), Glynn's I-Thou encounter (Chapter 12), Putnam's moral experience (Chapter 13), O'Hear's aesthetic experience (Chapter 14). The model of critical realism seems to be applicable as well.

## 16.3 The Conflicting Claims Objection[2]

### 16.3.1 Dealing with Conflicts between Presumptive Data

Many critics claim that since religious experiences are so various and mutually contradictory, we should regard all of them with suspicion. Even if we grant some force to religious experiences, different religious experiences cancel one another's force in the end (Flew 1966, pp. 126–7; Michael Martin 1986, pp. 87–8). However, the existing contradictions between religious experiences do not render the PCT inapplicable to them. To apply the PCT to some experiences is to have *initial* trust in them and, if they are defeated, to salvage as much as possible from them. It does not entail that they are all or mostly reliable. There is no contradiction in saying that we should have initial trust in conflicting experiences. Indeed, almost all sorts of experience or doxastic practices produce conflicting beliefs sooner or later. So why do we think that the presence of contradictions in religious experience should debar us from having initial trust, at least to some degree, in religious experience?

Consider the conflict of witnesses in the courts. It would indeed be stupid to reject all their accounts just because they conflict! It seems to be a rational strategy to try to reconcile their reports as much as possible. For example, a common core[3] can be identified. Many historical accounts of a momentous historical event, for example, China's Cultural Revolution, are also contradictory. It is difficult to determine the exact course or nature of this event, but it would be preposterous to deny that the Cultural Revolution happened. All the above examples count against the skeptical policy and show that conflict of presumptive data is not irremediable.

### 16.3.2 The Common Core of Religious Experience

The most important contradiction concerns the *nature of the ultimate reality*. Is it personal or impersonal? Numinous experiences and theistic experiences seem to indicate that it is personal, while monistic mystical experiences seem to show it is impersonal. However, even this contradiction is not irremediable. Suppose the ultimate reality is, indeed, personal. It is possible that a personal being can manifest himself in a nonpersonal way. The manifestation can still be veridical. Consider Yahweh's epiphany to Elijah. God can be said to be manifested in the earthquake and the whirlwind, but this is not yet a personal manifestation. If the epiphany stops at this level, the experient may even think that God is impersonal. However, the situation is transformed when the "still small voice" is added to the scene. The whole experience becomes an unambiguous personal manifestation. So a nonpersonal manifestation does not entail that the underlying reality is anti-personal. This is even more plausible when we realize that orthodox theists always maintain that God is more than personal, that is, the human category of "personal" can't exhaust the nature of God. Indeed, the Old Testament scholar Rowley says, "we find *personal and impersonal factors* woven together in what the Hebrews believed to be God's manifestation of himself" (Rowley 1956, p. 45).

In the end, there is a conflict only if one claims that the Ultimate is *essentially personal*, and the other claims that the Ultimate is *essentially impersonal*. However, "we rarely, if ever, run across claims to the effect that someone was aware of experiencing God's essential nature or some aspect of God as essential. In all cases I collected or examined I found neither claim made" (Wall 1995, p. 320). Of course, it can also be maintained that an Impersonal Absolute can manifest itself in personal ways. For example, some schools of Hinduism make the distinction between the *saguna-Brahman* (the personal manifestation of Brahman) and the *nirguna-Brahman* (the Impersonal Absolute and Ultimate). If the above analysis is correct, it means that there is no necessary conflict between the majority of reports of RE, which may place the emphasis on either the personal or impersonal aspects of the Ultimate without claiming that the Ultimate is exclusively personal or exclusively impersonal. (I will explore the conflict between theism and monism in Chapter 17.) So it is by no means impossible to organize the diverse religious experiences into a coherent framework. Of course, some revisionist moves are inevitable, but the CTA does not forbid them, provided the resulting worldview is more coherent.

In line with the above suggestions, although there is a significant degree of conflict among the religious experiences *at the highest level of description*, a certain common core can still be extracted from them *at a lower level of description*. Caroline Davis suggests the following as the common core:

(i)  the mundane world of physical bodies, physical processes, and narrow centres of consciousness is not the whole or ultimate reality.

(ii) ... there is a far deeper "true self" which in some way depends on and participates in the ultimate reality.

(iii) Whatever *is* the ultimate reality is holy, eternal, and of supreme value; it can appear to be more truly real than all else, since everything else depends on it.

(iv) This holy power can be experienced as an awesome, loving, pardoning, guiding (etc.) presence with whom individuals can have a personal relationship...

(v) ... at least some mystical experiences are experiences of a very intimate union with the holy power...

(vi) Some kind of union or harmonious relation with the ultimate reality is the human being's *summum bonum*, his final liberation or salvation, and the means by which he discovers his "true self" or "true home." (Davis 1989, p. 191)

All the religious experiences point to the fact that there is another realm *up there* or *beyond* the naturalistic world. So even if REs have internal conflicts, they can arguably still lend support to ARE insofar as they tilt the balance away from naturalism. This is the Stage One of my ARE. It is important to factor in the enhancer of the rainbow of experiences here as a balance against the alleged defeater of internal conflicts. As we have argued extensively in Part B, many human experiences possess a depth dimension that points to some kind of transcendent reality. This is coherent with and supportive of the conclusion of Stage One of ARE. To proceed to Stage Two, we need to do some more conceptual work first.

### 16.3.3 Reclassification of Religious Experience

To evaluate the epistemic status of TE relative to other kinds of RE, the Rule of Ground Level Sifting is helpful. What we need to do is to segregate the presumptive data into consistent subsets and then choose the one that has maximal weight. So let us reclassify REs in the following way:

A. *Theistic experience*
B. *Theism-compatible non-TE*

These REs, though not specifically theistic, are logically compatible with theism. They can be further divided into:

1. *theism-friendly non-TEs*: these experiences go quite well with theism, and they can be readily interpreted theistically without distortion or implausible reinterpretation.

2. *theism-neutral non-TEs*: these experiences are compatible with theism, and they can be interpreted theistically; however, they do not strongly suggest a theistic interpretation, and they can also be interpreted in a way which goes against theism.

3. *theism-unfriendly non-TEs*: these experiences are logically compatible with theism, but seem to suggest an interpretation that is in tension with theism.

C. *Theism-incompatible non-TEs*: These experiences, if veridical in their most ramified description, are incompatible with theism, because the Ultimate disclosed in these experiences is not personal.

The major conflict now occurs between TE and theism-incompatible non-TE. If we also take into consideration the theism-compatible non-TEs, then there are two competing groups of RE: the *pro-theistic group*, which consists of TE plus theism-friendly non-TEs, and the *anti-theistic group*, which consists of theism-incompatible plus theism-unfriendly non-TEs. (Since the theism-neutral non-TEs do not point in any specific direction, we can ignore them here.) I will try to decide which group has the greater weight in the next chapter.

# CHAPTER 17

# THEISTIC EXPERIENCE, CRITICAL TRUST, AND GOD

In this chapter, I argue that theistic experience is moderately well established, and hence, given the Principle of Critical Trust, merits prima facie trust. I then ague that TE is not defeated by its conflict with monistic experiences.


## 17.1 The Phenomenon of Theistic Experience

### 17.1.1 Theistic Experience as a Cross-Cultural Tradition

The experience of God is not confined to Westerners. Some kind of God was known to the ancient Chinese. The most common Chinese translations of the word "God" are Shang-ti (上帝), which means "the Emperor above," and the Lord of Tien (which means "Heaven") (天主). Neither Shang-ti nor Tien are terms created by the missionaries. They are, in fact, widely used in the ancient Chinese classics, and point to the belief in a personal God. The name Shang-ti has already appeared in the oracle bones, and it stands for the Supreme Lord of the universe.

In the *Doctrine of the Mean*, Confucius said, "By the ceremonies of the sacrifices to Heaven and Earth they served Shang-ti." In the *Book of Poetry*, there is a Hymn of Zhou (《周頌》) which praised Shang-ti, "Lord Wu with mighty power, Above all else will tower, Cheng the lord and Kang lord, Shang-ti likewise will laud." Another poem said, "A good crop of barley and wheat, Will soon be ready to reap, Oh by Glorious Shang-ti blest."

Shang-ti is One who can receive sacrifice, One who can bless. He is also One whom we should serve. Shang-ti or Tien (Heaven) cannot just mean the physical nature or some impersonal force, because He was regarded as a fearful God who had a moral will. Besides being the source of judgment, Shang-ti is also the source of goodness or happiness: "The great emperor of heaven grants happiness (or goodness) to the people below. The one who can follow the human nature of the people and make the people follow the instruction single-heartedly is not other but the sovereign."

It is widely recognized that one of the major thinkers in ancient China, Mo Tzu, believed in a personal God. He advocated universal love because Heaven also loved people. For Mo Tzu, there was nothing better than following Heaven. Heaven is all-inclusive and impartial in its activities, abundant and unceasing in its blessings, and lasting and untiring in its guidance. Heaven desires us to love one another and forbids us to harm one another.

Some scholars argue that Confucius (551–479 B.C.) is only a humanist, but I think this interpretation is wrong. It seems true that Confucius did not put a strong emphasis on Heaven, but he did have some kind of faith in a personal Heaven. He said, "At fifty I understood the Will of Heaven. At sixty, my ear was an obedient organ for the reception of truth. At seventy, I could follow what my heart desired, without transgressing what was right." (*Analects*, tr. James Legge). Besides talking about understanding Heaven and being understood by Heaven, Confucius also prayed to Heaven. He once said, "He who sins against Heaven has no place left where he may pray." When the Master fell ill, Chung Yu asked him to pray. Confucius answered: "My prayer has been in progress for a long time indeed." If Heaven were only the physical world or some impersonal principle for Confucius, it hardly made sense to pray to it.

So the ancient Chinese worshipped a single omnipotent Supreme Being in the form of Heaven alongside lesser spirits of the stars, mountains, and rivers. A contemporary Chinese scholar, He Guang-hu, thinks that the above view of Shang-ti and Heaven is the root of Confucianism, which believes in a personal God who is the Maker of the world and humankind, who is powerful, righteous, loving, and willing to communicate with human beings. So Chinese also have experiences of God, though the theistic tradition cannot be said to be very strong (Kwan and Han 2008).

The Korean theologian Joo-han Kim points out that in ancient Korean culture, there was also the concept of *Hannim*, which means "Lord/God of heaven." The term *theos* was translated as *Hananim*, which means "the god who resides in heaven above, and controls the world below" (Kim 2010, p. 16). Christianity was only introduced in Korea in 1884, slightly more than a century ago; but now around one-third of Koreans are either Christians or Catholics. Kim thinks that the rapid growth of Christianity in Korea may be partly due to the fact that the Christian concept of God is closely related to the concept of *Hannim*. Even now, in the Korean national anthem there is a phrase that the god of heaven will protect and guide the nation. I have no intention of saying that *Hannim* is exactly identical to the Christian God. My contention here is only that a broadly theistic tradition has also existed in the Korean culture from very early times, and there are "significant commonalities between the faith of *Hannim* and the concept of the biblical God." For example, "although we do not find any theory of creation in the concept of *Hannim*, it is evident that *Hannim* is believed to be the Ultimate source of all existent things" (Kim 2010, p. 19).

Concerning the Indians' RE, many Western scholars seem to have the impression that the monistic experience of the Advaita Vedanta is the dominant form. However, Advaita (non-dualism) is just one among many schools in Hinduism. There is also the theistic tradition represented by Madvha's Dvaita (dualism), which is very similar to Western forms of theism. The panentheistic tradition represented by Ramanuja's Visishtadvaita (modified non-dualism) is also influential, and this also contains significant theistic elements. Moreover, Bhakti (loving worship of God) is one of the three important ways to practice Hinduism. Indeed, "for Hindus participating in any of the organized devotional movements, *bhakti* is the central and organizing strand of both their individual and communal existence" (Carman 1983, p. 200).

For example, Ramanuja is a strong advocate for bhakti. He insists on the personal conception of Brahman, and regards the "close personal relation between devotee and Lord is both an external relation between a finite being and the Supreme Person and an internal relation of belonging, of being an infinitesimal part within an Infinite Whole" (Carman 1983, p. 200). The common analogy used is that the finite selves form the body of the Supreme Self, just as the physical form provides the body for each finite self.

For Hindu *bhaktas*, the goal is a vision of God and a single-minded relation with God. In practice, bhakti is largely theistic. The metaphor of the body of God can be interpreted in various ways and perhaps, to some degree, it is acceptable to Christians. After all, "Christians might recall that they are committed to seeing at least part of the finite universe, the Church, as the body of the Supreme Lord, and to the hope that eventually Christ will be 'all in all', so that the cosmos will be some day, if it is not now, the body of the Lord" (Ward 2000, pp. 68–9).

So TE is indeed an ancient cross-cultural tradition.

### 17.1.2 Religious Experience and Theistic Experience in the Contemporary World

Though I have doubts about the secularization theory (Kwan 2001), the secularists are correct to point out that modern life is hardly supportive of religious life and RE. In fact, Hay points out a "taboo" on admitting to religious experience. Many "respondents said they had never told anyone else about their experience, even relatives as close as their husbands or wives" for "fear of being thought mentally unbalanced" (Hay 1994, pp. 10–11).

In such a kind of inhibitive culture, it is indeed surprising how religious faith and RE have held up quite well. According to Schaffer and Lamm (1995, p. 393), the distribution of religious faith is as follows:

| Religion | Percentage of total population |
| --- | --- |
| None | 16 |
| Christianity | 34 |
| Islam | 18 |
| Hinduism | 13 |
| Buddhism | 6 |
| Other religions | 13 |

Religious believers are still the overwhelming majority of the world's population (84%), while nonreligious people are the minority (16%). Certainly many "believers" counted here are not much more than nominal believers. However, it is reasonable to believe that a substantial portion of the religious people have had some form of RE, and past studies of RE show that people who do not profess to any religion sometimes have RE, too. Note that Christians and Muslims together constitute 52 percent of the population, and the dominant form of RE in these theistic traditions is certainly TE. Hindus and Buddhists together amount to 19 percent of the population. However, we cannot conclude that the major form of their RE has to be monistic. As explained above, many ordinary Hindus' religious lives also consist of the worship of God (bhakti).

We have some quantitative data about the situation in the Western world. For example, the "BBC's 'Soul of Britain' survey in 2000 found that 76 per cent of the population...had some kind of spiritual experience" (Hick 2006, p. 17). The category of spiritual experience is considerably broader, but other statistics show that the proportion of people having RE (largely theistic) is not low:

> In the United States a 1975 National Opinion Research Center inquiry in which people were asked "Have you ever felt as though you were close to a spiritual force that seemed to lift you out of yourself?" found that 35 per cent of those asked said that they had, and a Princeton Research Center...survey in 1978 also recorded 35 per cent. In Britain at the same time a National Opinion Poll of a sample of 2000 reported 36 per cent. (Hick 2006, p. 35)

The real proportion may be higher, because of the taboo factor I have mentioned. The above results were obtained with the more impersonal method of a poll. Hay and Morisy find out that when they interview people and try to build up mutual trust and let them take time to recall, the positive response rate rises dramatically between 62 and 67 percent (Hay 1994, p. 11). Similar surveys have been done throughout the English-speaking world, and similar results were obtained. Hawker summarizes some of these findings: "a large proportion of the Western population has had firsthand experience of God or a presence or power:...43% positive response in the United States (1985), 44% in Australia (1983), and 44% in Canada (1990)" (Hawker 2000, p. 87).

Quantitative data about TE in other countries are available only in a few places. A survey about the Chinese RE was done from 2004 to 2008 using the Hardy question. It was found that a total of 56.7 percent of respondents had some RE. Among them 25.7 percent experienced the Will of heaven, and 6.1 percent the Christian God (Yao and Badham 2007, pp. 200–1). These are broadly theistic experiences. Others had experiences of ancestors, the Buddha, the God of fortune, ghosts, and the Dao or Qi. It should be noted that since 1949, the Chinese people have been subject to atheistic indoctrination in the schools, universities, media, and various other places. There had also been several decades of severe suppression of religion.

Apparently despite all these, the basic human response to the transcendent dimension had survived.

In Turkey, a predominantly Muslim country, a similar national survey was done by Cafer Yaran of Istanbul University in 2006 and 2007. Around 63.7 percent had some form of RE, including awareness of the presence of God, and so on (Rankin 2008, p. 237). In India, there had been a survey in South India in 2006, in which 68.4 percent of the people interviewed had a valid religious experience. Most of them were Hindus, Christians, and Muslims. The most common type of RE for Hindus was a sense of power (and not the monistic experience; Rankin 2008, p. 238).

Although we still do not have empirical data in many places, the data we have on the whole show that a broadly TE is indeed very widespread. Christianity is nowadays truly a world religion, and there are a large number of Christians on every continent. For example, there are at least, say, 30 to 40 million Chinese Christians. In the above survey, if the 6.1 percent figure is representative of the whole population of 1.3 billion, the number of people having a Christian TE will reach 79.3 million! We still need to add other forms of TE or proto-TE. The above data also show that TEs are common among Muslims, and a vague kind of proto-TE is also common among Hindus. If we factor in the experiences of numerous Christians living in diverse places, perhaps hundreds of million of people have had at least one TE. In short, TE indeed has a broad base across cultures and religious traditions, even in contemporary society.

Some critics charge that TE is a kind of odd experience (Vardy 1990, p. 103), and hence it should be subject to initial skepticism. However, it seems wrongheaded to label a kind of experience shared by at least tens of million of people odd. It seems that the dominant secular models have illegitimately led to a dismissal of a kind of *widespread and normal type of experience*. Besides statistics, the previous chapters of Part B have extensively argued that TEs are continuous with our ordinary experiences and the depth dimension of the entire rainbow of experiences. They do not seem to be merely excrescence, but instead flow from the inner dynamics of human nature. There is no reason to label TE as odd.

### 17.1.3 *Typology of Theistic Experience*

a. Numinous Experience

Otto's description of the numinous is still a good one: *mysterium tremendum et fascinans*. Yandell spells it out in this way: the subject "seems to experience an awesome...majestic and overpowering being and the subject...has a feeling of being a creature in the presence of the creator...the subject seems to experience a being who is unique in kind and intensely alive" (Yandell 1984, pp. 9–10).

b. Theistic Mysticism

Whereas in a numinous experience, God is felt to be other than the subject, in theistic mysticism, God is experienced in a union of the soul with

God. God is searched from within in this type of love mysticism, for example, as with the experiences of Teresa of Avila.

c. Sense of Presence of God

This is the more commonplace intuitive awareness of God. This awareness is often fused with a feeling of calm assurance and peace. Whereas extraordinary types of TE usually last for a relatively short duration, it is possible for some to maintain the sense of presence of God for a relatively long period (Brother Lawrence).

d. Divine-Human Encounter

In this type of TE, God is experienced as the Eternal Thou.

e. Experience of Grace

Awareness of God's unconditional demands may also occasion awareness of one's moral failings as "sinning against God" and awareness of one's moral impotence as "spiritual death." This may also open up the possibility of experiencing divine forgiveness of sin and renewal of moral personality through reconciliation with God. Characteristic emotions are a sense of guilt, the peace of forgiveness, and the joy of liberation.

f. Experience of Personal Growth in God

We should also note the personalizing character of some TEs. A person who experiences God may also experience personal growth at the same time: heightened sensitivity to people and moral values, a revitalized conscience, a greater concern for people, a willingness to sacrifice, and so on. In a word, he finds himself becoming more like an (integrated) person and his telos fulfilled in his life in God.

g. Baptism in the Spirit

It is "an overwhelming sense of being set free from sinful selfishness...[Signs include] deep interior peace [and]...the gift of tongues" (Dorr 1978, p. 40). There are a lot of these nowadays, since the charismatics constitute one of the fastest growing groups in contemporary world.

h. Corporate TE

Many TEs occur in the context of the "flight of the alone to the Alone." However, in Christianity, the corporate nature of these experiences is always emphasized:

> after Pentecost, the Spirit descends on the disciples.... then it is said that the disciples were all 'of one heart and soul'.... So the descent of the Spirit forms the community and the community is such that in it everything is shared, even at the economic level (Griffiths 1989, p. 223).

So experience of God and experience of community are often inseparable, and I would call this kind of TE a corporate TE.

i. Mediated TE

This is a TE that is mediated by other kinds of experience, for example, experiences of nature, art, conscience. Many examples have been given in previous chapters.

j. Sensory TE

A sensory TE is an experience of God that is mediated by sensory experiences, for example, visions, auditions, dreams, stigmata.

k. Interpretive TE

This is a spontaneous interpretation of an event as God's action or message, but the event can be clearly described without using religious concepts. Experiences of God through answered prayers, guidance, miracles, healing, tongues, and so on are examples of interpretive TE.

l. Intuitive Apprehension of God

All the above types are more or less mediated by some feelings, but some mystics also report a non-sensory awareness or intellectual vision of God in which all phenomenal content is absent. I call this an intuitive apprehension.

### 17.1.4 *Theistic Experiences Within a Common Ontology*

All the above kinds of TE are actually experienced by believers. It is foolish to elevate a certain kind of TE to the exclusion of other kinds. God's relations to the world and to man are so multifaceted that it is unreasonable to think there is only one way to approach Him. Consider an experience of drinking a cup of coffee, which actually consists of visual, olfactory, tactile, and gustatory experiences of the coffee. Considered in themselves, the smell of coffee and the visual sensations of a brown liquid are as diverse as any two things can be. Yet they are connected as modalities of the same SE of the same object. Similarly, God can be approached in many directions and manifested in diverse ways; yet the whole lot can be coherently explained by the nature of the same God:

a. Since God is the transcendent and holy creator, numinous experience and experience of contingency are to be expected.

b. If human beings are created in the image of God and their selves are ultimately grounded in God's sustaining activity, then God can also be approached from within (Theistic mysticism).

c. Since God is Himself the Absolute Good, it is no surprise to have experiences of His unconditional imperative, as well as love and succour, and also mediated TEs through conscience and morality.

d. Since God is personal, we can have experiences of personal encounter, divine speech, emotional healing, and so on.

e. God's wisdom and power over nature makes it possible for Him to reveal His purposes through providential and miraculous acts (mediated and interpretive TE).

f. God as the source of personality and community nicely explains the personalizing character of TEs and the occurrence of corporate TEs.

g. God as Redeemer is correlated with our experiences of grace and conversion.

h. God can act directly on the mind and hence intuitive apprehension is possible.

So the experience of God is marked by a rich diversity in unity. Arguably, this pattern is already there in the Biblical portrayal of the divine inter-action with man. For example, Rowley says, "His voice is still heard in Nature and in history, in individual experience and in the personality of men and women who are attuned to his spirit... Of greater significance than any of these separately, however, is that combination of factors dovetailing into one another" (Rowley 1956, p. 47). In the New Testament, Paul talks about a God who is above us, inside us, and among us (Ephesians). These descriptions can be nicely correlated with numinous experience, mystical or oblique experience of God, and corporate TE.

The same intricate pattern of experience of God is also reported by per-sons in contemporary secular society. Consider Jackie Pullinger's experience of God. She experienced God's calling to serve Him and finally she settled down inside the Walled City of Hong Kong, trying to preach the gospel to the drug addicts, Triad gangsters, and prostitutes. Now her work is still an expanding ministry. Her story consists of many "inner" and "private" experiences of God, and experiences of guidance, providence, comfort, and illumination that result in practical actions of social concern. She herself undergoes self-transformation, while many drug addicts experience conver-sion. There are also many experiences of tongues, healing, and miracles. Above all, all these experiences fit nicely together in her lifelong experience of God, which manifests beauty and an overarching purpose.

It is really important to keep sight of the *whole* of this evidential base. The full evidential force of TE can only be seen when the rich diversity and coherence of TEs are simultaneously recognized.

## 17.2 Conceptual Coherence of Theistic Experience

To be a well-established type of experience, the concept of TE needs to be conceptually coherent. Assuming the coherence of the concept of God, TE can still be incoherent, because *experience* of God might be shown to be impossible. Several reasons have been adduced for this claim: Jonathan Harrison rejected TE "partly on the grounds that one cannot have immedi-ate experience of dispositional characteristics, partly on the grounds that we can have immediate experience only of the contents of our own mind" (Harrison 1999, pp. 257–8). Forgie takes "theistic experience" to mean "an experience which is phenomenologically of God, that is, an experience which, if veridical, would *have to* constitute an accurate perception of God and *nothing else instead*" (Forgie 1998, p. 317; italics mine). But no experi-ence can be phenomenologically of God. So TE is impossible. Some other critics put the emphasis on the alleged impossibility of recognizing the infi-nite attributes of God in experience (Brian Davies).[1]

Initially, it sounds plausible to think it rather problematic to say the finite can experience the infinite, or the transcendent can be wholly given in the immanent. Simply put, God is just too big for humans to experience. However, puzzles immediately arise when we realize similar questions can be raised about the possibility of seeing a physical object. We think we can see the Yellow River or the Great Wall of China, but isn't it equally obvious that the Yellow River or the Great Wall are also too big for humans to see? I can see a physical object, and a physical object is essentially a three-dimensional object, having a front and a back, which cannot be given in our visual experience at the same time. So can I really see the object? Moreover, suppose Kripke is right that water is essentially $H_2O$. Then we need to ask: when we see water, how can the property of being $H_2O$ be given in our experience?

The basic problem about these kinds of questions about experience of God or physical objects is that they have presupposeed this requirement:

> For *S* to have an experience of an object *O* having an attribute *F*, either the whole being of *O* (or at least *O*'s essential properties) has to be *given* in the experience, or that an infallible indicator of the state of affairs (*O* is *F*) is present (and perceived as such) in the experience.

Requirements similar to the above are in fact made by the traditional foundationalists. If experience is our only access to the external world, once we allow a gap between the experience and the world, how then can we guarantee the possibility of empirical knowledge? I have argued in Part A that these requirements simply cannot be met even in our SE.

Consider our visual experience of water. What are given in the experience are two kinds of content: the propositional content of our epistemic seeming ("there is water over there"), and the nonconceptual content, which can be described in various ways: being appeared to water-ly, this and that kind of qualia or sense data. Water as a physical object cannot, in any literal sense, be given in our experience, which is a mental event. Indeed, this is a good ground for raising the question of whether any experience of a physical object is possible. This worry is further aggravated by the realization that the concept of a physical object is *the concept of something that can exist independently of all our experiences*—how can this property be given in our experience? This ability to exist independently is also a dispositional property. How can we perceive that? What features of our experience tell us that physical objects can do that? More experiences only tell us those objects can *continue to be perceived and experienced*, and it does not entail that they can exist *independently* of our stream of experience.

Contemporary understanding of physical objects further complicates matters. For example, Russell thinks that "if physics is true there must be so little resemblance between our percepts and their external causes that it is difficult to see how, from percepts, we can acquire a knowledge of external objects" (Russell 1948, p. 213). Since the "table as a physical object, consisting of electrons, positrons, and neutrons, lies outside my experience" (Russell 1948, p. 236), "I do not 'see' the furniture in my room except in a Pickwickian sense. When I am said to 'see' a table, what really happens is that I have a complex sensation which is, in certain respects, similar in structure to the physical table. The physical table, consisting of electrons, positrons, and neutrons, is inferred" (Russell 1948, pp. 237–8).

The problem then arises: if the physical table is inferred, then how do we justify this inference? The sensations certainly are not infallible indicators of the presence of the table. Even the alleged direct awareness of the table can be faked. As Alston admits "the intrinsic indistinguishability of hallucinations and the real thing," he has to concede that "even if hallucinations do not prove that perceptual experience is never a direct awareness of external objects, they certainly prove that it isn't always that" (Alston 1999, p. 238). Of course the propositional content of our experience can also be mistaken.

At this point, I think it is pertinent to ask what kind of approach we should adopt in relation to these questions. I suggest we cannot decide what capacities for experience and recognition are possible in an a priori manner. Instead it is more fruitful to look and see what actual experiences people claim to have and what sort of things they claim to recognize. If a concept of experience renders most of our actual experiences impossible, then perhaps what needs to be changed is the concept itself. In this spirit, I would suggest that there is no need to insist on too strong a connection between experience and its object. As long as the appearance of a transparent colorless liquid reliably indicates the presence of water ($H_2O$) *in our context,* and the water causes in an appropriate way our visual experience, then we can see water ($H_2O$). Our experiences are fallible, and its reliability cannot be guaranteed.

It follows that when we have an experience of O, we do not need to require that O's essential properties be given in the experience. In this way, experiences of the Yellow River, the Great Wall, or a three-dimensional object are no longer puzzling. Given this framework, we can see that Forgie's concept of TE and Harrison's objection depend on too narrow an understanding of experience. Since it is an empirical fact that an awful lot of people seem to have experiences of God, in the absence of a good reason to think otherwise, one should conclude that theistic experiences are indeed possible.

## 17.3  The Evidential Force of Theistic Experience

### 17.3.1  Intra-Coherence of Theistic Experience

Let us judge whether TEs deserve PFJ by the criteria of intra-coherence formulated in Chapter 4. As for clauses (a), (b), and (c) in that criteria, we have noted that many people in almost every age, culture, and in many religions seem to have at least some plainer TE, such as the sense of presence of God. Even nowadays, in some countries, the majority of people have some TEs. In other countries, TEs are at least shared by members of theistic communities that are significant minorities in the society. So conditions (a) and (c) are certainly satisfied.

For many persons who have had TEs, they may have had just a few of them. However, we have also mentioned the dramatic experiences of God that quite a number of individuals (e.g. Jackie Pullinger) have throughout their lives, and there are many more somewhat in the middle of these two groups. So condition (b) is reasonably satisfied for many, and eminently satisfied for a smaller number. I have also argued for the explanatory coherence between the TEs, and the conceptual coherence of TE. If my arguments are correct, conditions (d) and (e) are also satisfied. So barring the demonstration of conceptual incoherence of theism itself, we can conclude that TE is a relatively well-established type of experience.

### 17.3.2 Super-Reliability Fallacy Again

The critics may argue that our criterion of intra-coherence of a type of experience has too low a requirement. For example, theistic experiences still fall short of being universal and are much less frequent to many people than other established types of experience, such as SE or memory. However, the critics' requirements are too stringent here. First, universality among human beings is certainly not a necessary condition for PFJ. Obviously, a kind of experience shared by just a minority of people can nevertheless still be veridical. Actually, not all people can see or hear. Conceivably a nuclear war could happen that would cause all but one person to be blind. Furthermore, many are tone-deaf. It seems to be quite clear that even if many fewer people share the sense experiences we have, they are still at least prima facie justified for us.

If we count all the people all of history, people who have had TE may outnumber those who haven't. Moreover, in view of the fact that TEs occur to many diverse kinds of people, it is not implausible to say that the capacity for TE is at least potentially universal. If this is true, the contingent fact that TEs are not actually universal is not that damaging. The near universality of our current SEs is also contingent. Suppose there are aliens in many different places in the universe, and they all possess very distinct types of senses. Humankind is only a particular community of perceivers. So our SE may not be really universal in the universe. Would this hypothetical fact show that our SE cannot even be regarded as having PFJ? Hardly.

Furthermore, in most of our cognitive situations, when we have some initial presumption for the reliability of the experients, a sufficient number short of the entire community are adequate to convince us their reports are at least worthy of initial support. Take science as an example; the majority of people, in fact, do not know how to give reasons for the existence of black holes or quarks. However, as long as the scientific community agrees that they have good reasons to believe those exotic entities, it is reasonable for me to trust them, even though the scientists involved are just the minority among human beings. It is also the case for testimony to events one has not witnessed. Suppose one person tells me that he has seen a rare bird species in Hong Kong. It has some weight for me, but I may still doubt it (even not having strong reasons to doubt his integrity or reliability as a witness). However, when 30 people tell the same story to me, my initial worry should be sufficiently dispelled. Suppose I later learn of 300 people who also give the same testimony. The degree of PFJ of that testimony will be further enhanced, but it does not seem to be essential for its PFJ. Further suppose 30 percent of the population have seen the rare bird (most of them only once or twice), but 70 percent have never seen it. Are the majority here warranted in refusing to grant even PFEF to the experiences of those 30 percent? I don't think so.

I suggest that the critics may have committed the Super-Reliability Fallacy, which strictly requires a BSJ to reach the level of super-reliability before it can be regarded as having PFJ. The critics are right in pointing out the ways in which TE differs from sensory experience, and it indeed follows that TE has intra-coherence *to a lesser extent* than sensory experiences. However, the hasty inference that TE is therefore not well established is a non sequitur, and is like arguing that since a scientist is less brilliant than Einstein, he must be an incompetent scientist. The super-reliability requirement will not only endanger the PFJ of TEs, but also that of moral experience, aesthetic experience, and so on. This consequence is also implausible.

We are not yet arguing for the veridicality of TEs: we are only asking that they deserve kinds of initial trust similar to what we give to many kinds of experience, and that they not be written off. Is it reasonable to believe that all "God-experients" are either deceiving themselves or others? Gutting, for one, does not think so:

> religion, throughout human history, has been an integral part of human life, attracting at all times the enthusiastic adherence of large numbers of good and intelligent people. To say that something that has such deep roots and that has been sustained for so long in such diverse contexts is nothing but credulity and hypocrisy is…extraordinary. (Gutting 1982, pp. 2–3)

So TE is not extraordinary. It is part and parcel of the human situation. Instead, it is the overly skeptical attitude toward TE that is extraordinary. Suppose we come to know the life story of a person who has dramatic experiences of God *throughout his life*. We find that person honest, sane, and intelligent. We also find his story corroborated by many others' stories throughout history in many cultures. Isn't it rash to say that *all of them are entirely and chronically deluded*? And for that person, he or she is not even entitled to trust his or her experiences at least initially? This does not seem to be reasonable.

## 17.4  Coherence and Conflict of Theistic Experience with Other Religious Experiences

### 17.4.1  Theism-Neutral Religious Experiences

In Chapter 16, we argued that pure consciousness events (PCEs) are theism-neutral. The main reason is that a PCE has no propositional content, and hence it cannot contradict theism or anything else. In many cases, people have both PCEs and TEs, and they do not see any contradiction between them. I also argue that nature mysticism or extrovertive mysticism is at least theism-neutral. It can be interpreted in either a monistic or theistic way. The kind of unity sensed in nature mysticism can reflect either the unity of all things rooted in their common source—their Creator God—or the kind of metaphysical unity envisaged by monism. In fact, in the last chapter, I also argue that many characteristics of extrovertive mysticism are theism-friendly.

### 17.4.2  Theism-Friendly Religious Experiences

Second, let us assess the weight of the Pro-Theistic Group. I have contended that TE is a well-established type of experience, and it is plausible to think it has the highest degree of intra-coherence among REs. So TE is weighty in itself. Furthermore, many kinds of religious experiences are compatible with theism and can readily be interpreted theistically, and hence theism-friendly:

a. Ecstasy and peak experience
b. Encounter of the Light Being in a near-death experience
c. Experience of evil spirit, angels, or departed saints
d. Experience of contingency
e. Experience of design

The first type, (a), suggests a kind of spiritual depth in human beings that is more consonant with theism than with naturalism. If (b) and (c) are veridical, then there exist immaterial beings outside the bounds of nature. This is compatible with theism, but incompatible with naturalism. Types (d) and (e) point somewhat in the direction of a Transcendent Creator-Designer. If these experiences are veridical, they are certainly friendly with theism, and can even offer significant support for theism. I think these experiences are not that uncommon (see Chapter 9). Anyway, as far as RE is concerned, the Pro-Theistic Group has considerable weight.

### 17.4.3  Theism-Unfriendly Religious Experiences

Now let us assess the weight of the Anti-Theistic Group. The prime examples of theism-incompatible non-TE are monistic mysticism and the experience of

Nirvana. Since these experiences suggest the Ultimate is essentially imper-sonal, it conflicts with theism. I'll examine this conflict later.

Let us now discuss theism-unfriendly non-TEs. Perhaps the experience of minor deities: for example, visions of Kali or Buddha or Apollo, belong to this group. However, they are not *directly* incompatible with theism, because it is logically possible that both God and these minor deities exist at the same time. The tension only arises because we have a further assumption that if God exists, He would not have created these minor deities. Otherwise, we can just regard these beings as spiritual creatures in God's world. However, perhaps given some plausible assumptions, these experiences may be *theism-unfriendly*. Since the conflict is not directly given in the experiences, I think it is quite possible to remove the tension by appropriate adjustment of our underlying assumptions and reinterpretation of those experiences. A theist does not need to choose between blanket rejection or blanket acceptance. He can adopt a more nuanced, case-by-case approach toward these experi-ences of minor deities.

### 17.4.4  Conflict of Theism and Monism

Let us now arbitrate the dispute between theism and monism. Let us take the Advaita Vedanta school of Hinduism as an example of monistic claims:

a. Brahman as the Impersonal Absolute is the Ultimate Reality in which there is no distinction and differentiation.
b. Atman is Brahman, that is, every human self is metaphysically identical to Brahman; hence every self is metaphysically identical to another self.
c. The world is ultimately *maya* (illusion).

Obviously, these claims conflict with theism, which asserts that the Ultimate is a Personal God who creates the world and distinct selves. Theism also claims that although all the latter are contingent upon the con-tinuous creative act of God, they are nonetheless real and distinct from one another. In my CTA, we have resources to resolve this conflict: the Principle of Comparision and the Principle of Conflict Resolution (see Chapter 4). The crucial point is whether theistic experience is a better-established type than monistic experience or vice versa. Let us briefly discuss this question.

### 1. Intra-Coherence

a. It seems to me the people who have monistic experiences (hereafter MEs) are confined to a relatively small group of mystics in various religious traditions, and mainly Eastern ones, whereas I have argued that theistic experience is present in various traditions and shared by a substantial portion of humankind.
b. Even for the mystics, monistic experiences come at rare moments of enlightenment. I have argued that theistic experiences can come fre-quently to a person in such a way that he experiences a "life-in-God."

c. I have argued that tokens of TE do form intricate coherence relationships, whereas monistic experiences do not exhibit many modalities; nor
do their tokens exhibit a complex pattern of coherence.
d. It seems to me the articulation of the monistic experience suffers from
many conceptual difficulties: how is an experience of Nirvana or the
Absolute possible? A noetic experience has an intrinsic structure, but the
Absolute is structureless. If it is literally ineffable, how can it be commu-
nicated and form a inter-subjective type of experience?

My conclusion is that TE has a higher degree of intra-coherence than ME.

## 2. Inter-Coherence

I have argued for the inter-coherence of TE in previous chapters. The following points evaluate the degree of inter-coherence of ME with various
kinds of noetic experience.
    a. SE:
It seems that SE discloses a world of multiplicity and change. Since SE is
one of the best-established types of experience, SE can serve as the defeater
of other types of experience. Now, ME apparently comes in conflict with
SE, and this seems to be a serious problem for ME. There is no analogous
problem with TE. For example, Gale thinks that, concerning monistic experiences, their "descriptions are often contradictory or in conflict with our best-
established empirical beliefs, such as that there exists a multiplicity of distinct
objects and events in space and time." (Gale 1991, p. 303) This criticism is not
new at all: this was pressed by Madhva in the thirteenth century *within the
Hindu tradition itself* (Copleston 1982, p. 80). The postulation of *maya* does
not clearly help: isn't it introducing multiplicity within Brahman itself?
    b. Moral experience:
Monism also seems to come in conflict with the basic assumption of moral
experience, that is, that there is an objective distinction between good and
evil, right and wrong. It is questionable how this can be preserved in a system in which All is One. Does it mean that in the end we can't distinguish
Hitler from Mother Teresa, and Stalin from Gandhi? If so, it is a mockery of
our ordinary consciousness, not to mention the morally dangerous doctrine
that Brahman is beyond good and evil. I, of course, am not saying that the
monistic mystics are less moral human beings. On the contrary, I agree that
they typically exhibit a high degree of moral consciousness and display virtues in their lives. What I am pressing is the *logical* problem: are the moral
experiences of the monistic mystics compatible with their monistic experiences? TE, as I have argued in Chapter 13, coheres with moral experience
much better.
    c. Interpersonal experience:
In Chapter 12 I argued that interpersonal experience reveals the otherness
of the *Thou*. Again this seems to be in conflict with the monistic doctrine
that all these distinctions are just illusory. On the other hand, IPE is coherent with TE. Furthermore, theism allows for ecstatic union of souls, and the

ecclesiological doctrine of the Body of Christ also suggests that, although human persons are distinct, they are destined for intimate communion. So some insights of monism are preserved.

d. Existential experience :

I have argued that in many existential experiences, man experiences himself as a finite being aspiring to be infinite (Chapter 11). This structure seems to be coherent with TE, but again it conflicts with ME which suggests that the human self *is* also infinite by nature. (Atman is Brahman.)

e. Experience of change:

According to monism, change is an illusion. But "Nothing seems plainer than that there are a multiplicity of things in the world around us and that these, and our experience of them, are constantly changing. To deny the reality of change, variety and multiplicity seems to be the most bizarre of all religious or metaphysical procedures" (Lewis 1969, p. 296).

My conclusion is that TE has a higher degree of intercoherence than ME. It can even be maintained that ME is actually incoherent with many types of noetic experiences.

As a summary, it seems possible to argue, with respect to clauses (a), (b), and (c) of the Principle of Comparison, that TE should be taken as the better-established subtype of RE. (Clause (d) is not relevant here, because neither TE nor ME presupposes the justifiability of the other.) Therefore, in accordance with the Principle of Conflict Resolution, TE would probably serve as the defeater of ME, rather than the other way round.

### 3. Cognitive Adjustment

Of course ME, in itself, can be claimed to be an established type of experience. Hence it is not plausible just to dismiss the whole type. Maritain suggests such an interpretation of monistic experience: "The Hindu experience does appear therefore, to be a mystical experience in the natural order...of that absolute which is the substantial *esse* of the soul and, in it and through it, of the divine absolute. And how could this experience, being purely negative, distinguish the one of these absolutes from the other? Inasmuch as it is a purely negative experience, it neither confuses nor distinguishes them. And since no content of the 'essential' order, no *quid*, is then attained, it is comprehensible that philosophic thought reflecting upon such an experience inevitably runs the danger of identifying in some measure the one and the other absolute, that absolute which is the mirror and that one which is perceived in the mirror. The same word 'atman' will designate the human Self and the supreme Self" (Maritain 1966, pp. 97–8).

The Advaitin would allow that the *bhakti* is a legitimate way to Brahman, but ultimately a loving devotion to Brahman, if he is consistent, must be regarded as based on ignorance. It is because devotion presupposes some sort of dualism and it conflicts with Advaita's non-dualism. So Smart says, "It does seem to me that theism can give us a profound and beautiful way of integrating the insights of prophets with those of contemplatives and combining the paths of devotional worship and mystical endeavour. But if you try to do it the other way round the main teachings of theism begin to disappear: devotion fades and the revelations wither. While theism can convincingly absorb and enrich the mystical path without detriment to the latter, the mystical path cannot absorb theistic belief without relegating it to second place" (Smart 1960, p. 72). If this is the case, then the theistic way of cognitive adjustment preserves more PFEF than the monistic way. In accordance with the Principle of Conservation, the former is to be recommended.

The other major type of theism-incompatible RE is the experience of Nirvana. I can only briefly say that this seems to be beset with many similar problems. Furthermore, it is supposed to be an experience of no-self, but it seems to come in conflict with our experience of self, which I have argued to be very fundamental (Chapter 10). Certainly the above is only the beginning of a critical dialogue between various religious traditions. Nevertheless, I have suggested some substantial reasons for why TE is not defeated by the major kinds of theism-incompatible RE.

# Chapter 18

# The Beauty of the Rainbow of Experiences and the Consilience of Theism

## 18.1 Holistic Empiricism as the Key to Reality

My arguments in Part B serve to reinforce my rejection of narrow empiricism. Schilling asks, "Why should we unquestioningly accept what is subject to examination by the senses as alone definitive of reality? If the key prescribed does not fit all the doors of human experience, it is better to look for another key...than to maintain categorically that all doors but one have nothing behind them" (Schilling 1974, p. 187).

Even nonreligious thinkers are dissatisfied with the narrow-mindedness of narrow empiricism. Lorenz criticizes those who deny moral perception: "Neglecting a cognitive capacity signifies denying access to available knowledge. This is the greatest offense a human can commit against the intellectual ideal of searching for truth...[It can be] compared to the actions of a person who...continuously keeps one eye closed and thereby robs himself of stereoscopic vision" (Lorenz 1988, p. 82). However, he also points out that "some critics of ontological reductionism keep both eyes open but, where the real world is actually a unity, they see double," for example, "Lord Snow sees two nonunifiable cultures" (Lorenz 1988, p. 83).

In a similar vein, I contend that neglecting and denying much of the rainbow of experiences signifies an "offense against the intellectual ideal of searching for truth." By marginalizing and ignoring the depth of our rainbow of experiences, we are mutilating our holistic cognitive capacities and closing ourselves off to an encounter with this wonderful world in *all* its dimensions. Looking at the world only through SE and science is, indeed, acting in a way similar to someone who keeps one eye closed. As a result, he can only have an impoverished or even distorted vision of the world, and he robs himself of the stereoscopic spiritual vision of our own existence and the world. Of course, we want a rich vision, but also a unitary vision. The arguments in the previous chapters show, exactly, that the rich deliverances of the rainbow of experiences, as integrated in the theistic worldview, do not lead to a double vision, but a unitary beautiful world in which we can find our spiritual home. The beauty and coherence of the rainbow of experiences manifest a kind of consilience within theism.

The above claims are backed up by detailed arguments about phenomenology, various kinds of experiential and theoretical coherence that suggests the plausibility of applying the PCT to the entire rainbow of experiences. We should note that different types of experience (e.g. SE, memory, IPE, introspection, moral experience, aesthetic experience, intellectual experience, and religious experience) are very diverse in phenomenology, ontology, and degree of reliability. Although we should apply the general framework of CTA, the kataphysical principle also advises us to respect the integrity and uniqueness of each realm of experience. At the same time, these different types of experience also have interlocking relationships with one another, and they are often fused together in intricate ways. Specifically, I point out that TE is analogous to and fused with various types of experience in many ways. If we place all these experiences before our mind, the arbitrariness and exclusiveness of narrow empiricism will be more clearly perceived. So here we have cumulative evidence for a PCT that should also be applicable to RE. Together with my more general arguments for PCT in Part A, I think the case for CTA is quite compelling.

To a large extent, holistic empiricism is a vindication of the *Lebenswelt*—the world of everyday existence. This task would be unnecessary if not for the domination of the naturalistic paradigm in the modern word, especially in mainstream philosophy. As Putnam points out, "Accepting…the *Lebenswelt*, the world as we actually experience it, demands of us who have…been philosophically trained that we both regain our sense of mystery (for it *is* mysterious that something can both be *in* the world and *about* the world) and our sense of the common (… it is only the weird notions of 'objectivity' and 'subjectivity' that we have acquired from Ontology and Epistemology that make us unfit to dwell in the common)" (Putnam 1990, p. 118). I do not regard all forms of ontology and epistemology as pernicious. My contention is that theistic ontology and the epistemology of holistic empiricism can do full justice to the *Lebenswelt* as we actually experience it, but narrow empiricism cannot.

## 18.2 Companions in the "Guilt"

Let us further explore Putnam's argument against positivism. He claims that if the positivist (or the narrow empiricist) insists on pruning away moral facts from the objective world, he would also need to prune away epistemic values that he holds. So the positivist or naturalistic quest for an entirely objective world cannot be realized consistently. This is Putnam's "Companions in the guilt" argument: "You say…that value judgments have no objective truth-value, that they are pure expressions of preference. But the reasons that you give—…disagreements…that these controversies cannot be settled 'inter-subjectively'; that our conceptions of value are historically conditioned; that there is no 'scientific' (reductive) account of what value *is*—all apply immediately…to judgments of justification, warrant, reasonableness—to epistemic values generally. So, if you are right, judgments of epistemic justification (warrant) are also entirely subjective…So…you have given us a reason for abandoning epistemic concepts, semantic concepts [and]...the notion of a *fact* altogether" (Putnam 1990, p. 117).

In response, Harman argues that "we suppose that in the end the same basic principles underlie everyone's reasoning, in the way that the same grammar may underlie the speech of different speakers who have different vocabularies and different skills at speaking" (Harman 1982, p. 570). Harman's principles are the familiar maxims of conservatism, simplicity, and predictive power. Putnam has several lines of reply. First, there is a dilemma. Consider the consensus criterion of objectivity. If the standard is set too high, the view becomes self-refuting, because there is never any significant consensus over positivism itself. If the standard is too low, many things—the infallibility of the Pope, for example—will turn out to be "objectively" justified in certain cultures.

Second, this philosophical position will be self-destructive in a more general sense. Suppose there are right answers in philosophy, but "this rightness...does not consist in the possibility of an argument that will be satisfying to the majority...The argument that Harman gives for regarding ethical truth as relative is precisely the argument that the man on the street gives for regarding *all the philosophy* as subjective" (Putnam 1990, pp. 34–5). He also points out that claims about moral disagreement are exaggerated: "That one should not, other things being equal, harm a benefactor is more universally accepted than is the relevance of *prediction* to the question of whether the earth came into existence five or six thousand years ago."

Putnam's arguments against positivism are very relevant to the central contention of this book. It can readily be seen that the major arguments against moral realism are pretty much the same as those against TE. In Part B, I show that it is not only TE that does not satisfy the demands of narrow empiricism, but also almost the entire rainbow of experiences. The combined weight of those experiences should be enough to overturn the straitjacket of narrow empiricism. The case will be strengthened if we can discern the coherence of this rainbow of experiences.

## 18.3 The Unity of Spiritual Experiences in the Greater Light

To take SE as the paradigm of our experience is mistaken. The majority of our experiences are spiritual, in the sense that they are concerned with meaning and intelligibility, and they are driven by ideals of love, truth, goodness, and beauty. When we explore the height and depth of our SE (encounter with the natural world), IPE, experience of self, moral experience, aesthetic experience, and intellectual experiences, every time we find intimation of transcendence, the sense of Presence, or even the possibility of an explicit TE. So in all the dimensions of human existence, we find the openness of humanity to a larger Being or Presence, and our existence seems to be illuminated from above by the Greater Light, as expressed in T. S. Eliot's poem (from *The Rock*):

O Greater Light, we praise Thee for the less,
The eastern light our spires touch at morning,
The light that slants upon our western doors at evening,
The twilight over stagnant pools at batflight,
Moon light and star light, owl and moth light,
Glow-worm glowlight on a grassblade.
O Light Invisible, we worship Thee!
We thank Thee for the lights that we have kindled,
The light of altar and of sanctuary;
Small lights of those who meditate at midnight
And lights directed through the coloured panes of windows
And light reflected from the polished stone,
The gilded carven wood, the coloured fresco.
Our gaze is submarine, our eyes look upward
And see the light that fractures through unquiet water.
We see the light but see not whence it comes.
O Light Invisible, we glorify Thee!
......
And we must extinguish the candle, put out the light and relight it;
Forever must quench, forever relight the flame.
Therefore we thank Thee for our little light, that is dappled with shadow.
We thank Thee who hast moved us to building, to finding,
to forming at the ends of our fingers and beams of our eyes.
And when we have built an altar to the Invisible Light,
we may set thereon the little lights for which our bodily vision is made.
And we thank Thee that darkness reminds us of light.
O Light Invisible, we give Thee thanks for Thy great glory!
(cited in MacGregor 1947, pp. 201–2)

Our daytime existence is illuminated by the sun. Only rarely do we look directly into the blinding light of the sun, but we can feel the presence of the sun nonetheless. The sunlight is just everywhere: reflected from everything we encounter in the world, and sometimes refracted into a form of rainbow. In the theistic perspective, we are blessed with diverse kinds of "little light," though "dappled with shadow."

J. A. Robertson points to our sense of proportion and perspective in life, a sense of values, a sense of humor, and so on, that show that there is a spiritual common sense in humanity, a sensitiveness to the laws of the Unseen World. So "religious intuition is not any isolated phenomenon in human nature. It is part of the regular tendency of the mind to form higher senses, intuitive faculties, in every direction" (cited in Baillie 1928, p. 229). My arguments here support a similar conclusion. Religious experience is not an isolated phenomenon in human nature. Instead of being odd, it is the manifestation of a general tendency of the human person to have intuitive faculties, spiritual experiences, and higher forms of experience, in every direction. There is an irreducible plurality and richness in the experiential indicators of God. The experiences by which mankind as a whole has contact with the Divine form a continuum. However, special senses or forms of experience can be differentiated within this continuum, but they seem to come from a general source. Baillie has an interesting idea: "The special sense which we now possess point back to a primordial...'general sensation' from which they have been gradually differentiated" (Baillie 1928, p. 221).

Roger Penrose is also deeply impressed by the capacity of our mind to make contact with the absolute. He considers the qualities of "beauty" and "goodness" *absolute* ones, in the Platonic sense, and asks, "Might it be the case that our awareness is somehow able to make contact with such absolutes, and it is *this* that gives consciousness its essential strength? Perhaps there might be some clue, here, as to what our consciousness actually 'is' and what it is 'for'. Does awareness play some kind of role as a 'bridge' to a world of Platonic absolutes?" (Penrose 1995, p. 401). My answer is yes, but I contend that the above answer is an incomplete one. As the discussions of moral and intellectual experiences show, a merely Platonic realm cannot provide a satisfactory answer. I suggest our awareness of these absolutes is rooted in our primordial contact with the Divine Presence in our *imago dei*.

It seems true to say that it is ultimately the unitary mind that senses or perceives anything. The eyes alone can see nothing without the mind. In our original encounter with reality, our experiences do not come into boxes. Only after we have extensive experiences and sustained reflection, can we then distinguish them into several kinds according to their phenomenology and ontology. If we take the rainbow of experiences seriously, our mind seems to be not only in contact with the physical world, but also with a wider Being, which includes the world of meaning, the realm of the sacred, and the presence of the finite thou's, as well as the Eternal Thou. As the Bible says, everyone who is born into this world is enlightened by the True Light. This unitary source is the origin of all our experiences, in all their possible height and depth.

Sweetman has also adopted the metaphor of rainbow: "For what we call values are perhaps only a kind of refraction of reality, like the rainbow colors that emerge from a prism when white light is passed through it" (Sweetman 2008, p. 61). Besides values, existential experience, aesthetic experience, and so on there are also other rainbow colors. But since the entire rainbow is the refraction of the unitary source of Divine Light, they should be coherent with one another, and coherent with TE in particular. In other words, TE is the key to the consilience of the rainbow of experiences because TE leads us directly to the source of the rainbow—the Sun. Austin Farrer says, "However orderly our spectrum of the sciences, we cannot put theology in. Is it between the green and yellow?...No. The theologian is not picking a colour from the rainbow; he is looking at the sun" (Farrer 1967, p. 20). I would rather put theology into the spectrum of rainbow as well, because theology is also one human project to reach beyond the rainbow. It is God who transcends the rainbow, but at the same time provides the unifying focus of everything. However, in so far as TE points to God, TE has a central role in guaranteeing the coherence of the rainbow of experiences.

## 18.4 Consilience within the Theistic Worldview

The claim of experiential coherence is further supported by theoretical coherence. While the force of an individual consideration is not decisive, the cumulative weight is significant. It seems that "human experience, when its inner order and coherence are drawn out by reason, proves to have a theistic order and coherence that are only fully explicable in terms of the reality of God" (Nichols 1991, p. 1).[1]

The main contention of theism is that man is created in the image of God and destined for a union with God. This explains our different kinds of experience. The experience of self is God's basic gift to a created spirit. As created spirit, not all of ourselves are transparent to us. We need to learn to understand ourselves, become ourselves. Especially because we are implicitly striving for a union with God, we are capable of self-transcendence. This is the basis of many human experiences, especially existential experiences.

Our SE makes possible our contact with the common external world. This is the theater for our dramas of soul making, and makes possible the search for truth and beauty and the exercise of responsibility over the world, and other people. That is why SE is wonderfully adaptable for aesthetic experience, especially experience of music and visual arts. Our interpersonal experience (love and community) reflects the Trinitarian nature of God. Shared experiences of beauty, truth seeking, and moral practice can provide substance for the IPE, and make possible a community bathed in Truth, Goodness, and Beauty. Moral experience is an implicit experience of God's calling and summons.

As the above experiences point to the transcendent, they also point to the veridicality of REs. "To anyone persuaded of even some probabilistic force in the accumulation of these rational arguments,...we should expect transcendent reality to be encounterable experientially by human subjects" (Hebblethwaite 1988, p. 96). In this way, those human experiences that serve as the "signals for transcendence" and the TEs that have explicit reference to transcendent reality support one another in relation to a theistic worldview.

## 18.5 The Incongruity between Naturalism and the Human Spirit

In contrast, the rival hypothesis $H_n$ fails to exhibit coherence with these data of human experiences. It is doubtful that it is compatible with the fact of (libertarian) freedom. Its categories are more or less incongruous with those of the human experiences. It has to appeal to reductions, ad hoc hypotheses, denial of the prima facie data, "fluke explanations," and so on. On $H_n$, these diverse human experiences are just unrelated excrescences and epiphenomena. So, for each phenomenon, it has to cook up a tailored-made "explanation." Perhaps it *could* be true; yet it does not fare very well in the coherence test against our human experiences. While the accumulation of convergent indicators makes a strong case, the repeated appeals to "fluke explanations" (spandrel is its more respectable name) only add up to incredibility.

For the naturalists, excepting SE and perhaps IPE, all other types of experiences are not to be expected, and each of them seems to be independent of the others. Even the deeper dimensions of SE and IPE are not to be expected on naturalism. For example, we can have IPE without a depth moral dimension embedded into it—animals can interact with one another without recognizing the sanctity of the animal nature of others. Some people speculate that our knowledge of others' mental states arose because it could help us predict others' behavior. From this perspective, the reason for the existence of IPE is its tactical usefulness. But then what about the joy of communion, the intrinsic value we feel in a union of hearts, and so on?

Perhaps moral experiences are good for the formation of a community, but is there any need to experience the moral demand as categorical or unconditional? Is there any need to see human life as sacred? Moreover, as social animals, we can all be aesthetically blind—aesthetic experiences do not clearly contribute to survival. REs do not have a clear function, either. Evolutionary psychologists speculate the existence of a Hyper-sensitive Agency Detection Device (HADD) or some innate Theory of Mind (ToM). Well, all these are possible, but then the experience of God would be akin to the experience of very powerful aliens. Should we expect the mystical experiences of God to happen in the deepest recess of our souls? Should we expect that TEs can at the same time quench our deep-seated craving for meaning and wholeness? Concerning these existential experiences, the most obvious fact is that they seem to complicate our lives unnecessarily. The time and energy "wasted" over the quest for meaning can better be used to hunt a deer or find a mate, can't it?

So why should two types of experience (TE and existential experience), which should have emerged accidentally and independently, find themselves interlocked with one another? Why should we have intellectual experience at all? What is the use of unlimited questioning or logic? The idea of necessity does not seem to be necessary for survival at all. Why should the world be beautiful at so many levels? Why should our mind possess the capacity to unlock its secrets? There are so many questions that are most puzzling for the naturalists. I am not suggesting logical incompatibility here. The first point is that human existence as we know it is too extravagant—there are certainly many more practical ways to improve our chances of survival and propagate our genes without the unnecessary baggage of uniquely human experiences. The second point is the incongruity of the categories of naturalism with the categories of the spirit. The handles for evolutionary naturalism to grip are mainly causal connection and survival, but for human existence, the major categories are meaning, value, sacredness, beauty, truth (even necessary truth), love, and so on. There is simply no natural way to map one set of categories onto the other set. It is not that they haven't tried.

It is interesting to note that some naturalists are aware of the problem of reductionism, and they do hope to preserve our rich experiences. The naturalist Randall has written the epilogue to a book called *Naturalism and the Human Spirit* (Krikorian 1944), which is an attempt to integrate the rainbow of experiences with naturalism. Randall agrees that "naturalism...must become as rich as the idealistic philosophies by incorporating the facts and experiences they emphasized...it must take over what is actually valid in the 'spiritual life' of the great religious visions. It must really interpret...man's moral, religious, and artistic experience, and not merely try to analyse them away" (Randall 1944, p. 376).

But it is doubtful whether their metaphysical framework can really allow them to realize this intention. For example, Randall claims that "there is room for religion, to be sure, since that is an encountered fact of human experience...There is room for celebration, consecration, and clarification of human goals...for man's concern with the eternal and with...the deathless and divine." This sounds really encouraging, but immediately we are confronted with Randall's hard-hitting words: "But for naturalism eternity is no attribute of authentic Being, but a quality of human vision; and divinity belongs, not to what is existent, but to what man discerns in imagination" (Randall 1944, p. 358). So religious experiences are reduced to human vision and imagination.

## 18.6 Conclusion

I try to build a plausible case for the claim that all major types of human experience are well integrated in the theistic scheme, and the naturalistic explanation does not provide a plausible alternative concerning the consilience of the rainbow of experiences. Given the wide scope of areas we need to look at, this cannot be satisfactorily done even in one book. Surely we have to look more into the detailed arguments and counterarguments available to both sides. However, I hope enough has been said for the Rainbow Argument to show that there is a reasonable prima facie case for theism that can greatly support both stages of the ARE.

# CONCLUSION

In Part A, I argue for some form of Principle of Critical Trust (Weak Token PCT and Moderate Type PCT) and explain how these principles can be integrated into an entire epistemological framework (Critical Trust Approach). I conclude that the PCT and CTA provide a plausible framework of epistemic evaluation in our post-foundationalist context.

In Part B, I argue for the application of the PCT to the rainbow of experiences, the entire range of uniquely human experiences. I contend that our experiences as a whole point to the transcendent realm and exhibit a kind of consilience in the theistic worldview. In particular, I argue that the Moderate Type PCT can be applied to theistic experience, which is also found to be able to withstand many critical objections. So my conclusion is that a plausible case can be made for the argument for theistic experience.

Of course, by the nature of the case, my ARE cannot be conclusive. Especially due to the limitations of space, I have not explicitly dealt with some important defeaters, such as the naturalistic explanation of religious experience. (However, I extensively discuss the general problems with naturalistic explanation of many human experiences.) Moreover, many more things need to be said for the CTA, more arguments are needed to further substantiate the Rainbow Argument, and many more defeaters need to be dealt with more thoroughly. All these mean another book project. I just hope my efforts here will advance the case for the cumulative ARE and show that it is a plausible argument.

In any case, the limitations of my argument here can be compensated for by the efforts of scholars working on a similar project. In particular, I think Caroline Davis (1989), Alston (1991), Gellman (1997, 2001), and Wall (1995) are strong on the rebuttal of defeaters. Of course, theistic experience may still be defeated by some cogent arguments, such as the problem of evil. But given the plausible case suggested in this book, I believe, at least for those who have experiences of God, that their experiences do give them some good *prima facie* reasons for belief in God.

I do not expect the argument from religious experience to gain consensus, but philosophical arguments rarely achieve this. The argument from religious experience is worthy of further exploration, together with the deep epistemological questions of the twenty-first century. It may well lead to fruitful developments in both philosophy of religion and epistemology.

# NOTES

## 1 Contemporary Resurgence of the Argument from Religious Experience

1. The last phrase is added to safeguard against the so-called deviant causal chains. This condition is hard to specify in detail. The same problem occurs for the explication of the concept of veridical sensory perception (Dancy, chapter 3). It should also be noted that this is offered as a sufficient condition for veridicality, and this may not be identical to its necessary condition.
2. "G-d" is Block's reverential way of referring to "God."

## 2 Ludwig Wittgenstein and the Rainbow of Experiences

1. Some of Wittgenstein's remarks might suggest that in the end his solution to the quest for meaning was a kind of non-realism: "Of course there are then no questions left, and this itself is the answer. The solution of the problem of life is seen in the vanishing of the problem" (*Tractatus* 6.52–6.521). As has been argued, the vanishing of the problem in our language does not entail a complete dismissal of the significance of that problem.

## 3 Toward Holistic Empiricism

1. For general discussions of blindsight, see Weiskrantz 1986.
2. See Lowe (1992) for a strong critique of IIT.
3. Of course, it is actually the *truth* of the ES I am talking about here.
4. Possibly with the exception of pure consciousness events.

## 4 The Critical Trust Approach

1. In itself, this point is not an adequate reply to the skeptical questions. Of course, the skeptics need to assume some knowledge of language and various basic facts about our experience. However, if their presuppositions are also undeniable to us, and their reasoning on the basis of those presuppositions are cogent, then we are still faced with a problem.

2. For similar complaints of this narrow concept of experience, see John Smith (1968, chapter 1) and Baillie (1962, chapter 3).
3. Bonjour further suggests that the idea of observation also has to be extended: "the line between the observable and the unobservable is *not* fixed... observation is not essentially tied to sense experience in the way it is for more traditional views, and thus any sort of reliable, cognitively spontaneous belief, no matter what sort of causal process it may result from, can in principle count as observational" (Bonjour 1985, p. 175). According to Bonjour, a spontaneous belief that has no accompanying experiential content at all can still be an observation.
4. Eberle (1998) has a good appreciation of this problem.
5. Swinburne also expresses his approval of the above "criticism" in conversation.
6. In fact, I am not sure about this. Perhaps the experience of apparition is rejected only because we already have sufficient defeaters of it. As Stephen Davis says: "Swinburne... can sensibly claim that the dead-aunt-in-the-office case *does* satisfy one of his listed 'negative conditions', namely, the one... that says that the event experienced is highly improbable on the background evidence... Thus Swinburne... does not have to allow that Gutting's experience is veridical" (Davis 1997, p. 135). But the adoption of the weak form is safer, and it is enough for my purpose.

## 5  A Post-Foundationalist Argument from Religious Experience

1. Although Flew later became a kind of theist (Flew and Varghese 2007), the ARE was not cited as the major reason for his conversion.
2. I leave open whether the process of creation is performed abruptly or gradually. The theistic hypothesis here does not entail Creationism as understood by the Fundamentalists. The naturalistic hypothesis here is a *metaphysical* hypothesis, which should be distinguished from the scientific theory of evolution as such. Even if science has established the fact of gradual evolution of life forms and emergence of complexity, this does not, in itself, warrant the claim that man is *entirely* a physical product. God can be the antecedent cause of the evolutionary process. In this book, I will avoid another big debate between evolution and intelligent design.

## 6  Critique of Narrow Empiricism

1. Obviously I am oversimplifying matters. There are many sophisticated positions that try to combine the apparently irreconcilable, for example, compatibilism. For the sake of exposition, I have to ignore these.

## 7 Arguments for the Principle of Critical Trust

1. Moreover, "we can compare our commonsense hypotheses about physical objects to, let us say, a Berkeleyean hypothesis about a very complex mind orchestrating the comings and goings of sensations. Which theory is simpler? Well Berkeley had just minds, mental states, and causation. The commonsense hypothesis has minds, mental states, causation, and physical objects. On any criteria of simplicity, Berkeley seems to win" (Fumerton 1992, p. 165).
2. Cf. Quine's criterion of an observation sentence: "that all reasonably competent speakers of the language be disposed, if asked, to assent to the sentence under the same stimulations of their sensory surfaces" (Quine and Ullian 1978, p. 33).

## 9 Experience of the Natural World, Critical Trust, and God

1. The following treatment is indebted to Evans 2010, pp. 70–3.
2. For the original sayings of Smart, please see J. J. C. Smart (1989, pp. 182–3).
3. For his criticisms of the idea of personal God, see Robert Goldman (1997, p. 4).

## 13 Moral Experience, Critical Trust, and God

1. In common language, sometimes "values" may stand only for likings or tastes, and this kind of value can indeed be changed easily, for example, from liking steak most to a vegetarian taste. There are other values that seem to guide our action and give us an identity, for example, the importance of one's kids. We are talking about this kind of value here.
2. See also the positive assessment of this argument from conscience in Wainwright (2005, chapter 2).
3. However, for Gaskin, the above considerations do not count against atheism, because moral considerations are only pragmatic, and not cognitive. However, it seems to me that Gaskin is dogmatically assuming that moral experience cannot reveal a "state of affairs as it really is." But can science really reveal the true nature of radical evil? "The demonic is, after all, sociological territory, except that human science fails to account for the abyss of evil" (Martin 2010, p. 169).
4. For further criticisms of Wielenberg, see Evans (2010, pp. 114ff) and Wainwright (2010).

## 14  Aesthetic Experience, Critical Trust, and God

1. The following account basically follows Batchelor (1999, pp. 240–3).
2. In my view, O'Hear's reasons for the rejection of the design argument are inadequate, and he is imposing an unrealistically high standard on natural theology.

## 15  Intellectual Experience, Critical Trust, and God

1. A similar argument is defended in Bonjour (1985, p. 194). A general defense of a priori intuition is available in his Appendix A there.
2. O'Hear apparently moves from atheism to a kind of agnosticism that seems open to some form of supernaturalism. This is discussed in Chapter 14.
3. The following treatment is heavily indebted to Rogers (2008).

## 16  Religious Experience, Critical Trust, and God

1. Other scholars who come to a similar conclusion include R. C. Zaehner and William Wainwright.
2. I can only have a relatively brief treatment of this problem here. For more detailed arguments, see Kwan (2003, 2009).
3. Indeed it is not the case that a "common core" has to be shared by all the eye-witness accounts. Sometimes it is sufficient that it is shared by the large majority of the accounts, provided that either the error of the deviant witness in that aspect can be explained or overwhelming explanatory power is attained by adopting the common core. Admittedly there are borderline cases in which we have to rely on our judgments.

## 17  Theistic Experience, Critical Trust, and God

1. Everitt also thinks that God "is not even a possible object of sensory experience" (Everitt 2004, p. 172). I think his objection basically hinges on a kind of favoritism toward SE, which is widely criticized in this book.

## 18  The Beauty of the Rainbow of Experiences and the Consilience of Theism

1. John Polkinghorne has offered a similar argument (Polkinghorne 1998, chapter 1), and come to a similar conclusion.

# BIBLIOGRAPHY

Adams, R. M. 1999. *Finite and Infinite Goods*. Oxford: Oxford University Press.

Alston, William. 1983. "Christian Experience and Christian Belief." In Alvin Plantinga and Nicholas Wolterstorff, eds., *Faith and Rationality: Reason and Belief in God* (Notre Dame, IN: University of Notre Dame Press), pp. 103–34.

Alston, William. 1984. "Concepts of Epistemic Justification." *The Monist*, Vol. 68: 57–89.

Alston, William. 1991. *Perceiving God: The Epistemology of Religious Experience*. Ithaca, NY and London: Cornell University Press.

Alston, William P. 1993. *The Reliability of Sense Perception*. Ithaca, NY and London: Cornell University Press.

Alston, William. 1999. "Perceptual Knowledge." In John Greco and Ernest Sosa, eds., *The Blackwell Guide to Epistemology* (Oxford: Blackwell), pp. 223–42.

Anderson, Paul M., ed. 1998. *Professors Who Believe: The Spiritual Journeys of Christian Faculty*. Downers Grove, IL: InterVarsity Press.

Anscombe, G. E. M. 1990. "The First Person." In Palle Yourgrau, ed., *Demonstratives* (Oxford: Oxford University Press), pp. 135–53.

Archer, Margaret S., Andrew Collier, and Douglas Porpora. 2004. *Transcendence: Critical Realism and God*. London: Routledge.

Aronson, Jerrold. 1984. *A Realist Philosophy of Science*. London: Macmillan.

Atwater, P. M. H. 1994. *Beyond the Light*. New York City: Avon Books.

Audi, Robert. 1988. *Belief, Justification and Knowledge*. Belmont, CA: Wadsworth Publishing Company.

Audi, Robert. 1998. *Epistemology: A Contemporary Introduction to the Theory of Knowledge*. London: Routledge.

Audi, Robert. 2001. *The Architecture of Reason: The Structure and Substance of Rationality*. Oxford: Oxford University Press.

Ayer, A. J. 1940. *The Foundations of Empirical Knowledge*. London: Macmillan and Co. Ltd.

Ayer, A. J. 1967. "Can There Be a Private Language?" In Harold Morick, ed., *Wittgenstein and the Problem of Other Minds* (New York: McGraw-Hill), pp. 82–96.

Ayer, A. J. 1973. *The Central Questions of Philosophy*. London: Weidenfeld and Nicolson.

Babuta, Subniv, and Jean-Claude Bragard. 1988. *Evil*. London: Weidenfeld and Nicolson.

Baelz, Peter. 1975. *The Forgotten Dream: Experience, Hope and God*. London: Mowbrays.

Baergen, Ralph. 1993. "The Influence of Cognition upon Perception: The Empirical Story." *Australian Journal of Philosophy*, Vol. 71, No. 1 (March): 13–23.

Bagger, Matthew C. 1999. *Religious Experience, Justification, and History*. Cambridge: Cambridge University Press.

Baier, Kurt. 1980. "The Meaningful Life." In Steven Sanders and David R. Cheney, eds., *The Meaning of Life* (Englewood Cliffs, NJ: Prentice-Hall), pp. 15–24.

Baillie, John. 1928. *The Interpretation of Religion: An Introductory Study of Theological Principles*. New York: Abingdon Press.

Baillie, John. 1962. *The Sense of the Presence of God*. London: Oxford University Press.

Baker, Lynne Rudder. 2003. "Must Science Validate All Knowledge?" In Anthony Sanford, ed., *The Nature and Limits of Human Understanding* (London: T & T Clark), pp. 165–208.

Barrett, William. 1987. *Death of the Soul*. Oxford: Oxford University Press.

Batchelor, Mary. 1999. *Stairway to Heaven: True Stories of Encounters with God*. London: Hodder and Stoughton.

Baum, Gregory. 1971. *Man Becoming*. New York: Herder and Herder.

Bealer, George. 2000. "A Theory of the A Priori." *Pacific Philosophical Quarterly*, Vol. 81: 1–30.

Berger, Peter. 1970. *A Rumour of Angels*. London: Allen Lane.

Bergmann, Michael. 2008. "Reidian Externalism." In Vincent F. Hendricks and Duncan Pritchard, eds., *New Waves in Epistemology* (New York: Palgrave Macmillan), pp. 52–74.

Bertocci, Peter. 1970. *The Person God Is*. London: George Allen and Unwin Ltd.

Bianchi, Eugene C. 1972. *The Religious Experience of Revolutionaries*. Garden City, NY: Doubleday.

Bhaskar, Roy. 2000. *From East to West: Odyssey of a Soul*. London: Routledge.

Bhaskar, Roy. 2002. *Meta-Reality: The Philosophy of Meta-Reality*. Vol. 1. London: Sage.

Block, Irving. 2007. *G-d, Rationality and Mysticism*. Milwaukee, WI: Marquette University Press.

Bonjour, Laurence. 1985. *The Structure of Empirical Knowledge*. Cambridge, MA: Harvard University Press.

Bonjour, Laurence. 1999. "The Dialectic of Foundationalism and Coherentism." In John Greco and Ernest Sosa, eds., *The Blackwell Guide to Epistemology* (Oxford: Blackwell), pp. 117–42.

Bonjour, Laurence. 2005. "In Defense of the A *Priori*." In Matthias Steup and Ernest Sosa, eds., *Contemporary Debates in Epistemology* (Oxford: Blackwell), pp. 98–105.

Bouquet, Alan Coates. 1976. *Religious Experience: Its Nature, Types, and Validity*. 2nd edition. Westport CT: Greenwood Press.

Bradie, Michael. 1990. "Should Epistemologists Take Darwin Seriously?" In Nicholas Rescher, ed., *Evolution, Cognition, and Realism: Studies in Evolutionary Epistemology* (Lanham, MD: University Press of America), pp. 33–8.

Brink, David O. 1989. *Moral Realism and the Foundations of Ethics*. Cambridge: Cambridge University Press.

Brown, Harold I. 1977. *Perception, Theory and Commitment*. Chicago: The University of Chicago Press.

Brunner, Emil. 1944. *The Divine-Human Encounter*. London: SCM.

Buber, Martin. 1970. *I and Thou*. New York: Scribner.

Campbell, C. A. 1957. *On Selfhood and Godhood*. London: George Allen and Unwin.

Camus, Albert. 1955. *The Myth of Sisyphus and Other Essays*. New York: Vintage.

Carman, John B. 1983. "Conceiving Hindu 'Bhakti' as Theistic Mysticism." In Steven T. Katz, ed., *Mysticism and Religious Traditions* (New York: Oxford University Press), pp. 191–225.

Carruthers, Peter. 1986. *Introducing Persons: Theories and Arguments in the Philosophy of Mind*. London: Routledge.

Cartwright, Nancy. 1993. "How We Relate Theory to Observation." In Paul Horwich, ed., *World Changes: Thomas Kuhn and the Nature of Science* (Cambridge, MA: The MIT Press), pp. 259–74.

Casserley, Langmead. 1955. *Graceful Reason*. London: Longmans, Green and Co.

Chatterjee, Margaret. 1963. *Our Knowledge of Other Selves*. London: Asia Publishing House.

Chatterjee, Margaret. 1983. *Gandhi's Religious Thought*. London: Macmillan.

Chihara, C. S., and J. A. Fodor. 1967. "Operationalism and Ordinary Language: A Critique of Wittgenstein." In Harold Morick, ed., *Wittgenstein and the Problem of Other Minds* (New York: McGraw-Hill), pp. 170–204.

Chisholm, Roderick. 1969. "On the Observability of the Self." *Philosophy and Phenomenological Research*, Vol. XXX: 7–21.

Chisholm, Roderick. 1976. *Person and Object*. London: George Allen and Unwin.

Churchland, Patricia. 1987. "Epistemology in the Age of Neuroscience." *Journal of Philosophy*, Vol. 84, No. 10: 544–55.

Clack, R. Jerold. 1973. "Chisholm and Hume on Observing the Self." *Philosophy and Phenomenological Research*, Vol. XXXIII: 338–48.

Clark, R. W. 1973. *Einstein: The Life and Times*. London: Hodder and Stoughton.

Clark, Ralph. 1984. "The Evidential Value of Religious Experiences." *International Journal for Philosophy of Religion*, Vol. 16: 189–202.

Clasby, Nancy Tenfelde. 1988. "Jungian Archetypes and the Transcendent Image." In John R. Jacobson and Robert Lloyd Mitchell, eds., *The Existence of God* (New York: The Edwin Mellen Press), pp. 83–90.

Clifford, Paul R. 1971. *Interpreting Human Experience: A Philosophical Prologue to Theology*. London: Collins.

Copleston, Frederick. 1982. *Religion and the One*. London: Search Press.

Cottingham, John. 2003. *On the Meaning of Life*. London: Routledge.

Cottingham, John. 2005. *The Spiritual Dimension: Religion, Philosophy, and Human Value*. Cambridge: Cambridge University Press.

Crosby, Cindy. 2009. "Review of *Called out of Darkness: A Spiritual Confession*." *Books and Culture: A Christian Review*, Vol. 15, No. 2 (March/April): 6–7.

Crosby, John F. 2001. "The Twofold Source of the Dignity of Persons." *Faith and Philosophy*, Vol. 18, No. 3 (July): 292–306.

Dancy, Jonathan, ed. 1988. *Perceptual Knowledge*. Oxford: Oxford University Press.

Davies, Brian. 1985. *Thinking About God*. London: Geoffery Chapman.

Davies, Paul. 1984. *Superforce*. London: Unwin Paperbacks.

Davis, Caroline. 1989. *The Evidential Force of Religious Experience*. Oxford: Clarendon Press.

Davis, Stephen T. 1997. *God, Reason and Theistic Proofs*. Edinburgh: Edinburgh University Press.

Devitt, Michael. 2005. "There is no *a Priori*." In Matthias Steup and Ernest Sosa, eds., *Contemporary Debates in Epistemology* (Oxford: Blackwell), pp. 105–15.

Donceel, Joseph F. 1979. *The Searching Mind*. Notre Dame, IN: University of Notre Dame Press.

Donovan, Peter. 1979. *Interpreting Religious Experience*. London: Sheldon Press.

Dorr, Donal. 1978. *Remove the Heart of Stone- Charismatic Renewal and the Experience of Grace*. Gill and Macmillan.

Dulles, Avery. 1971. "An Apologetics of Hope." In Joseph P. Whelan, ed., *The God Experience: Essays in Hope* (New York: Newman Press), pp. 244–63.

Dupre, Louis. 1977. *The Dubious Heritage*. New York: Paulist Press.

Dupre, Louis. 1981. *The Deeper Life*. New York: Crossroad.

Eberle, Christopher J. 1998. "The Autonomy and Explanation of Mystical Perception." *Religious Studies* 34:299-316.

Edwards, Denis. 1984. *Human Experience of God*. Dublin: Gill and Macmillan Ltd.

Edwards, Rem. 1972. *Reason and Religion: An Introduction to the Philosophy of Religion*. New York: Harcourt Brace Jovanovich.

Einstein, Albert. 1949. *The World As I See It.* New York: The Wisdom Library.

Einstein, Albert. 1950. *Out of My Later Years.* New York: Philosophical Library.

Einstein, Albert. 1956. *Lettres a Maurice Solovine.* Paris: Gauthier-Villars.

Einstein, Albert. 1993. *Einstein on Humanism.* New York: Carol Publishing Group.

Elgin, Catherine Z. 1996. *Considered Judgment.* Princeton, NJ: Princeton University Press.

Elgin, Catherine Z. 2005. "Non-foundationalist Epistemology: Holism, Coherence, and Tenability." In Matthias Steup and Ernest Sosa, eds., *Contemporary Debates in Epistemology* (Oxford: Blackwell), pp. 156–67.

Elvee, Richard, ed. 1982. *Mind in Nature.* New York: Harper.

Erikson, Erik. 1968. *Identity.* London: Faber and Faber.

Erikson, Erik H. 1969. *Gandhi's Truth: On the Origins of Militant Nonviolence.* New York: W.W. Norton.

Evans, C. Stephen. 2010. *Natural Signs and Knowledge of God.* Oxford: Oxford University Press.

Evans, C. Stephen, and R. Zachary Manis. 2009. *Philosophy of Religion.* 2nd edition. Downers Grove, IL: IVP Academic.

Everitt, Nicholas. 2004. *The Non-existence of God.* London: Routledge.

Evola, Julius. 1983. *Metaphysics of Sex.* London and The Hague: East-West Publications.

Ewing, A. C. 1973. *Value and Reality: The Philosophical Case for Theism.* London: George Allen and Unwin Ltd.

Farmer, H. H. 1935. *The World and God.* London: Nisbet and Co. Ltd.

Farrer, Austin. 1966. *A Science of God?* London: Geoffrey Bles.

Farrer, Austin. 1967. *Faith and Speculation: An Essay in Philosophical Theology.* London: Adam and Charles Black.

Fischer, Norbert. 2005. *The Philosophical Quest for God: An Introduction to the Philosophy of Religion.* Münster: Lit Verlag.

Flanagan, Owen. 1992. *Consciousness Reconsidered.* Cambridge, MA: MIT Press.

Flew, Antony. 1966. *God and Philosophy.* London: Hutchinson and Co. Ltd.

Flew, Antony, and Roy Abraham Varghese. 2007. *There is a God: How the World's Most Notorious Atheist Changed His Mind.* New York: HarperCollins.

Fodor, Jerry. 1998. *In Critical Condition: Polemical Essays on Cognitive Science and the Philosophy of Mind.* Cambridge, MA: MIT Press.

Forbes, Cheryl. 1986. *Imagination: Embracing a Theology of Wonder.* Portland, OR: Multnomah Press.

Forgie, J. William. 1998. "The Possibility of Theistic Experience." *Religious Studies*, Vol. 34: 317–23.

Forman, Robert K. C., ed. 1990. *The Problem of Pure Consciousness: Mysticism and Philosophy.* New York: Oxford University Press.

Foster, John. 1991. *The Immaterial Self.* London and New York: Routledge.

Frank, S. L. 1946. *God with Us.* London: Jonathan Cape Ltd.

Frankl, Viktor. 1969. *The Will to Meaning.* New York: Plume Book.

Freeman, James B. 2005. *Acceptable Premises: An Epistemic Approach to an Informal Logic Problem.* Cambridge: Cambridge University Press.

Fromm, Erich. 1976. *To Have or To Be?* New York: Harper and Row.

Fumerton, Richard. 1992. "Skepticism and Reasoning to the best Explanation." In Enrique Villanueva, ed., *Rationality in Epistemology* (Atascadero, CA: Ridgeview Publishing Company), pp. 149–70.

Gaita, Raimond. 1991. *Good and Evil: An Absolute Conception.* London: Macmillan.

Gale, Richard. 1991. *On the Nature and Existence of God.* Cambridge: Cambridge University Press.

Gale, Richard M. 2005. "On the Cognitivity of Mystical Experiences." *Faith and Philosophy*, Vol. 22, No. 4 (October): 426–41.

Garrett, Brian. 1997. "Anscombe on 'I.'" *The Philosophical Quarterly*, Vol. 47, No. 189: 507–11.

Gaskin, J. C. A. 1984. *The Quest for Eternity: An Outline of the Philosophy of Religion.* New York: Penguin Books.

Geering, Lloyd. 1994. *Tomorrow's God: How We Create Our Worlds.* Wellington: Bridget Williams.

Geivett, R. Douglas. 2003. "The Evidential Value of Religious Experience." In Paul Copan and Paul Moser, eds., *The Rationality of Theism* (London: Routledge), pp. 175–203.

Gellman, Jerome. 1997. *Experience of God and the Rationality of Theistic Belief.* Ithaca, NY: Cornell University Press.

Gellman, Jerome. 2001. *Mystical Experience of God: A Philosophical Inquiry.* Aldershot: Ashgate.

Gellner, Ernest. 1974. *Legitimation of Belief.* Cambridge: Cambridge University Press.

Gelven, Michael. 1990. *Spirit and Existence.* London: Collins.

Ginet, Carl. 1975. *Knowledge, Perception, and Memory.* Dordrecht, Holland: Reidel.

Globus, Gordon G., Grover Maxwell, and Irwin Savodnik, eds. 1976. *Consciousness and the Brain.* New York: Plenum Press.

Glover, Jonathan. 1988. *I: the Philosophy and Psychology of Personal Identity.* London: Penguin Books.

Glymour, Clark. 1980. *Theory and Evidence.* Princeton, NJ: Princeton University Press.

Glynn, Patrick. 1996. *God: The Evidence: The Reconciliation of Faith and Reason in a Postsecular World.* Rocklin, CA: Forum.

Goetz, Stewart. 2008. *Freedom, Teleology, and Evil.* London: Continuum.

Goetz, Stewart. 2010. "Naturally Understanding Naturalism." *Faith and Philosophy*, Vol. 27, No. 1: 79–90.

Goldman, Alan. 1988. *Empirical Knowledge.* Berkeley, CA: University of California Press.

Goldman, Alvin. 1986. *Epistemology and Cognition.* Cambridge, MA: Harvard University Press.

Goldman, Robert N. 1997. *Einstein's God: Albert Einstein's Quest as a Scientist and as a Jew to Replace a Forsaken God.* Northvale, NJ: Jason Aronson.

Gould, Stephen Jay. 2000. "More Things in Heaven and Earth." In Hilary Rose and Steven Rose, eds., *Alas, Poor Darwin: Arguments Against Evolutionary Psychology* (New York: Harmony Books), pp. 101–26.

Goulder, Michael, and John Hick. 1983. *Why Believe in God?* London: SCM.

Griffith-Dickson, Gwen. 2005. *The Philosophy of Religion.* London: SCM Press.

Griffith-Dickson, Gwen. 2007. "Religious Experience." In Chad Meister and Paul Copan, eds., *The Routledge Companion to Philosophy of Religion* (London: Routledge), pp. 682–91.

Griffiths, Bede. 1989. *A New Vision of Reality- Western Science, Eastern Mysticism and Christian Faith.* London: Collins.

Grube, Dirk-Martin. 1995. "Religious Experience after the Demise of Foundationalism." *Religious Studies*, Vol. 31: 37–52.

Gutting, Gary. 1982. *Religious Belief and Religious Skepticism.* Notre Dame, IN: University of Notre Dame Press.

Haack, Susan. 1994. "Double-Aspect Foundherentism: A New Theory of Empirical Justification." In Ernest Sosa, ed., *Knowledge and Justification* (Aldershot, England: Dartmouth), pp. 729–44.

Hacking, Ian. 1983. *Representing and Intervening.* Cambridge: Cambridge University Press.

Hallett, Garth. 2000. *A Middle Way to God.* Oxford: Oxford University Press.

Hamlyn, D. W. 1970. *The Theory of Knowledge.* London: Macmillan.

Harman, Gilbert. 1982. "Metaphysical Realism and Moral Relativism: Reflections on Hilary Putnam's *Reason, Truth and History.*" *The Journal of Philosophy* Vol. 79: 568–75.

Harre, Rom. 1993. *Social Being.* 2nd edition. Oxford. Blackwell.

Harris, James F. 2002. *Analytic Philosophy of Religion.* Dordrecht: Kluwer.

Harrison, Jonathan. 1999. *God, Freedom and Immortality.* Aldershot: Ashgate.

Hawker, Paul. 2000. *Secret Affairs of the Soul: Ordinary People's Extraordinary Experiences of the Sacred.* Kelowna, British Columbia: Northstone.

Hay, David. 1994. "'The Biology of God': What is the Current Status of Hardy's Hypothesis?" *International Journal for the Psychology of Religion*, Vol. 4, No. 1: 1–23.

He, Guanghu. 1995. "The Root and Flower of Chinese Culture." (何光滬,〈中國文化的根與花〉,《原道》第二輯, 1995年5月, 頁29–56。).

Heaney, John J., ed. 1973. *Psyche and Spirit.* New York: Paulist Press.

Hebblethwaite, Brian. 1988. *The Ocean of Truth.* Cambridge: Cambridge University Press.

Hesse, Mary. 1981. "Retrospect." In A. R. Peacocke, ed., *The Sciences and Theology in the Twentieth Century* (Stocksfield: Oriel Press), pp. 281–96.

Hick, John. 1967. *Faith and Knowledge.* 2nd edition. London: Macmillan.

Hick, John. 1999. "Gandhi: The Fusion of Religion and Politics." In Leroy S. Rouner, ed., *Religion, Politics, and Peace* (Notre Dame, IN: University of Notre Dame Press), pp. 145–64.

Hick, John. 2006. *The New Frontier of Religion and Science: Religious Experience, Neuroscience and the Transcendent.* Basingstoke, England, and New York: Palgrave Macmillan.

Hinde, Robert A. 1999. *Why Gods Persist: A Scientific Approach to Religion.* London: Routledge.

Hookway, Christopher. 2002. "Emotions and Epistemic Evaluation." In Peter Carruthers, Stephen Stitch, and Michael Siegal, eds., *The Cognitive Basis of Science* (Cambridge: Cambridge University Press), pp. 251–62.

Huemer, Michael. 2001. *Skepticism and the Veil of Perception.* Lanham, MD: Rowman and Littlefield.

Huxley, Aldous. 1994. *The Doors of Perception and Heaven and Hell.* London: Flamingo.

Issacson, Walter. 1999. "Person of the Century: Who Mattered—and Why." *Time* (December 31): 8–20.

Jackson, Frank. 1977. *Perception: A Representative Theory.* Cambridge: Cambridge University Press.

Jaki, Stanley L. 1978. *The Road of Science and the Ways to God.* Chicago: University of Chicago Press.

James, William. 1916. *Some Problems of Philosophy: A Beginning of an Introduction to Philosophy.* New York: Longmans, Green, and Co.

Jencks, Charles. 2000. "EP, Phone Home." In Hilary Rose and Steven Rose, eds., *Alas, Poor Darwin: Arguments Against Evolutionary Psychology* (New York: Harmony Books), pp. 33–54.

Jung, C. G. 1933. *Modern Man in Search of a Soul.* New York: Harcourt, Brace and World.

Jung, C. G. 1938. *Psychology and Religion*. Princeton, New Haven: Yale University Press.

Kant, Immanuel. 1993. *Opus Postumum*. Cambridge: Cambridge University Press.

Katz, Jerrold J. 1990. "Descartes's *Cogito*." In Palle Yourgrau. ed., *Demonstratives* (Oxford: Oxford University Press), pp. 154–81.

Katz, Steven T. 1983. "The 'Conservative' Character of Mystical Experience." In Steven T. Katz, ed., *Mysticism and Religious Traditions* (New York: Oxford University Press), pp. 3–60.

Keightley, Alan. 1976. *Wittgenstein. Grammar and God*. London: Epworth.

Kenny, Anthony. 2004. *The Unknown God: Agnostic Essays*. London: Continuum.

Kim, Joo-han. 2010. "Creative Dialogue on Ultimate Reality." *Madong (場): International Journal of Contextual Theology in East Asia*, Vol. 13 (15 June): 7–22.

Knudson, Albert C. 1937. *The Validity of Religious Experience*. New York, Cincinnati: The Abingdon Press.

Krikorian, Yervant H. 1944. *Naturalism and the Human Spirit*. New York: Columbia University Press.

Kuhn, Thomas. 1962. *The Structure of Scientific Revolution*. Chicago: University of Chicago Press.

Kurtz, Paul. 1989. *Living without Religion: Eupraxophy*. Buffalo: Prometheus.

Kvanvig, Jonathan. 1984. "Credulism." *International Journal for Philosophy of Religion*, Vol. 16: 101–9.

Kvanvig, Jonathan L., ed. 1996. *Warrant in Contemporary Epistemology: Essays in Honor of Plantinga's Theory of Knowledge*. Lanham, MD: Rowman and Littlefield.

Kwan, Kai-man. 2001. "A Critical Appraisal of a Non-Realist Philosophy of Religion: An Asian Perspective." *Philosophia Christi*, Series 2, Vol. 3, No. 1: 225–35.

Kwan, Kai-man. 2003. "Is the Critical Trust Approach to Religious Experience Incompatible with Religious Particularism? A Reply to Michael Martin and John Hick." *Faith and Philosophy*, Vol. 20, No. 2 (April): 152–69.

Kwan, Kai-man. 2004. "Review of Jerome Gellman, *Mystical Experience of God: A Philosophical Inquiry* (Aldershot: Ashgate, 2001)." *Faith and Philosophy*, Vol. 21, No. 4 (October): 553–60.

Kwan, Kai-man. 2009. "The Argument from Religious Experience." In William Craig and J. P. Moreland, eds., *The Blackwell Companion to Natural Theology* (Oxford: Blackwell), pp. 498–552.

Kwan, Kai-man, and Siyi Han. 2008. "The Search for God in Chinese Culture and Contemporary China." *Canadian Social Science*, Vol. 4, No. 3 (June): 27–41.

Lakoff, George. 2003. "The Embodied Mind, and How to Live with One." In Anthony Sanford, ed., *The Nature and Limits of Human Understanding* (London: T & T Clark), pp. 49–108.

Layman, C. Stephen. 2007. *Letters to Doubting Thomas: A Case for the Existence of God*. New York: Oxford University Press.

Leplin, Jarrett, ed. 1984. *Scientific Realism*. Berkeley: University of California Press.

Lewis, H. D. 1959. *Our Experience of God*. London: George Allen and Unwin.

Lewis, H. D. 1969. *The Elusive Mind*. London: George Allen and Unwin.

Linville, Mark D. 2009. "The Moral Poverty of Evolutionary Naturalism." In Paul Copan and William Lane Craig, eds., *Contending with Christianity's Critics: Answering New Atheists and Other Objections* (Nashville, TN: B and H Academic), pp. 58–73.

Liu, Xiaobo. 1989. *Tragedy, Aesthetics and Freedom*. Taipei: Storm & Stress Publishing Company. [This is a Chinese book: 劉曉波,《悲劇. 審美. 自由》, 台北：風雲時代, 1989。]

Liu, Xiaofeng. 1997. *Individual Belief and Cultural Theory*. Chengdu: Sichuan People's Publishing House. [This is a Chinese book: 劉小楓, 《個體信仰與文化理論》, 成都：四川人民出版社, 1997。]

Lorenz, Konrad. 1988. *The Waning of Humaneness*. London: Unwin Paperbacks.

Lowe, E. J. 1992. "Experience and Its Objects." In Tim Crane, ed., *The Contents of Experience* (Cambridge: Cambridge University Press), pp. 79–104.

Lycan, William. 1988. *Judgment and Justification*. Cambridge: Cambridge University Press.

Lyons, Jack C. 2009. *Perception and Basic Beliefs: Zombies, Modules, and the Problem of the External World*. Oxford: Oxford University Press.

MacGregor, Geddes. 1947. *Aesthetic Experience in Religion*. London: Macmillan.

MacIntyre, Alasdair. 1980. "Epistemological Crises, Dramatic Narrative, and the Philosophy of Science." In Gary Gutting, ed., *Paradigms and Revolutions: Applications and Appraisals of Thomas Kuhn's Philosophy of Science* (Notre Dame, IN: University of Notre Dame Press), pp. 54–74.

Mackie, John. 1977. *Ethics: Inventing Right and Wrong*. Harmondsworth: Penguin Books.

Mackie, John. 1982. *The Miracle of Theism*. Oxford: Clarendon Press.

Macquarrie, John. 1973. *Existentialism*. Harmondsworth: Penguin Books.

Macquarrie, John. 1982. *In Search of Humanity*. London: SCM Press.

Malcolm, Norman. 1993. *Wittgenstein: A Religious Point of View?* London: Routledge.

Marcel, Gabriel. 1948. *The Philosophy of Existence*. London: The Harvill Press Ltd.

Marcel, Gabriel. 1952. *Man Against Humanity*. London: The Harvill Press Ltd.

Maritain, Jacques. 1966. *Challenges and Renewals*. Cleveland and New York: Meridian Books, the World Publishing Company.

Marshall, Paul. 2005. *Mystical Encounters with the Natural World*. Oxford: Oxford University Press.

Martin, David. 2010. "A Relational Ontology Reviewed in Sociological Perspective." In John Polkinghorne, ed., *The Trinity and an Entangled World: Relationality in Physical Science and Theology* (Grand Rapids, MI: Eerdmans), pp. 168–83.

Martin, Michael. 1986. "The Principle of Credulity and Religious Experience." *Religious Studies* 22:79-93.

Martin, Michael. 1990. *Atheism: A Philosophical Justification*. Philadelphia: Temple University Press.

Maslow, Abraham H. 1970. *Religions, Values, and Peak-Experiences*. New York: The Viking Press.

Mawson, T. J. 2005. *Belief in God: An Introduction to the Philosophy of Religion*. Oxford: Clarendon.

Maxwell, Nicholas. 1998. *The Comprehensibility of the Universe: A New Conception of Science*. Oxford: Clarendon.

McAllister, James. 1996. *Beauty and Revolution in Science*. Ithaca, NY: Cornell University Press.

McGrath, Alister E. 2004. *The Science of God*. Grand Rapids, MI: Eerdmans.

McGuinness, Brian. 1988. *Ludwig Wittgenstein: A Life*, Vol. I: *Young Ludwig 1889–1921*. London: Duckworth.

McMullin, Ernan, ed. 1988. *Construction and Constraint: The Shaping of Scientific Rationality*. Notre Dame, IN: University of Notre Dame Press.

McNaughton, David. 1988. *Moral Vision: An Introduction to Ethics*. Oxford: Basil Blackwell.

Miles, Grahame. 2007. *Science and Religious Experience: Are They Similar Forms of Knowledge?* Sussex: Academic Press.

Mithen, Steven. 2002. "Human Evolution and the Cognitive Basis of Science." In Peter Carruthers, Stephen Stitch, and Michael Siegal, eds., *The Cognitive Basis of Science* (Cambridge: Cambridge University Press), pp. 23–40.

Monk, Ray. 1990. *Ludwig Wittgenstein: The Duty of Genius*. New York: Free Press.

Moser, Paul. 1989. *Knowledge and Evidence*. Cambridge: Cambridge University Press.

Moser, Paul K. 2010. *The Evidence for God: Religious Knowledge Reexamined*. Cambridge: Cambridge University Press.

Murdoch, Iris. 1977. *The Fire and the Sun*. Oxford: Oxford University Press.

Nagel, Ernest. 1944. "Logic without Ontology." In Yervant H. Krikorian, ed., *Naturalism and the Human Spirit* (New York: Columbia University Press), pp. 210–41.

Newman, John Henry. 1973. *An Essay in aid of A Grammar of Assent*. Westminster: Christian Classics.

Newton-Smith, William. 1981. *The Rationality of Science*. London: Routledge and Kegan Paul.

Nichols, Aidan. 1991. *A Grammar of Consent*. Edinburgh: T & T Clark.

Nieli, Russell. 1987. *Wittgenstein: From Mysticism to Ordinary Language*. Albany, NY: State University of New York Press.

Novak, Michael. 1971. "The Unawareness of God." In Joseph P. Whelan, ed., *The God Experience: Essays in Hope* (New York: Newman Press), pp. 6–29.

Nussbaum, Martha C. 1990. *Love's Knowledge: Essays on Philosophy and Literature*. Oxford: Oxford University Press.

Ogden, Schubert. 1967. *The Reality of God*. London: SCM.

O'Hear, Anthony. 1989. "Evolution, Knowledge, and Self-consciousness." *Inquiry*, Vol. 32: 127–50.

O'Hear, Anthony. 1991. "Immanent and Transcendent Dimensions of Reason." *Ratio* (New Series), Vol. 4: 108–23.

O'Hear, Anthony. 1997. *Beyond Evolution: Human Nature and the Limits of Evolutionary Explanation*. Oxford: Clarendon.

O'Hear, Anthony. 1999. *After Progress*. London: Bloomsbury.

O'Hear, Anthony. 2008. *The Landscape of Humanity: Art, Culture and Society*. Exeter: Imprint Academic.

Oppy, Graham. 2006. *Arguing about Gods*. Cambridge: Cambridge University Press.

Ott, Heinrich. 1974. *God*. Edinburgh: The Saint Andrew Press.

Overman, Dean L. 2009. *A Case for the Existence of God*. Lanham, MD: Rowman and Littlefield.

Owen, H. P. 1969. *The Christian Knowledge of God*. London: The Athleone Press.

Parfit, Derek. 1987. *Reasons and Persons*. Revised version. Oxford: Oxford University Press.

Parsons, Howard. 1969. "A Philosophy of Wonder." *Philosophy and Phenomenological Research*, Vol. XXX: 84–101.

Parsons, Keith. 1989. *God and the Burden of Proof*. Buffalo: Prometheus Books.

Peacocke, Christopher. 1992. "Scenarios, Concepts and Perception." In Tim Crane, ed., *The Contents of Experience* (Cambridge: Cambridge University Press), pp. 105–35.

Pedersen, O. 1989. "Christian Belief and the Fascination of Science." In Robert Russell, William Stoeger, and George Coyne, eds., *Physics, Philosophy and Theology* (Notre Dame, IN: University of Notre Dame Press), pp. 125–40.

Penrose, Roger. 1995. *Shadows of the Mind: A Search for the Missing Science of Consciousness*. New York: Vintage Books.

Penrose, Roger. 2007. *The Road to Reality: A Complete Guide to the Laws of the Universe*. New York: Vintage Books.

Perry, John, ed. 1975. *Personal Identity*. Berkeley: University of California Press.

Pike, Nelson. 1992. *Mystic Union: An Essay in the Phenomenology of Mysticism.* Ithaca, NY: Cornell University Press.

Plantinga, Alvin. 1983. "Reason and Belief in God." In Alvin Plantinga and Nicholas Wolterstorff, eds., *Faith and Rationality: Reason and Belief in God* (Notre Dame, IN: University of Notre Dame Press), pp. 16–93.

Plantinga, Alvin. 1993. *Warrant and Proper Function.* Oxford: Oxford University Press.

Polanyi, Michael. 1958. *Personal Knowledge.* London: Routledge and Kegan Paul.

Polkinghorne, John. 1991. *Reason and Reality.* London: SPCK.

Polkinghorne, John. 1998. *Belief in God in an Age of Science.* New Haven, CT and London: Yale University Press.

Pollock, John. 1986. *Contemporary Theories of Knowledge.* London: Hutchinson.

Popper, Karl. 1969. *Conjectures and Refutations.* London: Routledge and Kegan Paul.

Pratt, J. B. 1937. *Personal Realism.* New York: Macmillan.

Pullinger, Jackie. 1980. *Chasing the Dragon.* London: Hodder and Stoughton.

Putnam, Hilary. 1981. *Reason, Truth, and History.* Cambridge: Cambridge University Press.

Putnam, Hilary. 1990. *Realism with a Human Face.* Cambridge, MA: Harvard University Press.

Putnam, Hilary. 1996. *Renewing Philosophy.* Cambridge, MA: Harvard University Press.

Quine, W. V. O. 1969. *Ontological Relativity and Other Essays.* New York: Columbia University Press.

Quine, W. V., and J. S. Ullian. 1978. *The Web of Belief.* New York: Random House.

Randall, John Herman. 1944. "Epilogue: The Nature of Naturalism." In Yervant H. Krikorian, ed., *Naturalism and the Human Spirit* (New York: Columbia University Press), pp. 354–82.

Rankin, Marianne. 2008. *An Introduction to Religious and Spiritual Experience.* London: Continuum.

Ratzsch, Del. 2009. "Humanness in their Hearts: Where Science and Religion Fuse." In Jeffrey Schloss and Michael Murray, eds., *The Believing Primate: Scientific, Philosophical, and Theological Reflections on the Origin of Religion* (Oxford: Oxford University Press), pp. 215–45.

Rea, Michael C. 2002. *World without Design: The Ontological Consequences of Naturalism.* Oxford: Clarendon Press.

Rea, Michael C. 2005. "Naturalism and Ontology: A Reply to Dale Jacquette." *Faith and Philosophy,* Vol. 22, No.3 (July): 343–57.

Rescher, Nicholas. 1995. *Satisfying Reason: Studies in the Theory of Knowledge.* Dordrecht: Kluwer.

Rhees, Rush, ed. 1984. *Ludwig Wittgenstein: Personal Recollections.* Oxford: Oxford University Press.

Rice, Hugh. 2000. *God and Goodness.* Oxford: Oxford University Press.

Roberts, T. A. 1989. "Religious Experience." In S. R. Sutherland and T. A Roberts, eds., *Religion, Reason and the Self* (Cardiff: University of Wales Press), pp. 75–89.

Robinson, N. H. G. 1969. "The Logic of Religious Language." In *Talk of God: Royal Institute of Philosophy Lectures Volume Two (1967–1968)* (London: Macmillan), pp. 1–19.

Rogers, Katherin A. 2008. "Evidence for God from Certainty." *Faith and Philosophy,* Vol. 25, No. 1 (January): 31–46.

Rowe, William. 1982. "Religious Experience and the Principle of Credulity." *International Journal for Philosophy of Religion,* Vol. 13: 85–92.

Rowley, H. H. 1956. *The Faith of Israel.* London: SCM.

Ruse, Michael. 2003. "Evolutionary Naturalism." In Anthony Sanford, ed., *The Nature and Limits of Human Understanding* (London: T & T Clark), pp. 111–62.

Russell, Bertrand. 1948. *Human Knowledge: Its Scope and Limits.* London: George Allen and Unwin.

Russell, Colin A. 1985. *Cross-Currents: Interactions between Science and Faith.* Grand Rapids, MI: Eerdmans.

Russell, Jeffrey B. 1988. *The Prince of Darkness: Radical Evil and the Power of Good in History.* London: Thames and Hudson.

Samartha, Stanley J. 1976. "Mission and Movements of Innovation." In Gerald H. Anderson and Thomas F. Stransky, eds., *Mission Trends No.3: Third World Theologies* (New York: Paulist), pp. 233–44.

Sartre, Jean-Paul. 1947. "Republic of Silence." In A. J. Liebling, ed., *Republic of Silence.* New York: Harcourt, Brace & Co., pp. 498–500.

Sartre, Jean-Paul. 1966. *Being and Nothingness.* New York: Washington Square Press.

Sayre-McCord, Geoffrey, ed. 1988. *Essays on Moral Realism.* Ithaca, NY and London: Cornell University Press.

Schaffer, Richard T., and Robert P. Lamm. 1995. *Sociology.* 5th edition. New York: McGraw-Hill.

Schellenberg, J. L. 2007. *The Wisdom to Doubt: A Justification of Religious Skepticism.* Ithaca, NY: Cornell University Press.

Schilling, S. Paul. 1974. *God Incognito.* Nashville, TN and New York: Abingdon Press.

Scruton, Roger. 1996. *An Intelligent Person's Guide to Philosophy.* London: Duckworth.

Scruton, Roger. 1998. *An Intelligent Person's Guide to Modern Culture.* London: Duckworth.

Scruton, Roger. 2009. *Beauty.* Oxford: Oxford University Press.

Shields, Philip R. 1993. *Logic and Sin in the Writings of Ludwig Wittgenstein.* Chicago: The University of Chicago Press.

Shoemaker, Sydney. 1984. *Identity, Cause and Mind.* Cambridge: Cambridge University Press.

Shortt, Rupert. 2005. *God's Advocates: Christian Thinkers in Conversation.* Grand Rapids, MI: Eerdmans.

Shutte, Augustine. 1987. "A New Argument for the Existence of God." *Modern Theology,* Vol. 3: 157–77.

Sikorska, Grazyna. 1985. *Jerzy Popieluszko: A Martyr for the Truth.* Grand Rapids, MI: Eerdmans.

Sima, Zhongyuan. 1981. "The Death of a Priest." In Zhang Xiaofeng, ed., *Compassionate People* (Taipei: Erya Publishers), pp. 15–23. [This is a Chinese book: 司馬中原,〈一個神父之死〉, 載張曉風編,《有情人》, 台北：爾雅出版社, 1981, 頁15–23。]

Sloan, Douglas. 1983. *Insight-Imagination: The Emancipation of Thought and the Modern World.* Westport, CT: Greenwood Press.

Slote, Michael. 1970. *Reason and Scepticism.* London: George Allen and Unwin.

Smart, J. J. C. 1989. *Our Place in the Universe: A Metaphysical Discussion.* Oxford: Blackwell.

Smart, Ninian. 1960. *A Dialogue of Religions.* London: SCM.

Smith, John. 1968. *Experience and God.* New York: Oxford University Press.

Smith, Joseph Wayne. 1988. *Essays on Ultimate Questions: Critical Discussions of the Limits of Contemporary Philosophical Inquiry.* Aldershot: Avebury.

Smith, Quentin. 1986. *The Felt Meaning of the World: A Metaphysics of Feeling.* West Lafayette, IN: Purdue University Press.

Snowdon, P. F. 1990. "Some Criticisms of Brain-Transplant Arguments." Paper given in Royal Institute of Philosophy Conference 1990 on "Human Beings."

Song, Choan-Seng. 1976. "From Israel to Asia: A Theological Leap." In Gerald H. Anderson and Thomas F. Stransky, eds., *Mission Trends No.3: Third World Theologies* (New York: Paulist), pp. 211–22.

Sorabji, Richard. 2006. *Self: Ancient and Modern Insights about Individuality, Life and Death*. Chicago: The University of Chicago Press.

Stace, Walter. 1960. *Mysticism and Philosophy*. Philadelphia: J. B. Lippincott Co.

Stein, Edward. 1990. "Getting Closer to the Truth: Realism and the Metaphysical and Epistemological Ramifications of Evolutionary Epistemology." In Nicholas Rescher, ed., *Evolution, Cognition, and Realism: Studies in Evolutionary Epistemology* (Lanham, MD: University Press of America), pp. 119–29.

Steinbock, Anthony J. 2007. *Phenomenology and Mysticism: The Verticality of Religious Experience*. Bloomington: Indiana University Press.

Sternberg, Eliezer J. 2010. *My Brain Made Me Do It: The Rise of Neuroscience and the Threat to Moral Responsibility*. Amherst, NY: Prometheus Books.

Stoeber, Michael. 1992. "Constructivist Epistemologies of Mysticism: A Critique and A Revision." *Religious Studies* Vol. 28: 107–16.

Stoeber, Michael. 1994. *Theo-Monistic Mysticism: A Hindu-Christian Comparison*. New York: St. Martin's Press.

Stoker, Wessel. 2006. *Is Faith Rational? A Hermeneutical-Phenomenological Accounting for Faith*. Leuven: Peeters.

Stump, Eleonore. 1997. "Awe and Atheism." In Peter A. French, Theodore E. Uehling, and Howard K. Wettstein, eds., *Midwest Studies in Philosophy*, Vol. XXI: *Philosophy of Religion* (Notre Dame, IN: University of Notre Dame Press), pp. 281–9.

Stump, Eleonore. 2009. "Modes of Knowing: Autism, Fiction, and Second-Person Perspectives." *Faith and Philosophy*, Vol. 26, No. 5 (Special Issue): 553–65.

Sweetman, Brendan. 2007. *Religion: Key Concepts in Philosophy*. London: Continuum.

Sweetman, Brendan. 2008. *The Vision of Gabriel Marcel: Epistemology, Human Person, the Transcendent*. Amsterdam: Rodopi.

Swinburne, Richard. 1979. *The Existence of God*. Oxford: Clarendon Press.

Swinburne, Richard. 1986. *The Evolution of the Soul*. Oxford: Clarendon Press.

Swinburne, Richard. 2001. *Epistemic Justification*. Oxford: Oxford University Press.

Taber, John. 1986. "The Philosophical Evaluation of Religious Experience." *International Journal for Philosophy of Religion*, Vol. 19: 43–59.

Taschek, William W. 1985. "Referring to Oneself*." *Canadian Journal of Philosophy*, Vol. 15, No. 4: 629–51.

Taylor, A. E. 1930. *The Faith of a Moralist*, Vol. 1. London: Macmillan.

Tennant, F. R. 1956. *Philosophical Theology*, Vol. II. Cambridge: Cambridge University Press.

Thagard, Paul. 2002. "The Passionate Scientist: Emotions in Scientific Cognition." In Peter Carruthers, Stephen Stitch, and Michael Siegal, eds., *The Cognitive Basis of Science* (Cambridge: Cambridge University Press), pp. 235–50.

Tolstoy, Leo. 1980. "My Confession." In Steven Sanders and David R. Cheney, eds., *The Meaning of Life* (Englewood Cliffs, NJ: Prentice-Hall), pp. 15–24.

Toulmin, Stephen. 2001. *Return to Reason*. Cambridge, MA: Harvard University Press.

Trueblood, Elton. 1957. *Philosophy of Religion*. Grand Rapids, MI: Baker.

Tye, Michael. 1992. "Visual Qualia and Visual Content." In Tim Crane, ed., *The Contents of Experience* (Cambridge: Cambridge University Press), pp. 158–76.

Urban, William. 1951. *Humanity and Deity*. London: George and Allen Unwin.

Van Cleve, James. 2005. "Why Coherence is not Enough." In Matthias Steup and Ernest Sosa, eds., *Contemporary Debates in Epistemology* (Oxford: Blackwell), pp. 168–80.

Van Fraassen, Bas C. 1980. *The Scientific Image*. Oxford: Clarendon.

Vardy, Peter. 1990. *The Puzzle of God*. London: Collins, Flame.

Vaught, Carl G. 1982. *The Quest for Wholeness*. Albany: State University of New York Press.

Vendler, Zeno. 1984. *The Matter of Minds*. Oxford: Clarendon Press.

Vivas, Eliseo. 1944. "A Natural History of the Aesthetic Transaction." In Yervant H. Krikorian, ed., *Naturalism and the Human Spirit* (New York: Columbia University Press), pp. 96–120.

Vogel, Jonathan. 1998. "Cartesian Skepticism and the Inference to the Best Explanation." In Linda Martin Alcoff, ed., *Epistemology: The Big Questions* (Oxford: Blackwell), pp. 352–9.

Vogel, Jonathan. 2005. "The Refutation of Skepticism." In Matthias Steup and Ernest Sosa, eds., *Contemporary Debates in Epistemology* (Oxford: Blackwell), pp. 73–84.

Von Leyden, W. 1961. *Remembering: A Philosophical Problem*. New York: Philosophical Library.

Wainwright, William. 1981. *Mysticism*. Brighton: The Harvester Press.

Wainwright, William. 2005. *Religion and Morality*. Aldershot: Ashgate.

Wainwright, William J. 2010. "In Defense of Non-natural Theistic Moral Realism: A Response to Wielenberg." *Faith and Philosophy*, Vol. 27, No. 4 (October): 457–63.

Wall, George. 1995. *Religious Experience and Religious Belief*. Lanham, MD: University Press of America.

Ward, Keith. 1974. *The Concept of God*. Oxford: Blackwell.

Ward, Keith. 2000. "Comparative Theology: The Heritage of Schleiermacher." In J'annine Jobling and Ian Markham, eds., *Theological liberalism: Creative and Critical* (London: SPCK), pp. 60–74.

Waterhouse, Eric S. 1923. *The Philosophy of Religious Experience*. London: The Epworth Press.

Webb, C. C. J. 1966. "Our Knowledge of One Another." In J. N. Findlay, ed., *Studies in Philosophy: British Academy Lectures* (Oxford: Oxford University Press), pp. 25–39.

Weiskrantz, L. 1986. *Blindsight: A Case Study and Implications*. Oxford: Oxford University Press.

Westphal, Merold. 1993. *Suspicion and Faith: The Religious Uses of Modern Atheism*. Grand Rapids, MI: Eerdman.

Wiebe, Phillip. 1997. *Visions of Jesus: Direct Encounters from the New Testament to Today*. Oxford: Oxford University Press.

Wiebe, Phillip. 2004. *God and Other Spirits: Intimations of transcendence in Christian Experience*. Oxford: Oxford University Press.

Wielenberg, Erik J. 2009. "Defense of Non-natural Non-theistic Moral Realism." *Faith and Philosophy*, Vol. 26, No. 1 (January): 23–41.

Wigner, Eugene P. 1967. *Symmetries and Reflections*. Bloomington: Indiana University Press.

Wilker, Benjamin, and Jonathan Witt. 2006. *A Meaningful World: How the Arts and Sciences Reveal the Genius of Nature*. Downers Grove, IL: InterVarsity Press.

Williams, Paul. 2002. *The Unexpected Way: On Converting from Buddhism to Catholicism*. New York: T & T Clark.

Wilson, E. O. 1984. *Biophilia*. Cambridge, MA: Harvard University Press.

Wittgenstein, Ludwig. 1961. *Tractatus Logico-Philosophicus*. London: Routledge & Kegan Paul.

Wittgenstein, Ludwig. 1965. "A Lecture on Ethics." *Philosophical Review*, Vol. 74, No. 1 (January): 3–12.

Wittgenstein, Ludwig. 1969. *On Certainty*. Oxford: Blackwell.

Wittgenstein, Ludwig. 1979. *Notebooks 1914–1916*. 2nd edition. Oxford: Blackwell.

Wittgenstein, Ludwig. 1980. *Culture and Value*. Oxford: Blackwell.

Wynn, Mark. 1999. *God and Goodness: A Natural Theological Perspective*. London: Routledge.

Wynn, Mark R. 2005. *Emotional Experience and Religious Understanding: Integrating Perception, Conception and Feeling*. Cambridge: Cambridge University Press.

Wystra, Stephen. 1990. "Reasons, Redemption, and Realism: The Axiological Roots of Rationality in Science and Religion." In Michael Beatty, ed., *Christian Theism and the Problems of Philosophy* (Notre Dame, IN: University of Notre Dame Press), pp. 118–61.

Yan, Jiaqi. 1992. *The Simplicity of Politics: The Way to Understand Politics*. Taipei: Cheng Chung Book Co. [This is a Chinese book: 嚴家其,《政治多麼簡單——理解政治之路》, 台北：正中書局, 1992。]

Yandell, Keith E. 1984. *Christianity and Philosophy*. Grand Rapids, MI: Eerdmans.

Yandell, Keith E. 1993. *The Epistemology of Religious Experience*. Cambridge: Cambridge University Press.

Yandell, Keith E. 1999. *Philosophy of Religion: A Contemporary Introduction*. London: Routledge.

Yandell, Keith E. 2006. "Pantheism." In Donald Borchert, ed., *Encyclopedia of Philosophy*, Vol. 7, 2nd edition (Detroit, MI: Macmillan Reference USA), pp. 202–5.

Yao, Xinzhong and Paul Badham. 2007. *Religious Experience in Contemporary China*. Cardiff: University of Wales Press.

Yaran, Cafer S. 2003. *Islamic Thoughts on the Existence of God: Contributions and Contrasts with Contemporary Western Philosophy of Religion*. Washington, DC: The Council for Research in Values and Philosophy.

Zaehner, R. C. 1961. *Mysticism: Sacred and Profane*. Oxford: Oxford University Press.

# Subject Index

a priori intuition 10, 45, 69, 72, 116, 241, 243, 247

bhakti 218, 269–70, 282
biophilia hypothesis 152–3, 236

coherentism 124, 132–4
conscience 32, 35, 173, 200, 212–15, 217, 220, 223–4, 272–3
consilience 83, 84, 189, 284, 288–92
constructivism 55, 252, 258–9, 263
critical trust approach 1, 9, 12, 15, 47, 62, 66, 68, 77, 123–6, 130–3, 292

empiricism, consensus 80, 119
empiricism, holistic 1, 2, 9–10, 40, 68–9, 243, 284–5
empiricism, narrow 1, 9–10, 17, 33, 51, 60–1, 68–70, 95, 98–101, 103, 106, 136, 146, 193, 202, 284–6
evolutionary psychology 151–3, 249, 290
experience of contingency 90, 141, 252, 273, 279
experience of design 141, 145, 252, 279
experience of evil 210, 252, 279
experience of freedom 25, 95, 182–3
experience of self 9, 50, 51, 95, 103–4, 162–7, 171–2, 283, 286, 289
experience of solidarity 197–8
externalism 62–4
extrovertive mystical experience 22, 257, 260

feeling perception 52–7, 60
fidelity 23, 196, 204
first person perspective 163, 169, 171
foundationalism, classical 7, 17, 85, 88, 101
foundationalism, explanatory 107, 111, 114, 116, 125–6, 167
foundationalism, weak 7, 132–3

ground level sifting 265
gullibilism 47, 67, 126, 132

individuality 177–8, 194, 204–6, 261
ineffability 35, 55
intellectual dynamism 240, 245
intelligibility of the world 144–5, 154, 158–9
intentional experience 12, 50, 71
internalism 62–4
I-Thou relationship 58, 194–7, 202–5

kataphysical principle 54, 71, 79, 285

Lebenswelt 48, 69, 100, 118, 209, 210, 285
logical gap objection 85–6

mediated immediacy 42, 138, 190
monism 23, 89, 91–2, 204–6, 224, 253–6, 264, 279–82

natural beauty 142, 150, 152, 216, 229, 231, 236
naturalized epistemology 56, 101–3, 130, 157, 244, 295
near death experience 20
noetic experience 10, 49–52, 55, 61, 69, 72, 99, 100–44, 133, 252, 281–2
noetic-qualitative complex 41, 52–3, 59, 140, 191

participatory knowing 22, 57–60, 217
peak experience 95, 174, 184, 252, 255–7, 279
principle of credulity 1, 6, 8–9, 11, 18, 74, 116
principle of critical trust 8, 107, 109, 114, 267, 292, 295
principle of doubt 66–8
principle of simplicity 12, 71, 78, 112, 117
principle of testimony 12–13, 68, 80
privacy objection 86–8
pure consciousness event 252, 254, 279, 293

# NAME INDEX